TRANSNATIONAL PSYCHOLOGY OF WOMEN

PSYCHOLOGY OF WOMEN
BOOK SERIES

TRANSNATIONAL PSYCHOLOGY OF WOMEN

Expanding International and Intersectional Approaches

EDITED BY LYNN H. COLLINS, SAYAKA MACHIZAWA, AND JOY K. RICE

AMERICAN PSYCHOLOGICAL ASSOCIATION
Washington, DC

Published by
American Psychological Association
750 First Street, NE
Washington, DC 20002
https://www.apa.org

Order Department
https://www.apa.org/pubs/books
order@apa.org

In the U.K., Europe, Africa, and the Middle East, copies may be ordered from Eurospan
https://www.eurospanbookstore.com/apa
info@eurospangroup.com

Typeset in Goudy by Circle Graphics, Inc., Reisterstown, MD

Printer: Sheridan Books, Chelsea, MI
Cover Designer: Beth Schlenoff, Bethesda, MD

Library of Congress Cataloging-in-Publication Data
Names: Collins, Lynn H., editor. | Machizawa, Sayaka, editor. | Rice, Joy K., editor.
Title: Transnational psychology of women : expanding international and intersectional approaches / edited by Lynn H. Collins, Sayaka Machizawa, and Joy K. Rice.
Description: Washington, DC : American Psychological Association, [2019] | Series: Psychology of women | Includes bibliographical references and index.
Identifiers: LCCN 2019006273 (print) | LCCN 2019013253 (ebook) | ISBN 9781433831249 (eBook) | ISBN 1433831244 (eBook) | ISBN 9781433830693 (hardcover) | ISBN 1433830698 (hardcover)
Subjects: LCSH: Women—Psychology. | Women--Cross cultural studies. | Feminist psychology.
Classification: LCC HQ1206 (ebook) | LCC HQ1206 .T735 2019 (print) | DDC 155.3/33—dc23
LC record available at https://lccn.loc.gov/2019006273

http://dx.doi.org/10.1037/0000148-000

Printed in the United States of America

10 9 8 7 6 5 4 3 2 1

CONTENTS

CONTRIBUTORS

Lynn H. Collins, PhD, Psychology Department, La Salle University, Philadelphia, PA

Janet M. Conway, PhD, Department of Sociology, Brock University, St. Catharines, Ontario, Canada

Sara Crann, PhD, Department of Psychology, University of Windsor, Windsor, Ontario, Canada

Andrea L. Dottolo, PhD, Psychology Department, Rhode Island College, Providence

Oliva M. Espín, PhD, Department of Women's Studies, San Diego State University, San Diego, CA

Shelly Grabe, PhD, Department of Psychology, University of California, Santa Cruz

Alisha Guthery, MA, LMHCA, MHP, CATP, Mountlake Terrace, WA

Julietta Hua, PhD, Department of Women and Gender Studies, San Francisco State University, San Francisco, CA

Nicole Jeffrey, MA, Department of Psychology, University of Guelph, Guelph, Ontario, Canada

Sayaka Machizawa, PsyD, Bracket Global, Wayne, PA

Jeanne Marecek, PhD, Department of Psychology, Swarthmore College, Swarthmore, PA

Jennifer J. Mootz, PhD, Department of Psychiatry, Columbia University, New York, NY

Edwina Pio, PhD, Faculty of Business, Economics and Law, Auckland University of Technology, Auckland, New Zealand

Joy K. Rice, PhD, Department of Psychiatry, University of Wisconsin–Madison School of Medicine and Public Health

Elizabeth Schwab, PsyD, Business Psychology and Behavioral Economics, Chicago School of Professional Psychology, Chicago, IL

Sally D. Stabb, PhD, Department of Psychology and Philosophy, Texas Woman's University, Denton

Jessica Tjiu, MA, Department of Women and Gender Studies, San Francisco State University, San Francisco, CA

Mary Wyer, PhD, Department of Psychology, North Carolina State University, Raleigh

SERIES FOREWORD

It would be hard to overstate the timeliness and significance of this volume. As the book goes to press, a global political furor over migration reveals deeply entrenched racial, ethnic, and religious prejudices and hostilities against those who dare to defy contemporary geopolitical nation-state boundaries or who must do so to find food, shelter, and safety. News outlets provide daily and deafening updates on the political controversies and debates with images of national and global emergencies, and yet, rarely if ever do we hear about issues specific to the lives of women in these contexts. It is as if women do not exist. *Transnational Psychology of Women: Expanding International and Intersectional Approaches* hopes to convert that invisibility into insight by foregrounding feminist research that refuses to marginalize the world's women and that insists on recognizing and specifying the wide range of social, historical, economic, and cultural contexts with which women engage. The Society for the Psychology of Women (Division 35) Book Series of the American Psychological Association (APA) is designed to support and disseminate scholarship such as this that can contribute to advocacy and social activism on behalf of women and other disempowered groups.

The discipline of psychology is not an innocent bystander in the dismissal of the world's women; its primary historical focus on White and Western patriarchal concerns has made it better at justifying inequalities than challenging them, a point reiterated by this book's contributors. A cornerstone commitment of APA's Division 35, and this book series, is to transform the knowledge base of psychology into one that fosters advocacy by, for, and about the empowerment of a world filled with girls and women. This is an ambitious goal, never more evident than in the pages of this book. Here, the authors explore the transformative promise of transnational feminist perspectives—on globalization, gender-based violence, human trafficking, reproduction, domestic violence, acculturation, clinical practice, community interventions, research, and in the classroom.

The editors of this collection of original articles are a distinguished, determined, and arguably prescient team. When Lynn H. Collins, Sayaka Machizawa, and Joy K. Rice began this work in 2015 as organizers of an APA-sponsored summit on the transnational psychology of women, global humanitarian efforts dominated the news, to combat the Ebola virus, address the needs of families fleeing war and persecution, and to develop human rights and worker protection reforms. Five years later, the headlines are different, and yet—and yet—it is as if women still do not exist. If you are searching for a more comprehensive way to understand the world, look no further.

—*Mary Wyer*
Series Editor

ACKNOWLEDGMENTS

We would like to acknowledge and thank Mary Wyer, American Psychological Association (APA) Division 35 (Society for the Psychology of Women) book series editor for supporting our book proposal and the process leading to its publication. Her feedback, advice, and editorial assistance were invaluable. We would also like to thank Chris Kelaher, APA acquisitions editor, for his support and belief in the project, as well as Kristen Knight, development editor, Elizabeth Brace, production editor, and Erin O'Brien, copyeditor, for their additional valued guidance and assistance. We would also like to thank the keynote speakers, discussants, workshop leaders, fellow organizers, sponsors, and participants for their contributions to the International Psychology of Women Summit that inspired this book.

Lynn H. Collins would like to thank the late Gloria Gottsegen for encouraging her involvement in international psychology and the Division 52 International Committee for Women and the Division 35 Global and International Perspectives on the Psychology of Women Committee for providing opportunities to contribute. Sayaka Machizawa would like to thank Lynn H. Collins and Joy K. Rice for the continuous mentorship and guidance throughout summit organizing and book editing. She would also like to acknowledge Carol Enns, her mentor of 20 years, for introducing her to transnational feminism over 4 years ago. Joy K. Rice wants to especially acknowledge the ongoing, tremendous support of her husband of 50 years, psychologist David Rice, and her mentor, the late Frances Culbertson, who 40 years ago encouraged her to become involved in international psychology and continues to inspire her.

TRANSNATIONAL PSYCHOLOGY OF WOMEN

INTRODUCTION

LYNN H. COLLINS, SAYAKA MACHIZAWA, AND JOY K. RICE

As globalization spreads connections and increases mobility, psychologists are called on to diagnose and treat clients, help with disaster responses, consult on research, assist communities, and work with a wider range of populations in settings both inside and outside their home countries (Altmaier & Hall, 2008; Morgan-Consoli, Inman, Bullock, & Nolan, 2018). The people with whom psychologists work are increasingly more diverse in terms of their cultural frameworks, family structures, home communities, governance structures, and migration experiences. Their access to education, health care, food, resources, and representation varies greatly, as does their experience with traumatic migration and military conflict (Arnett, 2008). The number of people living outside their home country rose from 173 million in 2000 to 258 million in 2017. It is estimated that there will be 405 million international migrants by 2050. India, Mexico, Russia, China, and Bangladesh were the most common countries of origin (Hill, 2018). Countries receiving

http://dx.doi.org/10.1037/0000148-001
Transnational Psychology of Women: Expanding International and Intersectional Approaches, L. H. Collins, S. Machizawa, and J. K. Rice (Editors)

immigrants often benefit economically, but immigration's benefits to societies are often underestimated and the number of immigrants and their cost to societies overestimated. Consequent negative reactions to immigration have disrupted the social order and politics of countries they enter (Porter & Russell, 2018). The escalation of migration is likely to continue, especially from sub-Saharan Africa. Furthermore, both economic factors and global warming are likely to continue to drive people from warmer regions and lower elevations, especially agricultural regions, to cooler, higher elevation urban centers (Porter & Russell, 2018; Spilker, Koubi, Schaffer, & Böhmelt, 2018).

Globalization and migration have escalated, but psychologists' understanding of the world's population has not kept pace. Many populations are not adequately represented in the psychological literature (Altmaier & Hall, 2008; Arnett, 2008; Henrich, Heine, & Norenzayan, 2010; Morgan-Consoli et al., 2018). For instance, research published in American Psychological Association journals only includes participants from 5% to 7% of the world's population (Arnett, 2008; Henrich et al., 2010), which transnational feminist scholars refer to as the *Global Minority*. Additional research and new approaches are essential to understanding the other 93% to 95% that transnational feminist scholars call the *Global Majority*. The impact of globalization, migration, economic factors, social unrest, military conflict, climate change, and other changing realities have made such knowledge essential for psychologists.

In light of escalating population mobility and the dearth of psychological research on Global Majority populations, in 2015, members of the Society for the Psychology of Women's Global Issues Committee and International Psychology's International Committee for Women held a summit with the theme "From International to Transnational: Transforming the Psychology of Women." The goal of the summit was to facilitate a paradigm shift from an international to a transnational psychology of women. The summit was held in Toronto, Canada. The lead organizers were Sayaka Machizawa, Lynn Collins, and Joy Rice. The summit featured interdisciplinary speakers and discussants who introduced summit participants to transnational feminist approaches by presenting examples of their transnational feminist research. Workgroups then applied the approaches to psychological topics.

At the end of the summit, attendees were excited about the paradigm but wanted a more comprehensive description of the approach. We developed this book to begin to expand psychological research to increase understanding of the Global Majority, the 95% to 97% of the world's population not included in research to date, and to use a transnational psychological approach to critique the influence of traditional Western psychological paradigms in shaping theory, methods, analysis, results, and conclusions. This book describes, explains, and summarizes assumptions and analytics currently associated with transnational feminist approaches, in the tradition of Mohanty (1984, 2003a, 2003b) and Grewal and Kaplan (1994), to psychological research, scholarship, practice, and consultation.

The group was inspired by transnational psychology's potential for decolonizing mainstream Western psychology. *Decolonizing* psychological science and practice requires that psychologists enhance their awareness of the multiplicity of psychologies around the world and develop *strong reflexivity*, which involves more rigorously critically evaluating and openly acknowledging the conceptual, political, historical, and other frameworks that shape their beliefs (Kurtiş & Adams, 2013, 2015). Transnational psychological approaches use collaborative, grassroots, and community-level approaches to understanding people, welcoming Indigenous knowledge, and partnering with communities in an egalitarian manner. They require genuine respect for communities' questions and needs, incorporating local knowledge and the use of ethnography and other qualitative approaches. Through transnational psychological approaches, psychologists are exposed to new forms of knowledge and new means of knowledge acquisition that can help "denaturalize" the cultural models that shape our knowledge about psychology (Macleod, Marecek, & Capdevila, 2014). Ultimately, by understanding the psychological and practical interactions and impacts of local through global influences, working in partnership with affected communities, adjustments can be made at the individual, community, regional, and global levels that improve the situations of women in ways that are responsive to their and their communities' particular needs and priorities.

PURPOSE OF THE BOOK

This book recognizes the contributions of those who have been working from transnational feminist perspectives. This is the first book to present a comprehensive introduction to transnational psychology. Transnational psychological approaches are essential to understanding the 95% of the world's population not yet represented in Western psychological literature. It holds great promise for addressing new contexts created by escalating globalization, global power dynamics, increasing migration, and an ever more interconnected world. This ground-breaking book expands upon international and intersectional approaches by transcending nation-state comparisons and extending intersectionality to include historical, sociopolitical, economic, and other global factors to the analysis of interconnected oppressive institutions. It is the first book to incorporate intersecting psychological identity narratives created by displacement, migration, colonization, imperialism, and political context, as well as the day to day realities of people marginalized by Western domination.

This book also aims to offer readers alternative paradigms and ways to approach theory and knowledge related to its sources, methods, validity, and scope. This includes ways to identify the influences of dominant religions, governments, business interests, and patriarchy within psychology. It suggests ways to dismantle, deconstruct, and decolonize psychology—to free it from these dominant influences to achieve a broader, more representative grassroots understanding of psychological phenomena. We hope that our authors will inspire readers to explore, investigate, and incorporate transnational psychological critiques and approaches in their work, leading the way toward greater psychological awareness of populations worldwide. Most transnational feminist psychologies use postcolonial feminist terms that are uniquely suited for describing and analyzing Western forces and dynamics associated with globalization and structural inequalities. This book will help readers become more familiar with the language and theory associated with this approach.

Practitioners, academics, students, policy makers, and others interested in cutting-edge global work in psychology, psychiatry, counseling, nursing, social work, and women's studies will find transnational perspectives useful in helping them understand patients, students, clients, and colleagues. The new perspectives will raise their awareness of the complex, fluid, dynamic nature of identity and the need to closely examine local through global contexts in addition to intersections of identity. This book will be valuable to practitioners because it will lead them to ask different questions before engaging in assessment and intervention. Ethnographic and qualitative approaches to assessment will help uncover hidden aspects of clients' identities and experiences, enhance understanding of clients' contexts, and lead psychologists to reconsider potential points of intervention: individual, family, community, and even regional. This may involve new types of partnerships with local communities and lead psychologists to integrate Indigenous treatment approaches unique to clients' histories and particular communities.

This book will be valuable to faculty teaching courses in undergraduate and graduate psychology that have been limited by the focus of psychological research on people from WEIRD (Western, educated, industrialized, rich, and democratic; Henrich et al., 2010) societies, which only include 5% to 7% of the world's population. Transnational psychology also promotes a deeper understanding of the impact of globalization and power asymmetries on individuals, communities, and psychological phenomena. In light of this, faculty teaching and conducting research in counseling, sociology, women's studies, and international studies programs will benefit from using a transnational psychology framework, especially when teaching courses on the psychology of women, globalization, international psychology, cross-cultural psychology, cultural psychology, and gender.

Researchers interested in conducting studies in the Majority World will find the book valuable in reframing their work. Chapters suggest new approaches and methodology to help uncover the particularities of individuals and communities and the nature of cultural, regional, and global influences on them. They also provide guidance on minimizing risks of imposing Western approaches on the rest of the world that reinforce the dominant influence of the Global Minority.

CHAPTER AUTHORS

As Guthery, Jeffrey, Crann, and Schwab note in Chapter 7, it is important to acknowledge the positions of the chapter authors. We acknowledge that their positions, situations, and locations are associated with the experiences, challenges, and benefits that inevitably shape their perspectives and scholarship. The perspectives presented by the chapters represent one set among many possible sets of interpretations of current transnational scholarship. More connections have to be made if the voices of the Global Majority are to be made salient.

In our search for summit keynote speakers in 2014, we did a thorough interdisciplinary literature search and used our international organizations and other international networks to find psychologists working from a transnational feminist psychological perspective. We sought feminist psychologists who not only worked internationally but who also framed their work from a transnational perspective and had published on the topic. The resulting literature search, which we updated as we developed the book, was one source of potential authors for the book. The summit's call for programs and registration were both widely advertised through our international networks, organizations, websites, and social media and so had a global reach. We solicited chapter proposals from those who responded, including workgroup leaders, discussants, and participants, as well as keynote speakers. Finally, our international network produced some authors through word of mouth.

We acknowledge that the final collection of authors was influenced by the dominance of Western academe, including Western feminism, availability of journals in English, and access to technology and other resources. Our authors are women who vary in religion, ethnicity, privilege, socioeconomic status, and physical location. They also differ in age, marital status, parental status, and educational attainment. Most of the authors currently reside in the United States and Canada, although not all were born there, and some have lived in other regions for parts of their lives. As Pio writes in Chapter 6, some formally educated Majority World individuals, including Malala Yousafzai, Vandana Shiva, and Chandra Mohanty, migrated to the West to access resources and privileges to support their activism, scholarship, and means of engaging with the world. Other scholars move to the West to flee violence, poverty, and/or to access education, employment, and economic opportunities.

STRUCTURE OF THE BOOK

We organized this book to lead readers through the history of the development of transnational feminist psychology, followed by more in-depth coverage of a selection of specific topics. The topics were chosen based on their levels of contemporary relevance and interest, as evident in a review of the literature, number of summit submissions on topics, and contemporary global news. We also considered interest levels among international organizations and the representation of topics in psychology of women courses and texts.

Chapter authors describe their position and briefly introduce their perspective on transnational feminist psychology, then provide an overview of the status of transnational feminist work on their topic. We are hoping that the authors' different positions and explanations of terms and theory help to convey the current breadth of interpretations of the approach. In addition, there is some intentional repetition of definitions of terms, concepts, and theoretical foundations. These repetitions allow each chapter to be a freestanding essay, as well as a contribution to the whole. Furthermore, this repetition should help increase readers' familiarity with and understanding of the general approach and its vocabulary, providing a solid foundation in transnational feminist psychology.

Many chapters include a case study that illustrates the potential of transnational feminist perspectives for interpreting cultural and cross-cultural dynamics in specific contexts. The chapters and book end with a description of the authors' vision for the application of transnational feminist perspectives as well as theoretical and practical challenges to address in future work. We hope that readers will come away with a clearer idea of the range of transnational feminist approaches and their potential applications to the field of psychology.

To introduce readers to transnational perspectives, the first chapter gives a brief overview of transnational feminism's history, concepts, assumptions, analytics (critiques), and debates using language that is likely to be unfamiliar to mainstream psychologists, defining terms as they surface in the text. Many of the associated concepts, critiques, and terminology originated in various disciplines' postcolonial, postmodern, Third World, and Women of Color feminist scholarship, including intersectionality and critical race theory, as well as scholarship addressing globalization.

In the second chapter, Janet M. Conway builds on the overview, going into more historical and theoretical depth and detail. Conway gives a brief history of globalization and traces the interdisciplinary history of transnational feminist paradigms, describing how they frame the effects of globalization. She examines how transnational feminist scholars have conceptualized and critiqued the impact of neoliberalism, capitalism, and privatization on women, particularly women from the Global Majority. Conway describes how Third World feminist critics "advocated a transnational and cross-cultural feminist praxis committed to combating inequalities among women while being sensitive to differences arising from cultural, social, and global geopolitical locations." Their approach increases the possibility of anti-imperialist, anticolonial, antiracist, and anticapitalist transnational feminist solidarity that offers the possibility of building bridges across differences related to intersectionality (Sandoval, 2000; Yuval-Davis, 2009). Subsequent chapters introduce increasingly sophisticated terminology, additional theoretical analyses, and topic-specific research.

Transnational feminists are critical of oppressive structures in the production of knowledge that have led to inaccurate, homogenous, and harmful representations of marginalized people. The Global Majority is largely unrepresented in psychological research. In Chapter 3, Jennifer J. Mootz and Sally D. Stabb apply a transnational feminist perspective to psychological research to address these concerns. They present the pitfalls of traditional research and then describe and illustrate transnational feminist research analytics. Mootz and Stabb provide helpful examples from the literature and reflections from their experiences with research conducted in Uganda. They encourage readers to engage in critical inquiries related to political, economic, cultural, and other aspects of transnational movement and influences when developing research questions. They share methods and practices that allow researchers to examine the impact of noncontiguous and contiguous transnational flows and cultural dynamism, including an extremely useful table describing transnational feminist strategies and considerations for developing questions; approaching constructs and measurement; engaging in data collection, analysis, and interpretation; disseminating results; and connecting the results to action.

Globalization may improve conditions for some, but for others, it increases the number and complexity of life's challenges. Increased rates of migration pose challenges to understanding clients' identities and matching those in need of help with the resources available to support them. In Chapter 4, Lynn H. Collins explores the use of ethnography in clinical work. She encourages psychologists to enlist ethnography and community partnerships to help rediscover Indigenous and other traditional healing methods and integrate them into treatment approaches. There is great potential for psychologists working at the individual through regional levels to identify and implement constructive strategies for promoting personal and structural change.

The numbers of migrants have grown rapidly worldwide since 2000. Never have so many people left their countries of origin in search of better circumstances (Chapter 5, this volume; Hill, 2018; Porter & Russell, 2018; Spilker et al., 2018). In Chapter 5, Oliva M. Espín and Andrea L. Dottolo break new ground describing and illustrating their understanding of the transnational threads that interweave experiences of migration for women all over the world. Espín and Dottolo show that transnational feminist perspectives provide important theoretical, methodological, and pedagogical strategies for examining the gendered processes of migration. They explore underlying principles and methodologies of transnational feminist psychology and migration, immigration policies, women's agency, and gender processes in migration. In doing so, they reveal ways in which transnational feminism can be more explicitly and directly integrated into feminist psychology scholarship, specifically as it relates to issues of gender and migration.

Women around the globe are entering educational systems at higher rates; however, many women are unable to advance their education due to the interaction of globalization with cultural and family responsibilities, economic challenges, and nonresponsive institutional and public policies. In Chapter 6, Edwina Pio exposes the barriers to women's success and survival, including insufficient access to resources, inadequate support, and changing circumstances, resulting in marginalization, restricted opportunities, and thwarted degree completion, development of leadership skills, and acquisition of experience. Several case studies and policies are discussed with the goal of developing practices and policies to facilitate more equitable educational, leadership, and workforce advancement of women in a transnational context.

Failure to define and document domestic violence has led to gaps in societal and legal interpretations and protections cross-nationally. The global prevalence of domestic violence has been well documented, but psychologists have yet to construct definitions that effectively address all its forms. In Chapter 7, Alisha Guthery, Nicole Jeffrey, Sara Crann, and Elizabeth Schwab highlight the challenges of defining domestic violence by examining the definitions used by six international advocacy organizations and legal systems across 13 countries. Guthery et al. use transnational feminist concepts to address these challenges and offer transnational feminist-informed future considerations for addressing domestic violence in all its forms and definitional challenges.

In Chapter 8, Jeanne Marecek drives home the need for feminist psychologists to disengage from the notions of a global feminist movement and a universal psychology and steep themselves in the contexts of those whom they wish to study if they intend to enrich the knowledge they produce. Women's reproductive experiences span much of their life cycles, including menarche and menstruation; sexual debut and sexual activity; contraception, child-spacing, and abortion; fertility issues and the increasing array of assisted reproductive technologies; pregnancy, childbirth, and adoption; disorders of the reproductive system; and menopause. Marecek examines women's reproductive experiences through the lenses of international and transnational psychology, drawing attention to possible questions for transnational feminist psychological study. Marecek also integrates comparative and relative analytic frameworks to reveal the complex constellation of contextual factors affecting reproductive experiences—that is, cultural meanings, state regulation, and the individual's social location—making a persuasive case for developing more nuanced, multifaceted conceptualizations.

Transnational feminists confront forms of violence against women in a similar manner. The rise of human trafficking discourse has also added new dimensions to existing feminist debates about sex work. The violence of trafficking, for instance, is not embedded just in the condition of being exploited and abused, but it is also embedded in the ways legal and discursive systems of accounting delimit how victimhood can be claimed and by whom. Transnational feminist engagements with sex trafficking question the conventions of representation and knowledge production that pose false binaries between coercion and choice, rescued and rescuer, victim and criminal prostitute, Third World and First World (Suchland, 2015). Given the many aspects of transnational feminist criticisms of human trafficking, in Chapter 9 Julietta Hua and Jessica Tjiu propose that readers consider how gendered and sexualized violence becomes expected and commonplace. They seek to destabilize what we currently take for granted as human trafficking. Such a transnational feminist perspective asks about the historical, economic, political, cultural, and social contexts of human trafficking, sex work, and labor migration.

Building on earlier work about teaching transnational psychology (Collins, 2019), Collins, Mootz, Marecek, Guthery, Machizawa, Espín, Dottolo, Hua, Crann, Jeffrey, and Schwab join forces to present a helpful guide to introducing transnational feminist psychological approaches in middle school through college classes. The chapter describes assignments, activities, readings, and videos to illustrate concepts. Chapters from this volume can serve as foundational reading assignments.

Finally, in the last chapter, "Toward an Inclusive, Affirmative, Transnational Psychology," Joy K. Rice and Shelly Grabe offer an analysis of the basic themes of the transnational approach to psychology, incorporating key issues, insights, and ways of reframing psychology from transnational feminist psychological perspectives. The authors analyze possible reasons for the slow, scant use and application of the transnational paradigm in psychology. Important advantages and limitations of applying transnational psychological approaches to research are presented. The chapter ends with a look forward to future practices that would deepen our understanding and application of transnational feminist psychology and further our progress toward the development of an inclusive, affirmative transnational feminist psychology.

CONCLUSION

Psychologists who are otherwise well-informed and competent and who regularly avail themselves of multicultural training and continuing education may be unaware of how they perpetuate Western *hegemony* (practices that covertly serve to reinforce the cultural beliefs and practices of those in power) by imposing Western psychological approaches in their work. Transnational feminist psychology, also called *transnational psychology*, has the potential to open our minds to new ideas about the nature of human psychological functioning.

This book pulls together current scholarship on transnational feminist psychology and begins to convey the breadth of interpretations and applications of the theory. We aspire to demystify the history, language, concepts, assumptions, analytics (critiques), and debates associated with transnational psychological approaches. We agree with Desai, Bouchard, and Detournay (2010) and Espín and Dottolo (Chapter 5, this volume) that the transnational should not come to incorporate or replace other feminist critiques but instead inspire psychology to venture beyond its Western, androcentric theoretical framework. Nor do we believe that incorporating transnational critiques will correct the ills of that framework within psychology or its negative consequences for women's daily lives. We do hope that this book offers readers alternative frameworks and techniques with which to identify theoretical, research, and practice traditions that prevent psychologists from correcting inaccurate assumptions, deconstructing Western theories, and identifying and understanding the communities with which we work. Hopefully, readers will come away with a clearer understanding of the nature and range of transnational feminist psychological frameworks, methodologies, and applications. Our goal is to facilitate the use of these approaches and thereby move the field of psychology forward.

REFERENCES

Altmaier, E. M., & Hall, J. E. (2008). Introduction to international quality assurance for psychology. In J. E. Hall & E. M. Altmaier (Eds.), *Global promise: Quality assurance and accountability in professional psychology* (pp. 3–15).

New York, NY: Oxford University Press. http://dx.doi.org/10.1093/acprof:oso/9780195306088.003.0001

Arnett, J. J. (2008). The neglected 95%: Why American psychology needs to become less American. *American Psychologist, 63,* 602–614. http://dx.doi.org/10.1037/0003-066X.63.7.602

Collins, L. H. (2019). Teaching cultural and transnational psychology: Taking intersectionality across the globe. In J. A. Mena & K. Quina (Eds.), *Integrating multiculturalism and intersectionality into the psychology curriculum: Strategies for instructors* (pp. 181–196). Washington, DC: American Psychological Association.

Desai, J., Bouchard, D., & Detournay, D. (2010). Disavowed legacies and honorable thievery: The work of 'transnational' in feminist and LGBTQ studies. In A. L. Swarr & R. Nagar (Eds.), *Critical, transnational feminist praxis* (pp. 46–64). Albany, NY: SUNY Press.

Grewal, I., & Kaplan, C. (1994). Introduction. In I. Grewal & C. Kaplan (Eds.), *Scattered hegemonies* (pp. 1–33). Minneapolis: University of Minnesota Press.

Henrich, J., Heine, S. J., & Norenzayan, A. (2010). The weirdest people in the world? *Behavioral and Brain Sciences, 33,* 61–83. http://dx.doi.org/10.1017/S0140525X0999152X

Hill, A. (2018, September 10). Migration: How many people are on the move around the world? *The Guardian.* Retrieved from https://www.theguardian.com/news/2018/sep/10/migration-how-many-people-are-on-the-move-around-the-world

Kurtiş, T., & Adams, G. (2013). A cultural psychology of relationship: Toward a transnational feminist psychology. In M. K. Ryan & N. R. Branscombe (Eds.), *Handbook of gender and psychology* (pp. 251–269). London, England: Sage. http://dx.doi.org/10.4135/9781446269930.n16

Kurtiş, T., & Adams, G. (2015). Decolonizing liberation: Toward a transnational feminist psychology. *Journal of Social and Political Psychology, 3,* 388–413. http://dx.doi.org/10.5964/jspp.v3i1.326

Macleod, C., Marecek, J., & Capdevila, R. (2014). Feminism and psychology going forward. *Feminism & Psychology, 24,* 3–17. http://dx.doi.org/10.1177/0959353513515308

Mohanty, C. (1984). Under Western eyes: Feminist scholarship and colonial discourses. *Boundary, 12,* 333–358. http://dx.doi.org/10.2307/302821

Mohanty, C. T. (2003a). *Feminism without borders: Decolonizing theory, practicing solidarity.* Durham, NC: Duke University Press. http://dx.doi.org/10.1215/9780822384649

Mohanty, C. T. (2003b). "Under Western eyes" revisited: Feminist solidarity through anticapitalist struggles. *Signs, 28,* 499–535. http://dx.doi.org/10.1086/342914

Morgan-Consoli, M. L., Inman, A. G., Bullock, M., & Nolan, S. A. (2018). Framework for competencies for U.S. psychologists engaging internationally. *International Perspectives in Psychology: Research, Practice, Consultation, 7,* 174–188. http://dx.doi.org/10.1037/ipp0000090

Porter, E., & Russell, K. (2018, June 20). Migrants are on the rise around the world, and myths about them are shaping attitudes. *The New York Times*. Retrieved from https://www.nytimes.com/interactive/2018/06/20/business/economy/immigration-economic-impact.html

Sandoval, C. (2000). *Methodology of the oppressed*. Minneapolis: University of Minnesota Press.

Spilker, G., Koubi, V., Schaffer, L., & Böhmelt, T. (2018, October 15). There's grim news on climate change. Will it lead to mass migration and conflict? *The Washington Post*. Retrieved from https://www.washingtonpost.com/news/monkey-cage/wp/2018/10/12/how-does-climate-change-push-migration-and-conflict-heres-what-our-interviews-reveal/?utm_term=.b7c6d2f92726

Suchland, J. (2015). *Economics of violence: Transnational feminism, postsocialism and the politics of sexual trafficking*. Durham, NC: Duke University Press. http://dx.doi.org/10.1215/9780822375289

Yuval-Davis, N. (2009). Women, globalization, and contemporary politics of belonging. *Gender, Technology and Development, 13*, 1–19. http://dx.doi.org/10.1177/097185240901300101

1

TRANSNATIONAL PSYCHOLOGY OF WOMEN

LYNN H. COLLINS, SAYAKA MACHIZAWA, AND JOY K. RICE

This chapter describes the development of a transnational psychology of women. Transnational psychology expands current approaches to the psychology of women by incorporating transnational feminist perspectives on the impact of globalization and consequent exposure to multiple cultural frameworks; family, community, and governance structures; and migration experiences. It also incorporates Global Majority perspectives, reminding readers that knowledge is socially constructed and should be questioned. The more viewpoints incorporated into psychological knowledge, the richer that knowledge will be. We hope that by developing better understandings of increasingly complex intersections of identities and contexts, we can move the psychology of women beyond Western psychological paradigms and approaches to research, theory, practice, and consultation.

In this age of globalization, the populations with whom psychologists work are increasingly mobile and diverse, whether within or outside

http://dx.doi.org/10.1037/0000148-002
Transnational Psychology of Women: Expanding International and Intersectional Approaches, L. H. Collins, S. Machizawa, and J. K. Rice (Editors)

the psychologist's home country (Altmaier & Hall, 2008; Morgan-Consoli, Inman, Bullock, & Nolan, 2018). Psychologists are called on to diagnose and treat clients, help with disaster responses, consult on research projects, assist with community interventions, or work in settings where the person or population involved is not adequately represented in the psychological literature (Altmaier & Hall, 2008; Arnett, 2008; Henrich, Heine, & Norenzayan, 2010; Morgan-Consoli et al., 2018). New approaches are essential because psychologists work with clients who have complex identities developed from exposure to multiple cultural frameworks, family structures, communities, governance structures, and migration experiences. Their experiences also vary in terms of education, health care, food availability, income, power, exposure to military conflict, and population density (Arnett, 2008).

Western psychology is based largely on psychological research conducted in Western, educated, industrialized, rich, democratic (WEIRD) countries. It has limited, if any, generalizability to those living in other regions (Arnett, 2008; Henrich et al., 2010). Henrich et al. (2010) found that there is great variability in experimental results of studies conducted across the globe on visual perception, fairness, cooperation, spatial reasoning, categorization and inferential induction, moral reasoning, reasoning styles, self-concepts and related motivations, and the heritability of IQ. In fact, research participants from WEIRD societies were frequently outliers when compared with the distribution of the general human population, undermining the justification for universalizing (e.g., assuming that the findings of studies conducted in WEIRD societies apply to all humans). Arnett (2008) described psychology in the United States as an incomplete science, noting that American Psychological Association journals focus too much on U.S. citizens, which make up only 5% of the world's population. He said that psychologists often unjustifiably generalize research findings to the other 95%, assuming psychological processes to be universal.

Like postcolonial feminists, our chapter authors avoid terms such as *undeveloped country* and *Third World country* because the use of these terms has become pejorative and perpetuates power inequities (Ashcroft, Griffiths, & Tiffin, 2000). Third World feminism was created in response to White second wave feminism, which continued the Western feminist tradition of analyzing only gender oppression. In contrast, Third World feminism examines multiple oppressions in the context of various social locations (Herr, 2014). Third World feminism describes the historical context of Third World women's oppression and resistance and respects their agency and voices. Unlike transnational feminism, Third World feminism tends to concentrate on local and national contexts and does not see nation-states and nationalism as necessarily detrimental to feminism (Herr, 2014). The term *Third World women* refers to women who live in regions previously called

Third World countries, who are considered part of the Majority World or Global Majority.

In addition, the term *undeveloped country* suggests that there is a single path of progress toward the goal of becoming like Western, capitalist regions (Alam, 2008). It suggests that undeveloped countries are inferior to developed ones and reinforces stereotypes about poor communities. Instead, transnational feminists use the alternative term *Majority World* to refer to regions where roughly more than 80% of the world's population lives. The term *Minority World* is used to refer to regions with less than 15% of the world's population, formerly called the *West* or *developed world*. Some authors use directional labels (e.g., *global North, South, East, West*) instead of the terms *developed* and *undeveloped countries*. Mohanty (1991) recommended using the one-third/two-thirds global paradigm of Minority World and Majority World instead of directional labels. The terms are capitalized because they are proper names and describe significant geographical places.

Some have tried to remedy the lack of information about these populations by exporting Western (United States and Western European) psychology, using the same methods to research, treat, and advise in other regions. This colonial approach (an approach in which an outside group inserts itself and takes over a region, similar to imperialism) is also problematic because it still applies Western psychological assumptions in work with other populations. Nor is "adding and stirring" information from research on other populations into predominantly Western conceptual frameworks a solution.

Although progress has been made in advancing competence in multicultural approaches, this training has also been based on Western research, practice, cultural beliefs, and traditions and has to be reevaluated for use with other communities (Morgan-Consoli et al., 2018). Henrich et al. (2010) and Arnett (2008) questioned whether psychologists are even justified in assuming that research conducted on undergraduates from WEIRD societies is generalizable to all sectors of the United States' and Western Europe's populations because these research participants do not adequately represent the full range of variability in the U.S. population (Henrich et al., 2010). At present, many psychologists who are otherwise well informed and competent and who regularly avail themselves of multicultural training and continuing education may be unaware of how they perpetuate Western hegemony (practices that covertly serve to reinforce the cultural beliefs and practices of those in power) by imposing Western or Global Minority psychological science on their clients.

Kurtiş and Adams (2013) called for a transnational feminist psychology that involves the active decolonization of psychology to open our minds to new ideas about the nature of human psychological functioning. Decolonizing psychological science and practice requires that psychologists deepen their awareness of the multiplicity of psychologies around the world and develop *strong reflexivity*, a term used by Sandra Harding (1991) to specify a rigorous form of reflexivity, one that requires acknowledging, critically evaluating, and openly admitting the conceptual, political, historical, and other frameworks that shape our beliefs. The term *strong reflexivity* is similar to the postcolonial feminist term *reflexivity* and the postmodern term *self-reflexivity*, although it is more thorough (Collins, 2019; Harding, 1991; McHugh, 2007). Some object to *self* because the self is a concept associated with Western individualism and is not emphasized or even recognized in some cultures. Strong reflexivity requires critical consciousness regarding one's position in the world and its relationship to what and how one knows. Strong reflexivity critiques one's knowledge, perspective, and location by identifying the factors that shape what one considers the "truth."

Strong reflexivity starts with awareness of *situated knowledge* (Haraway, 1988), the perspective shaped by experiences in one's location, position, or place in the world. Situated knowledge is then examined and critiqued. What one "knows" about a group (knowledge) depends on opinions (perspectives) developed by virtue of one's characteristics (e.g., race, gender, socioeconomic status, education, ethnicity) and personal experiences, and it is thus subject to these biases. Strong reflexivity requires that one ask the questions "What assumptions am I making because of my ethnicity, class, education level, sex, gender, age, religion, ableness, theoretical perspective, life experiences, and so forth?" and "How does my perspective lead me to select and conceptualize my research and scholarship?" Kuehner, Ploder, and Langer (2016), Finlay (2002), and Amer, Howarth, and Sen (2015) provided additional explanations and examples of strong reflexivity. Reflexivity helps to "denaturalize" the cultural models that shape our knowledge, including psychological knowledge, calling into question their normalcy (Macleod, Marecek, & Capdevila, 2014).

Transnational psychological approaches require grassroots methods of understanding communities around the world, welcoming Indigenous knowledge and partnering with communities in an egalitarian manner. They require genuine respect for communities' questions and needs, incorporating local knowledge and using ethnography, autobiography, and other qualitative approaches. In the process, psychologists may be exposed to new forms of knowledge acquisition and different forms of information that have the potential to enrich understanding. Although not a panacea, transnational psychology, also called *transnational feminist psychology*, is a paradigm that holds promise for helping to decolonize Western psychology and creating opportunities for a better understanding of human nature. Decolonization entails identifying and questioning histories of Western power and political and cultural domination and attempting to overcome associated racialized, capitalistic, institutional, and gender oppression. For the purposes of this book, however, authors may use *transnational psychology* as an umbrella term, with the understanding that it encompasses transnational psychology's many variants. Furthermore, some authors may use the terms *transnational psychology* and *transnational feminist psychology* as if they are synonymous.

TRANSNATIONAL FEMINISM

The term *transnationalism* itself is not connected with a theory but is useful when seen as an umbrella concept or paradigm (Vertovec, 2009). Transnationalism breaks away from traditional nation-state centered analyses and focuses on connections that exist separately from and beyond state-defined borders, laws, institutions, and national identities and the narratives associated with them. It is more focused on the human phenomena associated with globalization than is globalism, which pertains to the expansion of business interests, economic systems, and policy. The study of transnationalism examines how networks form, their characteristics, how they are maintained, and their influences on governance (Vertovec, 2011). Transnationalism is also concerned with the movement of people, companies, goods, money, and other objects across borders and its impacts. Examples of transnational phenomena include the expansion, distribution, and networks of businesses, organizations, workers, social groups, ethnic and religious communities, crime syndicates, social movements, and professionals around the globe (Vertovec, 2011). Chapters 2 and 11 present more detailed, interdisciplinary descriptions of the development of transnationalism and transnational feminisms.

Transnational feminisms developed in response to changes brought about by escalating globalization and rejection of the utopic and universalized politics of "global sisterhood" (Mohanty, 1991). Transnational feminist approaches pertain to the interdisciplinary study of the complex, uneven, changing, unequal relationships among women around the world. These approaches evolved out of postcolonial and Third World feminist movements within sociology, history, political science, law, and other disciplines. Transnational feminist approaches were created to address the new contexts created by escalating globalization, power dynamics, rapidly increasing migration, an increasingly interconnected world, and other phenomena that transcend nation-state boundaries. Transnational feminisms also consider the impact of the movement of people, companies, goods, money, and other objects across borders.

Transnational feminist approaches reject the concept of global sisterhood (as presented in Morgan, 1984), which was developed largely by White, middle-class feminists from WEIRD countries. Global sisterhood is problematic because it portrays women's experiences as homogeneous and emphasizes the role of gender-based oppression in determining women's fates to the exclusion of many other forms of oppression (Mohanty, 1991). There is no one unified, homogeneous transnational feminism because transnational feminist approaches are articulated by groups existing in different physical, economic, political, geographic, ethnic, and religious *situations* (variables or characteristics that influence their perspectives, also called *positions* and *locations*). Transnational feminist work often focuses on small, specific populations to reduce the degree of universalizing. *Universalizing* means applying broad norms, values, research results, or concepts to all people and cultures, regardless of the contexts in which they are located. Universalists assume all people are essentially the same (Teo, 2014). Transnational feminisms highlight the unique, diverse needs and agendas of different communities and cultures.

Transnational feminist approaches take a comparative rather than relative analytic approach to uncover the nuances of women's experiences within their communities (McHugh, 2007). A *comparative analytic approach* focuses intensely on the entity studied, looking at it from a variety of perspectives, examining the influences of various contexts and characteristics (e.g., historical, cultural, developmental, physiological, social, theoretical). It is similar to a case study of a community or population. Although research involving direct comparisons between groups (e.g., comparisons of age, culture, religion, nation-state) may be reviewed, such direct comparisons are more the focus of *relativistic analytic approaches*, also called *relativistic approaches* (McHugh, 2007).

Transnational feminist approaches favor social constructivist over essentialist explanations for human behavior and mental processes. The *social constructivist* perspective holds that characteristics and meanings have social causes—that they are created by society. Social constructivism holds that characteristics exist because people have agreed they exist and so they behave as if they exist. *Essentialism* holds that a community's characteristics are inherent—that they are fundamental to that group. Essentialism often assumes that group attributes have biological underpinnings (Morton, 2013).

Swarr and Nagar (2010) suggested that transnational feminism be viewed as an analytic lens or a critical stance on knowledge production and activism. Chiu (2015) wrote, "It is a political framework—a way of seeing that potentially offers a feminist escape from overdetermined colonial and colonizing, liberal and neoliberal, Western paradigms, narratives, processes, methodologies, practices, and applications" (p. 6). Conway provides a more detailed, interdisciplinary analysis of the origins and principles of transnational feminisms in Chapter 2.

TRANSNATIONAL FEMINIST PSYCHOLOGIES

Transnational feminist psychologies, also called *transnational psychologies*, are new and still evolving. Few psychologists have adopted transnational feminist psychological approaches. Discussion of transnational psychology seems to have begun in different areas within psychology in the late 2000s. Publications followed shortly thereafter. It developed in response to increased incidence and interest in diaspora groups. *Diaspora groups* are populations that have been involuntarily displaced from their homelands and have become dispersed across the globe because of such things as disagreements within the group, living and work conditions, war or globalization and associated imperialism (Ember, Ember, & Skoggard, 2005a, 2005b). Transnational psychology was also influenced by the study of intersections and the colonial and imperialist aspects of globalization. Sunil Bhatia (2007) suggested that a global and transnational cultural psychology was needed to examine the complexities associated with identities created in diasporas. He found the existing "narrow, atomic, and bounded notion of a community and culture outdated" in the context of globalization and associated diasporas (Bhatia, 2007, p. 11). Bhatia (2007) noted that the new context meant people could have multiple places they called "home," multiple languages, and even multiple selves. Some years later, Shelly Grabe and Nicole Else-Quest (2012) proposed a transnational feminist psychology shaped by the application of transnational feminism to the field of psychology. They also proposed a "transnational intersectionality" that expanded intersectionality to include local and global historical, sociopolitical, human rights, nationhood, economic, and political forces to the analysis of how oppressive institutions are interconnected.

Transnational feminist psychology was also articulated by Tugce Kurtiş and Glenn Adams (2013) in response to the need to resolve the tension between liberation-oriented forms of psychology, specifically feminist and cultural psychology perspectives. They developed their definition of transnational feminist psychology based on interdisciplinary discussions in postcolonial and feminist studies. Kurtiş and Adams envisioned a transnational feminist psychology that would use the context-sensitive focus of cultural psychology to reconsider and denaturalize the overgeneralizing theories of traditional Western science. Their approach views people in Majority World settings as resources (rather than ignorant and helpless) in the challenging of traditional scientific thought. It uses cultural–psychological critiques to question expansion-oriented relationality and uncover frameworks that illuminate pathways for the liberation of both women and men.

Even leading scholars in international psychology are only beginning to integrate the paradigm into their work (Machizawa & Enns, 2015), although some have used associated perspectives, such as intersectionality, liberation psychology, Indigenous psychology, cross-cultural psychology, and cultural psychology. As with transnational feminism, there is no unified definition of transnational psychology because it has emerged from multiple disciplines and different areas of psychology. It is shaped by diverse scholars' unique locations, situations, and standpoints. Transnational feminist psychologies have been influenced by insights from postcolonial, postmodern, Third World, and Women of Color feminisms (these concepts are described later in the chapter). There are, however, some themes that often run through the approaches.

Transnational feminist psychological approaches aim to incorporate the voices and experiences of those in the 95% of the world's population (the Global Majority), including diaspora groups, as yet unrepresented by Western psychology. Diaspora groups share their culture, knowledge, and practices with others as they travel, which constitutes another type of cross-border flow. The foundational anthropological studies of Schiller, Basch, and Blanc (1995) demonstrated how immigrants create and recreate their culture and identities as they transverse borders, cultures, and societies, struggling to keep connections with their countries of origin while continuing to view themselves as a community. They concluded that people are fundamentally changed by their contact with different cultures, technology, media, and relationships. Transnational psychologies view identities formed by the migration process as multifaceted, fused, hybridized, fluctuating, and sometimes fragmented (Bhatia, 2007; Rasmussen, 2015). Migration researchers have also noted that transnational networks take form within fluid social spaces, creating being and identity in two places simultaneously (Smith, 2005; Vertovec, 2009), as Espín and Dottolo discuss in Chapter 5 of this volume.

Transnational feminist psychologies are responsive to criticisms of feminism and psychology emanating from intersectionality and critical race theory (also described later in the chapter). As a result, transnational feminist psychologies offer strategies to challenge hegemonies (institutions, traditions, beliefs, and practices that move culture in a direction that benefits the dominant group) within existing ways of thinking, seeing, and doing. It is more attentive to the realities of the Global Majority women's lives than its precursors. It has been criticized as being not sensitive enough, however, due to the dominance of the Global Minority in academic epistemological circles (Grewal & Kaplan, 1994; Mohanty, 1991). Within psychology, transnational feminist psychologies are most closely related to cultural psychology, liberation psychology, and feminist psychologies. As Espín and Dottolo (Chapter 5, this volume) point out, transnational feminist psychologies do not simply subsume all other approaches to date.

Definitions of transnational feminist psychology are fluid, dynamic, and multifaceted, as is its conceptualization of identity. Because one of its assumptions is that much depends on where you are situated (what your specific life situation and context are), people in different locations will develop different transnational psychologies. There is a debate about whether *transnational feminist psychology* or *transnational psychology* is the preferable term. Some Global Majority women (women not represented in mainstream Western psychology) object to Western feminism's emphasis on gender as the primary analytic. Some see the term *transnational feminist psychology* as compromising transnational psychology's mission by elevating one of the multitude of characteristics affecting lived experience over others. This is consistent with Kurtiş and Adams's (2015) belief that transnational psychology's goal is to liberate both women and men; however, they too use the term *transnational feminist psychology*. Others are concerned that once *feminist* is dropped from the label, women's struggles will be forgotten. If, however, transnational psychology is proactively focusing on those who are most negatively affected by local and global dynamics, then it will necessarily include analyses of gender oppression within communities. The *transnational psychology of women* is defined as the application of transnational or transnational feminist psychology to the psychological study of women. Furthermore, in this chapter, transnational psychology is used as an umbrella term, with the understanding that it encompasses transnational psychology's many variants.

Development of Transnational Feminist Psychology

What follows is a brief description of some of the historical events, theoretical perspectives, and associated debates that were important in the development of transnational feminist psychology. Because these perspectives are also defined differently depending on the specific field and scholars' positions, it is important to read further regarding their varied and nuanced definitions and applications. Janet Conway presents a more in-depth, detailed, scholarly account in Chapter 2.

Impact of Globalization

In the late 1970s, many countries began to lift tariffs and other restrictive practices and open their markets to global commerce (Scheer, Stevens, & Mkandawire-Valhmu, 2016; Wolf, 2014). Treaties, organizations such as the World Trade Organization and the International Monetary Fund, private companies, and financial markets created policies such as "special economic zones" that provide benefits to developing areas; however, transnational labor laws made it more difficult to advocate for better wages, working conditions, and rights. Although the financial status of the wealthiest in high-income countries improved, it worsened for others, who often migrated to less developed countries where they earned lower wages under worse working conditions (Gelfand, Lyons, & Lun, 2011; McHugh, 2007; Mohanty, 2003a). Globalization often undermined local economies, exacerbating oppression, reinforcing hierarchies associated with class, gender, and race, and disrupting families and educational opportunities (McHugh, 2007; Mohanty, 2003a). Local farming declined, and access to necessities (food, water, health care, housing, utilities, education, and safety) was reduced. The nature of employment opportunities changed, and wages, benefits, rights, and state-provided services declined (Lindio-McGovern, 2007). In some regions, globalization brought greater repression and militarization.

Global forces also interacted with and were adapted to local laws, customs, and political, economic, and social contexts through a process called *glocalization* (Yuval-Davis, 2009). Glocalization is often characterized by more rapid *creolization*, in which traditional and modern cultures mix together to become part of a new distinct culture. This was the result of both contiguous and noncontiguous cross-border flows. *Contiguous flows* are influences that cross the borders of adjacent states or regions—for instance, culture and practices accompanying company employees, military personnel, and other migrants entering a location. *Noncontiguous flows* are types of exposure to culture, practices, and other influences from nonadjacent regions. Examples of sources of noncontiguous flows are the Internet, cell phones, and radio and television broadcasts, which transfer information globally in real time (Smith, 2005; Vertovec, 2009).

Transnational migration research in the 2000s brought new understandings and applications. Migrating families often lean heavily on women, increasing their workload at home and work, while increasing dependence on men to mediate between them and their new social, economic, and legal environment (Yuval-Davis, 2009). As the environment becomes more unpredictable and uncontrollable and as women gain access to workspaces previously not permitted, men often invoke and enforce fundamentalist beliefs and traditions that bolster gendered power differentials that favor and reassure men.

By the 1990s, postcolonial and postmodern feminisms encountered issues related to globalization. With increasingly rapid globalization, Western imperialism escalated. Westerners were in the minority globally (hence the term *Global Minority*), and yet their ideas, culture, and aggressions were unduly influential over the rest of the world (the Majority World). In many cases, Western imperial forces were more damaging and disruptive than local patriarchal and racial forces even when they were allegedly there to "help." Sometimes local gender and racial disparities, tensions, and threats among Majority World populations paled in comparison to the threat posed by the capitalistic, Minority World forces. Women in the Majority World came to see people of all colors and sexes from WEIRD (Henrich et al., 2010) countries as the real threat; they were perceived as aligned with colonial and imperial forces (Shiva, 2002). Although imperial groups were led by men, those subjected to their exploitation and oppression perceived imperial group women as complicit because they benefited from the situation (Abu-Lughod, 1990; Christopher, Wendt, Marecek, & Goodman, 2014; Falcón, 2016; Mohanty, 2006; Shiva, 2002). It was (and still is) necessary for the privileged few to recognize and redress this inequality to build transnational alliances.

Globalization disproportionally entailed more disadvantages for women in the Global Majority than those in the Global Minority. Indigenous women were (and still are) particularly vulnerable to the impact of globalization (Shiva, 2002). Globalization intensified structural inequalities; however, it also transformed feminists' and women's ways of organizing by opening new avenues for them to form transnational alliances. Globalization also promoted the magnitude and significance of grassroots involvement across the globe (Ferree & Tripp, 2006). Technological advancement in the 1990s accelerated mobilization of women in that it created opportunities for them to form a collective identity to work toward shared goals. In other words, we entered a new era where activism can take place transnationally to address a number of women's issues associated with globalization and capitalism.

Theoretical Precursors Outside of Psychology

Postmodernism and postcolonialism were both influential in the development of transnational psychological perspectives. These two perspectives share some concepts and methods with each other and with transnational feminism. Like transnational feminism, their definitions vary, partly depending on the field within which they are being applied (e.g., arts, anthropology, history, political science, sociology) and partly with scholars' positions. Postmodern approaches became popular in the 1980s and 1990s. Postmodern approaches objected to and critiqued passive acceptance of dominant ideologies, including objective reality, morality, human nature, social progress, and other universalist perspectives. Universalist perspectives consider it acceptable to apply broad norms, values, research results, or concepts to all people and cultures, regardless of the contexts in which they are located. Universalists assumed all people are essentially the same (Teo, 2014).

Postmodern feminism has drawn attention to the socially constructed basis of knowledge, examining the influence of culture, history, political forces, and power in determining dominant theories and discourses. It has also emphasized the importance of acknowledging one's position and subjective perspective when presenting ideas and "facts." Advocates have argued that *pluralism*, the consideration of many different perspectives and sources of information, is important when trying to approximate truth. Postmodern feminism has been characterized as less activist than transnational and most other forms of feminism (Mardorossian, 2002).

Recently, the Minority World (i.e., the United States and Western Europe) has been the primary source of imperialistic forces, which are often associated with capitalism and neoliberalism. *Imperialism* occurs when a group expands its power through land acquisition, diplomacy, or force. It is closely associated with *colonization*, which occurs when an outside group extends its influence over other people and lands, forcing its rule and associated culture, beliefs, and practices on them and exploiting them. *Neoliberalism* refers to a version of liberalism that supports free-market capitalism with little government regulation.

Postcolonialism focuses on the consequences of colonization for those taken over and exploited in the context of capitalism and neoliberalism. Postcolonial feminism's concepts are useful in examining groups' relationships with power structures (Brabeck & Brown, 1997; Kurtiş & Adams, 2015). Postcolonial feminism critiques Western thought including psychological paradigms (Ralston, 2009). It seeks to incorporate the concerns of Third World feminists but is still accused of having a Western, elitist bias because it has become institutionalized within Western academe (Grewal & Kaplan, 1994; Mohanty, 1991). As such, it contributes to uneven knowledge production between Majority and Minority Worlds. Postcolonial feminism is particularly useful in deconstructing and decolonizing Western ideas. Advocates demand that psychologists deepen awareness of psychologies around the world and critically evaluate and openly admit conceptual, political, historical, and other frameworks that shape our beliefs. Postcolonial feminist approaches insist that psychologists identify and question histories of Western power and take action to overcome associated racialized, capitalistic, institutional, and gender oppression.

Postcolonial feminism discourages simplistically conceptualizing binary, differently valued entities (e.g., pairs of characteristics such as good or bad or male or female in which one part of the pair is preferred). It also examines capitalism's impact on daily life, exploitation of labor forces, intersections of identity, gender stereotypes associated with women's bodies, and traditional masculine notions of national identity (Schutte, 1998). Postcolonial feminists also pointed out how Western feminists' attempt to "save" Third World women actually took their voices away by telling their stories for them and reframing these stories through Western lenses (Spivak, 1988). Postcolonial feminism criticized Western feminism for positioning Third World women as the agentless oppressed who need to be rescued (Spivak, 1988).

Like postmodern and postcolonial feminists, transnational psychology scholars seek information and understanding of the culture, history, values, and local and global sociopolitical forces impinging on the communities with whom they collaborate on studies, interventions, and other projects. They push the feminist mantra, "the personal is political" to a more sophisticated level of analysis by interviewing multiple individual members within the community to achieve a more pluralistic understanding of the particularities of the group (see Chapter 8). Transnational psychologists engage in strong reflexivity, a rigorous form of critical consciousness, to identify the impact of position and culture on their epistemological location (ways of knowing and perspective). It is achieved by identifying the historical, cultural, and social influences on their values and research hypotheses, design, and results (Harding, 1991; McHugh, 2007). More information about strong reflexivity can be found in *Qualitative Inquiry*'s special issue on "European Contributions to Strong Reflexivity" (Kuehner, Ploder, & Langer, 2016).

Another theoretical influence, critical race theory, is related to both postmodern and postcolonial feminism. It questions ideas about race and deals with the oppression and exploitation of People of Color by Whites. Critical race theory examines the social construction of race, power, and law and exposes White privilege. It critiques the imposition of White culture, ideas, and behaviors on People of Color. It shares with postmodern and postcolonial approaches a commitment to the importance of qualitative data such as narratives and a rejection of liberalism and *essentialism* (the idea that phenomena such as race and gender are biologically determined rather than socially constructed). Women of Color feminism is related to critical race theory. Women of Color feminism developed in response to the recognition that gender was not the primary factor that determined women's fates and that women's experiences were not as homogeneous as implied by the White mainstream Western feminist idea of global sisterhood (hooks, 1984; Mohanty, 1991; Morgan, 1984).

Intersectionality is an analytic framework developed by Women of Color feminists that originally examined influences on the oppression of Women of Color (Crenshaw, 1989) but has been expanded to study the intersecting oppressions of other groups as well. This is in contrast to White mainstream Western feminisms, which focus on the impact of gender-based power differentials on women and the process of women's liberation from them. Women of Color feminism criticized mainstream, Western feminist psychologies for being too universalist in treating women's experiences as homogeneous. Women of Color feminists developed an intersectional approach, related to post-structuralism and synonymous with kyriarchy (Pui-lan, 2009). In current forms, intersectionality and kyriarchy move beyond the focus on patriarchy and examine how multiple systems of discrimination and oppression overlap and are often compounded when individuals are members of more than one disadvantaged social category or group. These newest approaches go beyond Western feminist approaches by examining the interaction of power differentials and systems affecting those marginalized due to race, gender, class, age, sexual orientation, and ability. Although Women of Color feminists have greatly expanded psychology's understanding of intersectionality, they have been criticized by transnational psychologists and Third World feminists for being neocolonialistic and for focusing on gender and racial oppression in WEIRD country contexts (Kurtiş & Adams, 2015, p. 389).

Third World Feminist thinking is influenced by Chandra Mohanty, a prominent transnational and postcolonial theorist, who believes it is essential that Third World women generate knowledge and feminist analyses from their own experiences of oppression and resistance within their particular local through national contexts (Mohanty, 1984). In 2003, Mohanty published her book *Feminism Without Borders*, which deconstructed the Western feminist discourse that constructed a monolithic image of Third World women as oppressed and victimized by universalized patriarchy. She also observed that Western feminists frequently portray themselves as the educators, and sometimes saviors, of Global Majority women (Mohanty, 1991). Rather than viewing patriarchy or Whites as their oppressors as White women and Women of Color do respectively, many Global Majority women see powerful, imperialistic, colonizing entities as their primary oppressors. Although White men may lead the oppressive entities (e.g., countries and companies), again, Global Majority women see members of the Global Minority as complicit, regardless of gender or color (Christopher et al., 2014; Deepak, 2012; Falcón, 2016; Mohanty, 2006).

Both Third World feminism and transnational feminism reject universalist notions. In their book, *Hegemonies: Postmodernity and Transnational Feminist Practices*, Grewal and Kaplan (1994) described how *hegemonies*, the ways that imperialist groups impose themselves on others, can take many different forms depending on women's unique contexts. Hegemonies cut across political, economic, cultural, and social domains at the local through global levels, subordinating women (Sato, 2016). These "scattered hegemonies" impact identity formation, relationships, and social hierarchies and serve to perpetuate inequality. Because these hegemonic practices are present in so many varied forms, they require a variety of decolonizing interventions to root out the sources of inequity and oppression (Grewal & Kaplan, 1994). This is an area ripe for psychological study. Consistent with this, both Third World feminism and transnational feminism object to the idea that all women experience the same type of gender-based oppression. They view experiences of oppression as additionally impacted by economic exploitation and social hierarchies linked to imperialism and colonialism but exacerbated by globalization. Grabe and Else-Quest (2012) called this phenomenon *transnational intersectionality*. Thus, both Third World feminism and transnational feminism reject the universalist notions at the heart of White mainstream

Western feminisms and attend instead to "complex and intersecting oppressions and multiple forms of resistance" (Herr, 2014, p. 2).

Third World feminists and transnational feminists differ in some ways. Third World feminists give more attention to analyses based on nation-state boundaries and nationalism than most transnational feminists do. However, transnational feminists attend to borders when land is of particular significance to a community. In many cases, transnational feminists see nation-states and nationalism as disadvantageous to feminist causes and focus on feminist entities operating at the transnational level beyond individual nation-states (Grewal & Kaplan, 2001; Nagar & Swarr, 2010). In addition, Third World feminist approaches tend to focus less on diaspora than do transnational feminist approaches.

Transnational Feminism's Development Within Psychology

Early American and European psychological approaches were universal, linear, and essentialist. They assumed that all humans have a common ancestry, a common internal structure, and therefore common psychic characteristics—characteristics defined by Western cultural norms and behaviors. Racial and cultural variants were conceptualized as overlying a common structure, like layers of an onion (Bhatia, 2007). Although these Western approaches dominated psychological theory and research, their primary research sample only represented a minority (7%) of the world's population (Worldometers, 2019) and until recently was predominantly male. When limited to U.S. scholarship, that number dips to 5%. The results from this research are often inappropriately generalized to the other 93% to 95%—the Global Majority (Arnett, 2008; Henrich et al., 2010; Worldometers, 2019).

Cross-cultural psychology focuses on differences and similarities between cultures, rather than nations, to understand universals and variations. It uses a relativistic analytic approach, whereas transnational feminism uses a comparative analytic approach. Psychologists working from this perspective have expanded our understanding of cognition, language, social behaviors, acculturation, and cultural identity and elevated awareness of immigrant identity and its progression through stages (Bhatia, 2007).

Cross-cultural psychology is often confused with *international psychology*. Phenomena are typically considered "international" when they involve interactions or transfers between nation-states. Diplomacy, contracts, disputes, and other interactions involving the governing bodies of nation-states and the movement and comparison of people and things between two nation-states are considered international (Vertovec, 2011). Consistent with this, international psychology refers to any number of psychology-related activities (research, meetings, businesses, organizations) conducted across nation-state borders, rather than a unique theoretical perspective (Bullock, 2013). International psychology research typically focuses on comparisons between nation-states as defined by geographical and governmental borders. Researchers see patterns within a nation-state or region as universal, homogeneous, and static. Sometimes such cross-border comparisons are mistakenly referred to as transnational, but transnational psychology focuses on the unique local and global influences on individual communities, which are not defined by nation-state borders.

Unlike international psychology, transnational psychology deemphasizes nation-state and cultural boundaries that assume static populations, except in cases in which land is important to the groups' cultural heritage (e.g., as in the case of diaspora groups displaced from their homelands). Although background knowledge of a region and broad-brush cross-border comparisons may be useful in expanding general understandings of the range of potential influences and contexts in regions, they may not be representative of the community of interest and can also engender the development of stereotypes and inaccurate assumptions. Instead, transnational psychologists tend to look closely at the current and historical cultural, economic, and political influences on a community from local to global and how they shape the day-to-day realities in that community. They may also look at these realities for an individual within that community. Grabe and Else-Quest (2012) recommended using both microlevel and macrolevel analyses of indicators of systemic and structural dynamics affecting psychological well-being from regions across the globe to counter Western perspectives. Multiple levels of analysis (individual through global) should be included and integrated and their interactions examined if we are to understand the many contexts within which relevant, effective forms of community empowerment may potentially be achieved (Zimmerman, 1990).

Indigenous psychology developed around the same time as transnational feminism, in reaction to the colonization and hegemony of Western psychology. Indigenous psychology focuses on peoples' unique, native behavior and thinking not imported from other regions. It is described as

> a set of approaches to understanding human behavior within the cultural contexts in which they have developed and are currently displayed. . . . [Indigenous psychology] attempts to root psychological research in the conceptual systems that are indigenous to a culture, including the philosophical, theological, and scientific ideas that are part of the historical and contemporary lives of people and their institutions. (Allwood & Berry, 2006, p. 241)

Indigenous psychologies raise awareness and increase understanding of Indigenous constructs, philosophies, practices, and their applications and inclusion in global discourse within psychology. Indigenous psychological approaches struggle with the charge that they are universalist because they view culture as static and stable, and they do not address globalization (Bhatia, 2010; Kim & Berry, 1993; Roopnarine & Chadee, 2016).

Cultural psychology and liberation psychology are probably the areas of psychology closest to transnational psychology. *Cultural psychology* views human behavior and mental processes as the product of a progressive, dynamic, reciprocal, and organic interaction among or between the human psyche, culture, and experience (Shweder, 1990). Although it has not addressed the specific contexts of globalization, migration, and diaspora groups, this approach has impacted the evolution of newer models (Bhatia, 2007; Martín-Baró, 1994). Transnational psychology expands on cultural psychology by incorporating the study of migration and diasporic groups and critiquing identity narratives created by migration, colonization, culture, diasporic communities, political context, individual experiences, and Western perspectives.

Both liberation psychology and transnational psychology identify and demonstrate how local and global centers of power and dominance (especially capitalism) result in inequality between people of different socially constructed groups, including gender, nationality, class, and ethnicity. *Liberation psychology* explores and examines the dynamic psychological processes and behaviors of oppressed and impoverished communities. It is concerned with how they seek emancipation and escape from sociopolitical and structural aspects of oppression (Adams, Dobles, Gomez, Kurtiş, & Molina, 2015; Kurtiş & Adams, 2015). Important concepts of liberation psychology include *conscientization* (achieving a deep understanding that allows the identification of contradictions), *critical realism* (combining philosophies of science and social science to articulate the connection between the natural and social worlds), deconstructing reality, liberation of oppressed majorities, and nontraditional research methods (Freire, 2000). Both liberation and transnational psychology recognize that the Global Majority often finds itself in oppressive sociopolitical contexts (Sloan, 2002). Tugce Kurtiş and Glenn Adams (2013) proposed transnational psychology as a paradigm to resolve the tension between liberation-oriented forms of psychology, specifically feminist and cultural psychology perspectives, in the hope that by bringing forward the silenced perspectives of marginalized people, transnational psychology can liberate people in Global Majority settings (Kurtiş & Adams, 2015).

FREQUENT CONSIDERATIONS IN TRANSNATIONAL PSYCHOLOGIES

The following is a list of considerations often associated with transnational feminist psychologies that have the potential to move the field of psychology forward. These characteristics also interact dynamically, creating more complex and nuanced conceptualizations of human behavior. Chapter authors describe how some of these considerations interact and are applied in transnational psychology. The following list serves as an introduction to some of the common themes and issues characteristic of transnational psychology. Transnational psychological approaches often

- *address the contexts of globalization and diaspora groups.* Transnational psychology was initially developed in response to the increased incidence and interest in diasporas. Sunil Bhatia (2007) wrote that a global and transnational cultural psychology was needed to examine the complexities associated with identities created in the context of globalization and diasporas. Bhatia (2007) noted that as a result of globalization, "home" was not a single place or space but many, being multilingual was necessary, and individuals enacted multiple salient identities. He felt these realities warranted a new approach. Although the impact of globalization may be greatest on Majority World populations, it also affects Minority World residents.
- *question the utopic idea that sisterhood is global.* As noted earlier, the concept of global sisterhood (Morgan, 1984) is problematic because it portrays women's experiences as homogeneous and emphasizes the role of gender-based oppression in determining women's fates. The idea of global sisterhood was developed largely by White, middle-class feminists from WEIRD countries. Transnational feminism draws attention to the many different kinds of challenges women face given scattered hegemonies that may require different actions to address (Grewal & Kaplan, 1994). It is because of the impacts of these scattered hegemonies that global sisterhood is an inadequate theoretical ideal. Ideally, women should be able to support each other without glossing over differences. Some feminists advocate for identifying common dilemmas and supporting each other on those, but unfortunately, the issues selected have been those primarily important to the Global Minority. Even if the focus were on issues affecting the largest number of women, it would be preferable to work toward a more comprehensive approach that protects all women.
- *respect and elevate new and silenced voices.* The viewpoints of women who have been previously excluded could radically reframe feminist thought, politics, and practice (Mohanty, 2003b). Oppressed groups are less invested in the status quo and therefore more likely to reveal its limitations, whereas

members of dominant groups are more likely to be invested in continuing to conform to their dominant culture and therefore are more likely to obscure reality (Miller, 1986). Elevating new and silenced voices, including those of diaspora groups, has the potential to reveal information about the contexts and perspectives of Global Majority communities. Unfortunately, speaking up and being understood, respected, and heard is largely a privilege of those holding power (Alexander, 2006). Ironically, even when Minority World individuals spend time critiquing Minority World perspectives, they may inadvertently reinforce their importance. Popular media often downplays Global Majority women's strengths, advantages, life satisfactions, and opportunities and instead diminish, infantilize, and pathologize them, depicting them as helpless victims in need of rescue. This reinforces the historical colonial image of uninformed, ignorant Global Majority women in "underdeveloped" countries (Cronin-Furman, Gowrinathan, & Zakaria, 2017; Mohanty, 1991) and reinforces Western imperialist traditions. Such portrayals may lead viewers to underestimate the agency and competence of Global Majority women, leading others to disregard their viewpoints and ignore local programs and initiatives. Global Majority women are thereby silenced and agentless (Cronin-Furman et al., 2017).

Ideally, media biases should be corrected, and disempowered communities should speak for themselves. Mohanty (1991) encouraged people with privilege to use their access to power and resources to elevate Majority World voices to displace imperial, patriarchal ones. This can be facilitated by increasing the presence of Majority World voices in public forums and through narrative and qualitative data collection techniques. Elevating Global Majority voices helps to decenter the frameworks created by people in WEIRD settings, displacing Minority World influence, ultimately resulting in a more pluralistic understanding of communities. Increasing the representation of Majority World voices in decision-making forums is key to empowering people in Majority World settings to develop agendas for change that speak directly to their needs and experiences (Kurtiş & Adams, 2015).

- *consider positionality extremely important.* Transnational psychological approaches emphasize the importance of attending to *positionality*, the notion that how one understands the world is influenced by one's values, views, and social and spatial positions. Transnational psychology underscores that no research is value free, and thus it is critical to examine how one's social and spatial positions impact the knowledge production process. Consistent with this, it encourages strong reflexivity (Harding, 1991).

- *examine the impact of human rights policies and legislation on communities.* Human rights policies and legislation are often unduly influenced by Minority World perspectives and priorities. Furthermore, their benefits may only be experienced by privileged groups. In many cases, despite the development of laws that ostensibly improve women's rights, gender inequities, and women's status, these laws are often not enforced at the local level and do not change culture and tradition. Laws and policies related to the treatment of women may have little influence at the community level because they conflict with local norms and culture (Abeyasekera & Marecek, 2008). Considerable work still has to be done to ensure communities have a voice in shaping laws and that local norms and culture actively integrate and respect laws related to human rights.

- *critique dominance and exploitation of culturally different others.* Transnational psychology critiques the dominance and exploitation of culturally different others and avoids binaries. *Avoiding binaries* entails not conceptualizing groups as divided into dichotomous pairs, one of which is good, or preferred, and the other lesser, as in good or bad, male or female, developed or undeveloped. Transnational psychology also encourages the critique of dominant ideologies, including objective reality, morality, human nature, social progress, and other universalist perspectives. Transnational psychology seeks to deconstruct and decolonize Global Minority (Western) psychological ideas that celebrate individuality and independence.

  Transnational psychology also identifies and demonstrates how local and global centers of power and dominance (especially capitalism) result in inequality between people of different socially constructed groups, including gender, nationality, class, and ethnicity. It also explores and examines the dynamic psychological processes and behaviors of oppressed and impoverished communities and how they seek emancipation and escape from sociopolitical and structural aspects of oppression (Adams et al., 2015; Kurtiş & Adams, 2015).

- *believe that knowledge is socially constructed and not owned by any one group.* Transnational psychology does not conceptualize psychology as universal, linear, and essentialist. It views knowledge as influenced by culture, history, political forces, and power. Transnational psychology encourages psychologists to actively seek information and understanding of the culture, history, values, and local and global sociopolitical forces impinging on the communities with whom they collaborate. Transnational psychologists also acknowledge that no one group owns "knowledge" and work to bring forward the silenced perspectives of marginalized people in recognition of the advantages of the *plurality of knowledge*—that many different types and forms of knowledge exist and should be taken into consideration to better approximate "truth."

- *examine microlevel through macrolevel contexts and unique local through global influences*. Transnational psychological approaches focus on the unique local and global influences on individual communities, which are not defined by nation-state borders. Transnational psychological approaches deemphasize nation-state and cultural boundaries that assume static populations, except in cases where land is important to the group's culture and heritage. Else-Quest and Grabe (2012) recommended enhancing both micro- and macrolevel knowledge regarding local, state, regional, and global historical, economic, political, and other forces and including it in analyses. Transnational psychological approaches study individual communities by using ethnography and qualitative research approaches to better understand microlevel dynamics, the nuances of individuals' and communities' lives.

- *extend the notion of intersectionality*. Transnational psychological approaches view experiences of oppression as additionally impacted by the economic exploitation and social hierarchies associated with imperialism, colonialism, and globalization. Grabe and Else-Quest (2012) referred to this extended form of intersectionality as *transnational intersectionality*. Transnational psychological approaches also extend the notion of intersectionality by adding consideration of historical, sociopolitical, economic, and other local and global influences to the analysis of how oppressive institutions are interconnected. They view the resulting influences and experiences as dynamic, fluid, and synergistic, rather than merely additive. Transnational psychological approaches view human behavior and mental processes as the product of a progressive, reciprocal, organic interaction among the human psyche, culture, and experience. They incorporate intersections of identities, human rights, nationhood, and economic and political forces, and in this approach identities that are formed by the migration process are multifaceted, fused, hybridized, fluctuating, and sometimes fragmented.

- *aim to develop egalitarian ways to collaborate and intervene in the context of asymmetrical power relations.* To understand a community, it is important that community members partner with those with resources to implement studies or interventions, simultaneously managing the asymmetrical power relations that might interfere with the process. It is critical that the relationship be egalitarian and mutually beneficial and that the questions and needs of those with more resources do not take precedence.

- *develop and use appropriate assessment and research methods.* Rather than focusing on broad cross-border or cross-cultural comparisons, most transnational psychological work homes in on what is happening at the community, family, or even individual levels to explore the impact of global and local phenomena on human well-being. Like postmodern and postcolonial feminist work, transnational psychological research and scholarship frequently use narrative and qualitative research methods. Traditional, Western macrolevel indices such as mortality rates, educational access and systems, life expectancy, employment opportunities, family resources, Western mental health data, and political participation (Mancini-Billson & Fluehr-Lobban, 2005) reflect institutions' (the state, nongovernmental agencies and the United Nations) effectiveness in improving conditions through legal and policy reforms but have limitations (Abeyasekera & Marecek, 2008). These measures do not necessarily represent actual conditions within every community, nor for each individual within each community. Current Western psychological assessment instruments and research techniques may become less valid and relevant as migration escalates. As identities become more fluid and life experiences become more variable, the nature of instruments and procedures will have to change. The processes currently used to validate and standardize psychological measures and instruments may no longer be relevant.

CONCLUSION

Transnational psychology raises our awareness of the impact of globalization, migration, capitalism, global corporations, and global organizations. It extends the notion of intersectionality by adding considerations of historical, sociopolitical, economic exploitation, and social hierarchies in the contexts of imperialism, colonialism, and globalization (Grabe & Else-Quest, 2012), while also stressing that the interactions among these factors are dynamic. Transnational psychology refocuses on the multitude of "scattered" ways that people can be dominated and mistreated and encourages us to attend to them simultaneously, rather than solely championing groups associated with our identities. It reminds us that knowledge is socially constructed, that nobody has the right to own or control it, that it should always be questioned, and that the more viewpoints incorporated into that knowledge, the richer our knowledge will be. Transnational psychology does not promise a utopia. It will be a continual struggle to ensure human rights that fit communities' values and needs, to collaborate equitably in the context of power asymmetries, and to find methodologies that sufficiently consider all the relevant considerations in micro through macro analyses of phenomena. It will be a challenge to work perpetually to raise awareness of new and silenced voices. Nevertheless, if one mission of psychology is to improve human well-being, psychologists must consider the new perspectives and approaches to research, theory, practice, and consultation that transnational approaches uncover. The chapters that follow provide illustrations and offer inspiration regarding how transnational psychology can challenge hegemony within psychology, expand international and intersectional approaches, and truly focus on enhanced global human well-being.

REFERENCES

Abeyasekera, A., & Marecek, J. (2008). Women's well-being: Between the local and the global. *Psychology of Women Quarterly, 32*, 483–484. http://dx.doi.org/10.1111/j.1471-6402.2008.00460_1.x

Abu-Lughod, L. (1990). Can there be a feminist ethnography? *Women & Performance, 5*, 7–27. http://dx.doi.org/10.1080/07407709008571138

Adams, G., Dobles, I., Gomez, L. H., Kurtiş, T., & Molina, L. E. (2015). Decolonizing psychological science: Introduction to the special thematic section. *Journal of Social and Political Psychology, 3*, 213–238. http://dx.doi.org/10.5964/jspp.v3i1.564

Alam, S. (2008). Majority World: Challenging the West's rhetoric of democracy. *Amerasia Journal, 34*, 87–98. http://dx.doi.org/10.17953/amer.34.1.l3176027k4q614v5

Alexander, M. J. (2006). *Pedagogies of crossing: Meditations on feminism, sexual politics, Memory and the Sacred*. Durham, NC: Duke University Press.

Allwood, C. M., & Berry, J. W. (2006). Preface: Special issue on the indigenous psychologies [Special issue]. *International Journal of Psychology, 41*, 241–242. http://dx.doi.org/10.1080/00207590544000022

Altmaier, E. M., & Hall, J. E. (2008). Introduction to international quality assurance for psychology. In J. E. Hall & E. M. Altmaier (Eds.), *Global promise: Quality assurance and accountability in professional psychology* (pp. 3–15). New York, NY: Oxford University Press. http://dx.doi.org/10.1093/acprof:oso/9780195306088.003.0001

Amer, A., Howarth, C., & Sen, R. (2015). Diasporic virginities: Social representations of virginity and identity formation amongst British Arab Muslim women. *Culture & Psychology, 21*, 3–19. http://dx.doi.org/10.1177/1354067X14551297

Arnett, J. J. (2008). The neglected 95%: Why American psychology needs to become less American. *American Psychologist, 63*, 602–614. http://dx.doi.org/10.1037/0003-066X.63.7.602

Ashcroft, B., Griffiths, G., & Tiffin, H. (2000). *Post-colonial studies: The key concepts.* London, England: Routledge.

Bhatia, S. (2007). Rethinking culture and identity in psychology: Towards a transnational cultural psychology. *Journal of Theoretical and Philosophical Psychology, 27–28*, 301–321. http://dx.doi.org/10.1037/h0091298

Bhatia, S. (2010). Theorizing indigenous psychology [Review of book *Indigenous and Cultural Psychology: People in Context* by U. Kim, K. Yang, & K. Hwang (Eds.)]. *Theory & Psychology, 20*(1), 137–140. https://dx.doi.org/10.1177/0959354309345640

Brabeck, M., & Brown, L. (1997). Feminist theory and psychological practice. In J. Worell & N. Johnson (Eds.), *Shaping the future of feminist psychology: Education, research, and practice* (pp. 15–35). Washington, DC: American Psychological Association. http://dx.doi.org/10.1037/10245-001

Bullock, M. (2013). International psychology. In D. K. Freedheim & I. B. Weiner (Eds.), *History of psychology* (pp. 562–596). Hoboken, NJ: Wiley.

Chiu, M. (2015). *Drawing new color lines: Transnational Asian American graphic narratives.* Hong Kong: Hong Kong University Press.

Christopher, J. C., Wendt, D. C., Marecek, J., & Goodman, D. M. (2014). Critical cultural awareness: Contributions to a globalizing psychology. *American Psychologist, 69*, 645–655. http://dx.doi.org/10.1037/a0036851

Collins, L. H. (2019). Teaching cultural and transnational psychology: Taking intersectionality across the globe. In J. A. Mena & K. Quina (Eds.), *Integrating multiculturalism and intersectionality into the psychology curriculum: Strategies for instructors* (pp. 181–196). Washington, DC: American Psychological Association.

Crenshaw, K. (1989). Demarginalizing the intersection of race and sex: A Black feminist critique of antidiscrimination doctrine, feminist theory and antiracist politics. *University of Chicago Legal Forum, 1989*(1). Retrieved from https://chicagounbound.uchicago.edu/cgi/viewcontent.cgi?article=1052&context=uclf

Cronin-Furman, K., Gowrinathan, N., & Zakaria, R. (2017). *Emissaries of empowerment.* New York: Colin Powell School for Civic and Public Leadership, The City College of New York.

Deepak, A. C. (2012). Globalization, power and resistance: Postcolonial and transnational feminist perspectives for social work practice. *International Social Work, 55*, 779–793. http://dx.doi.org/10.1177/0020872811414038

Else-Quest, N. M., & Grabe, S. (2012). The political is personal: Measurement and application of nation-level indicators of gender equity in psychological research. *Psychology of Women Quarterly, 36*, 131–144. http://dx.doi.org/10.1177/0361684312441592

Ember, M., Ember, C., & Skoggard, I. (Eds.). (2005a). *Encyclopedia of diasporas: Immigrant and refugee cultures around the world: Vol. I. Overviews and topics.* New York, NY: Springer.

Ember, M., Ember, C., & Skoggard, I. (Eds.). (2005b). *Encyclopedia of diasporas: Immigrant and refugee cultures around the world: Vol. II. Diaspora communities.* New York, NY: Springer.

Falcón, S. M. (2016). Transnational feminism as a paradigm for decolonizing the practice of research: Identifying feminist principles and methodology criteria for US-based scholars. *Frontiers, 37*, 174–194. http://dx.doi.org/10.5250/fronjwomestud.37.1.0174

Ferree, M. M., & Tripp, A. M. (2006). *Global feminism: Transnational women's activism, organizing, and human rights.* New York: New York University Press.

Finlay, L. (2002). Negotiating the swamp: The opportunity and challenge of reflexivity in research practice. *Qualitative Research, 2*, 209–230. http://dx.doi.org/10.1177/146879410200200205

Freire, P. (2000). *Pedagogy of the oppressed* (30th anniversary ed.). New York, NY: Continuum.

Gelfand, M. J., Lyons, S. L., & Lun, J. (2011). Toward a psychological science of globalization. *Journal of Social Issues, 67*(4), 841–853. http://dx.doi.org/10.1111/j.1540-4560.2011.01731.x

Grabe, S., & Else-Quest, N. M. (2012). The role of transnational feminism in psychology: Complementary visions. *Psychology of Women Quarterly, 36*, 158–161. http://dx.doi.org/10.1177/0361684312442164

Grewal, I., & Kaplan, C. (1994). Introduction. In I. Grewal & C. Kaplan (Eds.), *Scattered hegemonies* (pp. 1–33). Minneapolis: University of Minnesota Press.

Grewal, I., & Kaplan, C. (2001). Global identities: Theorizing transnational studies of sexuality. *A Journal of Lesbian and Gay Studies, 7*, 663–79. http://dx.doi.org/10.1215/10642684-7-4-663

Haraway, D. (1988). Situated knowledges: The science question in feminism and the privilege of partial perspective. *Feminist Studies, 14*, 575–599. http://dx.doi.org/10.2307/3178066

Harding, S. (1991). *Whose science? Whose knowledge?* Ithaca, NY: Cornell University Press.

Henrich, J., Heine, S. J., & Norenzayan, A. (2010). The weirdest people in the world? *Behavioral and Brain Sciences, 33*, 61–83. http://dx.doi.org/10.1017/S0140525X0999152X

Herr, R. S. (2014). Reclaiming Third World feminism: Or why transnational feminism needs Third World feminism. *Meridians, 12,* 1–30. http://dx.doi.org/10.2979/meridians.12.1.1

hooks, b. (1984). *Feminist theory from margin to center.* Boston, MA: South End Press.

Kim, U., & Berry, J. W. (Eds.). (1993). *Indigenous psychologies: Research and experience in cultural context.* Newbury Park, CA: Sage.

Kuehner, A., Ploder, A., & Langer, P. C. (2016). Introduction to the special issue: European contributions to strong reflexivity [Special issue]. *Qualitative Inquiry, 22,* 699–704. http://dx.doi.org/10.1177/1077800416658069

Kurtiş, T., & Adams, G. (2013). A cultural psychology of relationship: Toward a transnational feminist psychology. In M. K. Ryan & N. R. Branscombe (Eds.), *Handbook of gender and psychology* (pp. 251–269). London, England: Sage. http://dx.doi.org/10.4135/9781446269930.n16

Kurtiş, T., & Adams, G. (2015). Decolonizing liberation: Toward a transnational feminist psychology. *Journal of Social and Political Psychology, 3,* 388–413. http://dx.doi.org/10.5964/jspp.v3i1.326

Lindio-McGovern, L. (2007). Conclusion: Women and neoliberal globalization inequities and resistance. *Journal of Developing Societies, 23,* 285–297. http://dx.doi.org/10.1177/0169796X0602300216

Machizawa, S., & Enns, C. Z. (2015). Transnational psychological practice with women: Perspectives from East Asia and Japan. In C. Z. Enns, J. K. Rice, & R. L. Nutt (Eds.), *Psychological practice with women: Guidelines, diversity, empowerment* (pp. 225–256). Washington, DC: American Psychological Association. http://dx.doi.org/10.1037/14460-009

Macleod, C., Marecek, J., & Capdevila, R. (2014). Feminism and psychology going forward. *Feminism & Psychology, 24,* 3–17. http://dx.doi.org/10.1177/0959353513515308

Mancini-Billson, J., & Fluehr-Lobban, C. (2005). *Female well-being: Towards a global theory of social change.* New York, NY: Zed Books.

Mardorossian, C. M. (2002). Toward a new feminist theory of rape. *Signs, 27,* 743–775. http://dx.doi.org/10.1086/337938

Martín-Baró, I. (1994). *Writings for liberation psychology.* Cambridge, MA: Harvard University Press.

McHugh, N. A. (2007). *Feminist philosophies A–Z.* Edinburgh, Scotland: Edinburgh University Press.

Miller, J. B. (1986). *Toward a new psychology of women* (2nd ed.). Boston, MA: Beacon Press.

Mohanty, C. (1984). Under Western eyes: Feminist scholarship and colonial discourses. *Boundary 2, 12,* 333–358. http://dx.doi.org/10.2307/302821

Mohanty, C. T. (1991). Under Western eyes: Feminist scholarship and colonial discourses. In C. T. Mohanty, A. Russo, & L. Lourdes Torres, L. (Eds.), *Third World women and the politics of feminism* (pp. 51–78). Bloomington: Indiana University Press.

Mohanty, C. T. (2003a). *Feminism without borders: Decolonizing theory, practicing solidarity*. Durham, NC: Duke University Press. http://dx.doi.org/10.1215/9780822384649

Mohanty, C. T. (2003b). "Under Western eyes" revisited: Feminist solidarity through anticapitalist struggles. *Signs, 28*, 499–535. http://dx.doi.org/10.1086/342914

Mohanty, C. T. (2006). US Empire and the Project of Women's Studies: Stories of citizenship, complicity and dissent. *Gender, Place & Culture, 13:1*, 7–20. http://dx.doi.org/10.1080/09663690600571209

Morgan, R. (1984). *Sisterhood is global*. New York, NY: Feminist Press at CUNY.

Morgan-Consoli, M. L., Inman, A. G., Bullock, M., & Nolan, S. A. (2018). Framework for competencies for U.S. psychologists engaging internationally. *International Perspectives in Psychology: Research, Practice, Consultation, 7*, 174–188. http://dx.doi.org/10.1037/ipp0000090

Morton, T. A. (2013). An essential debate: Science, politics, difference, and the gendered self. In M. K. Ryan & N. R. Branscombe (Eds.), *The SAGE handbook of gender and psychology* (pp. 378–393). London, England: Sage. http://dx.doi.org/10.4135/9781446269930.n23

Nagar, R., & Swarr, A. L. (2010). Introduction: Theorizing transnational feminist praxis. In A. Swarr & R. Nagar (Eds.), *Critical transnational feminist praxis* (pp. 1–20). Albany, NY: SUNY Press.

Pui-lan, K. (2009). Elisabeth Schüssler Fiorenza and postcolonial studies. *Journal of Feminist Studies in Religion, 25*, 191–197. http://dx.doi.org/10.2979/fsr.2009.25.1.191

Ralston, M. (2009). Towards a truly transnational feminism. *European Journal of Women's Studies, 16*, 400–401. http://dx.doi.org/10.1177/13505068090160040805

Rasmussen, S. (2015). Understanding honor in religious, cultural, and moral experience: Commentary on "Diasporic virginities: Social representations of virginity and constructions of identity amongst British Arab Muslim women" by Howarth, Caroline; Amer, Amena; and Sen, Ragini. *Culture & Psychology, 21*, 20–36. http://dx.doi.org/10.1177/1354067X14551301

Roopnarine, J. L., & Chadee, D. (2016). Introduction: Caribbean psychology—more than a regional discipline. In J. L. Roopnarine & D. Chadee (Eds.), *Caribbean psychology: Indigenous contributions to a global discipline* (pp. 3–11). Washington, DC: American Psychological Association.

Sato, C. (2016). Two frontiers of development? A transnational feminist analysis of public–private partnerships for women's empowerment. *International Political Sociology, 10*, 150–167. http://dx.doi.org/10.1093/ips/olw006

Scheer, V. L., Stevens, P. E., & Mkandawire-Valhmu, L. (2016). Raising questions about capitalist globalization and universalizing views on women: A transnational feminist critique of the World Development Report Gender Equality and Development. *Advances in Nursing Science, 39*, 96–107. http://dx.doi.org/10.1097/ANS.0000000000000120

Schiller, N. G., Basch, L., & Blanc, C. S. (1995). From immigrant to transmigrant: Theorizing transnational migration. *Anthropological Quarterly, 68*, 48–63. http://dx.doi.org/10.2307/3317464

Schutte, O. (1998). Cultural alternity: Cross-cultural communication and feminist thought in North–South dialogue. *Hypatia, 13*, 53–72. http://dx.doi.org/10.1111/j.1527-2001.1998.tb01225.x

Shiva, V. (2002). *Water wars: Privatization, pollution, and profit*. London, England: Pluto Press.

Shweder, R. A. (1990). Cultural psychology: What is it? In J. W. Stigler, R. A. Shweder, & G. Herdt (Eds.), *Cultural psychology: Essays on comparative human development* (pp. 1–44). Cambridge, England: Cambridge University Press. http://dx.doi.org/10.1017/CBO9781139173728.002

Sloan, T. (2002). Reseña de "psicología de la liberación" de Ignáio Martín Baron [Review of "Psychology of liberation" by Ignáio Martín Baron]. *Interamerican Journal of Psychology, 36*, 353–357.

Smith, M. P. (2005). Transnational urbanism revisited. *Journal of Ethnic and Migration Studies, 31*, 235–244. http://dx.doi.org/10.1080/1369183042000339909

Spivak, G. C. (1988). Can the subaltern speak? In C. Nelson & L. Grossberg (Eds.), *Marxism and interpretation of culture* (pp. 271–313). Chicago, IL: University of Illinois Press. http://dx.doi.org/10.1007/978-1-349-19059-1_20

Swarr, A. L., & Nagar, R. (2010). *Critical transnational feminist praxis*. Albany, NY: SUNY Press.

Teo, T. (Ed.). (2014). *Encyclopedia of critical psychology*. New York, NY: Springer.

Vertovec, S. (2009). *Transnationalism*. New York, NY: Routledge.

Vertovec, S. (2011). Transnationalism. In G. T. Kurian (Ed.), *The encyclopedia of political science* (p. 1684). Washington, DC: CQ Press.

Wolf, M. (2014). Shaping globalization. *Finance & Development, 51*(3), 22–25.

Worldometers. (2019). *Current world population*. Retrieved from http://www.worldometers.info/world-population/

Yuval-Davis, N. (2009). Women, globalization, and contemporary politics of belonging. *Gender, Technology and Development, 13*, 1–19. http://dx.doi.org/10.1177/097185240901300101

Zimmerman, M. A. (1990). Taking aim on empowerment research: On the distinction between individual and psychological conception. *American Journal of Community Psychology, 18*, 169–177. http://dx.doi.org/10.1007/BF00922695

2

THE TRANSNATIONAL TURN: LOOKING BACK AND LOOKING AHEAD

JANET M. CONWAY

Transnational came into use in the 1990s as a way to name the dramatically increasing flows of people, things, images, and ideas across the borders of nation-states in an era of "globalization." Distinct from the "international," which privileges nation-states as the key actors in mediating international relations, the transnational invokes more diverse and fluid forms, scales, and agents involved in contemporary cross-border relations.[1] For the 2015 summit of the Society for the Psychology of Women, "From the International to the Transnational: Transforming the Psychology of Women," we were asked to contemplate transnationalism as a paradigm shift in terms of "our awareness,

---

[1]See Naples (2002) for a discussion of the "politics of naming," surveying the contested usages of transnational versus global or international for feminism.

Ideas in this chapter were first described in my keynote address for "From International to Transnational: Transforming the Psychology of Women," a summit organized by the Society for the Psychology of Women (American Psychological Association Division 35), Toronto, Ontario, Canada, August 4, 2015.

http://dx.doi.org/10.1037/0000148-003
Transnational Psychology of Women: Expanding International and Intersectional Approaches, L. H. Collins, S. Machizawa, and J. K. Rice (Editors)

understanding, conceptualization and support of our sisters around the globe." This call echoed others across the social sciences since the 1990s in response to the forces of globalization as a set of economic, political, and technological processes, understood as both material and discursive, that worked to erode national boundaries and identities in favor of global integration.

This chapter takes up that challenge so that we may think, know, and act across boundaries in ways that build reciprocal solidarities with others locally and globally, rather than implicitly or explicitly reproducing the hierarchies that mark global world order. This chapter is thus an exercise in *critical globalization studies*, which contest deepening inequalities in power and wealth obscured through discourses naturalizing and or celebrating globalization.[2] In what follows, I specify what is meant by the paradigm of transnationalism in the social sciences, especially as it relates to developments and discourses related to globalization. By paradigm of transnationalism, I mark a shift in seeing and studying the world from one centered on the national as the taken-for-granted unit and scale of analysis for understanding the social (see Khagram & Levitt, 2008b). I then discuss how the transnational has been taken up in feminist studies. I differentiate between transnational feminism as the politics of cross-border solidarities in activist networks and transnational feminism as a normative analytic—a theoretical practice in Gender and Women's Studies. I pose some questions about transnational feminism as an analytic lens and approach, arising both from my work on transnational feminist networks and from challenges posed by Indigenous feminists. The chapter concludes with some thoughts on what it means at the moment to globalize, transnationalize, and decolonize our knowledge and politics to contest global inequities and promote reciprocal solidarities. To decolonize is to recognize the degree to which histories of European colonialism have shaped what and how we know in academia, while discrediting other traditions of knowledge as unscientific and to ameliorate this by provincializing Western knowledge as one tradition among many.

"GLOBALIZATION" IN THE 1990s

The appearance of transnationalism as a paradigm in the social sciences is associated historically with the material transformations, theoretical debates, and political struggles over globalization in the 1990s.[3]

---

[2]For a discussion of critical globalization studies, see Appelbaum and Robinson (2005).

[3]For a comprehensive overview of the globalization debates and the issues at stake at the time, see Held, McGrew, Goldblatt, and Perraton (1999). For later, more diverse and critical perspectives, see Appelbaum and Robinson (2005), el-Ojeili and Hayden (2006), Sassen (2007), and Turner (2010). For consideration of the continuities between colonization, development, and globalization in the production of global inequality, see McMichael (2017). For studies of globalization and social movements opposed to globalization, see Munck (2007) and Moghadam (2013).

Geopolitically, the immediate post–Cold War period, inaugurated by the fall of the Berlin Wall, the velvet revolutions across Eastern Europe, and the dissolution of the Soviet Union, gave rise to a widespread interpretation in the West of the inevitable triumph of capitalism over communism as a superior social system. This perspective was advanced by global economic and political elites, including international institutions such as the World Bank and the International Monetary Fund, powerful "First World" countries led by the United States, multinational corporations, and wealthy individuals to serve a new intensified project for global economic growth. Assuming the inexorable moral force of the "free market" as the motor both of global economic development and of global democratization, they prescribed a set bundle of economic policies to be applied to every country, centered on commitments to free trade, privatization of government-owned corporations, and deregulation in key areas such as labor and environmental protections. This project is now commonly identified as *neoliberal globalization*, and it inaugurated a new round of capitalist expansion and accumulation.

The fall of communism and the rise of the doctrine of neoliberalism converged with transformations propelling the globalization of manufacturing that had been underway since the 1970s. The development and spread of new technologies made for cheaper, faster communication and transportation. These, in turn, enabled new global-scale management capabilities, such as the coordination of production involving factories in multiple countries. The appearance of the multinational corporation as a new organizational form and powerful new political actor accompanied these developments. New technologies propelled the creation of entirely new goods and services, perhaps most notably at the time in banking and finance. This led to new financial instruments, massive increases in cross-border financial flows, and pressures for deregulation in the new borderless world. In the context of these new technological capacities and economic transformations, the regulatory aspirations of the nation-state over something called the *national economy* appeared increasingly outdated for the times. Pillars of the post–World War II order—welfare states in the North and developmentalist states in the South—began to give way (Appelbaum & Robinson, 2005; el-Ojeili & Hayden, 2006).[4]

---

[4]The "North" refers to wealthy countries of the "First World," in North America and Europe and including Australia and New Zealand, in which "welfare states" were the postwar norm. *Welfare states* are those in which governments, through taxation, provide for the health, education and income security of citizens. The "South" refers to poor countries of the "Third World," of Asia, Africa, and Latin America. In the latter half of the 20th century, "developmentalist" states in the South, or those in which governments were actively trying to promote catch-up economic development through International Monetary Fund financing and World Bank projects were the norm. "Development" was the globally dominant doctrine for economic growth promoted by the United States and its allies in the Third World. By the 1990s, neoliberalism replaced state-led development as their policy prescription for global economic development.

The dominant discourse of globalization naturalized these developments as both inexorable and desirable. It advanced a utopian vision in which expanding global markets would produce global economic growth, which would lift all boats on a global wave of wealth and prosperity. If anyone thought to question this vision of the global good life, it did not matter. "There is no alternative," Margaret Thatcher famously opined (Harvey, 2005).

However, many did question it. The great globalization debates raged through the 1990s and gave rise to intense political confrontations, which are still playing out (see Khagram & Levitt, 2008b). The Battle of Seattle in 1999, a mass "antiglobalization" protest, disrupted the World Trade Organization meetings and drew attention to the winners and losers in the new world order of neoliberal globalization. It was the iconic moment in the convergence of worldwide antiglobalization movements (Yuen, Katsiaficas, & Rose, 2001). It was preceded and followed by multiple localized and transnational struggles: the Jubilee 2000 campaign against "Third World" debt, anti–free-trade organizing against NAFTA and the proposed Free Trade Area of the Americas, and protests against the G8 as the club of rich nations who were orchestrating the neoliberal agenda (Conway, 2016). Multiple democratic uprisings and antiausterity movements that continue to erupt around the world, from the Arab Spring to Occupy, are arguably in this lineage (Moghadam, 2013; Munck, 2007).

Was globalization really something new in the 1990s? If so, what was the nature and significance of its newness? Or was the newness of the rhetoric of globalization obscuring a (re)new(ed) elite strategy on a global scale to accumulate wealth and secure economic and political power? On the political left, critics argued that globalization was merely the latest phase of capitalism, unfolding according to its structural logic. Or they perceived it as *imperialism*, a process of domination and exploitation through economic, political, and military means from the powerful and wealthy West toward the rest of the world. (See Appelbaum & Robinson, 2005, for a sample of these debates.)

Analysts of neoliberal globalization debated the transformed role of the state in the new global context. Were national governments superseded by political–economic globalization such that power and authority were located "above" or "beyond" the national scale? Were international institutions such as the International Monetary Fund, World Bank, World Trade Organization, G8, or United Nations more suitable sites for political decision making in an era of globalization? Was the nation-state now an empty shell, devoid of power, agency, and democratic possibility, or were (some) states actively facilitating globalization? Was globalization a condition to be embraced or resisted?[5]

---

[5]On globalization and the role of the state, see Hirst and Thompson (1996) and Held, McGrew, Goldblatt, and Perraton (1999).

Within the antiglobalization movements, activists differentiated between the neoliberal project of globalization from above and the global justice project as globalization from below. The latter celebrated the increased contact and exchange assisted by the new information and communication technologies, cheap travel, and the new transnational organizational capabilities enabled by the Internet. Against all forms of hierarchy, they advocated an ethos of horizontalism in their organizing and imagining of a new, more democratic, peaceful, and equitable global order (Brecher, Costello, & Smith, 2000).

The emergence of transnationalism as a paradigm in the social sciences is situated in this historical context of the 1990s, of these material and discursive transformations associated with political–economic globalization and the intense political struggles and debates over its nature and direction. This also effected an epistemological shift in producing a new common sense of the world as a single place and raised new questions about how to study and theorize social phenomena, from the local to the global (Sassen, 2007).

THE PARADIGM OF TRANSNATIONALISM

Like processes of globalization, transnational phenomena are not new. Arguably, globalization began over 500 years ago with the European conquest of the Americas and the inauguration of the modern world political–economic system (Wallerstein, 2004). Transnationalism understood as border-crossing processes invokes histories of world religions, human migrations, histories of empire from ancient times to the present, missionary movements, the North Atlantic slave trade, the movement for the abolition of slavery, and other international movements for labor rights, suffrage, and decolonization. The newness of claims to the transnational for the contemporary period has to do with the intensification (in terms of speed, spread, and scope) of transnational connectivities associated with political–economic globalization, information and communication technologies and new media, and global travel and transportation. These involve globally unprecedented flows of people, commodities, money, ideas, cultural forms, and practices. These mobilities across global space are creating new *hybridities* (i.e., culturally mixed forms and identities) and processes of *deterritorialization*, where people and things are in motion and not as rooted in or defined by specific places as had been more common in the past.

Although globalization has been problematic across the social sciences since the 1990s, its study has been largely anchored in business, economics, political science, and sociology. In its critical expressions, it centers analysis of capitalism and the politics of counterhegemonic social movements and relies on Marxian-inspired, political economy analytics (e.g., Appelbaum & Robinson, 2005). Such critical discourses of globalization frequently rely on notions of the world economy as unfolding according to a single, structural logic—one imposed by capitalism as a political–economic system that is now global in scope. Critical theories are also attuned to the conflicts produced by the contradictions, instabilities, and inequalities endemic to capitalism. The global scope of this kind of theory demands generalization and tends to produce its own universalisms, although seeking more equitable outcomes than the neoliberal variant discussed earlier.

The paradigm of transnationalism can be seen as a response and corrective to the predominantly political–economic discourse of globalization, whether of the neoliberal or Marxian variant. By contrast, a transnational perspective, when understood to address a wide variety of cross-border flows, exchanges, and dynamics, is more partial and variable in scope and scale than the global—more Foucauldian than Marxian[6] in its underpinnings, a transnational approach allows for more multidirectional influences and complex crisscrossing of power in cross-border relations. Important genealogies of the paradigm of transnationalism can be located in migration studies that proved influential in the definition of the paradigm more generally (Basch, Glick Schiller, & Szanton Blanc, 1994; Glick Schiller, Basch, & Szanton-Blanc, 1992).

The paradigm of transnationalism is widely used across the social sciences and humanities and has been brought to bear on a wide range of cross-border practices beyond the narrowly "economic." Transnational studies attend to the cross-border practices of a greater range of actors, flows, and dynamics than do critical globalization studies and interprets them in more complex, multivalent ways not reducible to capitalist social relations (e.g., Khagram & Levitt, 2008a). In advancing the methodological, theoretical, and epistemological dimensions of transnationalism, Khagram and Levitt (2008a), for example, proposed, "What are assumed to be bounded and bordered social units are understood as transnationally constituted, embedded and influenced social arenas that interact with one another" (p. 5). Morphologically, the world is understood to consist of multiple sets of dynamically overlapping, interacting transnational social fields. The task of transnational studies, according to these authors, is to focus on the production of social differentiation that is effected through the exercise of boundary drawing and, further, to deconstruct boundaries and bounded units as effects of power. A transnational perspective then sees the drawing of boundaries and borders as itself an act of power and seeks to analyze all kinds of phenomena

---

[6]A transnational perspective is more Foucauldian in its understanding of power as diffused throughout a social formation, multidirectional and contradictory, rather than lodged in particular places, actors, or institutions and operating in a more zero-sum manner.

as always produced through cross-boundary dynamics and never as the product of a single bounded essence.

Like the turn to the global, the transnational also represents a critique and alternative to methodological nationalism in which nation-states, national societies, national identities, and the national scale are no longer the taken-for-granted units of social and political life and of social scientific study. Transnational approaches denaturalize the nation-state as the a priori unit of analysis and as the container of social life, social processes, and social identities (Wimmer & Glick-Schiller, 2008). Although this is a critically important advance, the transnational turn has also been critiqued for effacing the ongoing importance of states and the effects of state power. It has likewise been implicated in a conceptual flattening of global inequalities that are still significantly spatial in nature. Relatedly, the transnational turn is associated with discourses of globalizing modernity or the assumption that societies and subjectivities the world over are essentially subject to a single trajectory of development. This has made it difficult to discern ongoing geopolitical dynamics of imperialism and coloniality within this paradigm.

THE TRANSNATIONAL TURN IN FEMINIST STUDIES

Within feminist studies, the transnational turn has been grounded in transformations in women's organizing and feminist politics.[7] One transformation was the phenomenon of women's and feminist movements worldwide engaging with the economic restructuring associated with political–economic globalization. This included women organizing against free trade and in response to neoliberal structural adjustment programs, starting in the 1980s. Women's activism resisted the generalized decline in standards of living experienced by the world's majorities due to cuts to social spending, privatized health and education systems, loss of stable employment, decent incomes, and access to land, water, and other environmental resources (Hawkesworth, 2018; Marchand & Runyan, 2011; Naples & Desai, 2002). Where new employment opportunities for women opened in factories, for example, wages and working conditions were poor, driven downward by extreme price competition. These transformations shifted a greater burden of care onto women as they sought to compensate for lost incomes and essential services in whatever ways they could (Desai, 2002; Gabriel & Macdonald, 1994; Lindio-McGovern & Walliman, 2009; MacDonald, 2002;

---

[7]Much of the following section is derived from my article "Troubling Transnational Feminism(s): Theorising Activist Praxis" (Conway, 2017).

Moghadam, 2005; Naples & Desai, 2002; Parrenas, 2015; see also Chapter 1, this volume).

Another important transformation was the transnationalization of feminism and women's movements enabled by the United Nations (UN) declaration of International Women's Year and Decade (1975–1985). Its organizing of international conferences on the status of women globally prompted the formation of women's groups all over the world. Through the UN conferences, global policy prescriptions, as well as intense debates about differences in women's contexts and perspectives, were produced on such issues as reproductive rights, myriad forms of violence against women, women's roles and rights in economic and political development, and women's rights as human rights. Cross-border organizing among feminists was, of course, not new. There are many antecedents going back to the 19th century, but the processes of the late 20th century were new in their intensities, institutionalizations, and geographic scope and scale.

Since the 1990s, the term *transnational* has come to characterize contemporary feminist organizing, where it often carries simply descriptive meanings (Baksh & Harcourt, 2015). Angela Miles (2000) used the term interchangeably with *global feminism* to describe the phenomenon of localized feminisms around the world that are increasingly aware of each other and the global context of their struggles and are building sustained networks of collaboration. Valentine Moghadam (2005) used it to designate networks working in three or more countries. Pascale Dufour, Dominique Masson, and Dominique Caouette (2010) used it to mean the construction of cross-border feminist solidarities across place and scale. Millie Thayer (2010) used it with reference to localized feminisms interacting with and partially constituted through transnational flows. Others have used it to refer to feminist activisms at all scales as they interact with global economic restructuring.

In this literature, transnational feminism is conceptualized as an empirical phenomenon and the object of study. This scholarship draws on an eclectic range of analytic resources across the social sciences, including social movement theories; debates about globalization, global civil society, democratization, development, and modernization; and the geographical concepts of space, place, and scale. These empirically oriented studies are concerned with documenting contemporary feminist activisms and addressing their practical dilemmas (e.g., Basu, 1995, 2010; Ferree & Tripp, 2006; Miles, 2013; Ricciutelli, Miles, & McFadden, 2004). Such works offer a plethora of case studies of both localized activisms and transnational networks, most of which are anchored in the Global South. Normatively committed to grassroots feminisms and transnational solidarities, they offer rich conceptualizations and relevant insights for feminist activist practice while validating knowledge arising from that practice.

There is, however, a more politically fraught and theoretically laden genealogy of the transnational turn in feminist studies. The descriptor *transnational feminism* emerged historically in the 1980s in the context of UN-sponsored women's conferences and the growing contact among feminisms across the North–South divide. It denoted an explicit rupture in theory and practice from both the feminist project of "global sisterhood" and earlier expressions of feminist internationalism. Both of these had been critiqued by Third World feminists[8] as reproducing global geopolitical hierarchies in which Western, White, and liberal feminist perspectives and modes of organizing were entrenched as normative for women's movements across the world. Concretely in the context of the UN conferences, Third World feminists critiqued the economic inequalities of the international order and the violence associated with U.S. interventions in their regions as central to women's local struggles for social justice and to Third World feminisms. These issues had not been on the map of the predominantly White, middle-class, and liberal U.S. women's movements as central to global feminism. Western feminism had theorized male power and patriarchy as a universal problem and advocated global sisterhood in response. A politics of global sisterhood is premised on the notion that all women everywhere share a common oppression, which is imagined as the basis for taken-for-granted global solidarity. In emphasizing commonality, it downplays differences and inequalities among women within and across societies and unwittingly reinscribes hierarchies of power and privilege among them.

Internationalism is associated with a form (national-scale associations), site (international federation; interstate organizations), and axis (national–international) of organizing, with an advocacy focus primarily on national institutions underpinned by a political commitment to national sovereignty but within an orientation to international solidarity. Historically, feminist internationalism has had liberal and left variants and has usually appeared in the form of formal organizational coalitions in which national identity is the primary difference that is named and negotiated in building alliances—as opposed, for example, to race, religion, sexual orientation, and so forth. National identities are the taken-for-granted building blocks of cross-border coalitions. The World March of Women, discussed later, is a good example of contemporary left feminist internationalism, although it has also been

---

[8] I use the term *Third World feminists* because this is how these women self-identified and differentiated their position from the putatively "global feminism" promulgated at the United Nations by Western feminists. See Mohanty (1991) for a discussion and arguments about Third World women's standpoint. The term *Third World* reflects a specific historical period (post–World War II to the fall of the Berlin Wall) and the project for global development. Although the term is now widely rejected for the hierarchies of development that it instantiates, it was also historically claimed as a critical positionality by anticolonial movements, as is the case with Mohanty.

influenced by the transnational turn. Transnationalism differs from internationalism in its recognition of cross-border practices of various kinds and at variable scales; more fluid forms of identification, organization and representation; and the possibility of international solidarity, contact, and collaboration beyond statist or interstate terms. The shift from internationalism to transnationalism in feminist political orientations is reflective of the transnational turn taking place more broadly across the social sciences.

Transnationalism refuses to take national identities for granted as fixed or to privilege them as the only or best way to build solidarities across borders. Nor are nation-state borders the only borders that transnationalism seeks to traverse. A transnational perspective can inform coalition building among women from diverse backgrounds living in multicultural cities who seek common ground on an issue (e.g., violence against women) that they may experience, analyze, and resist differently.

In feminist thought, the transnational turn was exemplified by Inderpal Grewal and Caren Kaplan's *Scattered Hegemonies* (1994). This work revolves around a critique of the centrality of nations, nationalisms, and the national scale in feminist political imaginaries. Here, the transnational is a way of naming the circulation of feminist discourses across various kinds of difference without reinscribing national(ist) boundaries or invoking a global-to-local hierarchy among scales of activism. The transnational here refers to relations and flows across national frontiers while avoiding claims to the universal that accompany the term *global* and the historical project of global sisterhood (see also Kaplan, Alarcón, & Moallem, 1999).

The second strand of transnational feminist thought is associated with works appearing in the U.S. academy in the 1990s by Chandra Talpade Mohanty and colleagues (Alexander & Mohanty, 1997; Mohanty, Russo, & Torres, 1991). These works reflect major debates of the mid-1980s in transnational feminist organizing between "Third World" and "Western" feminisms, the latter signifying the globally dominant, liberal feminism of U.S.-based White, class-privileged women and of the aid and development establishments. Third World feminists accused Western feminists of projecting monolithic understandings of women's oppression based on their own culturally specific experience in the mode of global sisterhood described earlier. In so doing, Western feminists homogenized Third World women's experience, erasing their national, class, and cultural specificities and denying them historical subjectivity (Mohanty, 1991). For example, Western feminism, in focusing on gender equality to the exclusion of other axes of identity and discrimination in women's lives, failed to understand how feminism was interwoven with a host of other social struggles in various contexts (e.g., for national liberation in Palestine, against apartheid in South Africa, for Indigenous rights for Sami women in Scandinavia, or against racism for Black women in the U.S.).

Instead of Western liberal feminism masquerading as global sisterhood, Third World feminist critics advocated a transnational and cross-cultural feminist praxis committed to combating inequalities among women while being sensitive to differences arising from cultural, social, and global geopolitical locations. They envisioned the possibility of transnational feminist solidarity that was also antiimperialist, anticolonial, antiracist, and anticapitalist.

In a parallel fashion, movements of racialized women, particularly in the United States, were challenging the dominant feminism of middle-class, White-dominated women's movements and forging antiracist feminist politics premised on a multiplicity of oppressions and the intersections of race, class, and gender, among other axes of social differentiation and inequality (Hill Collins, 2000; Moraga & Anzaldúa, 1981). Intersectionality as an analytic approach crystallized at this time, particularly through the work of Black feminists, and converged with U.S. Third World feminist critique. Through the 1980s, U.S. Third World feminism was the site of groundbreaking political and theoretical work on coalition building across differences premised on what came to be known as *intersectionality* (Sandoval, 2000; Yuval-Davis, 1993).

From these interrelated historical processes and feminist political and theoretical engagements, transnational feminism crystallized as a *normative analytic*, or a critical approach, in feminist studies strongly marked by intersectionality coupled with a postcolonial perspective. The latter insisted on situating intersectional identities, oppressions, and struggles within a critical reading of global geopolitical contexts. This meant being conscious of histories of empire, colonialism, and anticolonial struggles and how they shape the present and resisting new forms of political–economic or military domination of some countries or regions over others. This was distinct from transnational feminism's usage as a simple descriptor for transnational feminist organizing, which was also growing exponentially through the 1980s and into the 1990s facilitated by the UN processes.

INSTABILITIES IN TRANSNATIONAL FEMINISM

Although transnational feminism as an analytic approach continues to be theoretically and politically influential, some important questions are emerging from (a) contemporary transnational feminist organizing and (b) Indigenous feminisms. In tension with the claims of transnational feminism are those that affirm the ongoing salience of nation-states, the national scale, national identities, and claims to sovereignty for feminist politics. Relatedly, others argue to reexamine the material significance of place and territoriality in contemporary political contestations. These challenge some of the central norms of a transnational feminist analytic approach.

From research conducted over a decade at the World Social Forum (WSF), many transnational feminist networks (TFNs) engaged with the anti-globalization movement appear to be directly in the lineage of transnational feminism outlined previously (Conway, 2011, 2012). They are grounded in Third World women's contexts and agency and are enacting transnational feminist practices and coalition politics as called for by Mohanty (1991) and Grewal and Kaplan (1994); that is, they are acutely aware of diversity and pluralism among feminisms and of the diversity of women's situations in various (national) contexts. These TFNs are internationalized, with robust South–South links and Southern leadership. They are explicitly connecting gender justice to economic justice and in spheres beyond the family, as advocated by Mohanty in her critique of Western feminism. All TFNs at the WSF are deeply engaged with problematics associated with globalization and economic restructuring. All are unequivocally opposed to neoliberalism as destroying livelihoods and deepening global economic inequality. All are antiwar and antiimperialist, especially vis-à-vis U.S. military interventions in their regions (Conway, 2013; see also Eschle & Maiguashca, 2010). They see such interventions as contemporary forms of colonialism, meant to extract resources and pacify restive populations for the benefit of the global superpower. In all these ways, the praxis of these TFNs reflects an embrace of the transnational feminist critique of the project of global sisterhood and a concomitant rejection of the latter's underpinnings in Western White liberal feminism.

Furthermore, these TFNs are transnational in their practices in that they eschew any rigid forms of organization or representation based on nation-state identities. They collaborate freely and seek to strengthen solidarities across national divides of many kinds without insisting that activists "represent" their countries. However, the national remains a salient category and focus for feminist politics in and of TFNs, and many tack back and forth between national and transnational modalities. There is no apparent philosophical critique of the national as it appears in the canonical texts of transnational feminism even as many aspects of their practice are supra- or postnational. The World March of Women, for example, is a global network of national agglomerations, even as the content and form of the national vary greatly within it (Conway, 2008). For example, the March recognizes Quebec, Catalonia, the Basque country, and Western Sahara as nations asserting autonomy or sovereignty vis-à-vis the states to which they are subject. Likewise, the March does not eschew globality. It reaches for the global scale and does not critique the "global" per se. It actively embraces the project of building a global feminist identity, although this is clearly both postessentialist and antiimperialist. *Essentialism* refers to the belief that something (here, feminist identity) has a pre-given nature, content, or essence that determines its meaning. The March speaks explicitly of a feminism under construction and open to revision. Yet, the project of building a collective identity is regarded as central to politics (Dufour & Giraud, 2007; World March of Women, 2008). So, the March is a hybrid form of cross-border feminism, resonant with older forms of feminist internationalism and orientations to global sisterhood, as well as to transnational feminism.

Many TFNs at the WSF define a materialist feminism driven by concerns about the living conditions of poor women in the South. Although transnational in their modes of organizing, they remain anchored in the politics of place. The World March of Women is a TFN anchored in localized grassroots women's groups, organized in national agglomerations. On the transnational feminist field, the World March has politicized a popular transnational feminism grounded in the organizations and lived realities of poor, rural, and working-class women. The March contests the transnational feminism of highly educated, professionalized, urbanized, mobile, and globalized middle classes that took shape according to the UN processes and that was less anchored to specific local contexts.

From Indigenous feminisms have come distinct but related questions about the ongoing salience of place-based identities and attachments to territory deemed central to Indigenous peoples' struggle against dispossession and for their cultural (and indeed political and economic) existence as peoples. Mi'kmaw scholar Bonita Lawrence (2005) problematized transnational feminism's reliance on postcolonialism and its implications for Indigenous peoples' survival struggles. She noted that postcolonial studies assume that decolonization has occurred and that (formerly) colonized peoples are not struggling for their right to exist as political entities. Indigenous peoples, however, remain colonized, their very existence under constant threat by the settler states in which they reside. Transnational feminism's blanket critique of nations and nationalism, coupled with its lack of contemplation of Indigenous peoples and settler colonialism, render it problematic for Indigenous peoples' political claims, which are advanced in the language of nationhood and sovereignty, anchored to particular territories. Likewise, transnational feminism's scholarly focus on mobility and migration and consequently on diasporic identities, when not politically articulated in relation to Indigenous land claims in settler colonial societies (e.g., the United States and Canada), delegitimize Indigenous peoples' place-based attachments.

DECOLONIZING OUR KNOWLEDGE

By way of conclusion, what does it mean to globalize, transnationalize, and decolonize our knowledge and politics? In my view, these are three related but distinct moves, all of which are necessary.

To globalize our disciplines is to pay attention to the knowledge, theories, experiences, and voices arising from geopolitical contexts other than our own. Given our positioning in the Global North, in the North American academy, it is particularly critical to interact in serious ways with perspectives arising from other world regions, beyond the West and the "First World." Furthermore, it is essential to critically position ourselves, these "others," and our interrelation in the historical context of a global political economy that continues to produce and structure gross inequalities. Such inequalities include the fact that most expert knowledge and scholarly publications are produced in and about the Global North. Feminist scholars are beginning to experiment with new forms of research and collaboration across the North–South divide in this light (e.g., Alvarez et al., 2014; Nagar, 2014; Swarr & Nagar, 2010).

To transnationalize our disciplines is to recognize how identities, places, and knowledge have been and continue to be constituted by translocal flows and exchanges of people, goods, money, ideas, images, and discourses. These trans-regional entanglements go back at least 5 centuries to the European conquest of the Americas and constitute the modern world that we have inherited. These flows have been and remain crisscrossed by power relations of all kinds but are notably marked by the power of nation-states and the unequal relations between them. Even with the seeming durability of nation-states in the face of globalization and the resurgence of imperial power, the persistence of cross-border flows and exchanges and their increasing scope, scale, speed, and intensity destabilizes notions of bounded cultures and fixed identities, both of the past and in the present. Having said that, "strategic essentialisms" remain an important, perhaps inescapable, feature of many subaltern struggles, as indicated in Lawrence's (2005) Indigenous feminist critique of transnational feminism. *Strategic essentialism* refers to the self-attribution of characteristics to a social group for the purposes of asserting their collective existence in a struggle for rights or recognition. To *transnationalize* our disciplines is to recognize how flows and diasporas have constituted our knowledge and how these dynamics have been and remain power laden and asymmetrical, while rarely being zero sum.

To *decolonize* our disciplines is to grapple with how profoundly the history of European colonialism has structured modern knowledge and politics, how it has rendered the non-West as nonexistent, and how it has created colonial difference. *Colonial difference*, or the knowledge arising from other (non-European) worlds, is that which has been invalidated or suppressed through the global hegemony of discourses centered on Western civilization (Mignolo, 2002; see also Escobar, 2007). To decolonize our knowledge is to recognize these historic processes of othering and the existence of "worlds and knowledges otherwise" (p. 179). This requires engaging humbly and respectfully with epistemic difference and the problem of translation across worlds (Santos, 2005). To engage in such a nondomineering dialogue with alterity demands the cultivation of new desires, dispositions, and capacities which are in considerable tension with the epistemological starting points of Western social science—including its best critical traditions, among which feminisms have been leading examples.

No domain of Western knowledge will remain untouched by these three operations: globalization, transnationalization, and decolonization. They are all underway, albeit unevenly. They are simultaneously political and epistemological and so are as profoundly conflictual as they will be deeply transformative.

REFERENCES

Alexander, M. J., & Mohanty, C. T. (Eds.). (1997). *Feminist genealogies, colonial legacies, democratic futures*. New York, NY: Routledge.

Alvarez, S., Costa, C. D., Feliu, V., Hester, R. J., Klahn, N., & Thayer, M. (Eds.). (2014). *Translocalities/Translocalidades: Feminist politics of translation in Latin/a América*. Durham, NC: Duke University Press. http://dx.doi.org/10.1215/9780822376828

Appelbaum, R. P., & Robinson, W. I. (Eds.). (2005). *Critical globalization studies*. New York, NY: Routledge.

Baksh, R., & Harcourt, W. (Eds.). (2015). *The Oxford handbook of transnational feminist movements*. Oxford, England: Oxford University Press. http://dx.doi.org/10.1093/oxfordhb/9780199943494.001.0001

Basch, L., Glick Schiller, N., & Szanton Blanc, C. (1994). *Nations unbound: Transnational projects, postcolonial predicaments, and deterritorialized nation states*. Luxembourg: Gordon and Breach.

Basu, A. (1995). *The challenge of local feminisms: Women's movements in global perspective*. Boulder, CO: Westview.

Basu, A. (Ed.). (2010). *Women's movements in the global era: The power of local feminisms*. Boulder, CO: Westview.

Brecher, J., Costello, T., & Smith, B. (2000). *Globalization from below: The power of solidarity*. Cambridge, MA: South End Press.

Conway, J. (2008). Geographies of transnational feminism: The politics of place and scale in the World March of Women. *Social Politics, 15*, 207–231. http://dx.doi.org/10.1093/sp/jxn010

Conway, J. (2011). Activist knowledges on the anti-globalization terrain: Transnational feminisms at the World Social Forum. *Interface, 3*(2), 33–64.

Conway, J. (2012). Transnational feminisms building anti-globalization alliances. *Globalizations, 9*, 379–393. http://dx.doi.org/10.1080/14747731.2012.680731

Conway, J. (2013). *Edges of global justice: The World Social Forum and its 'others.'* New York, NY: Routledge.

Conway, J. (2016). Anti-globalization movements. In N. Naples (Ed.), *The Wiley-Blackwell encyclopedia of gender and sexuality studies*. London, England: Wiley-Blackwell. http://dx.doi.org/10.1002/9781118663219.wbegss250

Conway, J. M. (2017). Troubling transnational feminism(s): Theorising activist praxis. *Feminist Theory, 18*, 205–227. http://dx.doi.org/10.1177/1464700117700536

Desai, M. (2002). Transnational solidarity, structural adjustment, and globalization. In N. Naples & M. Desai (Eds.), *Women's activism and globalization: Linking local struggles and transnational politics* (pp. 15–33). New York, NY: Routledge.

Dufour, P., & Giraud, I. (2007). When the transnationalization of solidarities continues: The case of the World March of Women between 2000 and 2006—a collective identity-building approach. *Mobilization, 12*, 307–322.

Dufour, P., Masson, D., & Caouette, D. (Eds.). (2010). *Transnationalizing women's movements: Solidarities without borders*. Vancouver, Canada: University of British Columbia Press.

el-Ojeili, C., & Hayden, P. (2006). *Critical theories of globalization*. Houndmills, England: Palgrave Macmillan. http://dx.doi.org/10.1057/9780230626454

Eschle, C., & Maiguashca, B. (2010). *Making feminist sense of the global justice movement*. Lanham, MD: Rowman & Littlefield.

Escobar, A. (2007). Worlds and knowledges otherwise: The Latin American modernity/coloniality research program. *Cultural Studies, 21*, 179–210. http://dx.doi.org/10.1080/09502380601162506

Ferree, M. M., & Tripp, A. M. (2006). *Global feminism: Transnational women's activism, organizing and human rights*. New York: New York University Press.

Gabriel, C., & Macdonald, L. (1994). NAFTA, women and organizing in Canada and Mexico: Forging a feminist internationality. *Millennium, 23*, 535–562. http://dx.doi.org/10.1177/03058298940230030601

Glick Schiller, N., Basch, L., & Szanton-Blanc, C. (Eds.). (1992). *Towards a transnational perspective on migration: Race, class, ethnicity and nationalism*. New York: New York Academy of Sciences.

Grewal, I., & Kaplan, C. (1994). *Scattered hegemonies: Postmodernity and transnational feminist practices*. Minneapolis: University of Minnesota Press.

Harvey, D. (2005). *A brief history of neoliberalism*. Oxford, England: Oxford University Press.

Hawkesworth, M. E. (2018). *Globalization and feminist activism* (2nd ed.). Lanham, MD: Rowman & Littlefield.

Held, D., McGrew, A., Goldblatt, D., & Perraton, J. (1999). *Global transformations: Politics, economics and culture*. Palo Alto, CA: Stanford University Press.

Hill Collins, P. (2000). *Black feminist thought: Knowledge, consciousness, and the politics of empowerment* (2nd ed.). New York, NY: Routledge.

Hirst, P., & Thompson, G. (1996). *Globalization in question: The international economy and the possibilities of governance.* London, England: Polity.

Kaplan, C., Alarcón, N., & Moallem, M. (1999). *Between woman and nation: Nationalisms, transnational feminisms and the state.* Durham, NC: Duke University Press.

Khagram, S., & Levitt, P. (2008a). Constructing transnational studies. In S. Khagram & P. Levitt (Eds.), *The transnational studies reader: Intersections and innovations* (pp. 1–18). New York, NY: Routledge.

Khagram, S., & Levitt, P. (Eds.). (2008b). *The transnational studies reader: Intersections and innovations.* New York, NY: Routledge.

Lawrence, B. (2005). Indigeneity and transnationality? An interview with Bonitia Lawrence. *Women and Environments, 68/69,* 6–8.

Lindio-McGovern, L., & Walliman, I. (2009). *Globalization and Third World women: Exploitation, coping, and resistance.* Farnham, England: Ashgate.

MacDonald, L. (2002, August). Globalization and social movements: Comparing women's movements' responses to NAFTA in Mexico, the USA, and Canada. *International Feminist Journal of Politics, 4,* 151–172. http://dx.doi.org/10.1080/14616740210135469

Marchand, M., & Runyan, A. S. (2011). *Gender and global restructuring: Sightings, sites and resistances* (2nd ed.). New York, NY: Routledge.

McMichael, P. (2017). *Development and social change: A global perspective.* London, England: Sage.

Mignolo, W. D. (2002). The geopolitics of knowledge and the colonial difference. *The South Atlantic Quarterly, 101,* 57–96. http://dx.doi.org/10.1215/00382876-101-1-57

Miles, A. (2000, Fall). Local activisms, global feminisms and the struggle against globalization. *Canadian Woman Studies—Les Cahiers de la Femme, 20*(3), 6–10.

Miles, A. (Ed.). (2013). *Women in a globalizing world: Transforming equality, development, diversity and peace.* Toronto, Ontario, Canada: Inanna.

Moghadam, V. M. (2005). *Globalizing women: Transnational feminist networks.* Baltimore, MD: Johns Hopkins University Press.

Moghadam, V. M. (2013). *Globalization and social movements: Islamism, feminism and the global justice movements* (2nd ed.). Lanham, MD: Rowman & Littlefield.

Mohanty, C. T. (1991). Under Western eyes: Feminist scholarship and colonial discourses. In C. Mohanty, A. Russo, & L. Torres (Eds.), *Third World women and the politics of feminism* (pp. 51–80). Bloomington: Indiana University Press.

Mohanty, C., Russo, A., & Torres, L. (Eds.). (1991). *Third World women and the politics of feminism.* Bloomington: Indiana University Press.

Moraga, C., & Anzaldúa, G. (1981). *This bridge called my back: Writings by radical women of color.* Albany, NY: Kitchen Table Press.

Munck, R. (2007). *Globalization and contestation: The new great counter-movement.* New York, NY: Routledge.

Nagar, R. (2014). *Muddying the waters: Co-authoring feminisms across scholarship and activism*. Chicago: University of Illinois Press. http://dx.doi.org/10.5406/illinois/9780252038792.001.0001

Naples, N. (2002). Changing the terms: Community activism, globalization and the dilemmas of transnational feminist praxis. In N. Naples & M. Desai (Eds.), *Women's activism and globalization: Linking local struggles and transnational politics* (pp. 3–14). New York, NY: Routledge.

Naples, N., & Desai, M. (2002). *Women's activism and globalization: Linking local struggles and transnational politics*. New York, NY: Routledge.

Parrenas, R. S. (2015). *Servants of globalization: Migration and domestic workers*. Palo Alto, CA: Stanford University Press.

Ricciutelli, L., Miles, A., & McFadden, M. H. (2004). *Feminist politics, activism, and vision: Local and global challenges*. Toronto, Ontario, Canada: Ianna Publications and Zed Books.

Sandoval, C. (2000). *Methodology of the oppressed*. Minneapolis: University of Minnesota Press.

Santos, B. S. (2005). The future of the World Social Forum: The work of translation. *Development*, 48(2), 15–22. http://dx.doi.org/10.1057/palgrave.development.1100131

Sassen, S. (2007). *A sociology of globalization*. New York, NY: Norton.

Swarr, A. L., & Nagar, R. (Eds.). (2010). *Critical transnational feminist praxis*. Albany, NY: SUNY Press.

Thayer, M. (2010). *Making transnational feminism: Rural women, NGO activists, and Northern donors in Brazil*. New York, NY: Routledge.

Turner, B. (2010). Theories of globalization: Issues and origins. In B. Turner (Ed.), *The Routledge handbook of globalization studies* (pp. 3–22). New York, NY: Routledge.

Wallerstein, I. (2004). *World systems analysis: An introduction*. Durham, NC: Duke University Press.

Wimmer, A., & Glick Schiller, N. (2008). Methodological nationalism, the social sciences, and the study of migration: An essay in historical epistemology. In S. Khagram & P. Levitt (Eds.), *The transnational studies reader: Intersections and innovations* (pp. 104–117). New York, NY: Routledge.

World March of Women. (2008). *A decade of international feminist struggle*. São Paulo, Brazil: Sempreviva Organização Feminista.

Yuen, E., Katsiaficas, G., & Rose, D. B. (2001). *The battle of Seattle: The new challenge to capitalist globalization* (pp. 3–20). New York, NY: Soft Skull Press.

Yuval-Davis, N. (1993). Beyond difference: Women and coalition politics. In M. Kennedy, C. Lubelska, & V. Walsh (Eds.), *Making connections: Women's studies, women's movements, women's lives* (pp. 3–10). Washington, DC: Taylor & Francis.

3

STRATEGIES AND CONSIDERATIONS FOR TRANSNATIONAL FEMINIST RESEARCH: REFLECTIONS FROM RESEARCH IN UGANDA

JENNIFER J. MOOTZ AND SALLY D. STABB

"Are you a missionary?" the woman asked excitedly on learning that my family and I were moving to Uganda. "No," the first author hastily replied. "I'm a researcher."

With the onset of globalization, increased mobility, and technological interconnectedness, international psychological research has proliferated. The problematic sequelae ensuing from uncritical and decontextualized psychological research endeavors within and beyond national borders are numerous, and research approaches that consider transnational contexts are needed to meet the global moment. Transnational feminist theory has such potential, though its value as a research approach has been largely overlooked in psychology. As feminist counseling psychologists who are committed to conducting culturally relevant and nonoppressive international research that benefits marginalized women and girls, we aim to describe and apply transnational feminist strategies and considerations for developing research questions, measuring psychological constructs, analyzing and interpreting data, and disseminating findings. In doing so, we draw from our experiences

http://dx.doi.org/10.1037/0000148-004
Transnational Psychology of Women: Expanding International and Intersectional Approaches, L. H. Collins, S. Machizawa, and J. K. Rice (Editors)

researching gender-based violence and mental health in conflict-affected communities, as well as from the work of others.

THE PROBLEM

Western psychological research has an extensive and disconcerting history of intruding on the lives of other groups, often reinforcing racist, colonial, classist, and sexist assertions about people who reside in a variety of contexts. Commencing in the 1880s, for instance, Western psychologists paired with anthropologists to assign psychological attributes to racial classifications, which anthropologists constructed through examination of physical characteristics, such as skin color, skull size, and facial features (Guthrie, 2004). As the precursor to cross-cultural psychology, in the late 1880s, the Cambridge Torres Straits Expedition, constituted mainly by Western psychologists and anthropologists, traveled to Torres Straits, where psychologists performed experimental hearing, visual, and memory tests, among others, on villagers. Their hypotheses were rooted in scientific racism (Richards, 1997; Rivers & Seligmann, 1901), and as a result, they concluded that the villagers exhibited less intelligence than their Western, White normative group. The results of these types of poorly designed studies reinforced and legitimized preexisting colonialist distinctions and classifications that have positioned White, Western men, and secondarily, White, Western women, at the uppermost spectrum of the intelligence hierarchy. Consequences of studies such as these held transnational implications, especially for women.

Colonialist hierarchical distinctions—reified through scientific racism and research such as the example listed earlier—have exacerbated local ethnic relations and tensions, some of which later erupted into wars and genocidal killings. Before the genocide in Rwanda, for instance, Belgian colonialists had shown a preference for the Tutsi over the Hutu ethnic group by instituting ethnic identification cards and reserving governmental positions and educational opportunities for the Tutsi—discriminatory processes that centralized distinctions of ethnicity. Over 800,000 people were killed, and 150,000 women were sexually assaulted during the subsequent Rwandan genocide (Meredith, 2005; United Nations, 2015). Early psychological researchers' erroneous assertions connecting psychological abilities (e.g., intelligence) to race also inspired eugenics philosophies in the United States that undergirded sterilization laws and practices, largely targeting minority women. It is worth noting that many U.S. feminist organizations backed eugenics practices, such as sterilization laws, likely because of these same cultural norms and racial prejudices (Ziegler, 2008).

TRANSNATIONAL FEMINIST RESEARCH

As international research by psychologists and feminists expanded, the harmful political implications of such work became manifest, and transnational feminist criticisms of the research process emerged. In her seminal writing, *Under Western Eyes*, Mohanty (1988) highlighted Western feminists' discursive construction of "Third World women" as a singular composite, noting ways in which this homogenizing discourse flows from ethnocentric privileges. Specifically, Mohanty outlined how Western feminist research portrayed women in developing countries as uniformly powerless as victims of violence, culture, and colonization. She critiqued Western feminists' use of numbers (e.g., high numbers of women who wear veils) to imply universality of gendered experience as well as the assumption that gender is a superordinate category, subsuming all other identities, national and otherwise. Indeed, international feminisms have a history of mobilizing around trafficking in women, veiling, and female genital cutting (Chowdhury, 2009). The political consequences of such activism and research have been to objectify Third World women further and present them as a homogenous group distinguished by limitations and lack of agency (Mohanty, 1988).

Transnational feminist writers have since built on Mohanty's (1988) treatise to advance critiques of benevolent global feminisms, notions of Western feminism as progress, the feminist development agenda, hegemonic (i.e., dominant) feminism, and universal human rights perspectives, all of which position Western feminists as heroic savers of the rest (Dewey & St. Germain, 2012; Hegde, 1998; Kurtiş & Adams, 2015; Smith, 2011). Universally designed best research practices and instruments often originate in privileged spaces, are constructed by privileged people, and may not adequately address issues that are embedded in local contexts (Dewey & St. Germain, 2012). For instance, universalized poverty metrics may not adequately capture gendered access to resources within households or determine which resources are considered necessary based on cultural values (Jaggar, 2013). Transnational feminism calls for a decolonization of psychological science (Kurtiş & Adams, 2015) and better representation of voices of Third World women who are often portrayed as oppressed victims of tradition (Hegde, 1998). For further discussion of transnational feminism, please see Chapters 1 and 2, this volume.

Transnational feminist researchers ask us to consider how we know what we know (epistemology) by considering two processes: contiguous and noncontiguous globalization (Tsuda, Tapias, & Escandell, 2014). *Contiguous globalization* is the transnational physical movement and relocation of people, material, and goods across the borders of neighboring nation-states and regions (Tsuda et al., 2014). *Noncontiguous globalization* deals with flows from nonadjacent regions in virtual spaces (e.g., social media, websites, radio shows, television programming) assisted by technology (Internet, radio, television broadcasts; see Chapter 1, this volume; Tsuda et al., 2014). Both contiguous and noncontiguous globalization influence local communities. Transnational feminist research has attended to both of these processes, sometimes concurrently within the same research project. The critical inquisition and recognition of noncontiguous and contiguous transnational flows is part of what distinguishes transnational feminist from international psychological research. In other words, rather than an uncritical focus on nation-states as entities, transnational feminists are interested in understanding how systems of power and oppression operate across such boundaries, both now and in the past, both virtually and physically (Chowdhury, 2009).

Developing Transnational Feminist Research Questions

Developing transnational feminist research questions necessitates critically interrogating the underlying assumptions of definitions and variables under study. Table 3.1 lists transnational feminist strategies and considerations for developing questions within research areas, constructs and measurement, data analysis and interpretation, and dissemination, representation, and action. Noting from whom and how research questions originated is vital. The lenses through which transnational feminists view gender-related struggles and strengths simultaneously broaden and narrow to capture transnational movement and influences.

When developing research questions, transnational feminist researchers engage in critical inquiries related to transnational movement and influences: politically, economically, and migratorily (see Chapters 1 and 2). Using a framework that recognizes and critically examines the impact of noncontiguous and contiguous transnational flows is what differentiates transnational feminist research from international research. Questions that interrogate processes of cultural dynamism (i.e., flexible cultural norms and meaning) and understanding of how people resist, accommodate, and appropriate transnational influences are salient.

The attention to place and geopolitical complexity is reflected in language that suggests a probing for this intersecting bullseye, otherwise referred to as *transnational intersectionality* (Grabe & Else-Quest, 2012) or the *in-between* (Hegde, 1998). For example, playing with the feminist mantra that the personal is political, Else-Quest and Grabe (2012) reminded feminist psychologists that the political is also personal in their article, recommending the use of national-level indicators on gender equity to examine psychological well-being. Other researchers have similarly located their work in the space both within and outside hegemonic perspectives, including, for instance,

TABLE 3.1

Research Areas and Transnational Feminist Strategies and Considerations

Research area		Transnational feminist strategies	Transnational feminist considerations
Developing questions		• Locate and interrogate the intersection between the global and local • Question transnational migratory experiences within global economic frameworks • Situate current problems within historical geopolitical contexts (e.g., colonization, armed conflict, and gender-based violence) • Avoid homogenizing agendas and questions • Interrogate epistemology itself • Operationalize culture as dynamic	• Who originates research questions? • How do questions advance out of epistemology? • What are the global flows and structures that shape local lives and experiences? • How do the research questions situate within the context of transnational flows? • What have been the migratory pathways of feminist psychological theory, and how have these pathways shaped local understanding? • How do individuals, communities, and practitioners appropriate transnational flows?
Methods	Constructs and measurement	• Contest psychological constructs • Acknowledge heterogeneity of local contexts • Incorporate use of rapid ethnographies and qualitative methods to establish and adapt measures for local context • Take a stance of epistemological uncertainty	• How does the migration of feminist psychological theory associate with larger global structures and flows? • What are the psychological constructs under study? • From where do the psychological constructs originate? • What has been the migratory path of the dissemination of constructs, and how do pathways relate to geohistorical context? • What global dynamisms have influenced directional travel? • How have importers appropriated theoretical content, such as posttraumatic stress disorder treatment, to fit context?

(continues)

TABLE 3.1
Research Areas and Transnational Feminist Strategies and Considerations   *(Continued)*

Research area	Transnational feminist strategies	Transnational feminist considerations
Data analysis and interpretation	• Integrate transnational feminist theory with other emancipatory theories (e.g., liberation psychology) • Ensure meaningful local participation in data analysis processes • Look both within and beyond national hierarchies and power structures to situate research actors • Articulate intersecting identities and work beyond binary constructions (e.g., Global South/Global North) • Use transnational feminist theoretical constructs to code and organize qualitative data (Mohanty, 1988) • Analyze data from a transnational performance perspective by describing ways in which performances shift depending on context and interactions with others • Ensure representatives on community advisory boards represent a range of privileged and oppressed identities as identified by diverse input • Include and integrate local interpretations with analyses	• How can other theories be interwoven with transnational feminist concepts for analysis? • From whose and which perspectives are data interpreted? • What, if any, binary constructions are represented in positioning and analytical frameworks? • How can binary constructions be contested? • Which identities do researchers perform in transnational contexts? • How do behaviors and discourse relate to global flows? • Beyond national identities, what other intersecting identities are represented in community advisory boards and in other strategies for triangulation (e.g., socioeconomic status, race or ethnicity, urban or rural)?

| Dissemination, representation, and action | • Consult with research participants about preferred method of research dissemination
• Convey research importance and problems without homogenizing experiences
• Include strengths-based perspectives
• Be intentional about representation
• Acknowledge researcher positioning as it relates to the advancement of colonial perspectives | • Who is saving whom in this research narrative?
• How is emancipatory research connected to colonial histories?
• Who represents whom, and how does that representation advance transnational feminist interests?
• How might others who are unfamiliar with local contexts interpret researchers' communications?
• Who conceptualizes and articulates best practices?
• How should findings influence policy?
• How will findings be disseminated at the participant level?
• What strengths-based frameworks can be applied to processes?
• What narratives and lived examples from research partners and participants contradict the narrative of women lacking power and agency? |

A View From Elsewhere: Locating Difference and the Politics of Representation From a Transnational Feminist Perspective (Hegde, 1998), *Locating Global Feminisms Elsewhere: Braiding U.S. Women of Color and Transnational Feminisms* (Chowdhury, 2009), and *Between Global Fears and Local Bodies: Toward a Transnational Feminist Analysis of Conflict-Related Sexual Violence* (Dewey & St. Germain, 2012).

In the broadening outward, transnational feminist research questions attend to influences that transcend national contexts, with emphases on dominant and often exploitative capitalist, geopolitical forces and events. Transnational feminist researchers pay attention to and ask questions about how economic expansion is used to control the Global South (neo-imperialism) and how a focus on industry deregulation, privatization, and expanding free trade (neoliberalism) may undermine local cultural under-standings (Bahkru, 2008; Chaudhry & Bertram, 2009; Chowdhury, 2009). These kinds of questions offer a concerted and openly political research approach that challenges oppressive global shifts. For example, in British Columbia, Canada, Lee and Pacini-Ketchabaw (2011) aimed to understand how the experiences of racialized immigrant girls' caregiving labor for their younger siblings connected to frameworks of transnational migration and global market economies. Bahkru (2008) offered feminist reflections on her research examining how contiguous and noncontiguous global flows strengthened transnational feminist networking efforts.

Broadening the analytical focus of research aims and questions can induce tension in that its implementation does not homogenize experiences (e.g., by conceptualizing women uniformly as victims of violence or culture). This tension is especially salient when perspectives originate in dominat-ing contexts and are akin to colonizing discourses of the subject (Mohanty, 1988). A fruitful transnational feminist strategy has been to reveal the global as it is found in the local and individual. For instance, to query women's narratives of trauma and reconstructive processes, research conducted with Mohajir women survivors in Karachi, Pakistan, examined how a variety of institutional contexts that fed imperialist, capitalist, and nation-building prerogatives impacted women's experiences with and responses to violence. Findings from this study revealed that women demonstrated resilience and political resistance within recovery processes that were nonlinear and that coping strategies differed depending on their age (Chaudhry & Bertram, 2009). Acknowledging heterogeneity and remaining mindful of local and even regional differences might serve to offset homogenization (Chowdhury, 2009; Denmark & Segovich, 2012). Transnational feminists have refer-enced the assessment of the global in the individual as the lived experience model (Dewey & St. Germain, 2012). Integrating community participatory approaches can further produce locally informed and valid methodologies that are useful for understanding local contexts.

Other considerations for developing transnational feminist research questions concentrate on dynamic cultural processes within which the individual participates (Hegde, 1998; Mendoza, 2002). Flows of persons and economies across borders shift cultural values and norms, making them a moving target for research questions that materialize from decontextualized theory and paradigms. Moreover, individuals and communities are continually negotiating their identities in relation to input from their environmental surroundings (Tsuda et al., 2014). Albeit not explicitly transnational feminist, Atlani and Rousseau (2000) provided an insightful example of research that illuminates how community members can reconfigure the meaning of rape according to context. Their example also poignantly illustrates how cultural dynamism relates to transnational migration through interviewing several members of a Vietnamese community who fled from the communist dictatorship. Before leaving Vietnam, a raped woman was considered a spoiled belonging of her husband, father, or son. Before embarking on their migratory journey, however, the community suspected that it was highly probable that pirates would sexually assault women on their journey overseas, and the meaning of rape was renegotiated. The community encouraged women to acquiesce for the benefit of the larger group. Unexpectedly and tragically, while on their journey, the pirates forced community members to participate in sexual assaults by selecting women and girls. When the refugees arrived in the refugee camps, the meaning of sexual assault was renegotiated yet again within a Buddhist framework such that raped women and girls were seen as paying atonement for past misdeeds of their own in a former life or that of their ancestors. The community discouraged women and girls from speaking about their assaults because, in doing so, they would be revealing past shameful deeds. Atlani and Rousseau used this example of cultural dynamism related to the understanding of sexual assault (data collected with ethnographic methods) as a case study. It is helpful to consider research questions about the practice and conceptualization of transcultural psychiatry in humanitarian settings, the defining of culture, and how these translate into therapeutic care for sexual assault victims (Atlani & Rousseau, 2000). This is an example of how meaning ascribed to sexual assault is dynamic and changes according to migratory contexts and experiences.

As engaged agents, individuals and communities can resist, accommodate, or appropriate transnational flows, depending on the flows' relevance to local context (Tsuda et al., 2014). Inquiring about these processes is fodder for transnational feminist research. For example, to answer the question of how transnational discourses of gender and development are understood in

Kampala, Uganda, Mills and Ssewakiryanga (2002) conducted focus groups with students and professors who demonstrated their understanding of transnational feminist movements by framing the 1995 World Conference on Women, held in Beijing, China, as representative of a European feminist agenda that overlooked rural Ugandan women's needs. Participants instead called for a Ugandan approach that consisted of negotiation between genders and consensus building (Mills & Ssewakiryanga, 2002). Albeit from a liberation psychology perspective, Lindorfer (2009) used two case studies from Eastern Africa to answer the question of how discourse in trauma interventions framed victimization. Lindorfer found that trauma-trained counselors in refugee camps in Uganda exhibited appropriation by dismissing aspects of imported Western trauma treatment models perceived as irrelevant for the environment and persons with whom they were working (Lindorfer, 2009). Thus, another possible approach for inquiry is questioning practitioners' appropriation of psychosocial interventions designed elsewhere, such as in the West.

Research Methods

Several components of research methods are important to consider when conducting research from a transnational feminist perspective. These include data collection techniques, interpretation of data and results, and psychological constructs and their measurement. Like other feminist methodological paradigms (Sprague, 2016), transnational feminist research methods are variable and include the gamut of methodological possibilities. In this sense, a transnational feminist approach does not diverge from other feminist or international approaches. Instead, what matters "is not the method used, but how it is used, both technically and politically" (Sprague, 2016, p. 30). Thus, transnational feminist researchers are not limited to specific methodologies (e.g., Chaudhry & Bertram, 2009), though research that has referenced itself as transnational feminist overwhelmingly (e.g., Bahkru, 2008; Bhattacharya, 2009), but not exclusively (e.g., Grabe, Grose, & Dutt, 2015), has implemented qualitative methodologies.

Partnerships

Forming multisite research partnerships is a commonly used strategy of transnational feminist researchers. For example, in their study of immigrant girls caring for their younger siblings, Lee and Pacini-Ketchabaw (2011) involved their participants as coresearchers who documented their experiences using journals, field notes, and documentary video. The girls then disseminated these data in presentations they crafted themselves to professionals, parents, and peers. Grabe et al. (2015) formed partnerships with leaders of self-mobilized, grassroots women's organizations in Tanzania and Nicaragua with egalitarian dialogue to conduct a mixed methods research study on the association of land ownership with intimate partner violence. They collaborated with their locally based partners to design and adapt quantitative surveys. Partnerships are crucial throughout the research process. Local partners, for instance, should be leading the development of research questions and directions in ways that are meaningful for the local context. Conversations about data ownership (who stores and owns the data) and authorship on publications are essential to have before research begins. Attention to equitability in authorship opportunities is also important. In collaborations that are multilingual, partners who speak languages of high-resourced settings can provide editing and other support. High-resourced partners could build statistical and analytical support into grant budgets to help local partners answer other hypotheses and questions that may arise during the research process. These partnerships can help ensure that constructs, such as liberation (e.g., ownership of land), illness, and well-being are locally defined; research is meaningful for local contexts; and methods are ethical.

Data Collection Techniques

Common data collection procedures and methods found in transnational feminist research have been snowball sampling for recruitment and focus groups, individual interviews, participant observations, photo elicitations, and case studies. Other useful approaches have included participatory action research and community-based participatory research, two closely related methods that fundamentally share power by making research a community function in all aspects, from research questions through data collection and use of results (Israel, Eng, Schulz, & Parker, 2005). These data collection techniques prioritize partnerships among researchers and communities and participation through giving voice to participants. When applied transnationally, they have provided a platform for participants' perspectives on globalization, migration, and oppressive power structures.

Interpretation of Data and Results

Researchers frequently have integrated transnational feminism with other theoretical orientations, including liberation psychology (e.g., Chaudhry & Bertram, 2009), Women of Color feminist theory (e.g., Dewey & St. Germain, 2012), participatory action approaches (e.g., Lee & Pacini-Ketchabaw, 2011; Torre & Ayala, 2009), and cultural psychology (e.g., Kurtiş & Adams, 2015), describing integration as a weaving (Saavedra, Chakravarthi, & Lower, 2009) or a braiding (Chowdhury, 2009). Commonly cited theoretical influences in transnational feminist writings were Grewal and Kaplan (1994), Mohanty (1988), Anzaldu¥a (1999), Crenshaw (1991), and Martín-Baró (1996).

Self-Reflexivity. *Self-reflexivity* is a differentiating component of feminist research that acknowledges the important role that researchers' intersecting identities have in shaping analysis and interpretation of findings. Self-reflexivity is used to develop a critical consciousness of intersecting areas of power, privilege, and marginalization. It is a central tenet of feminist methodology (Chowdhury, 2009) and likewise evidenced in transnational feminist literature (Grewal & Kaplan, 1994). Reflective topics under consideration have included acknowledging areas of benefit, privilege, oppression or marginalization, and moral and political commitments (Bahkru, 2008; Miraftab, 2004). In data analysis and interpretation, this means striving to be aware of our biases as researchers. Because ideological privileges may create blind spots, critical exportation and importation of psychological constructs require transnational disciplinary and epistemological consideration (Marecek, 2012). A stance of radical uncertainty—openness to revising positions based on new knowledge—as well as interdisciplinary research collaborations, may all enhance efforts to be reflective about psychological constructs (Wade, 2012). All forms of boundary crossing (Sprague, 2016), including epistemological boundaries, can help to challenge the myopias of privileged perspectives. For instance, the initial feminist discourse around female genital cutting, deemed as culturally insensitive and homogenizing (Smith, 2011), has significantly altered following postcolonial critiques put forward in the 1990s (Wade, 2012).

Avoiding the Binary. The second area of importance in considering feminist data analysis and interpretation is to be aware of the tendency to use binary categories, which often oversimplify what is complex and nuanced. Many transnational feminist research summaries or reflections have included examples of ways in which binary representations did not reflect their own positioning, the positioning of the women or girl participants in their studies, or methodological approaches. Insider or outsider (Bahkru, 2008; Miraftab, 2004), qualitative or quantitative, subjective or objective (Bhattacharya, 2009), us or them, North or South, free or not free, savior or victim, global or local (Chowdhury, 2009), Western or non-Western (Torre & Ayala, 2009), First or Third World, and West or rest (Hegde, 1998) exemplify contested representations.

To avoid the use of binary labels, transnational feminist analysts have drawn on the notion of intersecting identities, privileges, and oppressions and noted the intersections' fluctuations and operations within transnational contexts (Grewal & Kaplan, 1994). In her performance ethnography, for instance, Bhattacharya (2009) offered the useful analogy of front- and back-stage performances when illustrating how two female Indian graduate students negotiated their identities in response to interpersonal exchanges with non-Indian and Indian expatriates in the United States. The front stage was how and in which ways the students chose to engage with and present themselves to those from their host country. The back stage was understood as a metaphor where the oftentimes conflicting tensions and nuances of the self remained.

For instance, when engaging with White U.S. people at her host academic institution, one student conveyed White U.S. people's frequent use of stereotypes, many of which she did not relate to. This student felt more at ease asking questions and speaking freely with other Indian residents, but she also gave examples of Indian men's sexualization of her and subsequently not feeling fully comfortable in that context either. Bhattacharya (2009) then skillfully extended the performance ethnography to an analysis of her positioning as a researcher by documenting how she spoke and behaved for academic audiences. Reflective transnational feminist researchers might consider which identities they bring to the front stage in transnational contexts, and how transnational interactions evoke these performances. In addition, researchers could note how their behaviors and discourse relate to global power structures and flows.

Dynamic, Fluctuating Hierarchies and Preconceived Notions. Transnational feminist research additionally claims that intersectional performances and reflections do not erase national differences but rather acknowledge within-nation and between-nation hierarchies and how research teams, collaborators, participants, and projects fluctuate within those hierarchies to provide and interpret data. Miraftab (2004), an Iranian scholar in U.S. academia, conducted research with women heads of households in Mexico and found that her preconceived notions of privilege and insider or outsider status were not the identities deemed most important to her participants. For instance, Miraftab's childlessness and Iranian background where, as participants had learned from media, men could take children away from women, proved as more salient components to participants than other privileges associated with educational level or class. Her work chronicles how researchers' notions of privilege and oppression are culturally informed and that people with whom researchers engage in transnational contexts are active agents in defining power and privileges (Miraftab, 2004). A common strategy for achieving local input is to establish a community advisory board. From a transnational feminist perspective, it would be crucial to have representatives who exhibit a range of privileged and oppressed identities and to ensure that researchers are not predetermining or defining those identities, but rather that those identities are negotiated and identified through a wide range of feedback.

Psychological Constructs and Their Measurement

Much of feminist critique of quantitative methods has hinged on standardized measurement (Sprague, 2016). From a transnational perspective, a component of this problem is that psychological constructs rooted in Western theory continue to be exported irrespective of local interpretations (Summerfield, 1999). In *Crazy Like Us: The Globalization of the American Psyche*, for instance, Watters (2010) deftly illustrated how the pharmaceutical industry's expansion into the global market included a concomitant exportation of U.S. constellations of psychiatric symptoms and corresponding illnesses, such as the marketing of major depressive disorder as a mental illness in Japan to facilitate the advertising and sale of antidepressant medications. This example illustrates how globalized marketing procedures can attempt to reshape local conceptualization of mental distress for corporate gain. Universalizing mental health constructs can mask illnesses' social implications and etiology (Watters, 2010). Several examples of indiscriminate use of psychological constructs are available in the transnational feminist scholarship. To better understand how conceptualization of mental health constructs varies among contexts, formative qualitative research is essential. For instance, to better understand the circumstances and conceptualization of Sri Lankan adolescent girls who were hospitalized after deliberate self-harm in the form of suicide attempts, Marecek and Senadheera (2012) conducted individual interviews. Through these interviews, they documented themes of self-harm as a form of communication resulting from frustration with intergenerational conflicts regarding daughters' comportment stemming from exposure to transnational flows of people with different practices and ideologies into the community. These themes differ from Western notions of self-harm as an outgrowth of clinical depression and illustrate how methods, such as interviewing individuals, can enrich understanding of mental health constructs in diverse contexts.

The Self. Another example is the infatuation with the self as a psychological entity. The idea of self has evolved from Protestant and individualistic cultural values and is subsequently reflected in Western psychological terminology, such as "self-affirmation, self-awareness, self-comparison, self-concept, self-consistent, self-control, self-efficacy, self-esteem, self-determination, self-fulfillment, self-handicapping, self-image, self-identity, self-perception, self-regulation, [and] self-reference" (Shiah, 2016, p. 2). Furthermore, Kurtiş and Adams (2015) offered some international comparative examples demonstrating how Western feminist emphases on self-realization, self-disclosure in relationships, and a right to sexual satisfaction are exported in the name of liberation of women for whom the constructs have different psychological outcomes. They argued that the uncritical exportation of these Western understandings of the self in relation to others could unwittingly pathologize women's experiences. For instance, they found that Turkish women's self-silencing in relationships facilitated better relationship outcomes (Kurtiş & Adams, 2015). This example shows that even if mental health constructs, such as self-silencing, translate similarly across contexts, they do not always associate with similar psychological outcomes. Thus, in addition to critically interrogating mental health constructs, transnational feminist researchers should extend critical inquiry to assumptions about behaviors that are positive and contributory to well-being.

Posttraumatic Stress Disorder. Research with international mental health experts in humanitarian settings has indicated that there is a decided over-emphasis on posttraumatic stress disorder (PTSD), though the construct is irrelevant in some settings (Weiss, Saraceno, Saxena, & van Ommeren, 2003). When exposure to interpersonal violence in conjunction with mental health problems is under investigation, many researchers assess symptoms of PTSD and rely on the PTSD Checklist to establish probable mental illness (e.g., Gupta et al., 2014; Vinck & Pham, 2013). Debates have transpired regarding the universalization of PTSD, with anthropologists asserting that PTSD is a Western diagnostic that is imposed on victims in non-Western cultures, equating the imposition to cultural colonialism (Drozdek, 2007; Summerfield, 1999). Even if symptoms are experienced universally, they may not present the same clinical utility as they do in the West. *Category fallacy* occurs when one culturally bound category is thought to have a similar meaning in another context (Kleinman, 1987). Although symptoms may look similar across cultures, symptom constellations may not be given the same meaning or level of importance as they are in the West. Research methods should thus include formative investigations about subjective meanings ascribed to experience. For instance, Summerfield (1999) conducted a study with war-displaced people in Nicaragua and stated that although some exhibited PTSD symptoms, they did not attend to these symptoms as the most important feature in their experience. Instead, they focused on the importance of building their social worlds insofar as was possible in the face of crippling poverty and fears of future destabilization. Insights such as these are critical for the provision of culturally relevant interventions.

Similarly, informed by her work in humanitarian settings in Uganda and the Democratic Republic of Congo, Lindorfer (2009) suggested that psychology's emphasis on PTSD decontextualizes mental health experiences, conceals global power structures, and invites neocolonialist knowledge transfer for treatment from people who originate in countries with political processes that may exacerbate war conditions. In research examining the construct of PTSD across three national contexts (Iraq, Burmese refugees in Thailand, the Democratic Republic of Congo) and with three different populations (respectively, torture survivors, refugees, sexual violence survivors), no models of PTSD were found that fit the population responses in Iraq (Michalopoulos et al., 2015).

Recommendations Regarding Constructs and Their Measurement. Because psychological constructs may be conceptualized and understood variably across many contexts, to avoid some of the problems illustrated previously, psychological measurement should ideally be preceded by qualitative and ethnographic work to develop and adapt instruments in meaningful ways beyond establishing the reliability and validity of instruments. Ethnographic methods (Davis & Craven, 2016), usually involving intimately spending long periods with communities using observation, coupled with diverse forms of formal and informal qualitative interviewing, are commonly used in social science research. Although not transnational feminist, there exist some commendable examples of research strategies, such as rapid ethnographic practices, that could be readily adopted to fit a transnational feminist framework. Rapid ethnographic strategies often involve asking participants and key informants to freely identify problems they are facing (without interviewer prompts and questions about specific problems they might face), define those problems, and when possible, rank the problems in terms of importance—a process usually completed in participant observation, focus groups, individual interview format, or some combination thereof (Bolton & Tang, 2004; Harris, Jerome, & Fawcett, 1997; Trotter, Needle, Goosby, Bates, & Singer, 2001).

For instance, to articulate idioms of distress and examine the concurrent validity of idioms and Euro American PTSD and depressive constructs in South Sudanese refugees, Rasmussen, Katoni, Keller, and Wilkinson (2011) conducted a rapid ethnography and asked traditional healers to group identified symptoms, providing an opportunity for the local conceptualization of symptom classification. To develop a culturally relevant functional impairment scale for children in political violence-affected settings, Tol, Komproe, Jordans, Susanty, and de Jong (2011) used strategies of brief participant observation, daily diaries of children, and focus groups for their rapid ethnographic process. The implementation of these types of strategies can triangulate (i.e., facilitate the validation of data through cross verification with other research methods and sources of data) and enrich quantitative measurement of psychological constructs in transnational studies. A transnational feminist concern during the enactment of these processes would be to ensure representation of all members, representing the various levels of stratification in communities.

To further illustrate the transnational feminist approach to research in a way that is responsive to local conditions, my (JJM's) work regarding gender-based violence in Uganda is detailed in the following case example.

TRANSNATIONAL FEMINIST RESEARCH CASE EXAMPLE: GENDER-BASED VIOLENCE IN UGANDA

The following transnational feminist case example is drawn primarily from two research endeavors in the Teso Subregion of Northeastern Uganda. The first was a dissertation project—a feminist, community-partnered qualitative study (*n* = 77) with participants ages 9 to 80. The researcher partnered with two organizations. The first was a local nonprofit organization called Transcultural Psychosocial Organization Uganda (TPO Uganda), which already had active gender-based violence (GBV) programs and wished to collaborate on a research project. The second was a community-based volunteer group who had come together to address high rates of GBV in their community (see the section on Partnerships). The local partners had anecdotal evidence that rates of GBV were high in conflict-affected communities where they were providing programming, and they were interested in obtaining data through research that could help them better understand GBV and armed conflict in these communities. The research questions that framed this project were (a) how does the community conceptualize GBV? and (b) how does armed conflict relate to GBV (Mootz, Stabb, & Mollen, 2017)? Funded by the Fogarty International Center and National Institute of Allergy and Infectious Diseases, I then lived in Uganda for 1 year and undertook a second, related mixed methods project, using structured surveys (*n* = 605 women), a rapid ethnography (*n* = 21), and in-depth interviews (*n* = 15). Building on the findings from the first study, the second study quantitatively examined pathways, highlighted by community members, between armed conflict and intimate partner violence and qualitatively investigated mental health experiences of women who had experienced intimate partner violence.

I first learned about GBV in the context of armed conflict from media coverage of the conflict in Sudan. News segments about Sudanese refugee women reported that women were being sexually assaulted when they were leaving the refugee camp to perform gender-related duties, such as gathering firewood. Three primary Western perspectives on sexual assault in the context of war have been described: feminist, medical, and anthropological (Atlani & Rousseau, 2000). Some Westerners consider sexual assault to be traumatic no matter the context or how others perceive their experiences, even though the traumatic framing of sexual assault is a relatively recent construction (Atlani & Rousseau, 2000). This perspective resonated with my internal processes and biases informed by my upbringing in the United States and feminist educational training. Although some Western women perceive sexual assault as traumatic, other women may conceptualize this experience differently, especially in the context of war and depending on a host of other intersecting identities. It was this media coverage of international events, combined with feminist interest and earlier experience volunteering in sub-Saharan Africa, which undergirded my first research project in Uganda.

Uganda provides wonderful examples that illustrate how people are not bounded, monolithic entities. More than 50 languages are spoken by numerous and diverse ethnic groups across the country, representing a richly complex and culturally diverse people (Central Intelligence Agency, 2016); however, sources of demographic data are somewhat limited and often collected (or at least partially overseen and funded) by international, Western organizations. Although approximately one third of Ugandans live in extreme poverty (earning less than $1.90 USD per day), national indices and profiles do not always reveal the unequal distribution of resources between the rural and urban populations and how resources are managed and allocated between family members within households. Those who live in the rural Northern and Eastern parts of the country represent 84% of the country's poor, for instance (World Bank Group, 2016). A transnational feminist approach can be used to understand better the complexity of populations' intersecting cultures.

My Ugandan partners' programming and volunteer activities speak to prominent transnational policy and funding flows related to issues of GBV, a global problem around which transnational feminists have aligned (Reilly, 2011). Their partnership in working to prevent and respond to GBV, and the subsequent research path, was built on the momentum of these transnational flows and an area of relative transnational feminist alignment. For instance, the community volunteer group had received training in GBV issues from international nonprofit organizations, and the local nonprofit organization, TPO Uganda, received funding from international foundations for its GBV work.

The Region's Colonial History

TPO Uganda, the partnering organization to these research projects, determined the site of the research, a rural location in Teso, Northeastern Uganda, that has unique geopolitical elements that differentiate it from other regions in the country—important considerations for transnational feminist research. At the conclusion of British colonization of Uganda in 1962, ethnicity and religion primarily determined Ugandans' political affiliations, and the constructed tribal and ethnic divisions ripened Uganda for the decades of civil war that followed their independence from the British (Rice, 2009). Teso experienced armed conflict by the Lord's Resistance Army and decades of a much more protracted conflict perpetrated by a nomadic ethnic group called the Karamajong through cattle rustling raids. The Karamajong acquired thousands of AK-47s left behind by Idi Amin's ousted army in 1979, and the acquisition of weapons inflated bride price (the payment of cattle from men's families to women's families when marrying), one of four primary incentives to conduct cattle raids (Jabs, 2007). Their raids spilled over into neighboring regions, including Teso. In addition to Karamajong warriors sexually assaulting women and girls during raids, GBV appeared to escalate as a result of the social instability following these raids. Although the high prevalence of GBV in armed conflict situations has been well documented (Hossain et al., 2014; Peterman, Palermo, & Bredenkamp, 2011), transnational feminist connections between indirect transnational influences, such as global market economies, and ongoing armed conflict have been less effectively established.

The United Nations (UN) has served as a transnational platform for feminist lobbying and advocacy regarding violence against women (García-Del Moral & Dersnah, 2014). In 1993, the UN approved the Declaration on the Elimination of Violence Against Women, following an amendment to the Convention on the Elimination of All Forms of Discrimination Against Women (CEDAW), which interpreted violence against women as a form of discrimination (García-Del Moral & Dersnah, 2014). Uganda has benefited from a robust grassroots women's movement and ratified several international human rights treaties that prohibit violence against women: The African Charter on Human and People's Rights, the UN International Covenant on Civil and Political Rights, the UN Convention against Torture and other Cruel, Inhuman, and Degrading Treatment or Punishment, the UN Convention on the Rights of the Child and the UN's CEDAW (Amnesty International, 2007). CEDAW contains an optional protocol, which Uganda has not ratified, that allows women whose rights have been violated to seek redress. However, the 1995 Constitution of Uganda incorporated the principles of CEDAW, called for gender equality in all sectors, and included affirmative action measures to balance gender inequalities.

Methodology

My formative qualitative work revealed how community members conceptualized GBV and various direct and indirect pathways between armed conflict and diverse forms of GBV (Mootz et al., 2017). Using qualitative methods to understand these problems from the community's perspective corrected some research biases and critically informed future work in several ways. For example, although media coverage of conflict has highlighted combatants' sexual assault in armed conflict situations, reporting that shaped their interest in and work with GBV in armed conflict, the community inhabitants in Teso highlighted male intimate partners' battering of women as most common and problematic.

The community's insights inspired new research questions and directions and provided the foundation for testing pathways between armed conflict and intimate partner violence more specifically. For the quantitative arm of the project, the sampling strategy was to survey three districts in Teso that represented varying levels of exposure to conflict. Their local partners recognized that even within districts there was wide variability of exposure level, so they further narrowed their strategy to randomly select villages from selected subcounties within districts that their local partners determined as representing high, medium, and low exposures to conflict. Without the community's invaluable input and knowledge of the variability of context, the originally conceptualized sampling methods would not have adequately addressed the research questions, once again signaling the importance of partnerships in developing research designs.

Moreover, advances in and heightened access to technology in Uganda played an important role in quantitative data collection methods. They used an online software program to manage survey data, which allowed for the monitoring of data collection from any location. Local research assistants used tablets to administer surveys with women in rural villages. At the end of each day, the local team uploaded survey responses with the assistance of a mobile router.

There were several central constructs measured across the two research projects: armed conflict, GBV, intimate partner violence, alcohol misuse, gender equity, socioeconomic status, and mental distress, among others. Diverse methodological strategies were used to capture how women who participated in the studies understood these constructs. For instance, by first asking the open-ended question of what GBV is before trying to measure exposure to GBV, participants shared numerous forms of violence that fall outside of traditional definitions put forward by the UN and the World Health Organization (World Health Organization, 2016). These experiences included abuse of rights, infidelity, early marriage, land grabbing, poor family relations, failure to reveal HIV status, heavy labor, witchcraft, and abduction. Expanding the definition of GBV according to participants' understanding allowed for a fuller understanding of how armed conflict relates to violence against girls and women. Others have also found that instruments developed in the West to assess GBV have overlooked local forms of violence, such as men hitting women with a shoe as a form of discipline in Sri Lanka (Marecek, 2012) or dowry deaths in India (Nayak, 2003). A more pronounced transnational feminist emphasis might consist of examining how transnational religious, humanitarian, or psychological flows influence the understanding, perpetration, and experience of GBV in conflict-affected communities. Moreover, it would be worthwhile inquiring about how local appropriation shifts longitudinally and in relation to these flows.

It was precisely because of concern about measuring psychological symptoms with imported constructs that their local partners requested that psychological problems be measured as generalized distress rather than discrete mental illnesses. The strategy of my collaborators and I was to use mixed methods to triangulate women's experience of and understanding of mental problems. The research team lightly adapted a well-known and previously validated in Uganda quantitative survey of mental distress for local relevance and then followed up the quantitative portion by randomly selecting women who had experienced intimate partner violence to participate in a rapid ethnography, establishing women's understanding and prioritization of problems. The research team then did a second follow-up, in-depth interview to understand women's conceptualization of mental health experiences. Extending the local construction of mental health well-being to capture transnational movement would further provide an analytical focus for transnational knowledge production efforts. Although these processes may involve numerous, iterative interviews to establish clarification, when researching interpersonal violence, balancing participation with safety is an important ethical consideration.

Another principal construct in the research team's work was measuring gender (in)equity in relationships. To do so, the research team incorporated the International Men and Gender Equality Survey Questionnaire (International Center for Research on Women & Instituto Promundo, 2010), a survey that has been widely used in low-resource settings and that includes a variety of questions measuring attitudes toward women, acceptance of partner battering and violence, and division of household labor, among others. One subset of questions assesses attitudes toward same-sex relationships. As is portrayed in the documentary *God Loves Uganda* (Williams & Goldman, 2013), U.S. evangelical missionaries and politicians influenced Ugandan politicians to implement the Anti-Homosexuality Act (AHA), prohibiting same-sex relations or providing aid to people who engage in same-sex activity. Same-sex relations had been illegal in Uganda since British colonization, but the AHA increased the limits of punishment from 14 years to an initial punishment of up to death, later reduced to a maximum punishment of life in prison.

Mob justice, the murdering and assaulting of people by lay civilians, ensued following the initiation of these laws targeting lesbian, gay, bisexual, transgender, and queer (LGBTQ) people in Uganda (Bowcott, 2014). Though the AHA has since been annulled by the Ugandan judicial court (Gettleman, 2014), due to ethical considerations regarding the safety of the research team and participants, the research team omitted the items on same-sex relationships and attitudes. The items' occlusion has influenced findings and available interpretations. In juxtaposition to collaborative advocacy working toward the abolition of violence against women, LGBTQ topics have been a silent issue among transnational feminists (Brenner, 2003). Thus, in addition to guiding conceptualization, decreasing misrepresentation through homogenization, and improving validity, knowledge of local responses arguably enhances the ethicality of transnational psychological research.

Reflexivity and Work in Uganda

Several examples of researcher reflexivity and its impact on data analysis and interpretation were evident in my work in Uganda. It was clear that attention to my intersecting identities and cultural context would be crucial throughout the research process. When people in the United States learned that my family and I were moving to Uganda, many assumed we were missionaries. The chapter's epigraph illustrates my desire to distinguish my work from that of missionaries, the unease partially fueled by knowledge of historical geopolitical flows of colonization across Ugandan borders. Priests were the first Europeans whom the Ugandan people had seen. Not long after their arrival, more Protestant and Catholic missionaries followed, competing to convert people from Islam and Indigenous beliefs to their respective religions, heightening rivalries and factions to the brink of civil war (Rice, 2009). I share the same skin color and Western origin as initial missionaries and colonists. As a research fellow whose work was supported by funding initiated in the United States, in one sense, I represented an economic good that transgressed national boundaries and flowed from the Global North to the Global South to conduct research about violence against women and girls. I delegated funding to a research team located in a region that has few economic means for livelihood. The direction of these flows became increasingly salient during a day of research team training when I learned that one of the team members had a 5-day-old infant for whom a family member was caring in a nearby room. The team member worried that I would disapprove of her working on the project if I were made aware that she was 5 days postpartum. The team member's family depended heavily on the income. In many ways, my transnational migration with accompanying funding resembled historical geopolitical flows and power structures where my economic positioning created a power differential between the research team and me.

In discussing this chapter's content with my Ugandan mentor, the mentor and I acknowledged our intersecting identities, certain facets of which seeming to have commanded greater salience than others. For instance, I am a U.S., middle-class, female *muzungu* (White person) who has conducted international research with marginalized communities and women in the Global South. Because *transnational* is often used interchangeably with *Third World women* (e.g., Bhattacharya, 2009; Grabe & Else-Quest, 2012), and given my *muzungu* and nationality statuses, I questioned whether I could advance discussion that is anything but rooted in a neocolonial perspective. However, my mentor is a citizen of the Global South. My mentor's research projects exclusively transpired within the Ugandan national context, but many were funded by international organizations, such as the UN. Given these complexities, we deliberated whether they were transnational enough.

This discussion focused on entrenched binary representations that emphasize difference (e.g., Global North and Global South). For instance, despite our national demarcations, our positioning as middle class, academic feminists might demonstrate areas of connection as well as shared privileges (Mootz et al., 2017). A discussion of intersectionality and points of divergence itself could be indicative of an academic bias with grassroots activists working toward the elimination of GBV placing a stronger emphasis on similarities across transnational contexts (Mendoza, 2002).

To offset biases in interpretations that might emanate from their privileged identities and interfere with the collection of data, I hired a team of local research assistants who were from Teso and spoke Ateso, the local language. In addition to having the quantitative measures forward and back translated, the research team and I collectively reviewed the measures item by item, making linguistic adjustments where necessary to enhance meaning and understandability. We piloted the surveys with volunteers and revisited the items once more, again adjusting items that were irrelevant or difficult to understand. Perhaps most crucially, the local team created conceptual categories for all the problems that women listed in the rapid ethnography exercise. The local team also conducted the grounded theory open, axial, and selective coding (Strauss & Corbin, 1990). A coding team in the United States additionally coded the transcripts for another source of triangulation, showing a surprising amount of overlap between the two coding systems. Although the research assistants were from the area, they had substantially more education and resources than our women participants, many of whom were illiterate and lacked basic necessities. An additional source of triangulation might have been to obtain feedback about central themes from participants. Another transnational feminist strategy for analysis could be to attach transnational feminist theoretical codes to narrative data.

SUMMARY: RESEARCH DISSEMINATION, REPRESENTATION, AND FUTURE DIRECTIONS

Feminists have been critical of the role of oppressive structures in the production of knowledge that harmfully portray or are not representative of marginalized people. Situated within this established tradition, transnational feminist research likewise is a political and action-oriented project. When flows of researchers and participants across national borders occur, the question of representation when disseminating research findings becomes paramount. Reflecting on her research with South Asian immigrant women in the United States and battered women in India, Hegde (1998) questioned, "How can we develop a feminist perspective that can travel transnationally and confront the challenge of representing marginalized others?" (p. 276). For example, transnational feminists have admonished U.S. politicians' co-opting of feminist discourse to advance imperialist activities, such as the invasion of Afghanistan for the liberation of oppressed women (Brenner, 2003; Chowdhury, 2009).

Research that overlooks transnational considerations has the potential to homogenize and misrepresent participants' lived experiences. To contextualize research efforts and politicize the production of knowledge in an increasingly integrated world, transnational feminists have used largely qualitative strategies to assess how the global intersects with the local through all stages of research. Collaborating transnationally to promote social change has the potential of transforming international research projects into transnational ones.

Transnational feminist research methods are diverse and not prescriptive. In fact, transnational feminists frequently contest the quantitative–qualitative binary in addition to the other binary representations previously mentioned. Many Western psychological constructs—for example, PTSD—do not always represent local experiences and conceptualization of symptoms. In these cases, qualitative and ethnographic methods can well serve transnational feminist researchers in establishing or adapting measurements so items more closely represent the lived experiences in diverse contexts. In the analysis and interpretation of data, moving beyond all binary understandings of the self and others and attending to how intersectional performances interact in transnational contexts is a key strategy in transnational feminist approaches.

Researchers have a variety of outlets and opportunities to convey messages about research questions, findings, and interpretations through formal and informal publications, presentations, social media, and commonplace conversations. As the production of and communication about research is a political project, how will others who are unfamiliar with local contexts interpret researchers' communications? Intentional representation for social change can help align communication with political interests, and knowledge-to-policy strategies can be better examined and articulated in transnational feminist research. In disseminating findings at the community level, one strategy could be to balance issues of powerlessness with a strengths-based framework that investigates facets of resilience and agency. In Uganda, the research team shared their results with community workers and leaders who then brought the information back to their communities.

However, in future research, I plan to include a question for participants about their preferred method of dissemination.

There are several promising next steps for transnational feminist research. First, transnational feminist researchers should continue to develop and adapt diverse methods that support the analytical framework of intersecting global and local phenomena. Advancing the integration of theory through interdisciplinary collaboration can enhance efforts to establish creative and novel methods. For instance, researchers who do not explicitly operate from a feminist perspective developed and refined many of the methods, such as rapid ethnographic assessment, detailed in this chapter. Next, global mental health momentum exists for increasing access to mental health treatment, especially for people residing in the Global South, and is gaining traction (Horton, 2007; Lancet Global Mental Health Group, 2007). Transnational feminist researchers should be active in global mental health efforts to align with communities, ensure efforts include attention to intersecting identities, and critically interrogate unanticipated effects of extending Western-based treatments and theories to diverse settings (Bhugra & Minas, 2007). Finally, applying a transnational feminist framework by considering the impact of globalization and resulting migration to psychological studies involving migrants and citizens of the Global North is needed.

To conclude, uncritical international psychological research can inadvertently homogenize populations because research questions and methods do not capture global and local intersections. By considering how flows across boundaries relate to systems of power and oppression, transnational feminist strategies and considerations can augment psychological research in numerous ways. When developing questions, researchers can interrogate intersections between the global and local. Using methods that contest Western-originated psychological constructs can enhance local relevance. Moving beyond binary interpretations and including multiple data analytics can strengthen data analysis and interpretation. Participatory partnerships forged with reflection, humility, and uncertainty for how power dynamics influence working relationships and research are fundamental. At all stages of research, it is critical to listen to partners and members of the community to support their efforts.

REFERENCES

Amnesty International. (2007). *Uganda, doubly traumatized: Lack of access to justice for female victims of sexual and gender-based violence in Northern Uganda.* Retrieved from https://tbinternet.ohchr.org/Treaties/CEDAW/Shared%20Documents/UGA/INT_CEDAW_NGO_UGA_47_10221_E.pdf

Anzaldúa, G. (1999). *Borderlands/la frontera.* San Francisco, CA: Aunt Lute.

Atlani, L., & Rousseau, C. (2000). The politics of culture in humanitarian aid to women refugees who have experienced sexual violence. *Transcultural Psychiatry, 37*, 435–449. http://dx.doi.org/10.1177/136346150003700309

Bahkru, T. (2008). Negotiating and navigating the rough terrain of transnational feminist research. *Journal of International Women's Studies, 10*, 198–216.

Bhattacharya, K. (2009). Negotiating shuttling between transnational experiences: A de/colonizing approach to performance ethnography. *Qualitative Inquiry, 15*, 1061–1083. http://dx.doi.org/10.1177/1077800409332746

Bhugra, D., & Minas, I. H. (2007). Mental health and global movement of people. *The Lancet, 370*, 1109–1111. http://dx.doi.org/10.1016/S0140-6736(07)61249-5

Bolton, P., & Tang, A. M. (2004). Using ethnographic methods in the selection of post-disaster, mental health interventions. *Prehospital and Disaster Medicine, 19*, 97–101. http://dx.doi.org/10.1017/S1049023X00001540

Bowcott, O. (2014, May 12). Uganda anti-gay law led to tenfold rise in attacks on LGBTI people, report says. *The Guardian.* Retrieved from http://www.theguardian.com/world/2014/may/12/uganda-anti-gay-law-rise-attacks

Brenner, J. (2003). Transnational feminism and the struggle for global justice. *New Politics, 9*(2), 25–33.

Central Intelligence Agency. (2016). *The world factbook.* Retrieved from https://www.cia.gov/library/publications/the-world-factbook/index.html

Chaudhry, L. N., & Bertram, C. (2009). Narrating trauma and reconstruction in post-conflict Karachi: Feminist liberation psychology and the contours of agency in the margins. *Feminism & Psychology, 19*, 298–312. http://dx.doi.org/10.1177/0959353509105621

Chowdhury, E. H. (2009). Locating global feminisms elsewhere: Braiding US Women of Color and transnational feminisms. *Cultural Dynamics, 21*, 51–78. http://dx.doi.org/10.1177/0921374008100407

Crenshaw, K. W. (1991). Mapping the margins: Intersectionality, identity politics, and violence against Women of Color. *Stanford Law Review, 43*, 1241–1299. http://dx.doi.org/10.2307/1229039

Davis, D., & Craven, C. (2016). *Feminist ethnography: Thinking through methodologies, challenges, and possibilities.* New York, NY: Rowman & Littlefield.

Denmark, F. L., & Segovich, K. E. (2012). The personal is international: Perspectives from the United Nations on transforming feminist research. *Psychology of Women Quarterly, 36*, 154–157. http://dx.doi.org/10.1177/0361684312441774

Dewey, S., & St. Germain, T. (2012). Between global fears and local bodies: Toward a transnational feminist analysis of conflict-related sexual violence. *Journal of International Women's Studies, 13*(3), 49–64.

Drozdek, B. (2007). The rebirth of contextual thinking in psychotraumatology. In B. Drozdek & J. Wilson (Eds.), *Voices of trauma: Treating survivors across cultures* (pp. 1–25). New York, NY: Springer Science + Business Media.

Else-Quest, N. M., & Grabe, S. (2012). The political is personal: Measurement and application of nation-level indicators of gender equity in psychological research. *Psychology of Women Quarterly, 36,* 131–144. http://dx.doi.org/10.1177/0361684312441592

García-Del Moral, P., & Dersnah, M. A. (2014). A feminist challenge to the gendered politics of the public/private divide: On due diligence, domestic violence, and citizenship. *Citizenship Studies, 18,* 661–675. http://dx.doi.org/10.1080/13621025.2014.944772

Gettleman, J. (2014, August 1). Uganda anti-gay law struck down by court. *The New York Times.* Retrieved from http://www.nytimes.com/2014/08/02/world/africa/uganda-anti-gay-law-struck-down-by-court.html?_r=0

Grabe, S., & Else-Quest, N. M. (2012). The role of transnational feminism in psychology: Complementary visions. *Psychology of Women Quarterly, 36,* 158–161. http://dx.doi.org/10.1177/0361684312442164

Grabe, S., Grose, R., & Dutt, A. (2015). Women's land ownership and relationship power: A mixed methods approach to understanding structural inequities and violence against women. *Psychology of Women Quarterly, 39,* 7–19. http://dx.doi.org/10.1177/0361684314533485

Grewal, I., & Kaplan, C. (1994). *Scattered hegemonies: Postmodernity and transnational feminist practices.* Minneapolis: University of Minnesota Press.

Gupta, J., Falb, K. L., Carliner, H., Hossain, M., Kpebo, D., & Annan, J. (2014). Associations between exposure to intimate partner violence, armed conflict, and probable PTSD among women in rural Côte d'Ivoire. *PLoS One, 9*(5), e96300. http://dx.doi.org/10.1371/journal.pone.0096300

Guthrie, R. V. (2004). *Even the rat was white: A historical view of psychology* (2nd ed.). Upper Saddle River, NJ: Pearson Education.

Harris, K. J., Jerome, N. W., & Fawcett, S. B. (1997). Rapid assessment procedures: A review and critique. *Human Organization, 56,* 375–378. http://dx.doi.org/10.17730/humo.56.3.w525025611458003

Hegde, R. S. (1998). A view from elsewhere: Locating difference and the politics of representation from a transnational feminist perspective. *Communication Theory, 8,* 271–297. http://dx.doi.org/10.1111/j.1468-2885.1998.tb00222.x

Horton, R. (2007). Launching a new movement for mental health. *Lancet, 370,* 806. http://dx.doi.org/10.1016/S0140-6736(07)61243-4

Hossain, M., Zimmerman, C., Kiss, L., Kone, D., Bakayoko-Topolska, M., Manan, D. K., . . . Watts, C. (2014). Men's and women's experiences of violence and traumatic events in rural Cote d'Ivoire before, during and after a period of armed conflict. *BMJ Open, 4*(2), e003644. http://dx.doi.org/10.1136/bmjopen-2013-003644

International Center for Research on Women & Instituto Promundo. (2010). *International Men and Gender Equality Survey (IMAGES) Questionnaire.* Retrieved from http://www.icrw.org/publications/international-men-and-gender-equality-survey-images

Israel, B. A., Eng, E., Schulz, A. J., & Parker, E. A. (2005). Introduction to methods in community-based participatory research for health. In B. Israel,

E. Eng, A. Schulz, & E. Parker (Eds.), *Methods in community-based participatory research for health* (pp. 3–26). San Francisco, CA: Jossey-Bass.

Jabs, L. (2007). Where two elephants meet, the grass suffers: A case study of intractable conflict in Karamoja, Uganda. *American Behavioral Scientist, 50,* 1498–1519. http://dx.doi.org/10.1177/0002764207302466

Jaggar, A. M. (2013). Does poverty wear a woman's face? Some moral dimensions of a transnational feminist research project. *Hypatia, 28,* 240–256. http://dx.doi.org/10.1111/hypa.12022

Kleinman, A. (1987). Anthropology and psychiatry: The role of culture in cross-cultural research on illness. *The British Journal of Psychiatry, 151,* 447–454. http://dx.doi.org/10.1192/bjp.151.4.447

Kurtiş, T., & Adams, G. (2015). Decolonizing liberation: Toward a transnational feminist psychology. *Journal of Social and Political Psychology, 3,* 388–413. http://dx.doi.org/10.5964/jspp.v3i1.326

Lancet Global Mental Health Group. (2007). Scale up services for mental disorders: A call for action. *The Lancet, 370,* 1241–1252. https://dx.doi.org/10.1016/s0140-6736(07)61242-2

Lee, J. A., & Pacini-Ketchabaw, V. (2011). Immigrant girls as caregivers to younger siblings: A transnational feminist analysis. *Gender and Education, 23,* 105–119. http://dx.doi.org/10.1080/09540251003674063

Lindorfer, S. (2009). In whose interest do we work? Critical comments of a practitioner at the fringes of the liberation paradigm. *Feminism & Psychology, 19,* 354–367. http://dx.doi.org/10.1177/0959353509105626

Marecek, J. (2012). The global is local: Adding culture, ideology, and context to international psychology. *Psychology of Women Quarterly, 36,* 149–153. http://dx.doi.org/10.1177/0361684312441775

Marecek, J., & Senadheera, C. (2012). 'I drank it to put an end to me': Narrating girls' suicide and self-harm in Sri Lanka. *Contributions to Indian Sociology, 46,* 53–82. http://dx.doi.org/10.1177/006996671104600204

Martín-Baró, I. (1996). Toward a liberation psychology. In A. Aron & S. Corne (Eds.), *Writings for a liberation psychology: Ignacio Martín-Baró* (pp. 17–32). Cambridge, MA: Harvard University Press.

Mendoza, B. (2002). Transnational feminisms in question. *Feminist Theory, 3,* 295–314. http://dx.doi.org/10.1177/146470002762492015

Meredith, M. (2005). *The fate of Africa.* New York, NY: Public Affairs.

Michalopoulos, L. M., Unick, G. J., Haroz, E. E., Bass, J., Murray, L. K., & Bolton, P. A. (2015). Exploring the fit of Western PTSD models across three non-Western low- and middle-income countries. *Traumatology, 21*(2), 55–63. http://dx.doi.org/10.1037/trm0000020

Mills, D., & Ssewakiryanga, R. (2002). 'That Beijing thing': Challenging transnational feminisms in Kampala. *Gender, Place and Culture, 9,* 385–398. http://dx.doi.org/10.1080/0966369022000024641

Miraftab, F. (2004). Can you belly dance? Methodological questions in the era of transnational feminist research. *Gender, Place and Culture, 11*, 595–604. http://dx.doi.org/10.1080/0966369042000307988

Mohanty, C. (1988). Under Western eyes: Feminist scholarship and colonialist discourses. *Feminist Review, 30*, 61–88. http://dx.doi.org/10.1057/fr.1988.42

Mootz, J. J., Stabb, S. D., & Mollen, D. (2017). Gender-based violence and armed conflict: A community-informed socioecological conceptual model from northeastern Uganda. *Psychology of Women Quarterly, 41*, 368–388. http://dx.doi.org/10.1177/0361684317705086

Nayak, M. V. (2003). The struggle over gendered meanings in India: How Indian women's networks, the Hindu Nationalist Hegemonic Project, and transnational feminists address gender violence. *Women & Politics, 25*, 71–96. http://dx.doi.org/10.1300/J014v25n03_04

Peterman, A., Palermo, T., & Bredenkamp, C. (2011). Estimates and determinants of sexual violence against women in the Democratic Republic of Congo. *American Journal of Public Health, 101*, 1060–1067. http://dx.doi.org/10.2105/AJPH.2010.300070

Rasmussen, A., Katoni, B., Keller, A. S., & Wilkinson, J. (2011). Posttraumatic idioms of distress among Darfur refugees: Hozun and Majnun. *Transcultural Psychiatry, 48*, 392–415. http://dx.doi.org/10.1177/1363461511409283

Reilly, N. (2011). Doing transnational feminism, transforming human rights: The emancipatory possibilities revisited. *Irish Journal of Sociology, 19*, 60–76. http://dx.doi.org/10.7227/IJS.19.2.5

Rice, A. (2009). *The teeth may smile but the heart does not forget: Murder and memory in Uganda.* New York, NY: Picador.

Richards, G. (1997). *Race, racism, and psychology: Towards a reflexive history.* New York, NY: Routledge.

Rivers, W. H. R., & Seligmann, C. G. (1901). *Reports of the Cambridge anthropological expedition to Torres Straits.* Retrieved from https://archive.org/details/reportsofcambrid02hadd/page/2

Saavedra, C. M., Chakravarthi, S., & Lower, J. K. (2009). Weaving transnational feminist(s) methodologies: (Re)examining early childhood linguistic diversity teacher training and research. *Journal of Early Childhood Research, 7*, 324–340. http://dx.doi.org/10.1177/1476718X09336973

Shiah, Y. J. (2016). From self to nonself: The nonself theory. *Frontiers in Psychology, 7*, 124. http://dx.doi.org/10.3389/fpsyg.2016.00124

Smith, C. (2011). Who defines "mutilation"? Challenging imperialism in the discourse of female genital cutting. *Feminist Formations, 23*, 25–46. http://dx.doi.org/10.1353/ff.2011.0009

Sprague, J. (2016). *Feminist methodologies for critical researchers.* New York, NY: Rowman & Littlefield.

Strauss, A., & Corbin, J. (1990). *Basics of qualitative research: Grounded theory procedures and techniques.* London, England: Sage.

Summerfield, D. (1999). A critique of seven assumptions behind psychological trauma programmes in war-affected areas. *Social Science & Medicine, 48,* 1449–1462. http://dx.doi.org/10.1016/S0277-9536(98)00450-X

Tol, W. A., Komproe, I. H., Jordans, M. J., Susanty, D., & de Jong, J. T. (2011). Developing a function impairment measure for children affected by political violence: A mixed methods approach in Indonesia. *International Journal for Quality in Health Care, 23,* 375–383. http://dx.doi.org/10.1093/intqhc/mzr032

Torre, M. E., & Ayala, J. (2009). Envisioning participatory action research entremundos. *Feminism & Psychology, 19,* 387–393. http://dx.doi.org/10.1177/0959353509105630

Trotter, R., II, Needle, R., Goosby, E., Bates, C., & Singer, M. (2001). A methodological model for rapid assessment, response, and evaluation: The RARE program in public health. *Field Methods, 13,* 137–159. http://dx.doi.org/10.1177/1525822X0101300202

Tsuda, T., Tapias, M., & Escandell, X. (2014). Locating the global in transnational ethnography. *Journal of Contemporary Ethnography, 43,* 123–147. http://dx.doi.org/10.1177/0891241614527085

United Nations. (2015). *Background information on sexual violence used as a tool of war.* Retrieved from http://www.un.org/en/preventgenocide/rwanda/about/bgsexualviolence.shtml

Vinck, P., & Pham, P. N. (2013). Association of exposure to intimate-partner physical violence and potentially traumatic war-related events with mental health in Liberia. *Social Science & Medicine, 77,* 41–49. http://dx.doi.org/10.1016/j.socscimed.2012.10.026

Wade, L. (2012). Learning from "female genital mutilation": Lessons from 30 years of academic discourse. *Ethnicities, 12,* 26–49. http://dx.doi.org/10.1177/1468796811419603

Watters, E. (2010). *Crazy like us: The globalization of the American psyche.* New York, NY: Free Press.

Weiss, M. G., Saraceno, B., Saxena, S., & van Ommeren, M. (2003). Mental health in the aftermath of disasters: Consensus and controversy. *Journal of Nervous and Mental Disease, 191,* 611–615. http://dx.doi.org/10.1097/01.nmd.0000087188.96516.a3

Williams, R. R. (Producer & Director), & Goldman, J. (Producer). (2013). *God loves Uganda* [Motion picture]. United States: Full Credit Productions.

World Bank Group. (2016). *The Uganda poverty assessment report 2016.* Retrieved from http://pubdocs.worldbank.org/en/381951474255092375/pdf/Uganda-Poverty-Assessment-Report-2016.pdf

World Health Organization. (2016). *Violence against women.* Retrieved from http://www.who.int/mediacentre/factsheets/fs239/en/

Ziegler, M. (2008). Eugenic feminism: Mental hygiene, the women's movement, and the campaign for eugenic legal reform, 1900–1935. *Harvard Journal of Law and Gender, 31,* 211–235.

4

TRANSNATIONAL PSYCHOLOGICAL PERSPECTIVES ON ASSESSMENT AND INTERVENTION

LYNN H. COLLINS

This chapter introduces readers to the current status and potential applications of transnational psychology to practice, including assessment, diagnosis, intervention, and consultation. It describes some of the dilemmas that psychologists face as they work to engage in informed, competent assessment, therapeutic, and consultative practice with populations from or living outside of psychologists' home communities. Clients who are globally mobile and/or a member of the 95% of the world's population who are not yet represented in the psychological literature present unique dilemmas (Henrich, Heine, & Norenzayan, 2010; see also Chapter 5, this volume). This chapter describes how a transnational feminist psychology could inform psychologists in meeting these challenges.

Due to escalating globalization and consequent migration, psychologists are increasingly called on to diagnose and treat clients, assist with disaster response, consult on research, assist with community problems, develop

http://dx.doi.org/10.1037/0000148-005
Transnational Psychology of Women: Expanding International and Intersectional Approaches, L. H. Collins, S. Machizawa, and J. K. Rice (Editors)

policy, and work with a wider range of populations in settings both inside and outside their home countries (Altmaier & Hall, 2008; Morgan-Consoli, Inman, Bullock, & Nolan, 2018; see also Chapter 1, this volume). The number of people living outside their home country has risen from 173 million in 2000 to 258 million in 2017. It is estimated that there will be 405 million international migrants by 2050 (Hill, 2018). Consequently, clients and communities are much more diverse in terms of their cultural frameworks, family structures, home communities, governance structures, and migration experiences than they were in the past. Their access to education, health care, food, resources, and representation varies greatly, as does their experience with traumatic migration and military conflict (Arnett, 2008). In addition, individuals may be simultaneously influenced by an ever-growing number of other cultures, experiences, and conditions over time as they move around the globe, rendering the characteristics of cultural groups and communities less static and homogeneous.

It has never been safe to assume that an individual or community shares one's background, even when they appear to. Thus, transnational psychological approaches are needed when working within one's community of origin or communities in which one is a voluntary or involuntary, temporary or permanent resident (Machizawa & Enns, 2015). Transnational psychological approaches take into consideration a full range of factors affecting communities and hold promise for understanding and increasing human well-being in an informed, respectful, effective manner. Transnational psychological approaches and principles suggest ways to explore the many dynamic, changing characteristics of the individuals and communities with which one works. The World Health Organization (WHO; 2007) defined *health* as "a state of complete physical, mental and social well-being and not merely the absence of disease or infirmity" (para. 5). Unlike the Western biomedical paradigm, this definition does not treat the body, mind, and society as separate systems. Like WHO, transnational psychology takes a holistic approach to health and healing that recognizes the roles of relationships among "individuals, communities and the universe" in maintaining and restoring health and well-being (WHO, 2007, para. 5). Political contexts also play a role (Abeyasekera & Marecek, 2008). In this chapter, *healing* is defined broadly as any process that results in the alleviation of suffering and restoration of health and well-being. Beyond restoring indicators of physical health, healing is a subjective, sometimes spiritual experience that may involve restoring meaning, connections, and sense of personal wholeness. Additional meanings may be uncovered as psychologists attain a more comprehensive understanding of the world's peoples. Transnational psychologists seek to uncover beneficial Indigenous and other local healing and coping approaches and create a greater variety of effective strategies for supporting human well-being. This chapter was intentionally placed after the chapter on research because we have much to learn about the psychological practice and consultation involving 95% of the world not included in psychological research (Henrich et al., 2010).

Although the term *intervention* has come to have negative associations because interventions have sometimes been conducted in imperialistic, colonizing ways, it is used in this chapter because it is broader than *psychotherapy* and can include a variety of positive modifications regarding individuals, families, communities, and regional systems that are designed by or in collaboration with communities that take forms other than traditional "therapy." Although the term *community* is frequently used in this chapter, transnational psychology's focus is different from that of traditional community psychology. In transnational psychology, there is more emphasis on the impact of globalization, migration, and other influences on the community system. Transnational psychologists recognize that a local or regional community is inseparable from the larger global community because "transnational linkages influence every level of social existence" (Grewal & Kaplan, 1994, p. 13). Transnational feminists use alternative terms such as *Majority World* to refer to regions where roughly more than 80% of the world's population lives and *Minority World* to refer to regions with less than 15% of the world's population, formerly called the *West* or *developed world* (Silver, 2015).

DEFINING WOMEN'S WELL-BEING

Traditional Global Minority macrolevel indices of women's well-being include mother–infant mortality rates, education access and systems, life expectancy, employment, family structure, resources, and political participation (Mancini-Billson & Fluehr-Lobban, 2005). These can be useful in demonstrating societal institutions' influence on conditions that play roles in women's health and advancement. These numbers reflect in part institutions' (the state, nongovernmental agencies, and the United Nations) success in paving the way for better conditions through legal and policy reforms (Abeyasekera & Marecek, 2008). These measures, however, do not ensure women's well-being. In many cases, despite the development of laws that ostensibly improve women's rights, gender inequities, and women's status, these laws are often not enforced at the local level and do not change culture and tradition. In times of war and political unrest, even basic rights (access to safety, shelter, and food) is not a given (Abeyasekera & Marecek, 2008).

Definitions of well-being must consider factors beyond Global Minority mental health criteria (Abeyasekera & Marecek, 2008). The well-being of individuals is tied to material resources, protection of their human rights, and freedom from violence and oppression, which contribute to the health of their political systems (and their voice within them), communities, and relationships (Abeyasekera & Marecek, 2008; Prilleltensky, 2007; Prilleltensky & Fox, 2007). This is in addition to components of traditional feminist conceptual frameworks that include other contextual factors, identities, positions, developmental influences, personal histories, traumatic experiences, and vulnerabilities, in addition to coping mechanisms, competencies, and strengths (Machizawa & Enns, 2015). At the same time, Abeyasekera and Marecek (2008) emphasized that "the well-being of individuals is grounded in their social lives; personal well-being cannot be separated from the well-being of relationships, communities, and the body politic" (Abeyasekera & Marecek, 2008, p. 483) and should not be measured solely in the Global Minority capitalist terms of improvement in status and material wealth.

A universal scoring system for girls' and women's female well-being may not be possible (Abeyasekera & Marecek, 2008). It is unlikely that there are universal meanings of well-being that would be equally valid for college students in Kuwait, Sami communities in the Murmansk Oblast of Russia, and communities in rural Uganda. Populations vary widely in their sociopolitical, cultural, and historical contexts (Abeyasekera & Marecek, 2008). Their emphasis on individual versus family or community success, what constitutes success, and what mechanisms can effectively bring about change could also vary. Efforts to create objective, standardized assessment methods may result in the loss of important contextual information, rendering the results meaningless or misleading.

APPLICATION OF TRANSNATIONAL PSYCHOLOGY TO PRACTICE

Several models have been developed regarding the attitudes, approaches, and skills required for international work in psychology, including the cross-national cultural competence model (Heppner, Wang, Heppner, & Wang, 2012), dynamic-systemic process model (Gerstein, Hurley, & Hutchison, 2015), and framework for competencies for U.S. psychologists engaging internationally (Morgan-Consoli et al., 2018). Transnational approaches may share some characteristics with international and cross-cultural approaches but also consider factors resulting from the dynamically fluctuating natures of identities shaped by globalization and migration and have a lens less focused on nation-state borders or static, universalized notions of cultural groups.

The following is the list of considerations often associated with transnational feminist psychologies from Chapter 1 and how they apply to assessment, interventions, and consultation.

Transnational psychology encourages psychologists to

- *Address the contexts of globalization and diaspora groups.* International and cross-cultural approaches focus on comparisons between nation-states and cultures, respectively, treating each as if it were static, and thereby universalizing the characteristics of residents and members. The importance of understanding the role of culture has been emphasized and integrated into training programs through courses and field experiences (e.g., practica, internships) on multiculturalism, cross-cultural psychology, and specific issues and populations. Having knowledge about regions, nation-states, and cultures can broaden understanding but may lead to essentialist assumptions based on the idea that all residents of a nation-state or region or members of a cultural group share the same attributes. Coursework and training may also give the impression that the beliefs and practices of such cultures are fixed and unchanging (Atlani & Rousseau, 2000). Populations have become increasingly diverse and less static. Immigrants create and recreate their culture and identities as they transverse borders, cultures, and societies, struggling to keep connections with their countries of origin while continuing to view themselves as a community (Glick Schiller, Basch, & Szanton Blanc, 1995).

  In 2007, Sunil Bhatia proposed a transnational cultural psychology that could better address the experience of immigrants and diaspora groups. Bhatia found that the new context meant people could have multiple places they called "home," multiple languages, and even multiple selves. Thus, people are fundamentally changed by their contact with different cultures, technology, media, and relationships (Glick Schiller et al., 1995). In transnational psychologies identities formed by the migration process are seen as multifaceted, fused, hybridized, fluctuating, and sometimes fragmented (Bhatia, 2007; Rasmussen, 2015). Consistent with this, transnational psychology intake interviews include an ethnography that asks about a wider variety of influences resulting from a more mobile, fluid existence. Responding to the needs of diaspora groups involves attending to the unique nature of their experiences as they traversed borders. It requires accessing information about all the cultures, traditions, and beliefs to which they have been exposed. The same applies to any community with a changing membership and multiple cultural, local, regional, and global influences. In

Chapter 5, this volume, Espín and Dottolo describe transnational psychological perspectives on the experience of migration including that of diaspora groups.

■ *Question the utopic idea that "sisterhood is global."* Women of Color, Third World feminists, transnational feminists, and now transnational psychologists criticize the idea that sisterhood is global (as proposed by Morgan, 1984), pointing out that women experience different forms of oppression and hegemonic influences in a variety of contexts. Transnational psychological approaches are not focused solely on gender oppression but consider different forms of oppression affecting women and men in conjunction with their surrounding contexts, with a goal of liberating both (Kurtiş & Adams, 2015). Transnational feminist approaches draw attention to the unique kinds of challenges people face, which Grewal and Kaplan (1994) called scattered hegemonies that require specific actions to address.

Rejection of global sisterhood involves both recognition of intersections of identities with their scattered hegemonies and the paradoxes of White Western feminist "liberation." Intersections of identities are discussed in a later section. Transnational psychology is Kurtiş and Adams's (2013) attempt to resolve the discrepancy between feminist ideas about liberation and cultural psychology perspectives that view some goals of Western feminism as contrary to the interests of women's—and all people's—well-being. For instance, Western White feminists partly endorse the oppressive androcentric context by recommending assertiveness, leadership, and other forms of training that develop skills typically associated with Global Minority men. Western White feminist psychologists might recommend interventions that promote expansion-oriented forms of relationality ("those emphasizing mutual exploration, authentic self-expression, and self-expansive merging in emotion-focused intimacy with a partner of one's choosing"; Kurtiş & Adams, 2013, p. 259) to encourage self-expression and maximization of satisfying connections (e.g., assertiveness, leadership training). However, from a cultural psychology perspective, maintenance-oriented relationships (those that focus more on relationships and responsibility to kin) are also viable paths to well-being.

Following cultural psychology's lead, transnational psychology also "denaturalizes" androcentric relationality by pointing out that expansion-oriented forms of relationality are not "natural" but instead an adaptation to environments characterized by neoliberal individualism and androcentric constructions of relationship—an adaptation that carries with it risks, including the lack of an enduring relationally based safety net (Kurtiş & Adams, 2013). In transnational and cultural psychology, the cultural context is examined and the many ways of behaving that can lead to well-being beyond Western androcentric norms are identified. Transnational psychologists point out that in many contexts, current Western, White feminist approaches only work for the privileged; the less fortunate cannot afford to disregard family tradition and responsibilities because women especially do not typically have sufficient resources to serve as an independent safety net. Such practices serve to reproduce racial, ethnic, and class privilege. Kurtiş and Adams (2013) encouraged psychologists to create new contexts, including "more humane forms of relationality that can better serve the interests of gender equality and global social justice without reinforcing neocolonial tropes and practices" (Kurtiş & Adams, 2013, p. 266).

- *Respect and elevate new and silenced voices.* In the tradition of Mohanty, transnational psychology actively elevates new and silenced voices to help reframe feminist thought, politics, and practice (Mohanty, 2003). Transnational psychologists implore people of privilege to use and share their access to power and resources to elevate others' voices (Alexander, 2006) so that previously silenced people can express their perspectives and reveal the limitations of Global Minority thought. The aim of transnational psychology is to reveal information about Global Majority communities to help displace Western ideas and influence with the goal of developing a more pluralistic perspective. Ideally, disempowered communities should speak for themselves. Increasing their representation in decision-making forums so that they can share their perspectives may help to further liberate people in Majority World settings (Kurtiş & Adams, 2015).

Another way to make silenced voices heard is through rapid or brief ethnography. Feminist ethnography can help uncover the context, characteristics, and situations of the populations seeking treatment, including local, Indigenous, and as yet unknown healing approaches. Craven and Davis (2013) defined *ethnography* as a process that documents "lived experience as it is impacted by gender, race, class, sexuality, and other aspects of participants' lives" (p. 14). Ethnography involves systematically studying peoples' agency and knowledge, as well as cultural, historical, social, political, familial, and other experiences from the perspective of the subjects being studied to deepen our understanding. Additional methods include oral histories and collaborative data analysis (Craven & Davis, 2013). In ethnography, the outsider may become a participant observer and spend extended periods with the group of interest to understand their perspectives (Manning, 2016).

In feminist ethnography, attention is paid to power differentials, an approach that informs the use of methods, and the process of feminist interpretations (Craven & Davis, 2013). Ethnography can help psychologists better expose, understand, and remedy unhealthy effects of globalization and neoliberalism. It has the potential to help address the influences of positionality and power when representing marginalized others, enabling their voices to be represented more accurately (Manning, 2016). It may help reveal opportunities for interventions to increase well-being. Feminist ethnography holds promise for the sharing of multiple perspectives, increasing the frequency of critical dialogue and reframing issues related to domestic violence, racism, reproductive rights, and therapeutic intervention (Craven & Davis, 2013).

- *Consider positionality extremely important.* Morgan-Consoli et al. (2018) emphasized the need to attend to the dual lens of one's culture and the host culture in international psychology work. Doing so requires specific knowledge and self-reflection (Morgan-Consoli et al., 2018). One's position is not static but changes depending on one's context. Consistent with this, *reflexivity*, critical consciousness regarding the impact of one's relational positions on epistemological location, is essential to transnational practice. Transnational feminist psychology underlines that there is no value-free research or therapy, and thus it is critical to examine how one's social and spatial positions impact the knowledge production and therapeutic process and to be aware of others' standpoints. Transnational psychologists should critically examine their value systems, beliefs, culture, and situations. They should develop self-awareness about their multiple social identities and how they have been shaped by their gender, geopolitical, economic, and current and historical contexts. They should reflect on how those identities and contexts have influenced their access to economic, political, gender-based, social, and other sources of power and privilege. If they understand the nature of privilege and its impact on culture and practices, they should be able to decenter its influence and instead attend to the experiences of those with nondominant identities (Mohanty, Russo, & Torres, 1991). Psychologists should also consider how the less privileged see those who are more privileged (including psychologists) and how they see themselves. Psychologists can begin this process through reading, coursework, participation in professional organizations, and participation in international travel, study, and conferences before engaging in fieldwork. Cultural immersion experiences are also helpful in decentering cultural perspectives and practices. Through these activities, psychologists will have the opportunity to develop personal and professional relationships, including mentoring and collaborative partnerships (Machizawa & Enns, 2015).

Hays's (2016) ADDRESSING framework provides an outline for the process of cultural self-assessment. ADDRESSING stands for identities associated with age, development, disability, religion (or spirituality), race or ethnicity, social status, sexual orientation, Indigenous heritage, nationality (colonization, migration), and gender. The assessment examines influences, identities, biases, privilege, strengths, and weaknesses (Hays, 2016). The process involves introspection, self-questioning, reading, research, and learning directly from diverse others. It is impossible to begin to understand all the dynamics involved, however, without full knowledge of clients' identities, value systems, beliefs, culture, and situations.

Although the ADDRESSING framework (Hays, 2016) is grounded in Western approaches, it is comprehensive and cues users to query important influences. One limitation is that the focus of the process is the self, which is not emphasized or even acknowledged by some groups. The system also presumes that additional background information about a person's community is available through the literature, which it may not be. Finally, the system does not address dynamics created by globalization, migration, and the experiences of diaspora groups.

Thus, although the ADDRESSING system may fill in the person-specific information and gaps in psychological knowledge through conversations with clients, psychologists need more information about the range of identities, value systems, beliefs, culture, therapeutic approaches, and situations in the 95% of the world excluded from study to effectively apply the system (Henrich et al., 2010). Otherwise, we may just be indoctrinating our clients and ourselves with dominant Western, Minority World psychological paradigms and beliefs. In the meantime, as we seek more information about communities around the world, Mootz and Stabb's table of "Research Areas and Transnational Feminist Strategies and Considerations" (see Chapter 3, this volume) suggests useful questions to ask when engaging in reflexivity, research, and clinical practice.

In summary, it is important to attend to positionality, a notion that how one understands the world is influenced by one's life experiences, personal values, views, and social and spatial positions. It is important to understand one's position and social location, and how access to power informs one's perspective and approach to working with others.

- *Examine the impact of human rights policies and legislation on communities.* Morgan-Consoli et al.'s (2018) list includes the need for awareness of other aspects of practice, such as histories of helping traditions, laws, human rights issues, national public policy, and mental health ethics codes or guidelines. Although there may be human rights policies and legislation that protect women within nation-states, human rights policies and legislation are often seen as unduly influenced by Minority World perspectives and priorities. Communities may have little influence on how they are shaped. In addition, the benefits of human rights policies and legislation may be experienced only by privileged groups and may not be enforced at the community level because they conflict with local norms and culture (Abeyasekera & Marecek, 2008). The result is that women are affected differently depending on the communities in which they participate. Considerable work still has to be done to ensure communities in both Minority and Majority World settings have a voice in shaping laws and that local norms and culture actively integrate and respect laws related to human rights. If asked to partner with a community to help advocate for better protections, ethnographies and qualitative assessments of women's realities may provide insights. Collaborating with communities to help them obtain real protections is a systemic way to potentially increase well-being.
- *Critique the dominance and exploitation of culturally different others.* Some Western and Global Minority psychologists and other providers view culture as an obstacle to the introduction of what they may view as new, modern, and scientific treatment approaches, superior to traditional, local remedies. Their

purported goal of learning more about a community may mask their real intention of understanding the community's beliefs just enough so that providers can effectively persuade community leaders and members to change beliefs to introduce Western interventions. Global Minority providers may also depict Global Majority women as helpless victims and pathologize them, then use their "rescue" to cover for capitalistic and other exploitive goals (Cronin-Furman, Gowrinathan, & Zakaria, 2017; Mohanty, 1991).

Transnational feminist psychologists work to prevent psychologists from essentializing and marginalizing views of the "other" associated with oppressive ideological systems. They critique the focus on sensational depictions of others' "barbaric" (e.g., honor killings, female genital mutilation, polygamy) or less sensationally different (sati, dowry, arranged marriage, self-silencing) behavior that pathologize communities and distract psychologists from examining more common realities of everyday life, including more prevalent subtle forms of gender and other oppressions (Kurtiş & Adams, 2013). They also critique how WEIRD (Western, educated, industrialized, rich, democratic) psychologists "other" women and pathologize their experiences by comparing them with androcentric norms (Kurtiş & Adams, 2013). Transnational psychologists encourage the rethinking of assumptions based on a closer examination of the day-to-day lives of people in a community, recognizing when practices are oppressive but also when practices assumed to be oppressive may be beneficial (Kurtiş & Adams, 2013). Hopefully, these efforts will help prevent misunderstandings and misguided recommendations.

Transnational feminist power analyses can also be helpful. They examine the power differentials in one's context and how associated forms of privilege and oppression influence thinking, feelings, and choices. They also identify forms of power that provide a sense of optimism and possibility and provide opportunities for action and empowerment (Enns, 2004) and opportunities to change pieces of existing systems to improve conditions for the community.

- *Believe that knowledge is socially constructed and not owned by any one group.* A community may not have "mental health professionals" per se or Western "technical expertise" or any formal laws or ethics codes or guidelines governing practice, but they may nonetheless use therapeutic techniques. It is important to recognize that Western or Minority World psychological practice may not be relevant or useful to communities outside the Western, White, middle-class community. Ethnography and other qualitative methods discussed previously can be used by psychologists to identify those who assist or counsel others in times of trouble and reveal the local, Indigenous, or hybridized treatment modalities of marginalized people in the interest of plurality of knowledge. The concept of plurality holds that many different types and forms of knowledge exist and should be taken into consideration. For example, interviewing multiple members of a wide variety of Global Majority communities may help to achieve a more pluralistic, and therefore more accurate, understanding of the communities' usual ways of dealing with difficult situations or psychological issues that disrupt well-being.

Knowledge of traditions and values may get lost and forgotten due to the intrusions of hegemonic influences of colonizers and social and historical changes, even if remnants of them can be found in contemporary life. Ethnography has the potential to encourage communities to serve as their own cultural researchers by engaging in community-based participatory research and case consultation regarding issues of interest to them. Ethnographic approaches can help to develop a better understanding of historical trauma and the development of culturally congruent therapies and intervention strategies (King, 2009).

Understanding the history of a community's traditions and how they are similar or dissimilar to contemporary practices can provide a perspective that is useful in understanding client's and communities' current struggles (Peters, Straits, & Gauthier, 2015). *Retraditionalization* is a form of decolonization in which cultural traditions are revisited and their values, practices, and principles applied to develop culturally informed interventions. Traditional practices can also be mixed with contemporary approaches to develop hybridized approaches to healing (BigFoot & Schmidt, 2010; Peters et al., 2015). Although it is important to use approaches that have been proven effective for a particular population (e.g., evidence-based treatments), Majority World communities are seldom included in treatment research. Even if they are included, the treatment approaches without community participation are likely to be limited and less effective than they might otherwise be or may even be experienced by community members as yet another form of colonization, adding to their existing history of traumatic colonization and associated hegemonies and oppression. To avoid doing harm, it is thus both necessary and useful to collect information about community healing traditions as well as those of the larger cultural group. Individual clients or communities can be asked what has been helpful in the past as well as what friends, family, and the community would usually recommend in a situation. This may elicit some traditional and unique approaches to healing that are used by the community because they are effective (Atlani & Rousseau, 2000; BigFoot & Schmidt, 2010; Griner & Smith, 2006; Peters et al., 2015; Wessells, 2009).

Psychologists also have to understand the relevant local dominant modes of psychological interventions and treatments and local regulatory requirements of practitioners (e.g., specific reporting requirements in the country, such as for domestic violence, child abuse, or sexual abuse) and supervisors. Morgan-Consoli et al. (2018) recommended researching the local norms and expectations about dual relationships, informed consent, and confidentiality as well as mental health professional licensing and supervisory requirements, but there may not be formal guidelines or procedures in many locales. They included a useful list of resources for international work and recommended determining whether any forms of Western therapy are inconsistent with the culture. It is also important to learn how the community currently deals with individual, family, and group tragedy and adversity to incorporate those approaches into psychologists' repertoires and/or the information used to develop culturally adapted techniques. Community-based programs designed to support and promote research, service, social change, and advocacy are being created and are open to developing collaborations with allies to support self-determination and healing in Native peoples of North America (Peters et al., 2015). Although most healing takes place in the context of interactions with community members, Atlani and Rousseau (2000) suggested that speaking to a therapist outside one's community may be helpful to clients in some cases, but more research has to be done to confirm the effects of such interventions.

- *Examine microlevel through macrolevel contexts and unique local through global influences on human well-being.* Until recently, most international research on the psychology of women focused on broad-brush nation-state comparisons rather than studying particular communities whose membership was not defined by nation-state boundaries. In contrast, most transnational psychologists take a microlevel through macrolevel focus on the unique local, regional, and global influences on individual communities and tend to deemphasize nation-state and cultural boundaries, which assume static homogeneous populations. The exception is that transnational psychology recognizes the importance of lands to certain diasporic groups' identity, culture, and heritage.

Whether working therapeutically with an individual client or partnering with a larger group within the community, it is important to understand the particularities of the specific local community in addition to understanding the broader cultural and regional history and context. Although macrolevel knowledge regarding state, regional, and global historical, economic, political, and other forces can be a useful foundation on which to build an understanding of a client or community's context, transnational approaches value and support understanding particularities of communities. This helps avoid generalizing (also known as *universalizing*) on the basis of broad categories such as nation-state or even major cultural or religious categories. Transnational psychologists often use ethnography and qualitative assessment approaches to better understand microlevel through macrolevel dynamics and the nuances of their influences on individuals and communities. For instance, in the case of the Native peoples of North America, there are not only many different tribes, each with their own history and traditions, but also many branches of those tribes, existing in unique circumstances.

Knowing a client's specific circumstances is critical to understanding their situation and perspective (Peters et al., 2015). Some of the problems to be managed or remediated, however, might be related to access to resources, community distress, or historical geopolitical dynamics, which are not the typical purview of clinical psychologists. Intervening at this intermediate systemic level might potentially improve the lives of more people in the community.

- *Extend the notion of intersectionality. Transnational intersectionality* includes a wider range of variables and extends the notion of intersectionality by adding consideration of historical, sociopolitical, economic, human rights, and other local and global influences to the analysis of how oppressive institutions are interconnected and their effects on people's lives (Grabe & Else-Quest, 2012). Morgan-Consoli et al. (2018) provided a list of needs and cultural contexts that should be considered in working with populations outside one's home population from a U.S. perspective. The list includes cultural contexts (e.g., individual, cultural, community), social environments (e.g., societal–structural), and historical–political contexts (e.g., colonization and political policies). In Chapter 3, Mootz and Stabb also include a table of "Research Areas and Transnational Feminist Strategies and Considerations" that comprises useful questions to ask when engaging in reflexivity, research, and clinical practice. Transnational approaches add awareness of regional and global forces on the community and migration history. They recommend considering cultural norms, local attitudes, and sites of resilience and agency within the local community, with the expectation that there will be both group and individual differences. They recommend that psychologists should not only gain knowledge of local cultural beliefs about relevant constructs (e.g., family, autonomy, gender, corporal punishment, mental health, psychopathology) but also understand the cultural norms related to gendered, familial, sexual identity, and other interpersonal interactions.

Peters et al. (2015) pointed out that mainstream assessment of ethnocultural backgrounds of clients is often limited to a single checked box, which does not begin to represent the historical contexts, culture, values, priorities, level of acculturation, and other unique characteristics of a person's ethnic heritage, let alone any information about their family unit or local community. Engaging in ethnography or another qualitative research approach as part of the assessment and conceptualization phase can help unearth invaluable information about how a context results in particular problems.

- *Aim to develop egalitarian ways to collaborate and intervene in the context of asymmetrical power relations.* The dearth of information available regarding therapeutic interventions with Majority World individuals highlights the need for more mutually beneficial partnerships in which an understanding of interventions can be developed and shared. Internationally focused clinical competencies require "openness and a commitment to collaboration with local psychologists and other mental health workers" (Morgan-Consoli et al., 2018, p. 181). Ethical clinical practice and supervision require working within the community's cultural context, applying psychological expertise with reflexivity and awareness of the boundaries of one's competence within the community context and avoiding exploitation (Morgan-Consoli et al., 2018).

Psychologists should partner with communities to better understand their needs and context, increase awareness of Indigenous approaches to healing, and support and explore whether additional approaches would be helpful. To advance the interests of a community, it is important that community members partner with those with resources to implement interventions but carefully negotiate consequent asymmetrical power relations that might interfere with the process. The equitable management of collaboration for the common purpose of increasing a community's well-being in the context of asymmetrical power relations is essential.

Partnerships can help psychologists learn the nuances of a region's history, culture, and contexts, including aspects of particular significance to the individuals or community with whom a psychologist is working (Peters et al., 2015). Awareness of community history, needs, contexts, and norms for demonstrating mutual respect is essential for effective collaboration. Cultural practice regarding the prescription and use of medications should be considered (Hays, 2016). Morgan-Consoli et al. (2018) recommended meeting with local psychologists, other health workers, and local regulating agencies to partner with them regarding care. It is also useful to explore the nature of other community roles to better understand which ones (e.g., elders, community leaders, spiritual leaders) are involved in supporting the health and well-being of the community and in what ways they are involved. Psychologists can partner and collaborate with healers and mentors to develop and build resources for increasing the well-being of the community that may include culturally congruent ceremonies and religious and spiritual approaches. Psychologists should respectfully explore traditional approaches and community resources offered by others that would be more consistent with their clients' or community partners' beliefs and possibly be more effective (Peters et al., 2015). This may be accomplished by connecting the client with a resource in the community (e.g., community representative, mentor, healer, leader).

Morgan-Consoli et al. (2018) advised psychologists not to engage in direct service unless they are integrated into the local context and speak the local language(s). They said that it is more appropriate to consult about clinical intervention than provide direct service. If a psychologist is already integrated into a local context and is fluent in the local language(s), competent practice still requires an understanding of how the community provides services with similar goals and purposes, including Indigenous approaches, and the psychologist has to be familiar with local diagnostic practices. When engaging in consultations involving program evaluation, it is also essential to be knowledgeable about the community, including the cultures and religions represented, day-to-day lives, values, beliefs, history, traditions, social structure, history, policies, and regional and global influences.

It is not advisable for psychologists who are not members of the community to assume that clients feel connected with their ethnic and cultural heritage and want them to use traditional healing approaches (Peters et al., 2015). Instead, psychologists may connect the clients to cultural healers, mentors, and other supports within the community. This demonstrates respect for the community's cultural healers, concern for the community, and a commitment to a positive collaborative relationship. Even if the client is not consciously familiar with these traditional approaches, they may nonetheless find them comfortable and familiar because they were developed in the context of cultural history, cultural memories, traditions, and behaviors over generations (Peters et al., 2015).

Again, ethnography may help reveal previously unnoticed dynamics that could be changed to increase the well-being of communities. Stacey (1988) expressed concern that although feminist ethnography might seem to be a respectful, egalitarian approach to assessment, this is merely a facade that could mask more profound forms of exploitation. Abu-Lughod (1990), however, showed how feminist ethnographers could use the approach to reveal how privileged women were complicit with the oppression of marginalized women when they promoted the notion of global sisterhood, based on the assumption of women's universal, shared experience.

- *Develop and use appropriate assessment and research methods.* Global Minority assessment practices may not only be biased and therefore lead to misdiagnosis, pathologizing, and inadequate conceptualizations but may also even be completely irrelevant because they are based on research done on a small fraction of the global population (Arnett, 2008). They may ignore contributing environmental factors and therefore be counterproductive or of no use in many Global Majority communities.

Western approaches to understanding the nature of a person, the issues with which they are struggling, and the effectiveness of interventions usually involves some form of standardized assessment. Assessing individuals from different cultures and who speak different languages with different versions of the same scale has been an ongoing struggle (Sireci, 2004) and a potential source of error (Moscoso & Spielberger, 2011). Although strongly influenced by Western practices, the International Test Commission Guidelines (2016) are useful for cross-cultural adaptation of achievement and aptitude tests and, to a degree, personality and emotional measures. Personality and emotional measures are more subjective and less clearly operationalized. Measures of personality and emotion are likely to show cultural and subcultural differences (Anastasi, 1988; Moscoso & Spielberger, 2011). Even when assessing achievement and aptitudes, it is difficult to disentangle group effects from language and cultural effects (Sireci, 2004). Some clinicians and researchers have bilingual individuals translate and back translate achievement and aptitude scales for use in new settings, which can be useful, but people who are bilingual may not be equally proficient in both languages, may have different backgrounds, and may differ from those who speak just one language on a number of dimensions.

Studies also have found that people from non-Western, collectivist cultures may be uncomfortable with items that query individual feelings and behaviors because they typically put more weight on situational factors (Moscoso & Spielberger, 2011) or cannot relate to the choice offered. Reactions to test items can only be understood in the context of the characteristics and situation of the group being assessed (Moscoso, 1997; Moscoso & Spielberger, 2011). Most challenging of all, this does not address serious problems with construct and test validity stemming from the nonequivalence of constructs related to emotion and personality in different cultures (Moscoso & Spielberger, 2011; Sireci, 2004). Anastasi (1988) recommended defining personality in terms of fundamental traits and states such as anxiety, depression, and anger, which appear to exist across cultures and are related to personality (Moscoso & Spielberger, 1999, 2011; Spielberger, 2006). Moscoso and

Spielberger (2011) also recommended paying careful attention to idioms because the same words can have different connotations for different regions, cultures, subcultures, and populations. Subpopulations can have complex social and cultural characteristics that are more different than similar, which means it is essential that meanings of words, phrases, and idioms are verified to be the same. It is important to focus on the meaning rather than the literal translation of words and idioms (Moscoso & Spielberger, 2011). Moscoso and Spielberger (2011) recommended creating a new, more equivalent set of items, even if this takes several rounds of translation and back translation. They also recommended that careful attention be paid to the difference between emotional states that vary in intensity and more stable personality traits. The language used to express emotion reflects the group's characteristic way of responding emotionally (Moscoso & Spielberger, 2011; Wierzbicka, 1994).

Like postmodern and postcolonial feminism, transnational feminist psychological researchers, practitioners, and scholars frequently use narrative and qualitative research methods in their work. Hays (2016) recommended collecting information about sociocultural historical events that may have influenced clients' development, using multiple sources of information, looking for culturally related strengths, and eliciting clients' conceptualizations, thoughts, and experiences related to health care and self-care. Although this approach improves on others, it assumes an individualistic focus and that the concept of "self" is relevant. Some view WEIRD models of self as an androcentric conception that valorizes separateness and personal agency characteristic of men's experiences and pathologizes the more relational nature of women's experiences (Kurtiş & Adams, 2013). It also makes universalist assumptions about culture. In many cases, a more systemic or community focus may be more helpful, and information about how they are impacted by local through global influences is necessary. In short, we need more detailed and inclusive assessment systems if we are to decenter Western conventions in psychological practice. The ADDRESSING approach already includes more variables than more contemporary assessment systems and can be expanded as more influences are known.

Hays (2016) recommended care when using standardized tests in light of potential biases from the test, procedures, environment, and tester. She recommended thinking more ideographically about a client's performance, comparing the performance of the client across time rather comparing with others, and hiring a cultural consultant for a better understanding of language differences and cultural influences. Clients who have experience with multiple cultural influences present a special challenge.

Diagnostic manuals such as the *Diagnostic and Statistical Manual of Mental Disorders* (fifth edition; *DSM–5*) published by the American Psychiatric Association (2013) and the *International Classification of Diseases* published by the WHO (2018) have been found to be gender and culturally biased even in Minority World contexts and have little relevance to how clinicians view problems in practice (Cosgrove & Krimsky, 2012).

The *DSM* especially emphasizes biological rather than sociocultural context and so encourages the use of biological treatments (e.g., medications). There is limited evidence of their validity and reliability (Cosgrove & Krimsky, 2012). If their utility is limited within Global Minority populations, their limitations may be even more significant for use within Majority World communities (Atlani & Rousseau, 2000; Hays, 2016). If using the *DSM–5*, Hays (2016) recommended complementing the diagnosis by thinking more systemically, considering relational disorders, and exploring cultural and environmental influences. Factors to consider in deciding on a diagnosis include vulnerability to specific disorders due to past experiences, current and past stressors, and strengths and supports. The resulting diagnosis should be explained in everyday language (Hays, 2016). Hays recommended including a cultural profile using the ADDRESSING framework. This becomes more challenging as the number of cultural and life experiences become more numerous.

The question remains whether Western psychological assessment, diagnosis, and research techniques will be relevant as migration escalates. As identities become more fluid and life experiences become more variable, the nature of instruments and procedures will have to change because there may not be a way to validate and standardize the instruments.

CASE EXAMPLES

The cases that follow illustrate transnational feminist approaches to intervention. Most use qualitative research methods to understand the nature of the context in which the issue (e.g., partner control, increased suicide rate) exists before considering which forms of intervention would be preferable to reduce partner control or suicide rates. The choice of point-of-intervention has to be informed by an understanding of family, community, and local, regional, and other systems that affect the issue being addressed, which may have an individual or group impact. Goals and treatment plans should be developed collaboratively (Hays, 2016). For examples of how interventions can go wrong, see Wessells (2009) and Christopher, Wendt, Marecek, and Goodman (2014).

Case 1. Intervening at the Community Level: Grabe (2012)

Grabe (2012) conducted a study related to the relationship between empowerment and domestic violence. She began by developing relationships with members of a community-based women's organization in Nicaragua. Through these women and other sources, Grabe developed an understanding of the sociopolitical context of the population. She practiced strong reflexivity by developing an acute awareness of the effect of her position, perspectives, and Western influences on her work. She used a critical communicative methodology, consisting of egalitarian dialogues between the researcher and participants of different organizations, and a mix of quantitative and qualitative research methods in her work with the participants. Her research team developed questionnaires, translated them into Spanish, then asked a local Nicaraguan to back-translate them. Team members also converted existing scales measuring gender ideology, relationship power, and partner control to a dichotomous format. They adapted questions from those created by organizations (e.g., International Center for Research on Women, WHO) and from established Western scales (e.g., the Attitude toward Women Scale; Spence, Helmreich, & Stapp, 1973; Sexual Relationship Power Scale; Pulerwitz, Gortmaker, & DeJong, 2000). In assessing outcomes from Grabe's project, Kurtiş, Adams, and Estrada-Villalta (2016) pointed out that in her study, the strongest positive outcomes on women's empowerment were associated with a cooperative, more community-oriented form of ownership (as consistent with local understandings) and included greater access to resources and a reduced level of domestic partner control. Although Grabe's primary focus was research rather than therapy, her study provides a model for how psychologists working in new communities can use their research skills to uncover information and develop a better understanding of the community context.

Case 2. Transnational Assessment and Conceptualization: Marecek and Senadheera (2012)

In another example, Marecek and Senadheera (2012) partnered with a community to investigate the high suicide rate in Sri Lanka. In preparation for the study, they first researched the history and context within which the increase in suicides occurred, using sources that included government and hospital records and cultural beliefs and attitudes about suicide. They also studied the social ecology of suicidal behavior, including its context in relationships, communication, local meanings, practices, and explanatory systems. They compared suicide rates across age, gender, religious communities, occupations, and urban and rural areas and examined the impact of wars and the globalized economy on the local community. After this preparation, using a qualitative approach, they used lengthy semistructured interviews with individuals hospitalized for self-harm and a family member. All participants were interviewed at least once, during hospitalization and, for some patients, a month after they left the hospital. The goal was to obtain a detailed narrative account of the circumstances, events, and consequences on which to base their theories regarding the increase in suicides. Their results indicated that the suicides were not the result of clinical depression or the increased availability of toxic pesticides. Instead, the suicide attempts were meant to communicate distress related to conflict between individuals engaging in self-harm and their parents regarding differences over standards of behavior stemming from changes brought on by globalization. Therefore, potential solutions involved improving communication between children and elders rather than limiting access to pesticides or implementing individual treatment for major depressive disorder, as had been suggested by other psychologists.

Case 3. Disaster Response Situations

Headlines draw attention to crises affecting Majority World communities and the need for services and resources. Although the intent of raising awareness of need is to garner support, get people involved, and encourage the donations of resources, often the result is to reinforce the perception of Majority World populations as helpless victims in need of rescue (Cronin-Furman, Gowrinathan, & Zakaria, 2017; Mohanty et al., 1991). In cases of disaster, it is a challenge to know how to intervene in a manner that is not only culturally sensitive but also community sensitive and effective. "Rescuers" and their interventions may do more harm than good (Christopher et al., 2014; Morgan-Consoli et al., 2018; Wessells, 2009). The affected community may be retraumatized by the influx of outsiders ("second tsunami" effect; Wessells, 2009, p. 849) with limited knowledge regarding the community's culture, practices, resources, and priorities, let alone the unique interpersonal and political dynamics that exist within the affected communities. In addition, these outsiders use the limited resources available, exhausting reserves and donations and interfering with efforts to provide them to local residents (Christopher et al., 2014; Wessells, 2009). Finally, the help they provide may be ineffective at best and damaging at worst because it is based on Global Minority priorities or how things work in the helpers' communities, regions, and countries. When it comes to helping communities deal with the psychological aspects of loss, intimate violence, suicide, substance use, and other trauma, Western or Minority World approaches may not only fail to help but may also even cause further harm (Christopher et al., 2014; Wessells, 2009).

Having a network of preexisting relationships with communities and comprehensive information about interventions could be extremely helpful in such emergencies. In emergency and disaster situations, there is not enough time to build relationships and gather enough information to form a comprehensive understanding of a community, its practices, what kinds of help may be needed in various emergencies, and how best to provide it. A preexisting understanding of communities' human psychology, beliefs, and behavior as Henrich et al. (2010) recommended, along with a network of community connections spanning the globe, could form the foundation of improved crisis responses. Interventions might be focused on limiting the intrusion of outsiders, providing, rather than individual psychotherapy, necessities and labor or other assistance that frees the community members to manage the more sensitive, interpersonal kinds of support themselves. All would depend on what the community itself has indicated it needs.

VISION FOR THE FUTURE OF TRANSNATIONAL FEMINIST APPROACHES TO INTERVENTION

To choose the best interventions for transnational populations, it is important to be familiar with a wide range of intervention strategies, which may include intervening at the individual, community, or regional level using local and Indigenous approaches, culturally adapted versions of mainstream Minority World psychotherapies, systems approaches, or interventions that require broader institutional or government-based changes. Pluralism will be valuable in the development of new approaches to enhance well-being. *Pluralism* is the consideration of many different perspectives, sources of information, assessment, and healing methods for dealing with issues to better approximate truth. A successful approach will require the sharing of information about how well-being is attained and maintained in communities around the world. Mutually beneficial networking and support with distant communities will help uncover new ways to detect and approach individual and community problems. Identifying the most effective ways to help people meet their needs and finding the best ways to collaborate with them to support their well-being requires compassion, empathy, an open mind, and creativity—that is, the flexibility to frame the complex aspects of identity related to histories of colonization, culture, intercultural adaptation, and hybridized identities. It requires curiosity to investigate complex contributing factors and creativity to put together the pieces with an approach that respectfully supports well-being.

Some traditional cultural healing techniques and Global Minority evidence-based treatments may already share characteristics. For instance, when I was giving a workshop on posttraumatic stress disorder for a group of Kuwaiti counselors, I shared Global Minority research on etiology and treatment. The group of counselors responded that although they could not use secular techniques, they used prayer and rituals in a similar manner to relaxation training, imagery, and cognitive therapy techniques. The counselors decided that they might try to encourage prayer and rituals in an intentional, targeted manner related to the trauma experiences to help those seeking help to cope. There is some evidence from Global Minority research that culturally adapted treatments for racial and ethnic groups may be more effective than conventional evidence-based treatments (Griner & Smith, 2006; Peters et al., 2015). As with any creative new psychological approach, it is helpful if the approach is consistent with the form and theory of other approaches that have been proven effective.

Hays (2016) pointed out that one of the reasons people may avoid talking about race, ethnicity, and culture is that diversity entails multiple perspectives, and multiple perspectives can lead to disagreements, even over the use of terms. As psychologists, we cannot avoid these topics. To work with clients with complex identities as therapists, researchers, and consultants, we have to effectively navigate difference and conflict without reinforcing dominant power structures (Hays, 2016), starting with our roles as experts and complicated by our other statuses. We have to show respect for and support and empower each other as well as our clients. The challenge is to do so in a manner that is informed by knowledge of our colleagues' and clients' histories, identities, and resulting perspectives. As Hays (2016) said, the main thing is that "two people who have extremely different upbringings, identities, and views of the world can come together, interact, learn from each other, and even appreciate one another" (p. 300). We are currently missing 95% of the information we need to accomplish this effectively.

Henrich et al.'s (2010) vision calls for a more representative, inclusive scientific understanding of the foundations of human psychology and behavior. They said, "Research programs need to increasingly emphasize large-scale, highly interdisciplinary, fully international research networks" (p. 122). This approach risks universalizing at the nation-state level. The results might be overgeneralized to small, unique communities and miss phenomena, including those associated with increasingly mobile populations. Consistent with their vision, however, understanding smaller groups for the purpose of collaboration in good times and crises will require maintaining "long-term, ongoing, research projects among diverse populations that collect data over the full life cycle using an integrated set of methodological tools, including wide-ranging experimental techniques, quantitative and qualitative ethnography, surveys, brain imaging, and biomarkers" (Henrich et al., 2010, p. 122). Although they avoided addressing the issue of psychopathology, saying it contained both individual and universalized aspects and was by definition not representative of the general population, without more information about research and appropriate assessment of difficult situations and psychological issues, it will be impossible to design effective collaborative approaches to prevention, healing, and empowerment.

It is important to remember that the considerations and principles described in this chapter can be useful and important whether one is working with someone whose identities, context, and history appear to be similar to one's own as well as those whose identities, contexts, and histories are visibly different. A careful, comprehensive consideration of clients' social, economic, political, health, education, and other realities allow those seeking to understand them to develop a better foundation for supporting their approach. Awareness of the plethora of contributing factors will allow psychologists to help clients identify and address and perhaps alter key factors of the clients' environments to encourage them and others affected by those factors to thrive. Some changes may be limited to the individual's behavior and mental processes, others at the family level, and still others at the community and even regional level, depending on the nature of the issue. Some may involve multiple levels. Furthermore, comprehensive, systemic case conceptualizations that permit considerations of factors in micro through macro contexts can support the overall health of the entire community.

POINTILLISTIC PLURALISM

Pointillism is an artistic practice that applies small dots of color to create an image best seen from a distance. A transnational feminist perspective in psychological practice is a bit like this: We strive to understand and truly see and appreciate human behavior in transnational contexts. In a crisis in today's world, ideally, people from different communities come to each other's assistance, whether it be to improve the well-being of individuals, communities, or larger populations. It could be in the context of managing day-to-day challenges or the aftermath of a natural disaster. To enable communities to be effective in providing assistance, more attention has to be paid to understanding communities, especially those that are distressed or at risk in some way (e.g., vulnerable to natural disasters, violence), in advance of crises. This commitment to research and planning would allow time to meet with the communities to determine what courses of action would be most appropriate and effective in their particular context should a crisis (e.g., earthquake, tsunami, mudslide) occur.

Even in noncrisis situations, it is important to gather knowledge and insight from the 95% of the world not included in psychological or other research because it would result in more comprehensive knowledge than we currently have. It would be helpful to have data on the nuances of day-to-day life and how communities deal with psychological and other problems. It would be good to know the nature of those serving in healing and helping roles, the kinds of assistance that would be most useful during emergencies, and the approaches used to enhance well-being. It is important that there will be simultaneous efforts to collaborate and network with communities and psychologists around the world to start to develop resources that include information about the particularities of each community.

Over time, this accumulated knowledge could serve as a resource to inform future interventions and crisis responses. This need not involve massive studies; information could be accumulated through an interdisciplinary network of individuals, including practitioners and researchers. Thus, in cases ranging from individual therapy to community interventions through disaster response, psychologists would have a resource to help them respectfully navigate the community's context. Rather than using a regional majority culture as a starting point and overgeneralizing that information to smaller communities, if we build our understandings pointillistically, community by community, we will likely end up with a much richer picture of both the commonalities and the diversity of communities within a region, providing a much richer context from which to partner in efforts to restore and support the well-being of community members. This work, dot by dot, is necessary, as with pointillism, to envisioning the whole with fresh insight and perspective if we are determined to improve human well-being.

REFERENCES

Abeyasekera, A., & Marecek, J. (2008). Women's well-being: Between the local and the global. *Psychology of Women Quarterly, 32,* 483–484. http://dx.doi.org/10.1111/j.1471-6402.2008.00460_1.x

Abu-Lughod, L. (1990). Can there be a feminist ethnography? *Women & Performance, 5,* 7–27. http://dx.doi.org/10.1080/07407709008571138

Alexander, M. J. (2006). *Pedagogies of crossing: Meditations on feminism, sexual politics, memory and the sacred*. Durham, NC: Duke University Press.

Altmaier, E. M., & Hall, J. E. (2008). Introduction to international quality assurance for psychology. In J. E. Hall & E. M. Altmaier (Eds.), *Global promise: Quality assurance and accountability in professional psychology* (pp. 3–15). New York, NY: Oxford University Press. http://dx.doi.org/10.1093/acprof:oso/9780195306088.003.0001

American Psychiatric Association. (2013). *Diagnostic and statistical manual of mental diseases* (5th ed.). Arlington, VA: Author.

Anastasi, A. (1988). *Psychological testing* (6th ed.). New York, NY: Macmillan.

Arnett, J. J. (2008). The neglected 95%: Why American psychology needs to become less American. *American Psychologist, 63,* 602–614. http://dx.doi.org/10.1037/0003-066X.63.7.602

Atlani, L., & Rousseau, C. (2000). The politics of culture in humanitarian aid to women refugees who have experienced sexual violence. *Transcultural Psychiatry, 37,* 435–449. http://dx.doi.org/10.1177/136346150003700309

Bhatia, S. (2007). Rethinking culture and identity in psychology: Towards a transnational cultural psychology. *Journal of Theoretical and Philosophical Psychology, 27–28,* 301–321. http://dx.doi.org/10.1037/h0091298

BigFoot, D. S., & Schmidt, S. R. (2010). Honoring children, mending the circle: Cultural adaptation of trauma-focused cognitive-behavioral therapy for American Indian and Alaska Native children. *Journal of Clinical Psychology, 66,* 847–856. http://dx.doi.org/10.1002/jclp.20707

Christopher, J. C., Wendt, D. C., Marecek, J., & Goodman, D. M. (2014). Critical cultural awareness: Contributions to a globalizing psychology. *American Psychologist, 69,* 645–655. http://dx.doi.org/10.1037/a0036851

Cosgrove, L., & Krimsky, S. (2012). A comparison of *DSM–IV* and *DSM–5* panel members' financial associations with industry: A pernicious problem persists. *PLoS Medicine, 9*(3), e1001190. http://dx.doi.org/10.1371/journal.pmed.1001190

Craven, C., & Davis, D. (2013). Introduction: Feminist activist ethnography. In C. Craven & D. Davis (Eds.), *Feminist activist ethnography: Counterpoints to neoliberalism in North America.* Lanham, MD: Lexington Books.

Cronin-Furman, K., Gowrinathan, N., & Zakaria, R. (2017). *Emissaries of empowerment.* New York: Colin Powell School for Civic and Public Leadership, The City College of New York.

Enns, C. Z. (2004). *Feminist theories and feminist psychotherapies: Origins, themes, and diversity* (2nd ed.). New York, NY: Haworth Press.

Gerstein, L. H., Hurley, E. J., & Hutchison, A. N. (2015). The dynamic-systemic-process model of international competencies for counseling psychologists and trainees. *Revista de Cercetare si Interventie Sociala, 50,* 239–261.

Glick Schiller, N., Basch, L., & Szanton Blanc, C. (1995). From immigrant to transmigrant: Theorizing transnational migration. *Anthropological Quarterly, 68,* 48–63. http://dx.doi.org/10.2307/3317464

Grabe, S. (2012). An empirical examination of women's empowerment and transformative change in the context of international development. *American Journal of Community Psychology, 49*, 233–245. http://dx.doi.org/10.1007/s10464-011-9453-y

Grabe, S., & Else-Quest, N. M. (2012). The role of transnational feminism in psychology: Complementary visions. *Psychology of Women Quarterly, 36*, 158–161. http://dx.doi.org/10.1177/0361684312442164

Grewal, I., & Kaplan, C. (1994). *Scattered hegemonies.* Minneapolis: University of Minnesota Press.

Griner, D., & Smith, T. B. (2006). Culturally adapted mental health interventions: A meta-analytic review. *Psychotherapy: Theory, Research, Practice, Training, 43*, 531–548.

Hays, P. A. (2016). *Addressing cultural complexities in practice: Assessment, diagnosis, and therapy* (3rd ed.). Washington, DC: American Psychological Association. http://dx.doi.org/10.1037/14801-000

Henrich, J., Heine, S. J., & Norenzayan, A. (2010). The weirdest people in the world? *Behavioral and Brain Sciences, 33*, 61–83. http://dx.doi.org/10.1017/S0140525X0999152X

Heppner, P. P., Wang, K. T., Heppner, M. J., & Wang, L.-F. (2012). From cultural encapsulation to cultural competence: The cross-national cultural competence model. In N. A. Fouad, J. A. Carter, & L. M. Subich (Eds.), *APA handbook of counseling psychology, Vol. 2. Practice, interventions, and applications* (pp. 433–471). Washington, DC: American Psychological Association. http://dx.doi.org/10.1037/13755-018

Hill, A. (2018, September 18). Migration: How many people are on the move around the world? *The Guardian.* Retrieved from https://www.theguardian.com/news/2018/sep/10/migration-how-many-people-are-on-the-move-around-the-world

International Test Commission. (2016). The International Test Commission guidelines on the security of tests, examinations, and other assessments. *International Journal of Testing, 16*, 181–204. http://dx.doi.org/10.1080/15305058.2015.1111221

King, J. (2009). Psychotherapy within an American Indian perspective. In M. E. Gallardo & B. W. McNeill (Eds.), *Intersections of multiple identities: A casebook of evidence-based practices with diverse populations* (pp. 113–136). New York, NY: Routledge/Taylor & Francis Group.

Kurtiş, T., & Adams, G. (2013). A cultural psychology of relationship: Toward a transnational feminist psychology. In M. K. Ryan & N. R. Branscombe (Eds.), *The SAGE handbook of gender and psychology* (pp. 251–269). London, England: Sage. http://dx.doi.org/10.4135/9781446269930.n16

Kurtiş, T., & Adams, G. (2015). Decolonizing liberation: Toward a transnational feminist psychology. *Journal of Social and Political Psychology, 3*, 388–413. http://dx.doi.org/10.5964/jspp.v3i1.326

Kurtiş, T., Adams, G., & Estrada-Villalta, S. (2016). Decolonizing empowerment: Implications for sustainable well-being: Decolonizing empowerment. *Analyses of Social Issues and Public Policy, 16*, 387–391. http://dx.doi.org/10.1111/asap.12120

Machizawa, S., & Enns, C. Z. (2015). Transnational psychological practice with women: Perspectives from East Asia and Japan. In C. Z. Enns, J. K. Rice, & R. L. Nutt (Eds.), *Psychological practice with women: Guidelines, diversity, empowerment* (pp. 225–256). Washington, DC: American Psychological Association. http://dx.doi.org/10.1037/14460-009

Mancini-Billson, J., & Fluehr-Lobban, C. (2005). *Female well-being: Towards a global theory of social change.* New York, NY: Zed Books.

Manning, J. (2016). Constructing a postcolonial feminist ethnography. *Journal of Organizational Ethnography, 5*, 90–105. http://dx.doi.org/10.1108/JOE-01-2016-0002

Marecek, J., & Senadheera, C. (2012). 'I drank it to put an end to me': Narrating girls' suicide and self-harm in Sri Lanka. *Contributions to Indian Psychology, 46*, 53–82. http://dx.doi.org/10.1177/006996671104600204

Mohanty, C. T. (1991). Under Western eyes: Feminist scholarship and colonial discourses. In C. T. Mohanty, A. Russo, L. Torres, L. (Eds.), *Third World women and the politics of feminism* (pp. 51–80). Bloomington: Indiana University Press.

Mohanty, C. T. (2003). "Under Western eyes" revisited: Feminist solidarity through anticapitalist struggles. *Signs, 28*, 499–535. http://dx.doi.org/10.1086/342914

Mohanty, C. T., Russo, A., & Torres, L. (1991). *Third World women and the politics of feminism.* Bloomington: Indiana University Press.

Morgan, R. (1984). *Sisterhood is global.* New York, NY: Feminist Press at CUNY.

Morgan-Consoli, M. L., Inman, A. G., Bullock, M., & Nolan, S. A. (2018). Framework for competencies for U.S. psychologists engaging internationally. *International Perspectives in Psychology: Research, Practice, Consultation, 7*, 174–188. http://dx.doi.org/10.1037/ipp0000090

Moscoso, M. S. (1997). Medicion de la colera y hostilidad: Implicaciones en tratamiento psicologico con pacientes VIH/SIDA [Measurement of cholera and hostility: implications in psychological treatment with HIV/AIDS patients]. *Revista Peruana de Psicologia, 2*, 39–64.

Moscoso, M. S., & Spielberger, C. D. (1999). Measuring the experience, expression, and control of anger in Latin America: The Spanish multi-cultural State–Trait Anger Expression Inventory. *Interamerican Journal of Psychology, 33*(2), 29–48.

Moscoso, M. S., & Spielberger, C. D. (2011). Cross-cultural assessment of emotions: The expression of anger. *Revista de Psicología, 29*, 343–360.

Peters, W. M. K., Straits, K. J. E., & Gauthier, P. E. (2015). Psychological practice with Native women. In C. Z. Enns, J. K. Rice, & R. L. Nutt (Eds.), *Psychological practice with women: Guidelines, diversity, empowerment* (pp. 191–256). Washington, DC: American Psychological Association. http://dx.doi.org/10.1037/14460-008

Prilleltensky, I. (2007). Poverty and power: Suffering and wellness in collective, relational, and personal domains. In S. Carr & T. Sloan (Eds.), *Psychology and poverty* (pp. 19–44). New York, NY: Kluwer/Plenum.

Prilleltensky, I., & Fox, D. R. (2007). Psychopolitical literacy for wellness and justice. *Journal of Community Psychology, 35,* 793–805. http://dx.doi.org/10.1002/jcop.20179

Pulerwitz, J., Gortmaker, S. L., & DeJong, W. (2000). Measuring sexual relationship power in HIV/STD research. *Sex Roles, 42,* 637–660. http://dx.doi.org/10.1023/A:1007051506972

Rasmussen, S. (2015). Understanding honor in religious, cultural, and moral experience: Commentary on "Diasporic virginities: Social representations of virginity and constructions of identity amongst British Arab Muslim women" by Howarth, Caroline; Amer, Amena; and Sen, Ragini. *Culture & Psychology, 21,* 20–36. http://dx.doi.org/10.1177/1354067X14551301

Silver, M. (2015, January 4). If you shouldn't call it the Third World, what should you call it? *NPR.* Retrieved from https://www.npr.org/sections/goatsandsoda/2015/01/04/372684438/if-you-shouldnt-call-it-the-third-world-what-should-you-call-it

Sireci, S. G. (2004). Using Bilinguals to Evaluate the comparability of different language versions of a test. In R. K. Hambleton, P. F. Merenda, & C. D. Spielberger (Eds.), *Adapting educational and psychological tests for cross-cultural assessment* (pp. 117–138). London, England: Psychology Press.

Spence, J. T., Helmreich, R., & Stapp, J. (1973). A short version of the Attitudes toward Women Scale (AWS). *Bulletin of the Psychonomic Society, 2,* 219–220. http://dx.doi.org/10.3758/BF03329252

Spielberger, C. D. (2006). Cross-cultural assessment of emotional states and personality traits. *European Psychologist, 11,* 297–303. http://dx.doi.org/10.1027/1016-9040.11.4.297

Stacey, J. (1988). Can there be a feminist ethnography? *Women's Studies International Forum, 11,* 21–27. http://dx.doi.org/10.1016/0277-5395(88)90004-0

Wessells, M. G. (2009). Do no harm: Toward contextually appropriate psychosocial support in international emergencies. *American Psychologist, 64,* 842–854. http://dx.doi.org/10.1037/0003-066X.64.8.842

Wierzbicka, A. (1994). Emotion, language, and cultural scripts. In S. E. Kitayama & H. R. M. Markus (Eds.), *Emotion and culture: Empirical studies of mutual influence* (pp. 133–194). Washington, DC: American Psychological Association. http://dx.doi.org/10.1037/10152-004

World Health Organization. (2007). *Health of indigenous peoples.* Retrieved from https://www.who.int/mediacentre/factsheets/fs326/en/

World Health Organization. (2018). *Manual of the international statistical classification of diseases, injuries, and causes of death* (11th rev.). Retrieved from https://icd.who.int/browse11/l-m/en

5

A TRANSNATIONAL FEMINIST PERSPECTIVE ON THE PSYCHOLOGY OF MIGRATION

OLIVA M. ESPÍN AND ANDREA L. DOTTOLO

Never have so many people lived outside their country of birth. The number of international migrants worldwide has continued to grow rapidly over the past 15 years, reaching 244 million in 2015, up from 222 million in 2010 and 173 million in 2000 (United Nations, 2016). According to the United Nations High Commission on Refugees "we are now witnessing the highest levels of displacement on record" (para. 1) with 65.3 million people displaced, 53% of them from Syria, Afghanistan, and Somalia (United Nations High Commission on Refugees, 2017). The Syrian and Middle Eastern refugee crisis affecting Europe and the recent child and youth migration emergency at the U.S. southern border, particularly during the summer of 2014 (Chisti & Hipsman, 2015) are concrete expressions of this phenomenon.

This chapter explores how transnationalism can be more explicitly and directly integrated into feminist psychology scholarship as it relates to issues of gender and migration. In our previous collaboration (Espín &

http://dx.doi.org/10.1037/0000148-006
Transnational Psychology of Women: Expanding International and Intersectional Approaches, L. H. Collins, S. Machizawa, and J. K. Rice (Editors)

Dottolo, 2015), we aimed to focus attention on gender and migration in psychology, specifically feminist psychology. Although transnational issues were presented in that volume, we would like to make explicit in this chapter our understanding of the transnational threads that interweave experiences of migration for women all over the world. We believe a transnational feminist perspective is an important theoretical, methodological, and pedagogical contribution that advances understanding of the gendered processes of migration.

Some of the underlying tools and strengths of our understanding of a transnational feminist psychology of migration are rooted in cultural psychology and liberation psychology. Adams, Dobles, Gómez, Kurtiş, and Molina (2015) explained that *cultural psychology* can offer a bidirectional approach to understanding culture and psychology. This includes the sociocultural constitution of psychological experience, meaning that no internal, individualized psychology is separate from culture. Conversely, the psychological constitution of sociocultural reality, reminds us that there are no social or cultural contexts that are not constructed by individuals and groups. Similarly, Kirschner and Martin (2010) explained that "just as the mind is constituted by the social, cultural, political, and historical contexts in which it emerges, so also is this true of the mind's products, including psychological knowledge itself" (p. 15). Shweder (1990), and later Bhatia (2007), also emphasized the important distinction between cultural psychology, as we are discussing here, and *cross-cultural psychology*, which tends to treat culture as an independent variable that can be compared across contexts.

Culture, with all its concrete and intangible components, is at the core of who we all are. We could not be humans without a cultural context that supports families and individuals and tells us who we are and what the world around us means. Culture creates our worldview and our identities as groups and individuals. However, we are aware that "culture" is not a static entity. "Change, conflict, and contradictions are resident *within* culture itself" (Phan, 2003, p. 13). The role of power is extensive in the formation of cultural norms and identity. Those who have more power can dictate terms of how and when "cultural" attitudes will be tolerated or rejected outright (Phan, 2003). And although cultural values and prejudices influence how immigrants are represented in psychological science and cultural values are influenced by power, it is also true that the members of immigrant groups are cultural agents.

Groups that are transforming their way of life through a vast process of acculturation focus on preserving "tradition" almost exclusively through the gender roles of women. Gender becomes the site to claim the power denied to immigrant men by the host society (Espín, 1999, 2006). However, expressions of male dominance among immigrants are nothing but the specific culture's version of the myth of male superiority that exists in most cultures, including mainstream U.S. and European cultures. In all cultures, those who have a stake in preventing the development of consciousness among women will not be pleased when those women take their lives into their own hands. In all cultures, there will be resistance to women's transformations of their roles by those invested in maintaining the status quo. "Returning women to their 'traditional roles' continues to be defined as central to preserving national identity and cultural pride" (Narayan, 1997, p. 20) by some immigrants of both sexes. Some cultures still subscribe to the traditional ideas of male superiority, but many reject it outright.

Veroff and Goldberger (1995) explained that some of the central elements of culture include "common rituals, beliefs, values, rules and laws . . . which can be distinctively identified according to culturally normative practices . . . that make up the fabric of how a society functions" (p. 10). We should tease out the responsibility to respect cultures against an easy assignment of power to represent the group to cultural spokesmen (Phillips, 2010). "In the name of equality between cultures, the guardians of conservative gender roles have been provided . . . an amplified voice on the public stage" (Phillips, 2010, pp. 1–2). Sensitivity toward other cultures does not imply unquestioning acceptance of patriarchal definitions of cultural identities and behaviors. "Since no society yet operates under conditions of gender justice, what is considered to be right and just within any given society must always be open to critical scrutiny" (Phillips, 2010, p. 17). Transnationalism considers the effects of the convergence of multiple cultures.

As Adams and his collaborators (2015) described, features of *liberation psychology* inform a transnational feminist perspective, including questioning the hegemonic epistemological positions (including imposed and internalized ways of knowing that benefit those in power) and attitudes toward women from other cultural backgrounds—from which feminist psychology is not exempt. A transnational feminist psychology must resist the urge to *essentialize* (or reduce to the most basic and "natural" qualities) the immigrant woman, or as Desai, Bouchard, and Detournay (2010) pinpointed, the "woman from the global South," as "the emblem of the 'most oppressed' and therefore the 'most outside'" (p. 53). This can result in Western or Northern feminist psychologists clamoring to collaborate with those "authentic" knowers, those immigrant outsiders (Desai et al., 2010). Simultaneously, a transnational feminist psychology can work toward undoing these characterizations by integrating decolonizing discourses, which are "typically absent in psychological discourses . . . (feminist or otherwise)" (Kurtiş & Adams, 2015, p. 389) and bring us back to the question of who holds the power over meanings in psychology and inside a given culture (Magnusson & Marecek, 2012; Narayan, 1997; Phillips, 2010).

We could add that from a transnational feminist perspective, not only gender justice but also all forms of justice should be open to critical scrutiny. This will demand awareness about the interlocking nature of oppression and the continued weight of its many worldwide forms, a daunting but necessary task, which requires we pay attention and question the nature of power and the structures that perpetuate the exercise of that power—something, we might add, psychologists are not very good at doing (Espín, 2006; Espín & Dottolo, 2015). This is why we need a transnational feminist psychology that would not reproduce psychology's tendency to create knowledge that conforms to the perspectives of a privileged minority of people in Western or Northern settings.

Feminist psychology emerged in the 1970s, but many of the key concepts of feminist thinking and women's studies have yet to make their mark on psychology as a discipline today. Psychologists still struggle with the central feminist tenet that issues of gender cannot be fully understood without the simultaneous analysis of race, class, sexuality, age, body ability, and other intersecting factors. Erica Burman (1998) contended 2 decades ago that feminist psychology has reproduced a model of woman that is homogenizing and reproduces hegemonic norms. This remains the case for the most part. As recently as 2008 a special issue of the journal *Sex Roles* (Shields, 2008) was devoted to exploring intersectionality in psychology, some 30 years after feminist scholars in other disciplines had begun using the term. If the pace has been slow in adopting intersectional approaches in psychology (e.g., Espín, 2005), it has been glacial in adopting transnational scholarship, but there is important and exciting work emerging nonetheless.

Transnational feminist perspectives have been advanced by feminist scholars theorizing about how mainstream feminist scholarship has consistently ignored so-called "Third World" women's movements and experiences as well as the impact of coloniality on women's lives. "The popularization and embracing of transnational feminisms as a discourse in feminist/women's and gender studies has coincided with a commitment to address the asymmetries of the globalization process" (Swarr & Nagar, 2010, p. 3) and to appreciate and incorporate the complexities of knowledge production across borders. Transnational feminists contend that ignoring transnational conditions and phenomena in understandings of intersectionality is reproducing knowledge and ways of knowing that replicate hegemonic academic discourses. *Hegemony* can be defined as "the command, influence, or predominance of one group over another" (Winter, 1996, p. 604). Hegemony is structural and institutional, involving authority, leadership, and identity. *Hegemonic power* is psychological, in that it involves convincing those that are being ruled that it is in their best interest to be ruled, intruding into all psychological processes, for both the power holders and targets of power (e.g., Freire, 1970).

Transnational feminists also question the assumptions of "a model based on the notion of an individual knowledge producer in academia (feminist studies included)" (Swarr & Nagar, 2010, p. 2). Transnational feminism proposes a set of understandings that attends to racialized, classed, and heteronormative practices fostered by globalization and patriarchies and grapples with the complex and contradictory ways in which these processes shape subjectivities and interweave epistemological self-reflexivity. In other words, it questions, contextualizes, and situates how knowledge itself is constructed and legitimated. It interrogates all forms of relations of power and incorporates knowledge from activist communities everywhere (Swarr & Nagar, 2010).

> Using a transnational perspective allows for a more systematic study of the social processes and institutions that have been routinely obscured by traditional migration scholarship. . . . New perspectives emerge on a number of issues, including the effect of migration on gender hierarchies and racialized identities; family dynamics; the significance of nation-states, membership and citizenship, and the role of religion. (Levitt & Schiller, 2008, p. 290)

We are aware that "feminists have an ambivalent relationship to transnationalism as both an academic discourse and a complex set of social practices" (Pratt & Yeoh, 2003, p. 159). Desai et al. (2010) warned that the *transnational* has come to define our current moment; the term has become an umbrella that encompasses and moves beyond other "previous" feminisms:

> What happens to Third World feminisms, to women of color feminisms, to diasporic feminisms (to name a few of the bodies of theory that have sought to interrogate the intersections of racial formation, sexuality, empire, capitalism, and colonialism) with the advent of the transnational? (pp. 48–49)

We recognize the pitfalls of minimizing or erasing important theoretical and political differences among feminist stances (e.g., liberal, Marxist, socialist, radical, lesbian, womanist) in the name of the transnational.

We both support and qualify this critique. We agree that the transnational should not come to subsume other feminist inquiries or see them as "collapsible and identical" (Desai et al., 2010, p. 49). However, we do argue that a transnational perspective should encourage psychology, as a discipline traditionally rooted in an androcentric, Eurocentric "physics envy," to move further "beyond" its epistemic frame. In trying to correct this "myopia," we do not want to fall into a utopian hope about transnationalism as a corrective force that would equalize gender relations in some normative Western idealized way but rather be aware that "patriarchal relations return in different guises in different times and places"

(Pratt & Yeoh, 2003, p. 161). We are aware that what has been written about transnationalism "is almost always gender-blind" (Pratt & Yeoh, 2003, p. 159). Indeed "there is nothing inherently transgressive or emancipatory about transnationalism" (Pratt & Yeoh, 2003, p. 160). We are conscious that the "effects of transnationalism on gender relations are contradictory and complex" (Pratt & Yeoh, 2003, p. 160). For example, if a lens of transnationalism is applied without taking gender (and race, class, and sexuality, etc.) seriously, researchers run the risk of not only avoiding asking appropriate questions but also ignoring the gendered data at their fingertips. But we still believe looking at immigration issues through a transnational lens can provide valuable insights.

TRANSNATIONAL FEMINIST PSYCHOLOGY AND MIGRATION

Perhaps no other phenomenon is more self-evidently transnational than the issue of international migration. However, "transnational migration studies form a highly fragmented, emergent field which still lacks both a well-defined theoretical framework and analytical rigor" (Portes, Guarnizo, & Landolt, 2008, p. 275). All over the world immigrants forge and sustain strong transnational networks based on "multi-stranded social relations that link together their societies of origin and settlement" (Basch, Schiller, & Blanc, 2008, p. 263). Understanding immigration through a transnationalism lens, therefore, allows an analysis of "the 'lived' and fluid experience of individuals who act in ways that challenge our previous conflation of geographic space and social identity" (Basch et al., 2008, p. 263).

In recent decades, social scientists have noticed a pattern that differs from the assimilation emphasis characteristic of previous waves of migration so that now the transnational defines the experience of migration as facilitated by modern communications. In the context of migration, *transnationalism* is defined as the process by which immigrants

> forge and sustain multi-stranded social relations that link together the societies of origin and settlement [and make it possible for immigrants to] take actions, make decisions, and develop subjectivities and identities embedded in networks of relationships that connect them simultaneously to two or more nations. (Basch, Schiller, & Blanc, 1994, p. 7)

Immigration has never been a process of simply moving from one country to another, where immigrants exorcise all contact, memory, and habits from the old country to "assimilate" into the new. However, in contemporary modes of travel and communication, transnational identities emerge in the context of being in multiple places "at once." For example, a Venezuelan living in

Mexico may carry on political discussions with family and friends about the situation in her country of birth that may influence their decision to participate or not in street protests. Or grandchildren of Haitian immigrants born in Canada who use Facetime with their grandparents will continue to use Creole in their conversations to be able to talk to the grandparents and therefore maintain the ancestral language and continue to develop and sustain a Haitian identity.

It is evident that "there is a qualitative difference in the transnational experience immigrants live today" (Pedraza, 2006, p. 46). They do not just keep their home country in their memory and imagination but are in touch with that country in the present because of the ways that social technologies (cell phones, social media, and other computer-mediated communications) have altered the migration experience for families and individuals alike (Bacigalupe & Camara, 2012). As an everyday example, an immigrant woman living in Saudi Arabia might call her mother in the Philippines to ask about details on the preparation of a traditional recipe. And then, she might improvise a little, using ingredients available in Saudi Arabia, so the resulting dish is a product of transnationalism.

But immigrant experience is not just influenced by the daily maintenance of bonds of love and loyalty for the family and nation left behind but also by their lack of acceptance in host societies (Pedraza, 2006). In fact, maintaining transnational ties "may serve to socially enhance the immigrants' lives" (Murphy, 2006, p. 81) because "the social networks may produce tangible resources, social capital and emotional support that may offset some of the alienating and stressful effects of immigration" (Murphy, 2006, p. 84). However, these ties can also produce some negative effects. Paradoxically, although transnationalism is related to high life satisfaction in immigrants, it is also related to higher depression, possibly because the constant contact may exacerbate the feelings of loss and mourning that are associated with migration (Murphy, 2006).

WOMEN AND TRANSNATIONAL MIGRATION

Women are particularly key to understanding transnational migration in a variety of ways. A transnational feminist understanding of the psychology of migration examines the experience of women migrants by exploring how gender, race, economics, politics, and nation are organizing structures of power relations in which women migrants are variously implicated and by which they are deeply affected in their daily lives. We argue that a transnational feminist mode of inquiry understands the importance of a social justice standpoint to rethink conventional wisdom about the psychological impact of migration on women. We also argue that it is essential to avoid a model of "woman" that reproduces hegemonic feminisms and norms in its understanding of women immigrants.

The topic of migration in relation to gender has been studied assiduously in recent years. "Conceptualizing gender as a process [rather than a variable], as one of several ways humans create and perpetuate social differences, helps to deconstruct the myth of gender as a product of nature while underscoring its power dimension" (Mahler & Pessar, 2001, p. 441). However, the work of understanding the impact of gender on transnational migration processes has been done mostly from an anthropological, historical, sociological, geographical, and/or public policy perspective and much less from a psychological one. Although women in certain immigrant groups have been studied from a psychological perspective, including some book-length works (e.g., Cole, Espín, & Rothblum, 1992; Kawahara & Espín, 2007, 2012), and some specific topics such as issues of sexuality have been addressed (e.g., Espín, 1999), with few exceptions, "psychologists have remained absent from the discussion of international migration and its gendered character" (Upegui-Hernández, 2012, p. 230). Specifically, transnational migration studies informed by feminist psychological perspectives have yet to articulate a well-defined theoretical framework. In this chapter, we aim to foster the development of that theoretical framework.

We use a transnational perspective not only to refer to immigrants—as an "empirical descriptive"—but also to the perspective and mode of knowledge production—as a "mode of critique" (Desai et al., 2010, p. 48). A transnational feminist analysis interrogates the usual psychological focus on differences between women and men and questions power structures (such as the state) that determine and influence personal choices while hiding the ideological dimensions of those choices. It recognizes that power structures influence the content, method, and epistemology behind all psychological knowledge (Magnusson & Marecek, 2012). Therefore, although data concerning women and girls provide valuable information, a transnational feminist analysis interprets these data through a gender lens that is seen as a central organizing axis of power, intimately and inextricably connected to social structures such as the state, nation, age, class, race, ethnicity, sexuality, and disability as well as other sociohistorical and context factors, and it emphasizes themes such as survival, resilience, and success. Even though from a transnational perspective intersectionality is necessary and fundamental to any analysis, we also contend that gender is a central axis of that analysis and integral to one that calls itself feminist. To say that gender and other domains of power are inseparable and co-constituted is not a justification or support of White hegemonic feminisms. In fact, we are precisely disrupting such ideologies, as so many others have done before and since, as we apply that analysis to transnational experiences of immigrant and refugee women.

"Globalization has enabled and accelerated mobility and made affordable forms of communication and sharing, relocated and created new types of work" (Rajagopalan, 2015, p. 232), but with it has come a "permanent and growing global undocumentedness" (Rajagopalan, 2015, p. 226). Many of those undocumented immigrants are women and children (e.g., Chen & Gill, 2015; Chisti & Hipsman, 2015).

Regardless of legal status, migrants, particularly women, support their families, and thus the economies of their countries of origin, through their cash remittances. For example, a Guatemalan woman working as a maid in the United States may send money back to her family in Guatemala, enabling her family to buy more food, construct a new home, or otherwise stimulate the economy of their village. These remittances are one of the multiple ways in which women affect and are affected by transnationalism. The importance of monetary remittances and their impact on economic development in countries with high rates of emigration are undeniable. These countries may be dependent on their diasporas' monetary flows (Cortina & Ochoa-Reza, 2013).

Moreover, the transnational impact of these remittances goes beyond their economic impact. New constructions, new garments, and gadgets that become accessible through these remittances to those who have not migrated themselves transform families and towns and influence thoughts and practices and, with them, the culture in the home countries (Riofrio, 2015). For example, a daughter who works as a nurse in Sweden may buy and send a phone to her mother who lives in a village in Colombia and periodically prepay the account on this Swedish phone, allowing her mother to regularly make international phone calls and have access to information about other places in the world. Buying a phone and keeping it charged becomes a form of remittance. And thus, remittances in this and many other circumstances become culturally transformative, another iteration of the transnational impact of women's migration. In addition, women migrants' increasing ability to move across borders serves to connect home and host country across national borders besides providing economic sustenance to their families and home countries (Yeoh & Ramdas, 2014).

Women migrants "have been identified as being more reliable remitters than men" (Upegui-Hernández, 2012, p. 232). However, countries who benefit from the work of their women citizens living and working abroad have done little to protect them and ensure their human and social rights (Upegui-Hernández, 2012), particularly when they are undocumented in the host country. They depend on these women but do not support them in any way, which leads to frequent exploitation and abuse, sexual and otherwise. "As is the case with any illicit and prohibited market, opportunities for exploitation, abuse (physical and sexual) and violence are rampant" (Upegui-Hernández, 2012, p. 234).

A transnational feminist psychology of migration is attentive to the many ways in which migration impacts the lived experience of women migrants as well as their role as providers and bridges in the multiple contexts in which they move. No matter how strong the similarities created by the experience of migration, vast differences in personal experience are present. Differences originate in the dissimilar countries of birth, ages at migration, historical period when the migration took place, circumstances surrounding it, premigration political and economic context, mental health issues, and each individual's specific life experiences. Upegui-Hernández (2012) urged us to take "seriously how the experience of migration and transnational life affects and shapes psychological and social well-being" (p. 229).

We hope it is clear that when we refer to *transnational migration*, we include traffic in information, money, politics, ideologies, and more that go beyond bodies moving across geopolitical boundaries.

GENDER ROLES, MIGRATION, AND TRANSNATIONALISM

It is important to understand that even though women migrate for a range of reasons and external constraints that they share with men, including issues of religion, education, war, sexuality, political instability, lack of natural resources, or other economic needs, the impact of these problems is always already gendered (Kofman, Phizacklea, Raghuram, & Sales, 2000). In addition, some specific factors are important causes of migration for women. "Marital discord and physical violence, unhappy marriages and the impossibility of divorce [as well as other instances of sexual or gendered oppression] often influence women's decision to migrate" (Kofman et al., 2000, p. 21).

Women's agency,

> viewed within the context of resisting oppression and exploitative structures . . . is particularly vital for a gendered account of migration, because it is so often assumed that women simply "follow" men and that their role in migration is reactive rather than proactive. (Kofman et al., 2000, p. 23)

In other words, it is important to keep in mind that women's migration is not only triggered by financial opportunities dictated by men but that immigrant women are also individual agents, often strategically seeking flight from patriarchal regimes (Kofman et al., 2000).

As such, at its roots, the phenomenon of transnational migration involves both voluntary and involuntary migration. And although the usual understandings of international migration distinguish between *true volun-tary immigrants* as motivated by economic reasons and refugees as *involuntary immigrants* motivated by fleeing situations of danger, this division is not as clear when women's motivations for migration are concerned. Is a woman fleeing marital violence in a country where the legal system does not protect her a voluntary immigrant looking for an independent economic situation, or is she a refugee fleeing a situation of danger and thus an involuntary immi-grant? The lines are blurry because economics and physical danger inter-weave to create for women the motivation and the will to migrate.

Although families are an important factor in migration, presenting immigrant women only as members of families, such as mothers, wives, or daughters misses the point that many women migrate alone and, in fact, encounter and negotiate the personal, economic, social, and political issues raised by migration on their own. Many women who migrate alone do so to provide financial support for the families left behind in the home country, as discussed earlier.

Transnational migration may offer women the opportunity to trans-gress and challenge established traditional gender roles and power structures. Women may view migration as a chance to leave unsatisfying partnerships or improve their gender role status by increasing control over household deci-sions and building personal autonomy. Many immigrant women perceive migration as providing a space and permission to cross boundaries and trans-form their sexuality and sex roles, including embracing a nonheterosexual identity (Espín, 1999, 2006). The opportunities in work, education, and rou-tines of life provided by the migration are present in women's stories regard-less of differences in the roles of women in their countries of birth.

Many women appear to benefit from the liberating effect of being "out-siders" in the new culture (Espín, 1999). However, transnational migration can also contribute to a situation where immigrant women embrace more traditional gender roles while embodying a "reimagined" home culture in their new cultural milieu (Mahalingam & Leu, 2005). Migration carries with it the possibility of limiting women's private spheres of influence and their moral authority within traditional cultural contexts. Women may benefit economically while their subordination as women may continue, although it may take different forms (Pessar, 2003). These tradeoffs and tensions create ambivalence and contradictions.

Transformations that occur in individual lives through migration impact the acceptable norms in countries of origin and, therefore, the lives of people who remain in the home country. Transnational migrants are transformed by their transnational practices, and these practices affect cultural norms, including gender norms, in the nation-states of their origin and settlement (Basch et al., 2008, p. 263). Immigrant women from India may have learned to eat fish and chips in the United Kingdom, but the British have now also made curry and chutney part of their everyday diet. Not only do immigrant women from many countries learn new iterations of their gender roles in their host countries but their counterparts in the country of birth may also start changing gendered behaviors as a consequence of comments or observations from their immigrant sisters. Because of the transnational networks that most immigrants participate in,

> they come in contact with the regulatory powers and the hegemonic culture of more than one state. . . . Individuals are, therefore, embedded in multiple legal and political institutions that determine access and action and organize and legitimate gender, race, and class status. (Levitt & Schiller, 2008, p. 285)

To talk about migration is obviously to talk about geographical movement. And geographical movement entails psychic transformations intertwined with memories and languages (Espín, 2015). Yet understanding migration from the perspective of transnationalism "challenges our previous conflation of geographic space and social identity" (Basch et al., 2008, p. 263), even though to talk about geography sometimes also entails fierce contestations of geographical space and lands (Alexander & Mohanty, 2010, p. 39).

METHODOLOGICAL CONSIDERATIONS FOR A TRANSNATIONAL FEMINIST PSYCHOLOGY OF MIGRATION

We believe that the personal experience of the researcher is not only valid but also essential in the development of studies that are meant to be contextual, reflexive, and relevant. We know that feminist psychologists started revealing that psychological knowledge frequently reflected varieties of male experience without acknowledging that it excluded women. Yet we are also cognizant that feminist psychology has frequently de-emphasized race, class, and other factors in its effort to universalize the psychology of women. The multiple critiques of a feminist psychology focused on the experience of a privileged minority of White, middle- or upper-class heterosexual women recognize that valid experiential knowledge should be enriched by a variety of knowledge and practices (e.g., Espín, 1991; Kurtiş & Adams, 2015). Transnational perspectives can transform feminist psychology by destabilizing and expanding our understanding and knowledge about women in the world. Understanding the meanings of global movements of women from a transnational feminist psychology perspective is entangled with uncovering the meanings of everyday contexts and relations that are so pervasive they are hardly visible at all.

As we have reiterated, a transnational feminist psychology of migration questions and explores "the linkages and intersections among gender, sexuality, ethnicity, class, nationality, migration, and transnationalism" (Yeoh & Ramdas, 2014, p. 1205). Feminist scholars across disciplines have insisted on the centrality of intersectional and transnational perspectives that make explicit that our identities and lived experiences cannot be separated from one another but mutually construct one another (e.g., Collins, 1990; Crenshaw, 1997; Dottolo & Stewart, 2008; Espín, 1997, 2005; Shields, 2008). As Mohanty (2003) stated, "women are workers, mothers, or consumers in the global economy, but we are also all those things simultaneously. Singular and monolithic categorizations of women in discourses of globalization circumscribe ideas about experience, agency, and struggle" (p. 527).

However, traditional psychology has been slow to understand and integrate these notions that capture the realities of lived experience. Intersectionality continues to be "a perspective in search of a method" (Shields, 2008, p. 306) in psychology and "disciplines that prize methodological approaches that do not easily lend themselves to empirical study of intersectionality" (Shields, 2008, p. 301). Reluctance to "deploying transnationalism as an analytic optic" (Yeoh & Ramdas, 2014, p. 1205) is also evident in psychology.

One of the reasons the discipline of psychology has remained behind in the study of issues of gender and transnational migration is its stubborn reliance on quantitative, positivist approaches (Suárez-Orozco & Qin, 2006). Even though quantitative, positivist methods contribute significantly to knowledge in psychology, they alone cannot capture the subjective experience and agency of migrants, particularly women, or the subtleties of gender ideologies. "Because [for the most part] psychologists insist firmly on a scientific methodology that emphasizes validity, reliability, and experimental designs, gender has been treated mainly as a dichotomous variable" (Donato, Gabaccia, Holdaway, Manalansan, & Pessar, 2006, p. 17). The slow advance of gender analysis in quantitative research has prompted alternative methodological innovations such as qualitative studies, narrative research, and other approaches that lend themselves to conceptualize "gender as a central social category organizing the identities, social practices and institutions influencing migration" (Donato et al., 2006, p. 17). A transnational feminist psychology that avoids the pitfalls of privileged blindness takes the risk of challenging traditional methods in the discipline of psychology and exploring new possibilities of inquiry (Marecek, 2003). It joins in trying to develop "a useful roadmap toward those answers" (Shields, 2008, p. 307) as they pertain to transnational migrant women.

Grabe and Else-Quest (2012) expanded and discussed the methodological implications of intersectionality in a transnational context:

> Transnational intersectionality places importance on the intersections among gender, ethnicity, sexuality, economic exploitation, and other social hierarchies in the context of empire building or imperialist policies characterized by historical and emergent global capitalism. Thus, because understanding gender oppression at the intersection of other imbalances of power is increasingly imperative in a globalized world, transnational feminist actors can and do make use of international data to advance local causes. For these reasons, there is a great utility in developing and using macro-level indicators of power. (pp. 159–160)

Furthermore, we believe that collaboration should be explicitly encouraged and valued in transnational feminist psychology endeavors. Transnational collaborations between feminist psychologists can make "a meaningful contribution . . . in overcoming methodological nationalisms" (Yeoh & Ramdas, 2014, p. 1207). We believe that a "multiplicity of feminist voices situated across diverse contexts and originating from different cultural and historical starting points" (Yeoh & Ramdas, 2014, p. 1207) and "participating in joint research collaborations between scholars inhabiting different worlds [can] create new opportunities for efflorescence" (i.e., growth and development; Yeoh & Ramdas, 2014, p. 1208). "Translocally grounded, collaborative projects that will open up avenues for answering critical questions" (Yeoh & Ramdas, 2014, p. 1208) can make a significant contribution to a transnational feminist psychology of migration.

Dottolo and Tillery (2015) suggested an approach they called *reflexivity-in-relation*, extending beyond the more solitary activity of reflection to rely on our scholarly communities, especially our trusted relationships, to mirror, interrogate, and query our positionality and connections to our research and practice. Swarr and Nagar (2010) argued that such collaboration can result in new epistemologies and "suggest that interweaving theories and practices of knowledge production through collaborative dialogues provides a way to radically rethink existing approaches to subalternity, voice, authorship, and representation" (p. 2). Spivak (1988) famously asked, "Can the subaltern speak?" referring to marginalized groups that have been rendered without voice or agency as a product of hegemonic structures. Swarr and Nagar also reminded us that "all academic production is necessarily collaborative" (p. 1). We need other voices not only to develop our own but also even to understand our own.

Finally, we believe and agree that

> It is imperative that the academy *not* be the only location that determines our research and pedagogical work; that we recognize those hierarchies of place within the multiple sites and locations in which knowledge is produced, and we maintain clarity about the origin of the

production of knowledge and the spaces where this knowledge travels. (Alexander & Mohanty, 2010, p. 27)

CONCLUSION

As coauthors, we have both written and edited several works together and have already experienced the uncertainty of where one of our thoughts begins and the other's ends. We hope to continue strengthening our understanding of a transnational feminist psychology of migration through future collaborations.

We believe that as transnational feminist psychology continues to develop, understand, revise, and critique notions of "transnational," it will be important to explicitly value multiple methodologies, multiple feminisms, feminist psychologies, narrative research, and interdisciplinarity—central tenets of the larger "story" of a transnational feminist psychology.

We also believe that the increased understanding of women's migration from transnational perspectives will enhance feminist psychology's theoretical knowledge as a discipline. And we hope it will have an impact as well on the everyday lives of women immigrants as nation-states and cultures become more aware of the transnational impact of women's migrations.

We hope that the development of a transnational feminist psychology of migration will generate more questions than answers about a psychology of migration, as all good theory and research do. For example, what other ways can we understand gendered experiences of migration? Who is not yet being seen, heard, or represented? What issues and topics are most in need of further investigation? How might the understandings of migration change over time, as communities become ever more connected? Who will shape the landscape as its contours continue to shift and boundaries and borders are redefined? How will psychology respond to and engage with scholarship on migration that prioritizes intersectionality, interdisciplinarity, and reflexivity, to name a few? How does the memory of experiences of migration and the languages in which they are described affect the nature of the transnational experience of women migrants?

However the answers to these questions unfold, surely a more just, more fully inclusive future will put the global movement of women migrants and transnational feminist perspectives on their experiences at the center.

REFERENCES

Adams, G., Dobles, I., Gómez, L. H., Kurtiş, T., & Molina, L. E. (2015). Decolonizing psychological science: Introduction to the special thematic section. *Journal of Social and Political Psychology, 3*, 213–238. http://dx.doi.org/10.5964/jspp.v3i1.564

Alexander, M. J., & Mohanty, C. T. (2010). Cartographies of knowledge and power: Transnational feminism and radical praxis. In A. L. Swarr & R. Nagar (Eds.), *Critical transnational feminist praxis* (pp. 23–46). Albany, NY: SUNY Press.

Bacigalupe, G., & Camara, M. (2012). Transnational families and social technologies: Reassessing immigration psychology. *Journal of Ethnic and Migration Studies, 38*, 1425–1438. http://dx.doi.org/10.1080/1369183X.2012.698211

Basch, L., Schiller, N. G., & Blanc, C. S. (1994). *Nations unbound: Transnational projects, postcolonial predicaments, deterritorialized nation states*. Langhorne, PA: Gordon and Breach.

Basch, L., Schiller, N. G., & Blanc, C. S. (2008). Transnational projects: A new perspective and Theoretical premises. In S. Khagram & P. Levitt (Eds.), *The transnational studies reader: Intersections & innovations* (pp. 261–272). New York, NY: Routledge.

Bhatia, S. (2007). Rethinking culture and identity in psychology: Towards a transnational cultural psychology. *Journal of theoretical and philosophical psychology, 27–28*, 301–321. http://dx.doi.org/10.1037/h0091298

Burman, E. (Ed.). (1998). *Deconstructing feminist psychology*. London, England: Sage. http://dx.doi.org/10.4135/9781446279243

Chen, A., & Gill, J. (2015). Unaccompanied children and the U.S. immigration system: Challenges and reforms. *Journal of International Affairs, 68*, 115–133.

Chisti, M., & Hipsman, F. (2015). The child and family migration surge of summer 2014: A short-lived crisis with a lasting impact. *Journal of International Affairs, 68*, 95–114.

Cole, E., Espín, O. M., & Rothblum, E. D. (Eds.). (1992). *Refugee women and their mental health: Shattered societies, shattered lives*. New York, NY: Haworth Press.

Collins, P. H. (1990). *Black feminist thought: Knowledge, consciousness and the politics of empowerment*. London, England: HarperCollins.

Cortina, J., & Ochoa-Reza, E. (2013). Women, children, and migration. In J. Cortina & E. Ochoa-Reza (Eds.), *New perspectives on international migration and development* (pp. 139–164). New York, NY: Columbia University Press. http://dx.doi.org/10.7312/columbia/9780231156806.003.0006

Crenshaw, K. (1997). Intersectionality and identity politics: Learning from violence against women of color. In W. K. Kolmar & F. Bartkowski (Eds.), *Feminist theory: A reader* (pp. 533–542). Boston, MA: McGraw-Hill.

Desai, J., Bouchard, D., & Detournay, D. (2010). Disavowed legacies and honorable thievery: The work of the "transnational" in feminist and LGBTQ studies. In A. L. Swarr & R. Nagar (Eds.), *Critical transnational feminist praxis* (pp. 46–62). Albany, NY: SUNY Press.

Donato, K. M., Gabaccia, D., Holdaway, J., Manalansan, M., & Pessar, P. (2006). A glass half full? Gender in migration studies. *The International Migration Review, 40*, 3–26. http://dx.doi.org/10.1111/j.1747-7379.2006.00001.x

Dottolo, A. L., & Stewart, A. J. (2008). "Don't ever forget now, you're a Black man in America": Intersections of race, class and gender in encounters with the police. *Sex Roles, 59,* 350–364. http://dx.doi.org/10.1007/s11199-007-9387-x

Dottolo, A. L., & Tillery, S. M. (2015). Reflexivity and research: Feminist interventions and their practical implications. In J. L. Amoreaux & B. J. Steele (Eds.), *Reflexivity and international relations: Positionality, critique, and practice* (pp. 123–141). New York, NY: Routledge. http://dx.doi.org/10.4324/9781315765013-7

Espín, O. M. (1991, August). *Ethnicity, race, class, and the future of feminist psychology.* Paper presented at the annual convention of the American Psychological Association, San Francisco, CA.

Espín, O. M. (1997). *Latina realities: Essays on healing, migration and sexuality.* Boulder, CO: Westview Press.

Espín, O. M. (1999). *Women crossing boundaries: A psychology of immigration and the transformations of sexuality.* New York, NY: Routledge.

Espín, O. M. (2005, January). *The age of the cookie cutter has passed: Contradictions in identity at the core of therapeutic intervention.* Paper presented at the National Multicultural Conference and Summit, Los Angeles, CA.

Espín, O. M. (2006). Gender, sexuality, language and migration. In R. Mahalingam (Ed.), *Cultural psychology of immigrants* (pp. 241–258). Mahwah, NJ: Erlbaum.

Espín, O. M. (2015). A geography of memory: A psychology of place. In O. M. Espín & A. L. Dottolo (Eds.), *Gendered journeys: Women, migration and feminist psychology* (pp. 29–53). London, England: Palgrave Macmillan. http://dx.doi.org/10.1057/9781137521477_2

Espín, O. M., & Dottolo, A. L. (Eds.). (2015). *Gendered journeys: Women, migration and feminist psychology.* London, England: Palgrave Macmillan. http://dx.doi.org/10.1057/9781137521477

Freire, P. (1970). *Pedagogy of the oppressed.* New York, NY: Continuum.

Grabe, S., & Else-Quest, N. (2012). The role of transnational feminism in psychology: Complementary visions. *Psychology of Women Quarterly, 36,* 158–161. http://dx.doi.org/10.1177/0361684312442164

Kawahara, D., & Espín, O. M. (Eds.). (2007). *Feminist reflections on growth and transformations: Asian-American women in therapy.* New York, NY: Haworth Press.

Kawahara, D., & Espín, O. M. (Eds.). (2012). *Feminist therapy with Latina women: Personal and social voices.* New York, NY: Routledge.

Kirschner, S. R., & Martin, J. (Eds.). (2010). *The sociocultural turn in psychology: The contextual emergence of mind and self.* New York, NY: Columbia University Press.

Kofman, E., Phizacklea, A., Raghuram, P., & Sales, R. (2000). *Gender and international migration in Europe: Employment, welfare and politics.* New York, NY: Routledge.

Kurtiş, T., & Adams, G. (2015). Decolonizing liberation: Toward a transnational feminist psychology. *Journal of Social and Political Psychology, 3*, 388–413. http://dx.doi.org/10.5964/jspp.v3i1.326

Levitt, P., & Schiller, N. G. (2008). Conceptualizing simultaneity: A transnational social field perspective on society. In S. Khagram & P. Levitt (Eds.), *The transnational studies reader: Intersections & innovations* (pp. 284–294). New York, NY: Routledge.

Magnusson, E., & Marecek, J. (2012). *Gender and culture in psychology: Theories and practices.* New York, NY: Cambridge University Press. http://dx.doi.org/10.1017/CBO9781139086318

Mahalingam, R., & Leu, J. (2005). Culture, essentialism, immigration and representations of gender. *Theory & Psychology, 15*, 839–862. http://dx.doi.org/10.1177/0959354305059335

Mahler, S., & Pessar, P. (2001). Gendered geographies of power: Analyzing gender across transnational spaces. *Identities, 7*, 441–459. http://dx.doi.org/10.1080/1070289X.2001.9962675

Marecek, J. (2003). Dancing through minefields: Toward a qualitative stance in psychology. In P. M. Camic, J. E. Rhodes, & L. Yardley (Eds.), *Qualitative research in psychology: Expanding perspectives in methodology and design* (pp. 46–69). Washington, DC: American Psychological Association. http://dx.doi.org/10.1037/10595-004

Mohanty, C. T. (2003). "Under Western eyes" revisited: Feminist solidarity through anticapitalist struggles. *Signs, 28*, 499–535. http://dx.doi.org/10.1086/342914

Murphy, E. J. (2006). Transnational ties and mental health. In R. Mahalingam (Ed.), *Cultural psychology of immigrants* (pp. 79–92). Mahwah, NJ: Erlbaum.

Narayan, U. (1997). *Dislocating cultures: Identities, traditions, and Third World feminism.* New York, NY: Routledge.

Pedraza, S. (2006). Assimilation or transnationalism? Conceptual models of the immigrant experience in America. In R. Mahalingam (Ed.), *Cultural psychology of immigrants* (pp. 33–53). Mahwah, NJ: Erlbaum.

Pessar, P. R. (2003). Engendering migration studies. In P. Hondagneu-Sotelo (Ed.), *Gender and U.S. migration* (pp. 20–42). Berkeley: University of California Press.

Phan, P. C. (2003). *Christianity with an Asian face: Asian American theology in the making.* New York, NY: Orbis Books.

Phillips, A. (2010). *Gender and culture.* Cambridge, England: Cambridge University Press.

Portes, A., Guarnizo, L. E., & Landolt, P. (2008). The study of transnationalism: Pitfalls and promises of an emergent research field. In S. Khagram & P. Levitt (Eds.), *The transnational studies reader: Intersections & innovations* (pp. 275–283). New York, NY: Routledge.

Pratt, G., & Yeoh, B. (2003). Transnational (counter) topographies. *Gender, Place and Culture, 10*, 159–166. http://dx.doi.org/10.1080/0966369032000079541

Rajagopalan, K. (2015). Global "undocumentedness." *Journal of International Affairs*, 68, 225–243.

Riofrio, J. D. (2015). *Continental shifts: Migration, representation, and the struggle for justice in Latin(o) America*. Austin: University of Texas Press.

Shields, S. A. (2008). Gender: An intersectional perspective. *Sex Roles*, 59, 301–311. http://dx.doi.org/10.1007/s11199-008-9501-8

Shweder, R. A. (1990). Cultural psychology: What is it? In J. W. Stigler, R. A. Shweder, & G. Herdt (Eds.), *Cultural psychology: Essays on comparative human development* (pp. 1–44). Cambridge, England: Cambridge University Press. http://dx.doi.org/10.1017/CBO9781139173728.002

Spivak, G. C. (1988). Can the subaltern speak? In C. Nelson & L. Grossberg (Eds.), *Marxism and the interpretation of culture* (pp. 271–313). Urbana: University of Illinois Press. http://dx.doi.org/10.1007/978-1-349-19059-1_20

Suárez-Orozco, C., & Qin, D. B. (2006). Gendered perspectives in psychology: Immigrant origin youth. *The International Migration Review*, 40, 165–198. http://dx.doi.org/10.1111/j.1747-7379.2006.00007.x

Swarr, A. L., & Nagar, R. (Eds.). (2010). Introduction: Theorizing transnational feminist praxis. In A. L. Swarr and R. Nagar (Eds.), *Critical transnational feminist praxis* (pp. 1–20). Albany, NY: SUNY Press.

United Nations. (2016). *International migration report 2015* (ST/ESA/SER.A/375). Retrieved from http://www.un.org/en/development/desa/population/migration/publications/migrationreport/docs/MigrationReport2015_Highlights.pdf

United Nations High Commission on Refugees. (2017). *Figures at a glance*. Retrieved from http://www.unhcr.org/en-us/figures-at-a-glance.html

Upegui-Hernández, D. (2012). What is missing in the transnational migration literature? A Latin American feminist psychological perspective. *Feminism & Psychology*, 22, 228–239. http://dx.doi.org/10.1177/0959353511415831

Veroff, J. B., & Goldberger, N. R. (1995). What's in a name? The case for "intercultural" psychology. In N. R. Goldberger & J. B. Veroff (Eds.), *The culture and psychology reader* (pp. 3–21). New York: New York University Press.

Winter, D. G. (1996). *Personality: Analysis and interpretation of lives*. New York, NY: McGraw-Hill.

Yeoh, B., & Ramdas, K. (2014). Gender, migration, mobility and transnationalism. *Gender, Place and Culture*, 21, 1197–1213. http://dx.doi.org/10.1080/0966369X.2014.969686

6

TRANSNATIONAL FEMINIST PERSPECTIVES ON WOMEN'S EDUCATION, WORK, AND LEADERSHIP

EDWINA PIO

Empower yourselves with a good education, then get out there and use
that education to build a country worthy of your boundless promise.
—Michelle Obama, "Michelle Obama to Young Americans:
Empower Yourselves With Education"

One book, one pen, one child, and one teacher can change the world.
—Malala Yousafzai, *I Am Malala: The Story of the Girl
Who Stood Up for Education and Was Shot by the Taliban*

The power by which the dominant knowledge system has subjugated all
others makes it exclusive and undemocratic.
—Vandana Shiva, *The Vandana Shiva Reader*

Women around the globe are devising and seeking opportunities for learning in multifarious ways. In the weaving of education, work, and leadership, many women are challenged by the interaction of globalization, family responsibilities, economic inequities, employment encounters, hegemonic "Western" lenses, and minimally responsive institutional and public policies. In addition, women's communities and sociopolitical contexts may constrain their abilities to compete, negotiate, and consider a smorgasbord of educational and occupational opportunities. Transnational feminist psychology is

http://dx.doi.org/10.1037/0000148-007
Transnational Psychology of Women: Expanding International and Intersectional Approaches, L. H. Collins,
S. Machizawa, and J. K. Rice (Editors)

an emerging domain, and its various avatars posit challenges and debates in its conceptualizations and terminology. Transnational feminist psychology intersects with tensions in the academic literature on feminism, psychology, and cultural studies and presents a multilayered puzzle that needs reconstruction and deconstruction to appreciate its genesis, its articulated responses, their interwoven components, and how these, in turn, shape new forms of empirical work and praxis in action.

This chapter presents an interpretation of literature on transnational feminist psychology; vignettes to highlight and decipher how transnational feminist psychology is enacted in the fields of education, work, and leadership for women, and the poignant hope for a future with pluralistic knowledge in and for each other. The chapter presents information that may be viewed as noncoherent by the guardians of hegemonic Western scholarship and knowledge; it is woven from up and down and through (Pio & Graham, 2018; Pio, Tipuna, Rasheed, & Parker, 2014) in seeking to present alternate realities that rupture "donor" models of magnanimity based on development aid and interventions (Grabe & Else-Quest, 2012; MacDonald, 2016) that often create generational crutches of dependency. For example, although advancing certain types of education is useful, the benefits and scalability are a far cry from the money poured into these interventions. I seek to move away from reinscribing homogenized images of Third World (or Majority World) girls and women who are perceived to need rescuing from poverty and oppression and hence constitute sites for investment from the Western, First, or Minority World. Although there is an impetus to disown labels of *First* and *Third World*, these labels continue to be used along with *Minority* and *Majority World*, as are images of diasporic women. Moving away from reinscribed homogenized images is a long journey, and what has been built up over centuries cannot be dismantled in a heartbeat or a single chapter.

On the basis of a quarter century of experience working and researching with women through qualitative methodologies in First and Third World settings, as a "Scholar of Color," I unfurl a collection of vignettes for reflection and praxis in action. This unfurling is illuminated against a backdrop that highlights how transnational feminist psychology seeks to rupture the homogeneity of Majority World women. This rupturing implicates the critical significance of the socioeconomic context within which women operate and negotiate their lived realities. These lived realities are depicted through the luminous and dark skeins of primary, secondary, and higher education in Majority World settings that impact notions of women and leadership. The poignant and pervasive hope in the eight vignettes is to create spirals of influence to facilitate alternative realities for diversely equitable educational, work, and leadership understandings of women globally. These alternatives include long-term solutions that holistically incorporate specific educational opportunities and skill sets within the spectrum of contexts in which girls and women breathe, survive, thrive, and flourish in their lives.

RUPTURING THE HOMOGENEITY
OF MAJORITY WORLD WOMEN THROUGH
TRANSNATIONAL FEMINIST PSYCHOLOGY

Nagar and Swarr (2010) argued for a transnational feminist praxis that is "critically aware of its own historical, geographical and political locations even as it is invested in alliances that are created and sustained through deeply dialogic and critically self-reflexive processes of knowledge production and dissemination" (p. 3). In the broadest possible sense, transnational feminist psychology emerges as a proposition made by Kurtiş and Adams (2015) to reexamine the postcolonial legacies of both feminism and psychology that, they suggested, have crafted a simple universal practice and a theory of liberation. Hence, current notions of women, their views, needs, and even pathologies are overshadowed by Western constructions that most of the time reflect the logic, desires, and depictions of White middle-class women in the industrialized world. Consequently, Kurtiş and Adams proposed a reconciliation between cultural psychology and postcolonial, transnational, feminist theories to provide a more comprehensive alternative to explore the complex relations between gender and culture. In "Decolonizing Liberation: Toward a Transnational Feminist Psychology," Kurtiş and Adams (2015) stated, "The liberatory impulse of feminist psychology falls short of its potential not only because of its grounding in neo-colonial legacies of hegemonic feminisms, but also because of its complicity with neo-colonial tendencies of hegemonic psychological science" (p. 388).

Such tendencies have shaped universal notions of women and gender oppression constructed in Western, educated, industrialized, rich democracies (or WEIRD) that not only fail to understand women in other cultures but also most of the time involve the idea that women in such other cultures are powerless or ignorant victims who look to their liberated sisters in WEIRD worlds for rescue. Yet, Kurtiş and Adams's (2015) critiques are hardly new. Years before them, a number of feminist scholars observed how postcolonial constructs of women had influenced not only the academic literature but also numerous social movements and the basis of policy design in many nongovernmental organizations and international organizations.

Chandra Mohanty, Gayatri Spivak, Uma Narayan, and I, together with many other scholars, initiated the articulation of a new type of feminist theory incorporating postcolonial views on gender (Mohanty, 2013; Narayan, 1998; Pio & Singh, 2016; Spivak, 1996). Postcolonial feminism explores the different contexts of women's lives, work, identity, and sexuality in light of colonialism and neocolonialism. The notion of a universal "woman," as well as the reification of the Third World "difference" that produces the "monolithic" Third World woman is contested. Postcolonial feminists have made reiterative calls to recognize differences and acknowledge the historical specificity of women's experiences in various times and places. Different constructs of women must go beyond promoting and reflecting the interests of a privileged minority in affluent centers (Adams, Dobles, Gómez, Kurtiş, & Molina, 2015).

Grabe and Else-Quest (2012) offered the concept of transnational intersectionality in studying power, gender, ethnicity, class, sexuality, and economic exploitation based on globalization and empire building through international macrolevel indicators and data. They stressed the need for resistance so that changes can be implemented according to social contexts and accountability.

Mainstream psychological propositions have traditionally accorded a key role to Western notions of women that resulted in the type of broad liberation theories opposed by postcolonial and transnational feminists. Indeed, Kurtiş and Adams (2015) argued that conventional psychological science pathologizes women's experience and portrays it as "other" to an androcentric norm. In this regard, "conventional varieties of feminist psychology generally share tendencies of conventional psychological science to either ignore Majority World women's experience or cast it as 'Other' to an ethnocentric norm" (p. 394). Such an approach limits the liberatory potential of feminist psychology and, at the same time, suggests its likelihood of reproducing systems of exclusion and domination to support psychology's claims of universality.

Despite divergent views, common concerns of transnational feminist psychology and its priorities and practices, other disciplines coalesce around ending gender oppression and creating spaces of possibility and agency (Else-Quest & Grabe, 2012; Kurtiş & Adams, 2013, 2015). In a nutshell, transnational feminist psychology takes as its primary standpoint that of people in Majority World settings to reimagine the liberatory potential of feminist psychological insights for complex and constantly changing societies. It signals attention to disrupting and destabilizing boundaries of race, nation, and gender (Kaplan & Grewal, 1999). Transnational feminist psychology does not disregard Minority World standpoints. The novel character of the emerging work in transnational feminist psychology means that it would be premature to claim an entire body of literature with common and widely shared methodological grounds. There are continuities—for instance, transnational feminist psychology linked to education can be feminism as radical praxis (Mohanty & Alexander, 2010), which ruptures narratives of inferiority, deficiency discourses of underachievement, poverty, and pathology linked to minority individuals. There is a surge toward research that is accountable and responsible through the various boundaries of nation-states (Kilpatrick & Pio, 2013; Okpalaoka & Dillard, 2012; Pio & Graham, 2018) and reciprocal dialogue with critical counterpoints through differently positioned feminists (Conway, 2017). The use of critical race theory and intersectionality along with perspectives from transnational feminist psychology can make the invisible visible in higher education to highlight the complex interdependent relationships between ethnicity, gender, and class resulting in achievement gaps (López, Erwin, Binder, & Chavez, 2018). It is important to note that voice and silence may not have global purchase and fluid interpretations may be closer to the reality of Majority World women's education, work, and leadership experiences (Peake & DeSouza, 2010; Pio & Singh, 2016). Please see previous chapters for further expositions of transnational feminist psychology.

LOCATING AND NEGOTIATING DEEP INEQUALITY

The range and complexity of challenges Global Majority women face are linked to gendered norms and structural systems of deep inequality in how such women are educated and the impact of these systems on their work and leadership trajectories, not only in their own source countries but also as diasporic women in First or Minority World settings. Although there are broad trends in locating and negotiating deep inequality, such as those presented in the yearly global gender gap reports (World Economic Forum, 2017), there is a need to constantly acknowledge the heterogeneity that exists in the Majority World with reference to gender, class, socioeconomic status, patterns of inequality, and access. Adjustments in the education sector by policy makers, with relevant content and meaningful delivery mechanisms, can result in increasing access to education and higher retention rates of learning, and thus serve as pathways to reduce inequality (Pio & Graham, 2018; Pio et al., 2014; Spear & da Costa, 2018).

CURRENT STATUS OF EDUCATIONAL ATTAINMENT

The World Economic Forum's (2017) global gender gap report indicated that although many countries have closed the gender gap in educational attainment, there continue to be wide gaps pertaining to out-of-school children of primary and secondary school age, educational attainment rates, and advanced and vocational degrees and variations across various fields of study. Among the 144 countries included in the Forum report, Chad is ranked the last among these countries at 144, Guinea at 143, Benin at 142, Yemen at 141, and Mali at 140. In terms of the gender gap or progress toward gender parity by region represented by the remaining gender gap or percentage needed to close this gap, the Middle East and North Africa are at 40%, South Asia at 34%, and sub-Saharan Africa at 32%, and these regions are classified as the developing world or Third World or Majority World (World Economic Forum [WEF], 2017).

The 2017 Global Gender Gap Report (WEF, 2017) noted that no single measure could adequately represent the complete situation of gender equality because inequality overlaps with a number of dimensions, including age, geography, caste, class, history, and education. In addition, the report "highlights that even though qualified women are coming out of the education system, many industries are failing to hire, retain and promote them, losing out on a wealth of capacity" (WEF, 2017, p. v). As the youngest Noble Peace prize winner, Malala Yousafzai, stressed, equality can start with education through one pen, one book, one teacher, which can make an enormous difference to improving opportunities for the girl child. Although this provision can initiate the road to equality, it can also be viewed as an easier option that massages altruism through a donor model (MacDonald, 2016) of dependency without providing long-term change. The more complex option is to move beyond such developmental initiatives and donor magnanimity. The easier option might be necessary to serve altruistic comfort with an evolutionary and slow rate of change, rather than offering sustainable change for enhanced opportunities and long-term well-being. But such progress would still be a far cry from recruiting women and moving them to leadership positions, particularly when this connotes praxis in action and destabilizes monolithic positions of power. Essentially, this chapter is a call to reflect on why we do what we do as transnational feminists in academia, business, community, and society. In the intersections of gender, work, and education, the socioeconomic context is vital to understand how (in)equality and poverty are knitted together resulting in large segments of our world lacking opportunity and accessibility for education, work, and leadership.

SOCIOECONOMIC CONTEXT

The Majority World continues to have challenging levels of poverty, lack of opportunities, and educational inequalities resulting in low attainment levels in education and social mobility, despite various development strategies and frameworks (Nakray, 2018; Tshabangu, 2018). Poverty issues impacting educational inequalities include overreliance on external donor aid, child labor, gendered inequalities, inadequate investments, and political and military conflict (Tshabangu, 2018). In sub-Saharan Africa, for example, being a girl might translate into being asked to drop out of school in preference for boys in the family attending school and not just expectations for early marriage but being married at an early age, doing household chores, and looking after younger children (Tshabangu, 2018). Njoh et al. (2018) emphasized the importance of electricity supply, access to water, and improved sanitation as crucial determinants for girls to attend school so that they are not overburdened by domestic chores. Hence, more time can be devoted to formal education rather than to fetching fuel wood and water, cooking and washing clothes, and looking after young children. Despite these varied and unique barriers, which seem insurmountable in traversing the road to equality, the strength, talent, and resourcefulness of many women in these difficult contexts challenge images of victimhood and instead highlight resourcefulness and creative ways of accessing education and opportunities.

PRIMARY SCHOOL ENROLLMENT

Transnational feminist psychology tends to focus on the particularities of communities; hence it is likely to show differences in how primary school enrollment takes place in various communities, countries, and regions. Psaki, McCarthy, and Mensch (2018), examining trends in gender and education policy outcomes in 24 sub-Saharan African countries, accentuated the need for a deeper understanding of school enrolment, grade attainment, and learning to understand gender inequalities in education truly. Increases in primary school enrolment are not necessarily linked to learning outcomes and post-primary school opportunities. Girls continue to face barriers pertaining to pregnancy, early marriage, and child-rearing responsibilities. There are gaps in grade attainment, progression, dropout, and ability to read and uneven enrolment, though this differs by specific education setting and variability among communities. Male advantage in labor markets continues. UNESCO's Education 2030 agenda (UNESCO, 2016) emphasizes not only school attendance but also the development and retention of key skills such as literacy and numeracy.

Gender-based exclusion from education (Nakray, 2018) in India continues to prevail, with political rhetoric and legislative frameworks barely touching the lives of girls in marginalized communities. The pervasive influence of caste, religion, ethnicity, and gendered hierarchies emphasizes the fact that "lack of access and adverse learning outcomes result in a lifetime of deprivation" (Nakray, 2018, p. 27). India has a sex ratio of 940 females to 1,000 males with a child sex ratio of 914 females per 1,000 males (Census 2011, 2011); female feticide and dowry continue to exert a strong influence in Indian communities. Although narratives of rape may exclude feminist activism, it is no secret that gender imbalance may lead men to seek sexual gratification through rape, female molestation, and acid violence and women in such contexts to commit suicide or remain outcasts stigmatized because of their sexual "impurity" (Bradley, Sahariah, & Siddiqui, 2017; Pio & Singh, 2016).

The problems in India are immense despite initiatives such as *Lek Soniyachi* (Precious Daughter) and *Apni Beti Apna Dhan* (My Girl, Our Wealth), which provide cash transfers to mothers on the birth of a girl child (USD 7) and savings bonds redeemable at 18 to 21 years (varying from USD 350 to USD 10,000), with payments for primary and secondary education. These educational schemes, although commendable, are unfortunately not carefully linked to the national education programs (Nakray, 2018); hence, they run the risk of not being able to deliver in the long run, according to the vagaries of political parties in power. Conditional cash transfer programs, which are conditional on children attending school for a specified time, are effective in increasing primary school enrolment and attendance in marginalized communities in Bolivia (Bauchet, Undurraga, Reyes-García, Behrman, & Godoy, 2018). These programs are dependent on the utility of formal schooling, the language in which the curriculum is taught, parents' ability to interact with teachers, cultural norms, trust in government officials, and costs of reaching school in terms of physical access (Bauchet et al., 2018). Circumnavigating these obstacles involves meaningful content in the local language and honoring cultural norms while negotiating their interpretation so that both girls and boys can enjoy the benefits of early education.

Langsten and Hassan (2018), in their study of trends and determinants of primary education completion in Egypt, emphasized that children from wealthy families have achieved universal primary education, and although educational attainment for girls and boys from rural areas has improved, there is a need to focus on the education of poor urban boys who seem to be left behind in commitments for education for all. Transnational feminist psychology seeks to get into the specific circumstances within communities to better understand situations and how community members and allies might improve them. Hence, it is in this scenario of specifics that a study on gender roles depicted in school books is presented, with the hope that varied scripts and images of roles girls can embrace in thinking about the future for employment and careers can be enhanced. Islam and Asadullah (2018), in a comparative content analysis of Malaysian, Indonesian, Pakistani, and Bangladeshi school textbooks, showcased how gender stereotypes in education confirm a pro-male bias, though there was country variation. For example, in their textbooks or recommended study books, Bangladesh had teacher, lawyer, TV anchor, social scientist, and queen for female professions; Malaysia had teacher and maid; Indonesia had singer and dancer; and Pakistan had nurse, midwife, poetess, and author. Female occupations depicted are mostly traditional and less prestigious, and there is an underrepresentation of females in both text and pictures, with portrayals of them being passive, subordinate, and submissive. Women are likely to be shown in service-oriented occupations with a limited range of roles, whereas men are shown in power-oriented activities with a wide array of roles and portrayed as visionary and legendary.

In considering primary education, there has been some success in student enrollment in majority countries due to free primary education, despite uneven learning outcomes. The large populations in these countries now set their sights on secondary education and connections to employment opportunities.

SECONDARY EDUCATION

Secondary enrollment rates in South Asia and sub-Saharan Africa continue to remain low (Cosentino, 2017). In a study conducted in Andhra Pradesh, India, Singh and Mukherjee (2018) investigated gender inequity in secondary education. Their article, titled "Whatever She May Study, She Can't Escape From Washing Dishes," emphasized that engaging in more than 2 hours of domestic work and paid work at the age of 12 years disadvantages girls in their educational outcomes, as does son preference in the case of India. This results in high dropout rates and poor attendance of girls relative to boys. Furthermore, socioeconomic status determines enrolment in education, and children from tribal areas and lower castes are less likely to transition from primary to secondary education. Thus, gender inequality intersects with other forms of disadvantage such as caste hierarchy and cultural mores. Improving learning and making sure that youth remain in school and learn necessitates enhanced curriculum relevance and stronger youth networks with more supportive cultural norms to achieve better educational outcomes (Cosentino, 2017).

Khurshid (2016) discussed domesticated gender inequality in Pakistan. Although educated (*pari likhi*) women in Pakistan achieve higher status and function in public spaces, they are also expected to be models of perfection with respect to their domestic role. However, in the process, they reproduce gender hierarchies in relation to uneducated (*unparh*) women, who are often excluded from decision making. This emphasizes that women's role in the domestic sphere has hardly changed, with women continuing to be primarily responsible for child-rearing and household work. For some individuals, migration serves as an opportunity to have access to education and work opportunities they are unlikely to have in their home countries (Pio & Essers, 2014; Walker, 2018). It is pertinent to note that the populations in the Majority World number in billions, hence although a few individuals do go "West" to the Minority World, these numbers are minuscule compared with those who remain in the Majority World. However, many of those formally educated individuals who do go West continue to be activists through their writing and research projects and other forms of engagement with the Majority World settings, specifically their source countries. Thus, Malala Yousafzai, quoted in the epigraph, now lives in the West but continues to work for girls in Pakistan and internationally; Vandana Shiva lectures around the world and has written over a dozen books in English but resides in India from where she continues her leadership role in environmental activism.

The emphasis on migration is linked to students from the Majority World who increasingly populate the portals of secondary and higher education in the Minority World (NAFSA, 2019). These international students are a significant source for maintaining the economic viability of schools and universities in the Minority World (Education Counts, 2018). In addition, India, according to data from 2015, has the largest number of migrants in Saudi Arabia working in construction, manufacturing, retail, domestic work, and health care, where they number 2,800,000. In the United States, they number 1,272,846 and work in education, information technology, software, hotels, and health. In Australia, they number 251,000, and in New Zealand, they number 45,000, working in education, health, and retail (National Skills Development Agency [NSDA], 2018).

Although India has a strong economy, its per capita income is among the lowest in the world, and there is low labor participation for its population of over 1.2 billion individuals (NSDA, 2018). There are 42 million international migrants who were born in Asia and currently live elsewhere, with India having the largest diaspora, or number of people living outside its borders (16.6 million persons), followed by Mexico, the Russian Federation, and China (United Nations, 2017). India is the top source of international migrants, with one in 20 migrants worldwide born in India, though it has one of the world's lowest emigration rates; only about one percent of those born in India live outside the country (Connor, 2017). India's religious minorities are more likely to migrate; about 19% of Indian migrant population is Christian, though the Christian population in India is only 3% (Connor, 2017). Migratory mobility highlights the intersection of gender, religion, and educational opportunities in the search for converting dreams into reality with spirals of influence for current and future generations of women.

HIGHER EDUCATION

Feminist agency is significant in counteracting institutional resistance to change and to mainstream gender in higher education to change the rules of the game (Verge, Ferrer-Fons, & González, 2018). This translates into the integration of gendered content in the curriculum to problematize current gendered norms and roles to expose, reinterpret, and challenge gendered stereotypes. In Bangladesh, for example, despite having higher education, women are unable to convert this education into appropriate employment (Ahmed & Hyndman-Rizk, 2018). Limited information technology competence, stereotyped subject selection, limited career aspirations, and lack of relevant job skills are identified as constraints in labor force participation. Although there are more women of color in academia in universities, female professors are underrepresented in higher ranks (Beddoes & Schimpf, 2018). Student experiences in higher education are varied, but a hegemonic discourse linked to Western ways of knowledge continues to be pervasive in curricula, supervision practices, and writing conventions (Corner & Pio, 2017; Keiha & Pio, 2015). University communities support gender inequalities through professional socialization discourses and standards that often disadvantage women who must balance work and family responsibilities. These discourses embed power relations that govern how topics can be discussed and which topics can be discussed within hegemonic ideas about fairness, collective good, and training (Beddoes & Schimpf, 2018). Hence, although women with higher qualifications have more job mobility, Women of Color still have to struggle for parity with their White sisters (Pio et al., 2014). Many women Scholars of Color in universities enact leadership for social justice to break inequitable patterns and connect with both their internal and external stakeholders (Murakami, Jean-Marie, Santamaría, & Lopez, 2017).

WOMEN AND LEADERSHIP

In writings about postfeminist sensibility, there is an emphasis on fluidity, flexibility, and subjectivity for a range of contexts and disciplines (Riley, Evans, Elliot, Rice, & Marecek, 2017). Hence, for example, more Women of Color are advancing to senior leadership positions in U.S. academe while holding onto their language, culture, and heritage and serving as role models for future generations (Huang, 2017). Enns (2010) observed how postmodernism has pushed scholars toward a questioning attitude and careful scrutiny of dominant knowledge claims, especially "those that imply that 'truth' or the 'self' can be understood as stable, ahistorical, or universal" (p. 334).

Postmodern feminism, she contended, should reject the search for a universal or distinctive female standpoint and accent how meaning is invented, structured, and renegotiated and how persons in authority maintain control over meanings. Mabokela and Mlambo (2017) highlighted race and gender disparities in academic leadership in Africa, despite increasing gender and race representation in enrolment in higher education, pointing out that universities have to harness their talented women to be globally competitive in the educational sector.

The next section translates and exemplifies the issues and tensions discussed through scholarship on women's education, work, and leadership, through voices of vignettes, which showcase and breathe life into major insights of transnational feminist psychology. The vignettes unfurl reflection and praxis in action through actual experiences and voices of Majority World women. As stated at the outset, this chapter is woven through with threads from research and experience and moves away from the more traditional or hegemonic linear positioning of chapters which are organized as a theoretical framework, methodology, findings, discussion, and conclusion. This is an attempt to move away from Minority World knowledge presentation to one where the world is experienced in a nonlinear fashion to encourage talking, reflection, and dialogue as equals, irrespective of one's geographical origins. This weaving is a threshold mat to move between First, or Minority, and Third, or Majority, Worlds.

As I write, I keep in mind that despite some porosity, the Minority Worlds continue to assert their dominance in how education, work, and leadership are enacted. It is with this backdrop that women seek to be educated and work in ways that may resemble Minority or First Worlds to gain acceptance and acknowledgment in the worlds of work and leadership (Pio, Kilpatrick, & LeFevre, 2017). Changing the rules of the game, or deconstructing the dominant lens, requires persistence, courage, and compassion. This is all the more applicable for those women who have had the luxury to be educated and who do not have to worry about a square meal a day, garments to clothe themselves, and a roof over their head—or translated into Hindi, one of the languages of India, minimal worry regarding *roti, kapda, aur makan*.

Of note in rule changing is the hegemonic use of *America*, which has come to primarily mean the United States of America, even though America includes South, Central, and North America. Emancipating this word from its current usage in common parlance and academic writing requires constant explanation, definitions, negotiations, and transitioning between worlds and words. Configurations of inequality are complex, systemic, structural, and multilevel (Collins, 2009), and there are only partial answers. It is with this paradoxical situation in mind that the voices of vignettes are to be read, gazed at, and reflected on.

VOICES OF VIGNETTES THROUGH THE IMPETUS
OF TRANSNATIONAL FEMINIST PSYCHOLOGY

The theoretical approaches tapped into by transnational feminist psychology, taken together, provide a lens through which we can see how women experience shifts of power and perspectives in their individual histories. Their accounts serve as processes of gazing back to shift positions of power and emphasize that local and global, First and Third Worlds are not necessarily fixed (Pio & Essers, 2014). In identifying myself as a Scholar of Color, I hold my hands out to entwine with Western feminist scholars whose intentions and actions mesh in their quest for not only better Western futures but also better futures for all women across the globe, premised on the notion that not all women want to work, not all women want formal education, and not all women consider men as oppressors and perpetrators of violence to body, mind, and soul (Pio & Essers, 2014). The voices of eight women, each in their unique contexts, are unfurled through three strands—education, work, and leadership. Despite their hegemonic use, the commonly understood *First* and *Third World* are terms sprinkled in the vignettes along with their counterparts *Minority* and *Majority*. This decision has not been taken lightly and has been made in the interests of the reader delving deeper into the core connotation of each vignette, rather than being "stuck" on the denotative word form. For clarity, the vignettes are organized within one of these dominant strands, but the women's accounts in full weave the themes together and provide insights into alternate patterns of pluralistic knowledge. Pseudonyms from the world of gems have been used to highlight the sparkle of diversity when viewed through transnational feminist psychology: What does it mean to be a refugee in education? What does it mean to be a migrant in education? How can these questions be answered with language that captures the varieties of ways women have demonstrated their enduring strengths across historically situated economic and social global contexts?

Education: Turquoise, Sapphire, and Emerald

Turquoise came to the country as a geographical, linguistic, and religious refugee, a child born in Pakistan to Middle Eastern refugees with dreams in their eyes, lashings on their backs, and the discomfort of negotiating numerous boundaries. Multiple geographies, multiple languages, and the Islamic faith formed the omnipresent backdrop of Turquoise's existence. She lived with her parents in a small village on the outskirts of a large city in Pakistan. Education for girls was frowned on, but her parents insisted that she go to the local school, and thus she was able to complete her early education. Her family had minimal resources, but they spent time with her in the evenings talking about the myths and legends of their homeland and giving thanks for being alive, with gratitude to the Pakistani people for letting them stay in Pakistan. In her adolescent years, she was selected to fly into a First World, English-speaking country with her parents. English was her fourth language when she went to secondary school. She looked different and behaved differently and was constantly teased. She spoke differently and brought in different food—different from the standard of "White" and different from the majority—and hence ridicule and bullying were her constant companions. But she learned to stand tall, to have multiple identities, and to seek a legal qualification at a prestigious university. She dressed like the majority culture because she felt that there were skirmishes to be engaged in beyond dress, and today she works with the Human Rights Commission and has been awarded a prestigious scholarship to do a master's degree in an Ivy League university in the United States. She is the founder of a nongovernmental organization for refugees from her source country and constantly speaks at public forums to shatter the notion of the "poor refugee woman who lives on state handouts."

Sapphire, too, came to a First World country as a refugee. She took a dangerous trip by sea, changing numerous boats, all of which were deemed nonseaworthy, accompanied by her parents and siblings, in a desperate attempt to evade conflict in her source country and enter an English-speaking, safe, and secure First World country. She was a child when she entered this new country and did her primary, secondary, and higher education through the institutions in this First World country. She speaks more than one language, wears the veil, and has made a documentary about her boat experiences as a research component for her undergraduate degree. She has a job in the education sector that continues to allow her access to higher education in a First World country. She supports other refugees through sharing her story and is proud to share information about her source country, religion, and food. She stated, "Don't save me! Provide access to opportunities."

Emerald is a legally resident migrant with two children and three grandchildren. She does not speak fluent English and cannot write in English, but her children and grandchildren are fluent in English as well as the language of their source country. She completed her primary education in a Majority World country in the local dialect of her region. She did not complete secondary education because she had to look after her siblings and was tasked with preparing the meals for her large joint family. In the new country, she learned English through nonformal education, such as free English classes for migrants, when she had the time to go to those classes. She has put her culinary skills to use and works as a chef of traditional foods in a café every evening and on alternate mornings spends time with two households cooking vegetarian food for their meals. She is proud of her achievements and would not dream of taking a handout. She has maintained her culture, language, and religion (Hinduism) while ensuring that her progeny have the cultural and linguistic skills to function and flourish in a First World country. She would not want to live again in her source country because she enjoys the gender equity and peace of her new country. She misses the reliable, cheap, and frequent transport in her home country. Her stumbling block is driving, and so she continues to use the unreliable public transport in this First World country. She stated, "Many women in my source country are uneducated. We want basic education, and we can then work with dignity."

These three vignettes show how agency is used to circumvent the images of "typical" Majority or Third World settings pertaining to lack of education, low levels of education, and accessibility to formal schooling, as well as images symbolically represented by non-White and non–English-speaking accents, which present an overriding imagery of victimhood and inadequacy.

Work: Quartz and Amethyst

Quartz, a postgraduate solo mother with two children, was determined to make a new life for herself. All her education in her source country was in English, and she is a Christian. From a Third World country, she obtained work in a First World, English-speaking country with the help of the church to which she belonged. The church provided her with emotional, financial, and other support while she honed her qualifications to be a certified teacher. She learned the Indigenous language of the original people of the land (sometimes referred to as *tribal people*) in which she now resides, and she is a fluent speaker and writer of English. Schools sought her expertise because her linguistic and cultural sensitivity ensured she was comfortable dealing with children who had violence at home and who continued to repeat the cycle of violence in school. Her stumbling block was driving, which she eventually surmounted—a cause for celebration. Today she continues to work with the church, schools, and underprivileged children from the First, Second, or Third World. Her vacations are spent in Third World countries educating women and children on literacy basics through cultural and religious acknowledgment. She stated, "*First* and *Third Worlds* are easy terms to understand some aspects of our lives, but they should not be used as lazy terms to homogenize women."

Amethyst wanted a more gender-equitable society to live in—her path for migration was through education. She has a doctorate and works in the higher education sector where she continues to experience a default mode of White hegemony and Western conceptualizations in interpreting pedagogy and student engagement. On many days, she goes home and cries because she is exhausted from jumping through hoops that her White Western counterparts do not have to go through or from the numerous times colleagues forget to include her on published lists for expertise or forget to send her e-mails that are sent to other colleagues. In the larger scheme of things, she knows that staying in this First World country and working in the higher education sector is a privilege. This is her choice, instead of going back to her source country. In her current leadership position, she is a role model and mentor to migrant ethnic women and suggests various alternatives to them in their search for education, work, and leadership. She continues to travel internationally and collaborate with international scholars. Her talks at various public fora and regarding policy interventions are part of her community outreach to disrupt notions of the weak, submissive, nonliterate migrant Third World woman. She stated, "Reflect on why you do what you do to 'other' women irrespective of their color, religion, and source country. If we dream and act in concert, we can truly change our worlds."

These two vignettes illustrate the life choices available to highly educated Majority or Third World women who live in Minority or First World settings. Neither Quartz nor Amethyst came from privileged backgrounds; they were ordinary, middle-class women in their source countries. The narratives highlight stumbling blocks not often problematized in transnational scholarship, including advocacy for social justice, the daily veiled insults from colleagues, transportation difficulties, and the challenges of confronting ubiquitous stereotypes.

Leadership: Citrine, Topaz, and Tanzanite

Citrine was an editor for a glossy magazine in the English language with a wide circulation in her source country, but her family wanted to live in a First World country, so they made the journey to this First World, English-speaking country as legally resident immigrants. She suffered tremendously because she looked like "a typical migrant," and despite her credentials, she was not recognized for her expertise. Her employers assumed that because she was from a Third World country, she would have to be coached to achieve the standards of the literary publications in the new country. Her employers soon realized that she could spin a story better than her "senior colleagues," and so she rose in the organization. But her dreams were short lived because she was constantly asked to prove herself, and junior colleagues thought she was just a token. Unable to take this barrage of stereotyping on a daily basis, she left the organization. She continued working in media as a freelancer, however, and today is employed by a media organization where she is the chief editor. Her family provides a net of emotional support to her. Interestingly, because her husband does not drive, she does the driving when they have to use the car. She credits much of her success to her husband and family who have supported her in her various media roles. What she misses most is the glitz and glamour of her high status in her Third World source country, a status based on her reputation and competence. In the First World receiving country, however, she rarely gets invited to such high-profile events. She stated, "Our men can be very supportive. We have to learn to renegotiate silence and patriarchy to give a little and take a little and sometimes let our hearts break a little as we live out our lives." Citrine was not fleeing conflict, war, famine, persecution, or difficult personal circumstances, but she chose to live in a First World country because she felt there would be less corruption, systems that worked, and more gender parity. Although she enjoys these aspects of her new homeland, she misses the occupational parity she had achieved with her colleagues in her highly competitive job in her source country.

Topaz wanted a new life, having faced many problems on a personal front in her source country. She did her research and knew she had a strongly accented spoken English, which in her host country was frowned on. Therefore, on reflection, she realized she would have to hone skills that favored her expertise, and because she had done some work as a beautician in her source country, she chose a similar trade in the host country. She completed several certificate courses in beauty treatments and then worked in a specialized beauty parlor that used alternative therapies similar to those in her source country. She received the support of her mother who encouraged her to open her own enterprise. In a few years, she opened her own beauty parlor and today owns a string of beauty parlors in one of the commercial centers of her receiving country, sources beauty products from her home country, and provides beautician-certified courses for which she employs White and non-White instructors. She is married and has a daughter. She has won awards for her business acumen. Her English continues to be heavily accented, she does not drive, and she does not intend to seek any further formal education. She stated, "I am happy here. I work hard and do not want to look back. My daughter has a better future here."

These two vignettes underscore the contentment that Third World women find in the First World with the opportunities to create a new life in a new country and the importance of not stigmatizing all men with the broad brushstroke of being autocratic and aggressive because it is in a community of both men and women that we live out our lives.

The final vignette is of Tanzanite, a highly educated woman with a postgraduate degree from her Third World source country, who migrated along with her highly educated and professionally qualified wealthy entrepreneurial family to a First World country. Tanzanite worked for some time in the hospitality industry because she was unable to get employment in her specialization, finance. She was intensely involved in community work for the less fortunate of her community in this First World country. Later, she attained postgraduate qualification in health care and worked in a hospital. She loved the work, and her colleagues treated her well. She felt called to go back to her Third World source country, however, and now works in a leadership position in a not-for-profit community organization. Tanzanite epitomizes the majority of highly educated women in Third World countries who choose to stay in the Third World country because of family ties, property, and their ability to have continuity in their contributions to their families, community, and society. They do not feel the need to immigrate to a First or Minority World county and they are not prepared to go through the rituals of being stereotyped based on skin color and accent and colonial mind-sets that give more credence to White women in the matrix of power in organizations and First or Minority World societies.

TRANSNATIONAL FEMINIST VISION: SPIRALS OF INFLUENCE IN A CONSTANTLY CHANGING WORLD

Reflecting on the experiences and perspectives in these vignettes, I emphasize that the voices emerge from dynamic relational processes of articulating one's positionality and power, and they can be used to garner support for poignant, pervasive radical feminist praxis (Kurtiş & Adams, 2015; Pio & Essers, 2014). I have presented an introduction to transnational feminism and explained the theory and themes—work, education, leadership—with multiple vignettes, to illustrate some of the context encountered by women in Majority and Minority World settings. The goal is to rupture hegemonic ways of perceiving women. In locating and negotiating deep inequality in the Majority World and barriers related to educational and economic global disparities, I highlight the situation of the girl child and the need for critical pedagogic frameworks to meaningfully transform gendered norms, structures, and institutionalized discourses at all levels of education. Consideration also has to be paid to the sociohistorical and economic legacies within which such gendered disparities are embedded.

The vignettes are presented to disrupt notions of underprivileged women from Majority World settings who need handouts and are inferior and lacking in voice. Including their narratives is meant to introduce dialogue about changing centers and margins, shifting geographical boundaries, and differing meanings. In giving them a voice, there is more than they voice as the vignettes, whereas being specific also encompasses the entanglement of women at meso- and macrolevel world settings. In the transformations of education, work, and leadership for ourselves and our sisters, daughters, aunties, mothers, grandmothers, and partners, there is the dream of a world where fluid realities are honored and blessed, where each day is an opportunity to reinvest and replenish our spirits and souls as we reach out to each other.

Transnational transformation can take place one day at a time, while also being deeply informed by long-term strategies and realities. There is no one best practice. Instead, I emphasize the need for multiple pathways that move toward a world where we breathe more easily, where there is more compassionate harmony and more evocative access to education, work, and leadership, worlds where our transnational feminist lenses become second nature, our third eye guiding us in the way we frame our work and behaviors to create spirals of influence with and through our colleagues, organizations, communities, and the many contexts in which we live our lives. Although theorists will see many of the approaches as problematic in some ways, the radical praxis necessary for transformation and creating spirals of influence is on-the-ground actions with enactment and performance of daily change for a more egalitarian planet.

Critical race theorists interrogate configurations of inequality and emphasize a sociohistorical context to reveal the lower likelihood of graduation for all individuals compared with high-income White women, though this excludes high-income Hispanic and Asian women (López et al., 2018). Critical race theory insists that racism is systemic, structural, multilevel, and not only limited to everyday forms of racism at individual levels (Collins, 2009). This is in line with transnational feminist psychology, which seeks to highlight the need to name, renegotiate, and reconstruct cultural and symbolic images of women and address structural inequalities in meaningful ways.

It is in this context that teacher training programs and their education can serve as transformative pathways for rupturing gendered norms to sustain new images of girls and women. Teacher training programs must include critical pedagogic frameworks if they are to be transformative in dismantling deep-seated beliefs about gender norms (Spear & da Costa, 2018). Education of teachers is crucial because they bring with them overt and covert beliefs and behaviors into the classroom; hence the importance of gender awareness training through deconstructing gender privileges and power and a deeper understanding of disenfranchised communities through productive dialogue and behavioral shifts in the classroom (Spear & da Costa, 2018). Gender inequality in education is emphasized in conflict-ridden areas such as Uganda, but gender-responsive approaches to education can enable peace building and gender equality (Datzberger & Le Mat, 2018). These women have unequal land rights and restricted access to justice and face sexual and domestic violence, often reinforced through structural barriers. Although primary education is achievable, there are wide gaps in secondary and tertiary education for girls. Supportive curricula that are gender sensitive and gender transformative, as well as more women in teaching professions, are initiatives that encourage gender equality and serve as pathways for empowerment and fracturing normalization of gender violence and inequality. Datzberger and Le Mat (2018) encouraged addressing root causes of structural inequalities with emphasis on sociohistorical causes and consequences, rather than an add-women-and-stir approach that does not holistically address women's issues.

Spirals of influence are not snobbish about terms of usage, and there is no animosity in how people choose to enact their pathways as women. There is a move to agency, to activating the pipeline rather than squashing it for leadership so that women are both shapers and receivers of making the world a better place for living with and for each other. Why do we do what we do? For our children, our sons and daughters who inherit our fragile planet.

REFERENCES

Adams, G., Dobles, I., Gómez, L. H., Kurtiş, T., & Molina, L. E. (2015). Decolonizing psychological science: Introduction to the special thematic section. *Journal of Social and Political Psychology*, 3, 213–238. http://dx.doi.org/10.5964/jspp.v3i1.564

Ahmed, R., & Hyndman-Rizk, N. (2018). The higher education paradox: Towards improving women's empowerment, agency development and labour force participation in Bangladesh. *Gender and Education*, 1–19. Advance online publication. http://dx.doi.org/10.1080/09540253.2018.1471452

Bauchet, J., Undurraga, E. A., Reyes-García, V., Behrman, J. R., & Godoy, R. A. (2018). Conditional cash transfers for primary education: Which children are left out? *World Development*, 105, 1–12. http://dx.doi.org/10.1016/j.worlddev.2017.12.021

Beddoes, K., & Schimpf, C. (2018). What's wrong with fairness? How discourses in higher education literature support gender inequalities. *Discourse*, 39, 31–40. http://dx.doi.org/10.1080/01596306.2016.1232535

Bradley, T., Sahariah, S., & Siddiqui, O. (2017). A critical reading of western newspaper narratives of rape in India and their implications for feminist activism. *Continuum*, 31, 126–137. http://dx.doi.org/10.1080/10304312.2016.1231787

Census 2011. (2011). *Population Census 2011*. Retrieved from https://www.census2011.co.in/

Collins, P. H. (2009). *Black feminist thought: Knowledge, consciousness and the politics of empowerment*. New York, NY: Routledge.

Connor, P. (2017). *India is a top source and destination for world's migrants*. Retrieved from http://www.pewresearch.org/fact-tank/2017/03/03/india-is-a-top-source-and-destination-for-worlds-migrants/

Conway, J. M. (2017). Troubling transnational feminism(s): Theorising activist praxis. *Feminist Theory*, 18, 205–227. http://dx.doi.org/10.1177/1464700117700536

Corner, P., & Pio, E. (2017). Supervising international students' theses and dissertations. *Academy of Management Learning & Education*, 16, 23–38. http://dx.doi.org/10.5465/amle.2015.0054

Cosentino, C. (2017). Supporting secondary education in developing nations. *Mathematica Policy Research*. Retrieved from https://www.mathematica-mpr.com/commentary/supporting-secondary-education-in-developing-nations

Datzberger, S., & Le Mat, M. L. J. (2018). Just add women and stir? Education, gender and peacebuilding in Uganda. *International Journal of Educational Development*, 59, 61–69. http://dx.doi.org/10.1016/j.ijedudev.2017.09.006

Education Counts. (2018). *Tertiary education*. Retrieved from https://www.educationcounts.govt.nz/statistics/tertiary-education

Else-Quest, N. M., & Grabe, S. (2012). The political is personal: Measurement and application of nation-level indicators of gender equity in psychological research. *Psychology of Women Quarterly*, 36, 131–144. https://dx.doi.org/10.1177/0361684312441592

Enns, C. Z. (2010). Locational feminisms and feminist social identity analysis. *Professional Psychology: Research and Practice*, 41, 333. http://dx.doi.org/10.1037/a0020260

Grabe, S., & Else-Quest, N. M. (2012). The role of transnational feminism in psychology: Complementary visions. *Psychology of Women Quarterly*, 36, 158–161. http://dx.doi.org/10.1177/0361684312442164

Huang, B. L. (2017). Woman of colour advancing to senior leadership in US academe. In H. Eggins (Ed.), *The changing role of women in higher education* (pp. 155–172). New York, NY: Springer. http://dx.doi.org/10.1007/978-3-319-42436-1_8

Islam, K. M. M., & Asadullah, M. N. (2018). Gender stereotypes and education: A comparative content analysis of Malaysian, Indonesian, Pakistani and Bangladeshi school textbooks. *PLoS One*, 13(1), e0190807. http://dx.doi.org/10.1371/journal.pone.0190807

Kaplan, C., & Grewal, I. (1999). Transnational feminist cultural studies: Beyond the Marxism/poststructuralism/feminism divides. In C. Kaplan, N. Alarcón, & M. Moallem (Eds.), *Between women and nation: Nationalism, transnational feminisms, and the state* (pp. 349–363). Durham, NC: Duke University Press.

Keiha, P., & Pio, E. (2015). For whose purposes do we educate? Wairua in business schools. In C. Mabey & W. Mayrhofer (Eds.), *Developing leadership: Questions business schools don't ask* (p. 189). London, England: Sage. http://dx.doi.org/10.4135/9781473919983.n16

Khurshid, A. (2016). Domesticated gender (in) equality: Women's education and gender relations among rural communities in Pakistan. *International Journal of Educational Development*, 51, 43–50. http://dx.doi.org/10.1016/j.ijedudev.2016.08.001

Kilpatrick, R., & Pio, E. (2013). I want to touch the sky: How an enterprise challenges stigma for sex-workers. *Equality, Diversity and Inclusion, 32,* 277–288. http://dx.doi.org/10.1108/EDI-12-2012-0114

Kurtiş, T., & Adams, G. (2013). A cultural psychology of relationship: Toward a transnational feminist psychology. In M. K. Ryan & N. R. Branscombe (Eds.), *The Sage handbook of gender and psychology* (pp. 251–269). London, England: Sage. http://dx.doi.org/10.4135/9781446269930.n16

Kurtiş, T., & Adams, G. (2015). Decolonizing liberation: Toward a transnational feminist psychology. *Journal of Social and Political Psychology, 3,* 388–413. http://dx.doi.org/10.5964/jspp.v3i1.326

Langsten, R., & Hassan, T. (2018). Primary education completion in Egypt: Trends and determinants. *International Journal of Educational Development, 59,* 136–145. http://dx.doi.org/10.1016/j.ijedudev.2017.10.013

López, N., Erwin, C., Binder, M., & Chavez, M. J. (2018). Making the invisible visible: Advancing quantitative methods in higher education using critical race theory and intersectionality. *Race, Ethnicity and Education, 21,* 180–207. http://dx.doi.org/10.1080/13613324.2017.1375185

Mabokela, R. O., & Mlambo, Y. A. (2017). Women, leadership, and organizational culture in higher education: Lessons learned from South Africa and Ghana. In H. Eggins (Ed.), *The changing role of women in higher education: Academic and leadership issues* (Vol. 17, pp. 75–92). New York, NY: Springer. http://dx.doi.org/10.1007/978-3-319-42436-1_4

MacDonald, K. (2016). Calls for educating girls in the Third World: Futurity, girls and the 'Third World Woman.' *Gender, Place and Culture, 23,* 1–17. http://dx.doi.org/10.1080/0966369X.2014.991699

Mohanty, C. T. (2013). Transitional feminist crossings: On neoliberalism and radical critique. *Signs, 38,* 967–991. http://dx.doi.org/10.1086/669576

Mohanty, C. T., & Alexander, J. (2010). Cartographies of knowledge and power: Transnational feminism as radical praxis. In A. L. Swarr & R. Nagar (Eds.), *Critical transnational feminist praxis* (pp. 23–45). Albany, NY: SUNY Press.

Murakami, E. T., Jean-Marie, G., Santamaría, L. J., & Lopez, A. E. (2017). Educational leadership among Women of Colour in United States, Canada, New Zealand. In P. Miller (Ed.), *Cultures of educational leadership: Intercultural studies in education* (pp. 53–75). London, England: Palgrave Macmillan.

NAFSA. (2019). *NAFSA international student economic value tool.* Retrieved from http://www.nafsa.org/Policy_and_Advocacy/Policy_Resources/Policy_Trends_and_Data/NAFSA_International_Student_Economic_Value_Tool/#econvaluenatl

Nagar, R., & Swarr, A. L. (2010). Theorizing transnational feminist praxis. In A. L. Swarr & R. Nagar (Eds.), *Critical transnational feminist praxis* (pp. 1–18). Albany: State University of New York Press.

Nakray, K. (2018). Gender and education policy in India: Twists, turns and trims of transnational policy transfers. *International Sociology*, *33*, 27–44. http://dx.doi.org/10.1177/0268580917745769

Narayan, U. (1998). Essence of culture and a sense of history: A feminist critique of cultural essentialism. *Hypatia*, *13*, 86–106. http://dx.doi.org/10.1111/j.1527-2001.1998.tb01227.x

Njoh, A. J., Ananga, E. O., Ngyah-Etchutambe, I. B., Deba, L. E., Asah, F. J., Ayuk-Etang, E. N. M., & Akiwumi, F. A. (2018). Electricity supply, and access to water and improved sanitation as determinants of gender-based inequality in educational attainment in Africa. *Social Indicators Research*, *135*, 533–548. http://dx.doi.org/10.1007/s11205-016-1512-1

National Skills Development Agency. (2018). *Grant Thornton report on overseas migration patterns from India*. Retrieved from http://www.shram.org/researchpapers/papers/20180117115945

Okpalaoka, C. L., & Dillard, C. B. (2012). (Im)migrations, relations and identities of African peoples: Toward an endarkened transnational feminist praxis in education. *Educational Foundations*, *26*, 121–142.

Peake, L., & DeSouza, K. D. (2010). Feminist academic and activist praxis in service of the transnational. In A. L. Swarr & R. Nagar (Eds.), *Critical transnational feminist praxis* (pp. 105–123). Albany: State University of New York Press.

Pio, E., & Essers, C. (2014). Professional migrant women decentering otherness: A transnational perspective. *British Journal of Management*, *25*, 252–265. http://dx.doi.org/10.1111/1467-8551.12003

Pio, E., & Graham, M. (2018). Transitioning to higher education: Journeying with Indigenous Maori teen mothers. *Gender and Education*, *30*, 846–865. http://dx.doi.org/10.1080/09540253.2016.1269157

Pio, E., Kilpatrick, R., & LeFevre, M. (2017). Navratna—the nine gems: Illuminating enablers, barriers and vignettes of South Asian women leaders. *South Asian Journal of Business Studies*, *6*, 1–17. http://dx.doi.org/10.1108/SAJBS-05-2016-0045

Pio, E., & Singh, S. (2016). Vulnerability and resilience: Critical reflexivity in gendered violence research. *Third World Quarterly*, *37*, 227–244. http://dx.doi.org/10.1080/01436597.2015.1089166

Pio, E., Tipuna, K., Rasheed, A., & Parker, L. (2014). Te Wero—the challenge: Reimagining universities from an indigenous worldview. *Higher Education*, *67*, 675–690. http://dx.doi.org/10.1007/s10734-013-9673-1

Psaki, S. R., McCarthy, K. J., & Mensch, B. S. (2018). Measuring gender equality in education: Lessons from trends in 43 countries. *Population and Development Review*, *44*, 117–142. http://dx.doi.org/10.1111/padr.12121

Riley, S., Evans, A., Elliot, S., Rice, C., & Marecek, J. (2017). A critical review of postfeminist sensibility. *Social and Personality Psychology Compass*, *11*(12), e12367. http://dx.doi.org/10.1111/spc3.12367

Singh, R., & Mukherjee, P. (2018). 'Whatever she may study, she can't escape from washing dishes': Gender inequity in secondary education—evidence from a longitudinal study in India. *Compare: A Journal of Comparative Education, 48*, 262–280. http://dx.doi.org/10.1080/03057925.2017.1306434

Spear, A. M., & da Costa, R. B. (2018). Potential for transformation? Two teacher training programs examined through a critical pedagogy framework. *Teaching and Teacher Education, 69*, 202–209. http://dx.doi.org/10.1016/j.tate.2017.10.013

Spivak, G. (1996). Diasporas old and new: Women in the transnational world. *Textual Practice, 10*, 245–287. http://dx.doi.org/10.1080/09502369608582246

Tshabangu, T. (2018). The intersectionality of educational inequalities and child poverty in Africa: A deconstruction. *Educational Research for Policy and Practice, 17*, 69–82. http://dx.doi.org/10.1007/s10671-017-9216-0

UNESCO. (2016). *Gender review: Creating sustainable futures for all.* Retrieved from http://gem-report-2016.unesco.org/en/gender-review/

United Nations. (2017). *International migration report 2017.* New York, NY: United Nations.

Verge, T., Ferrer-Fons, M., & González, M. J. (2018). Resistance to mainstreaming gender into the higher education curriculum. *European Journal of Women's Studies, 25*, 86–101. http://dx.doi.org/10.1177/1350506816688237

Walker, M. (2018). Aspirations and equality in higher education: Gender in a South African university. *Cambridge Journal of Education, 48*, 123–139. http://dx.doi.org/10.1080/0305764X.2016.1254159

World Economic Forum. (2017). *The global gender gap report 2017.* Geneva, Switzerland: Author.

7

USING TRANSNATIONAL FEMINIST THEORY TO EXPAND DOMESTIC VIOLENCE UNDERSTANDINGS

ALISHA GUTHERY, NICOLE JEFFREY, SARA CRANN,
AND ELIZABETH SCHWAB

In this chapter, we respond to the transnational feminist theorists' call to examine gender-based violence by considering disparate local meanings through the lens of various systemic forces (e.g., Nayak, 2003). We focus specifically on globalization, colonialism, and neoliberalism and attempt to include distinct, non-Western perspectives to challenge and expand current Western and international understandings of violence against women perpetrated by intimate partners and family members. These emerging reconceptualizations might be used by practitioners, advocates, and researchers but are not unified or consistent, a particular challenge that we discuss throughout this chapter.

Gender-based violence (GBV) perpetrated by intimate partners and family members occurs worldwide (Garcia-Moreno, Jansen, Ellsberg, Heise, & Watts, 2006; World Health Organization [WHO], 2013). This particular

http://dx.doi.org/10.1037/0000148-008

Transnational Psychology of Women: Expanding International and Intersectional Approaches, L. H. Collins,
S. Machizawa, and J. K. Rice (Editors)

form of GBV can include physical, emotional, psychological, sexual, and economic abuse and the use of controlling behaviors (WHO, 2013). In contrast to the decrease in most violent crime rates in Western nations, GBV has remained relatively stable and may be on the rise in some cases (Perreault, 2015; Walby, Towers, & Francis, 2016). Although it is difficult to assert a similar trend for non-Western regions (due to the lack of available crime statistics pertaining to GBV), the European Union Agency for Fundamental Rights (2014) estimated that in 2012 half of female homicide victims were killed by intimate partners or family members, and additional studies indicate an increase in homicides over the past 15 years in many non-Western regions, most notably Central America, Africa, and the Caribbean (United Nations Office on Drugs and Crime, 2011). GBV is tied to women's social, political, and economic inequality and systemic forces such as globalization, colonialism, and neoliberalism (Brenner, 2003; Dasai, 2002; Kanuha, 2002; Speed, 2014; WHO, 2013), yet current Western literature and international advocacy organizations tend not to account for these varied factors. Instead, they tend to promote Western hegemony (i.e., dominance) and remain monolithic (i.e., singular and unchanging) and focused on the individual.

In this chapter, we use the term *domestic violence* (DV) to refer to GBV perpetrated by intimate partners and family members. We recognize that it is a Western term and does not explicitly highlight the gendered and systemic nature of such violence as do umbrella terms—such as *gender violence* and *gender-based* violence—that are often used in research from or focused on non-Western countries. However, these terms, and others "[risk] losing specificity of women's bodies" (Schuller, 2015, p. 186). Although some activists and agencies prefer the terms *violence against women* or *domestic violence against* women[1] for this reason (Hester, 2005; Schuller, 2015), they too can be problematic because they are victim focused and risk obscuring those who perpetrate violence. Thus, in the absence of ideal language, we use *DV* for clarity and consistency and because it has become commonplace in international literature and is widely recognized (e.g., see Fulu, 2014; Zhang, 2009). We purposely do not define DV because our main objective is to critically analyze various terms and understandings from an interdisciplinary perspective by pointing out the oversimplification of DV by Westerners and others and embracing the need for more complex locally informed understandings of DV.

---

[1]Chinese activists and academics, for example, have challenged previous descriptions of DV by purposefully moving away from terms such as *da laopo* (wife beating) and *nuedai* (maltreatment) to the directly translated concept of *domestic violence against women* "as a means of including gender awareness" (Hester, 2005, p. 452).

POSITIONING OURSELVES

It is important to acknowledge that our social positions include both privileged and minority statuses. We are women, mothers, childless, single, married, Western, White, Jewish, college-educated, middle-class, and from the United States and Canada, with diverse backgrounds in psychology. We acknowledge the benefits and challenges that these positions have afforded us and that have shaped our writing of this chapter. This chapter represents our negotiated and shared perspectives but is, nonetheless, one among many possible interpretations of the scholarship we examine.

PROBLEMATIZING WESTERN DOMESTIC VIOLENCE UNDERSTANDINGS

Dominant contemporary understandings of DV in the Western social-scientific literature and used by international advocacy organizations tend to promote a singular representation of what DV looks like and how it occurs and to focus on individual behaviors and causes of violence. This can be seen in Western DV research and in commonly used terminologies and DV definitions. The psychology-oriented literature, in particular, has a strong tradition of studying GBV from a decontextualized and individualistic perspective (Salazar & Cook, 2002).

In their review of 10 years of psychological research on DV, sexual assault, and sexual harassment, Salazar and Cook (2002) concluded that psychology: (a) "maintains an orientation toward basic science and a focus on illuminating causal factors," (b) "views [GBV] as a problem that resides within individuals," (c) "studies violence against women in a limited range of populations," and (d) "tends to ignore the social, political, and historical context of the problem" (p. 418). This research has tended to focus on clinical and college samples at the expense of community and workplace samples, victims and perpetrators at the expense of other groups who play a role in preventing or maintaining GBV, and intrapersonal (risk) factors among victims and perpetrators at the expense of social, cultural, and political factors (Salazar & Cook, 2002). Although Salazar and Cook's review is dated, our engagement with the psychology-oriented research literature suggests that the problem persists.

Our review of the Western social-scientific literature also suggests a limited and individualistic focus on DV tactics. The types of violence included in most Western literature include physical, sexual, and psychological violence. Our review of the definitions of DV used by six nongovernmental, international advocacy organizations (see Table 7.1) further suggests the ascendancy of Western understandings in the international field.

Although a focus on these particular tactics has been useful in highlighting some forms that patriarchal domination and control can take, they may exclude additional forms of violence including social, legal, technological, honor-based, religious, and spiritual violence; violence or threats

TABLE 7.1

Definitions of Domestic Violence Used by Nongovernmental, International Advocacy Organizations

Organization	Definition
Amnesty International, 2005	"Domestic violence usually refers to abuse at the hands of a partner and ranges from verbal and physical aggression, to sexual violence and marital rape, through to homicide. Domestic violence can include an economic component. Usually the perpetrator is male and the victim female" (p. 3).
The Advocates for Human Rights, 2013	"Domestic violence is a pattern of abusive and threatening behaviors that may include physical, emotional, economic and sexual violence as well as intimidation, isolation and coercion. The purpose of domestic violence is to establish and exert power and control over another; men most often use it against their intimate partners, such as current or former spouses, girlfriends, or dating partners" (para. 1).
United Nations International Children's Emergency Fund, 2000	"Domestic violence . . . includes violence perpetrated by intimate partners and other family members and manifested through: *Physical abuse* . . . [including] traditional practices harmful to women such as female genital mutilation and wife inheritance. . . . *Sexual abuse*. . . . *Psychological abuse* which includes behaviour that is intended to intimidate and persecute . . . [and] *Economic abuse*" (p. 2).
United Nations (UN), 1993	The UN's umbrella definition of violence against women includes, among other forms, abuse perpetrated within the context of the family: "Physical, sexual and psychological violence occurring in the family, including battering, sexual abuse of female children in the household, dowry-related violence, marital rape, female genital mutilation and other traditional practices harmful to women, non-spousal violence and violence related to exploitation" (para. 16).
Women Against Violence Europe	Domestic violence "shall mean all acts of physical, sexual, psychological or economic violence that occur within the family or domestic unit or between former or current spouses or partners, whether or not the perpetrator shares or has shared the same residence with the victim" (Council of Europe, 2011, p. 3).
World Health Organization, 2016	"Intimate partner violence refers to behaviour by an intimate partner or ex-partner that causes physical, sexual or psychological harm, including physical aggression, sexual coercion, psychological abuse and controlling behaviours" (para. 2).

against family members, pets, and property; harassment and stalking; neglect; extreme jealousy; and persecution. In addition to homogenizing our understandings of DV, both common terminology and included tactics focus on patterns and behaviors at the level of the individual, to the exclusion of sociocultural conditions that enable DV. This decontextualized and individualized view of DV risks obscuring experiences of violence that are culturally and locally specific (see examples in the next section) and is problematic for both research and praxis.

Research and praxis that focus on the individual assume an innate or learned propensity for violence and cannot address the complex sociocultural conditions that support and shape women's DV experiences. Individualist perspectives do little to account for differences based on social positions and instead prescribe a universal understanding of the nature of DV. As a result, experiences of violence in the lives of racialized and non-Western women become "culturalized" and "treated as extraneous to the experiences of violence" of White and Western women (Carty & Mohanty, 2015, p. 9). It is also necessary to attend to nuanced localized experiences across the globe to avoid "blanket characterizations by which Southern women are unduly pigeonholed" as "accepting" violence as a result of culture (Rajan, 2018, p. 5). Clearly, current understandings of DV found in the Western literature (Salazar & Cook, 2002) and used by international advocacy organizations tend to bolster Western hegemony by promoting a largely singular understanding of DV focused on one individual's acts of violence against another.

USING TRANSNATIONAL FEMINISM TO EXPAND UNDERSTANDINGS OF DOMESTIC VIOLENCE: ATTENDING TO SOCIAL AND SYSTEMIC FORCES

In this section, we examine the broader social and systemic forces that contribute to DV. We argue that transnational feminism's focus on such forces should be used to inform more nuanced, inclusive, and contextualized understandings of DV. Specifically, we examine how local context and social intersections impact DV experiences and how globalization, colonialism, and neoliberalism contribute to the social and economic conditions of DV.

Impacts of Local Context and Social Positions on Domestic Violence

Understandings of DV must account for local contexts and social positions to reflect women's lived realities of violence and the forces that undermine their safety, freedoms, and well-being. What constitutes DV for a woman in one part of the world may not accurately capture the experience of another woman in a different part of the world (Schneider, 2000). In Table 7.2 we provide several examples of how local context impacts women's experiences and conceptualizations of DV.

Expanded understandings of DV must take these and other local particularities into account to fully understand and address women's diverse experiences. The impact of dowries on women's experiences of violence and the significance and meaning of dowry and marriage, for example, are made invisible in current Western understandings of DV. Moreover, what constitutes DV is embedded in local context and may not be consistent with dominant Western understandings—as in the case of Indigenous understandings of DV that include broader family violence (e.g., Day, Jones, Nakata, & McDermott, 2012)—and, thus, might not be captured in current conceptualizations that tend to focus on intimate partners. Failure to expand our understanding of DV risks overlooking particular abusive experiences, such as abandonment, while imposing victim status onto women and communities without regard for localized understandings of DV.

Differences based on social positions, including gender, race, ethnicity, class, sexuality, ability, geography, Indigeneity, immigration status—and the intersections thereof, can influence how DV is experienced and responded to by others (Bovarnick, 2007; Brassard, Montminy, Bergeron, & Sosa-Sanchez, 2015; Crenshaw, 1991; Sokoloff, 2008). For example, many racialized women experience poverty, child-care responsibilities, unemployment, and discriminatory employment and housing practices, all of which "[make] battered women of color less able to depend on the support of friends and relatives for temporary shelter" (Crenshaw, 1991, p. 1246). Transnational feminism adds an additional layer of analysis by attending to the sociocultural and historical contexts in which these intersections occur (Patil, 2013).

Expanded understandings of DV informed by transnational feminism are ones that take local particularities, transnational processes, and the intersections of various social positions into account (Patil, 2013). It is not simply about recognizing additional or different forms of DV; this would fail to adequately address the critiques of Western understandings of DV levied by us and others. Examining DV through the lens of transnational feminism requires moving beyond a focus on discrete behavioral acts of violence and instead understanding DV as a complex phenomenon that is cultivated within and facilitated and perpetuated by particular sociocultural, political, and global economic forces. However, this presents significant challenges to developing effective and contextualized but inclusive policies and interventions that address DV (we elaborate on this in the concluding section).

TABLE 7.2

Examples of the Impact of Local Context on Domestic Violence

Research location or context	Example of impacts on domestic violence
Many African countries	DV and relationship power inequity increase women's risk of HIV infection and account for a substantial proportion of these infections (Jewkes, Dunkle, Nduna, & Shai, 2010; Maman et al., 2002). This increased risk occurs through forced sex with an infected partner (some abusers may even use their infection as a control tactic), limited negotiation of condom use and other safer sex practices (e.g., because of fear of DV and retaliation), and abusers' increased sexual risk-taking behaviors (see Campbell et al., 2008, for a review).
Cultures in South Africa, Sudan, and Bangladesh	Dowries (negotiated payments of cattle or money) are often paid to the groom and his family (Khan, 2015; Kircher, 2013; Mazibuko, 2016). The payment of dowries may make it difficult for women to leave abusive relationships, particularly if their families cannot return the payment. Moreover, many men feel that their wives are their property and can be disciplined: "When you get angry you beat your wife because when you got married you paid many cows for her" (participant from Kircher, 2013, p. 27).
Varying cultures around the globe	Some communities experience forms of DV based on collective family structures and honor-based value systems, such as forced marriage, acid attacks, and honor-based violence (Gangoli, Razak, & McCarry, 2006; Gill, 2008) perpetrated on the grounds of protecting or restoring the honor of the family and "based on men's putative right to control women's sexual and social choices" (Dorjee, Baig, & Ting-Toomey, 2013; Gill, 2008, p. 246).
Tibet	Wife beating is understood by both women and men with and without histories of DV to be acceptable under certain conditions (Rajan, 2018). A husband's physical violence toward his wife is not necessarily considered abuse (e.g., when the beating is considered mild and the reason behind it was small or mundane)—although severe or unjustified beatings are considered unacceptable—and abuse can occur in the absence of physical violence (e.g., being abandoned for long periods of time).
Indigenous communities in the West	Many Indigenous communities in the West often include in their understandings of DV abuses within (extended) families, intimate relationships, kinship networks, and communities (Day, Jones, Nakata, & McDermott, 2012, p. 105; Victorian Indigenous Family Violence Taskforce, 2003).

Note. DV = domestic violence.

Impacts of Globalization on Domestic Violence

Four key features or effects of globalization have contributed to the social and economic conditions fostering DV or influencing women's particular experiences of DV: (a) economic uncertainties and changing workplace conditions, (b) women's economic inequality, (c) global cultural flow, and (d) migration. First, in the United States, globalization has transformed the industry-based economy to a service-dominated one, which has meant decreased job availability (especially for manufacturing jobs), job security, wages, health and pension benefits, and social services in many communities and households (Dasai, 2002). These economic conditions can contribute to DV through resulting poverty, stress, and increased workplace pressures (including pressures to work longer hours; Weissman, 2007). Importantly, a perpetrator's lack of employment is one of the strongest risk factors for domestic homicide (Campbell et al., 2003) because men's unemployment may threaten their masculinity, leading to the use of DV as a way to maintain patriarchal hierarchies.

Second, globalization has contributed to the inequality of women in the global workforce. Although globalization has afforded women access to jobs, stronger connections to markets, and new opportunities in the workforce (The World Bank, 2012, p. 244), women still make up less of the overall workforce than men but most of the informal sector (e.g., preparing products, domestic services; Dasai, 2002). These jobs provide low wages and no protections or benefits at the same time that governments are cutting funding for health, education, and other social services that would assist in elevating women's status (Dasai, 2002; Radford & Tsutsumi, 2004). These conditions have ushered in distinct opportunities for violence against and exploitation of women, "making poor women and girls especially vulnerable to entrapment, exploitation, abuse, and enslavement" (Radford & Tsutsumi, 2004, p. 2). These conditions have helped to define further the use of economic violence perpetrated not only by abusive partners but also through local and global forces.

More generally, globalization has disrupted local economies, state-provided services, and employment, housing, and food security (Lindio-McGovern, 2007; Mohanty, 2003), each of which may increase DV and impact women's specific DV experiences and help-seeking abilities. For example, women experiencing economic abuse in Ghana reported being unable to access appropriate medical support when injured by violent partners: "I could not go to the hospital because I was not having health insurance, and he also refused to give me money" (participant from Sedziafa, Tenkorang, Owusu, & Sano, 2017, p. 2633).

Third, globalization has contributed to an increased exchange or flow of interaction, ideas, and ideologies across the globe (i.e., cultural flow; Held,

McGrew, Goldblatt, & Perraton, 1999), and this has impacted the prevalence, causes, and consequences of DV (Fulu, 2014; Fulu & Miedema, 2015). For example, the Maldives has traditionally had lower rates of DV compared with many other South Asian countries, likely due to its flexible marriage and divorce practices, history of relatively equal gender relations, and ideology of masculinity that does not accept violence (Fulu, 2014). However, with the global reach of the media and "spread of Victorian style White weddings, and Bollywood love stories," marriage and divorce are becoming more restrictive, and new masculinity ideals that are more accepting of violence are emerging (Fulu & Miedema, 2015, p. 1435). As a result, DV is on the rise, and more women may be trapped in violent relationships without the option for divorce (Fulu & Miedema, 2015).

Finally, globalization has meant a change in migration (Castles, 2002), which itself can influence DV experiences, risk factors, and help seeking. Many immigrants experience isolation, limited access to services, legal dependency on their violent partners, fear of deportation, limited financial and occupational resources, and language barriers (Adams & Campbell, 2012; Erez, Adelman, & Gregory, 2009; Vidales, 2010). Abusers may also use these conditions to exert control over their partners (Erez et al., 2009). Cultural and lifestyle transitions postmigration can also impact DV. For example, loss of kinship networks—which often serve to resolve marriage conflict—and other new sources of stress, have contributed to DV in some Sudanese immigrant communities in the United States (Holtzman, 2000). Attending to these dynamics is crucial in an increasingly globalized world if we are to understand and address DV among diverse women.

Due in part to increased globalization and immigration, different forms of violence are appearing in the West, such as forms of DV based on collective family structures and honor-based value systems (Gangoli, Razak, & McCarry, 2006; Gill, 2008). Failure to include these particular forms of DV risks delegitimizing and erasing women's lived experiences and the physical, social, psychological, economic, and political consequences. However, when honor-based violence is included in Western understandings of DV, it is often "culturalized" (framed as cultural or religious practice) and sensationalized (Carty & Mohanty, 2015, p. 9) by the public and legal systems in Western countries. The common, selective focus on honor-based violence as distinct from other forms of GBV can create culturalist and racist explanations for DV and mask other systemic conditions supporting DV (Olwan, 2013). Although honor-based violence must be recognized in an effort to include diverse experiences, such inclusion must understand this violence within complex structural and systemic inequality frameworks that include gender inequality among other forces of globalization, neoliberalism, patriarchy, and poverty (Carty & Mohanty, 2015; Chowdhury, 2015; Gill, 2008).

Impacts of Colonialism on Domestic Violence

Colonialism has impacted cultural violence, and DV specifically, through male superiority (e.g., the oppression of women by men based on the rationale that men's way of thinking and knowing are superior to women's), influence over the forms of violence experienced (e.g., forbidden use of native language, manipulation of family structure and prayer practices), control of economic resources (e.g., exploitation or forcing the relocation of families), and control of the narrative of cultural identity (e.g., defining what is acceptable and exotic about a culture; Kanuha, 2002). Contextualizing DV within broader systems and structural frameworks of historical and contemporary oppression, such as colonialism, can help remedy such assumptions (Sokoloff, 2004).

Colonialism has also shaped women's experiences in many parts of the West. Specifically, it has contributed to the social and economic conditions fostering DV among colonized groups (e.g., Indigenous communities) and has influenced their particular experiences of DV. To illustrate, violent and patriarchal laws and assimilation practices in the West—such as Canada's Indian Act, large scale apprehension of Indigenous children by child protection services, the residential school system, and forced relocation of Indigenous communities—have collectively fostered conditions supportive of DV (Brassard et al., 2015; Centre de recherché interdisciplinaire sur la violence familiale et la violence faite aux femmes [CRI-VIFF], 2011). They have contributed to generational trauma and have normalized violence and disrupted family structures (e.g., matrilineal family structures) and cultural traditions (Brassard et al., 2015; CRI-VIFF, 2011). As a result, Indigenous communities in Canada and elsewhere face higher rates of DV (Boyce, 2016; Brassard et al., 2015). Indigenous communities also face continued discrimination, poor living conditions, and limited social and financial resources (Australia's National Research Organisation for Women's Safety, 2015; CRI-VIFF, 2011), all of which can impact DV experiences and supports.

Impacts of Neoliberalism on Domestic Violence

Neoliberal policies, including reduction in government spending, increase in privatization of services, and focus on individual responsibility (Harvey, 2005), contribute to the social and economic conditions that (a) increase women's likelihood of experiencing violence and (b) reduce access to DV support. With respect to the former, the relationship between state-sanctioned violence and domestic, "private" violence is apparent through an analysis of neoliberalization. In the context of Latin America, neoliberalization has led to increased poverty, inequity, unemployment, and drug trafficking, which have ultimately contributed to the rise in gangs that commonly promote misogynistic ideologies and violence against women (Speed, 2014). With respect to the latter, neoliberal policies work to shift the responsibility of supporting the needs of individuals from government to local communities, which often have limited resources and capacity. In the United Kingdom, for example, recent federal policy initiatives have led to a focus on short-term cost-saving policies, reducing government-funded DV services in tandem with increasing local community responsibility for running social services (Ishkanian, 2014), resulting in the isolation of women and children experiencing and fleeing abuse.

The rise and subsequent impact of neoliberal policies on DV can be seen in different countries around the world. To illustrate, in the context of neoliberal economic restrictions in the Caribbean—which have resulted in rising unemployment rates, the reduction of state support, and overall worsening economic conditions—women are disproportionately affected because they are expected to stretch family budgets while men are afforded the right to continue spending without personal sacrifice (Khalideen & Khalideen, 2002). Across the Caribbean, rates of DV have increased alongside increasing unemployment rates among men and the emotional and psychological impacts of coping with economic crisis (Mondesesire, 1995).

The ascendancy of neoliberalism has also individualized current Western understandings of DV (McDonald, 2005) that (as highlighted previously) tend to ignore the systemic conditions that enable DV and shape women's experiences (such as neoliberalism itself). The focus on individual behaviors reifies DV as an individual problem. Neoliberalism also contributes to the prevailing monolithic and hegemonic Western understanding of DV— one that "treats western practices as the measure of progress for women and for society and thus legitimizes neo-colonial domination" (Brenner, 2003, p. 27). Thus, transnational feminism can help to counter these neoliberal notions by questioning Western hegemony and attending to the various socio-cultural, political, and global economic conditions (including the impacts of neoliberalism itself) discussed throughout this chapter.

TOWARD A TRANSNATIONAL FEMINIST UNDERSTANDING OF DOMESTIC VIOLENCE

Thus far, we have argued for the utility of applying transnational feminism to address current limitations of Western understandings of DV. Specifically, we have argued that transnational feminism's attention to globalization, colonization, neoliberalism, and diverse and pluralistic experiences offers more nuanced, inclusive, and contextualized understandings of DV than are currently used in Western social-scientific literature and by international advocacy organizations. Attention to intersecting identities and the unique vulnerabilities and conditions faced by women in different contexts can inform the needs and experiences of diverse women and assist in creating more relevant and effective services, policies, and interventions (Crenshaw, 1991; Sokoloff & Dupont, 2005). As one example, children (and other family members) living within the often tight-knit family structures found in many Indigenous communities may be more heavily or differentially impacted by witnessing DV, and interventions should span multiple levels and generations (Burnette & Cannon, 2014).

Currently, there is no unified transnational definition or conceptualization of DV (Saltzman, 2004; Yamawaki, Ochoa-Shipp, Pulsipher, Harlos, & Swindler, 2012). DV definitions within and across regions tend to vary based on terminology used, inclusion beyond the partner dyad, types of violence included, and level of focus (United Nations International Children's Emergency Fund, 2000). We, like other scholars, are wary of the usefulness and appropriateness of a universal conceptualization of DV because, as we have examined throughout this chapter, experiences and understandings are embedded in diverse local contexts.

At the same time, we acknowledge the challenges for transnational research on and monitoring of DV resulting from this diversity. For example, prevalence rates are difficult to compare across countries because of inconsistencies in the definitions used (Heise & Garcia-Moreno, 2002). International feminist advocacy organizations (e.g., Women Against Violence Europe, n.d.) and others (Johnson, 2009; Saltzman, 2004) have argued that establishing common definitions of DV transnationally and across advocacy and legal efforts is a critical step in providing effective (transnational) prevention, support, and services. Scholars must continue to grapple with the tensions of advocating a universal conceptualization of DV.

Transnational feminism allows for the simultaneous recognition of local particularities and systemic forces and broader commonalities in the experience of DV—such as how traditional social mechanisms legitimize and reproduce violence against women and how the appropriation and control of women's bodies act to maintain existing gendered power relations (Bovarnick, 2007). As we have explored in this chapter, globalization, colonialism, and neoliberalism are implicated in the experience of DV for women around the world. Attending to and analyzing how these systemic forces contribute to DV allows scholars and advocates to better account for the nuanced and contextual realities of DV without requiring a universal understanding of DV.

Efforts to address DV globally are long-standing. Diverse transnational feminist networks such as the Women's Learning Partnership (WLP) for Rights, Development, and Peace; AF3IRM; the Centre for Women's Global

Leadership; and the International Alliance of Women, to name a few, work at local, national, and transnational levels to address GBV and other gendered issues. The WLP, for example, works in 16 countries in South and Central America, Africa, Asia, and the Middle East on issues of women's empowerment, leadership, citizenship, political participation, and human rights—issues that are deeply rooted in globalization, colonialism, and neoliberalism. Further, several of these networks are involved in global campaigns such as "16 Days of Activism Against Gender-Based Violence," highlighting the coordinated transnational effort to bring attention to GBV. Coupled with transnational feminism's emphasis on destabilizing national boundaries (Grewal & Kaplan, 2000), the more nuanced understandings of DV that we have advocated for in this chapter may help support the conditions for women around the globe to continue to work in solidarity to end violence against women.

REFERENCES

Adams, M. E., & Campbell, J. (2012). Being undocumented & intimate partner violence (IPV): Multiple vulnerabilities through the lens of feminist intersectionality. *Women's Health & Urban Life*, *11*, 15–34.

The Advocates for Human Rights. (2013). *Domestic violence: General information*. Retrieved from http://www.stopvaw.org/Domestic_Violence_Explore_the_Issue

Amnesty International. (2005). *Women, violence and health*. Retrieved from https://www.amnesty.org/en/documents/act77/001/2005/en/

Australia's National Research Organisation for Women's Safety. (2015). *Innovative models in addressing violence against Indigenous women: State of knowledge paper*. Retrieved from https://www.anrows.org.au/publications/landscapes-0/innovative-models-in-addressing-violence-against-indigenous-women-state

Bovarnick, S. (2007). Universal human rights and non-Western normative systems: A comparative analysis of violence against women in Mexico and Pakistan. *Review of International Studies*, *33*, 59–74. http://dx.doi.org/10.1017/S0260210507007309

Boyce, J. (2016). *Victimization of Aboriginal people in Canada, 2014* (Juristat, Statistics Canada Catalogue No. 85-002-X). Retrieved from https://www150.statcan.gc.ca/n1/pub/85-002-x/2016001/article/14631-eng.htm

Brassard, R., Montminy, L., Bergeron, A. S., & Sosa-Sanchez, I. A. (2015). Application of intersectional analysis to data on domestic violence against Aboriginal women living in remote communities in the province of Quebec. *Aboriginal Policy Studies*, *4*, 3–23. http://dx.doi.org/10.5663/aps.v4i1.20894

Brenner, J. (2003). Transnational feminism and the struggle for global justice. In J. Sai & P. Waterman (Eds.), *World social forum: Challenging empires* (pp. 26–37). Montreal, Quebec, Canada: Black Rose Books.

Burnette, C. E., & Cannon, C. (2014). "It will always continue unless we can change something": Consequences of intimate partner violence for indigenous women, children, and families. *European Journal of Psychotraumatology, 5*(1). http://dx.doi.org/10.3402/ejpt.v5.24585

Campbell, J. C., Baty, M. L., Ghandour, R. M., Stockman, J. K., Francisco, L., & Wagman, J. (2008). The intersection of intimate partner violence against women and HIV/AIDS: A review. *International Journal of Injury Control and Safety Promotion, 15,* 221–231. http://dx.doi.org/10.1080/17457300802423224

Campbell, J. C., Webster, D., Koziol-McLain, J., Block, C., Campbell, D., Curry, M. A., . . . Laughon, K. (2003). Risk factors for femicide in abusive relationships: Results from a multisite case control study. *American Journal of Public Health, 93,* 1089–1097. http://dx.doi.org/10.2105/AJPH.93.7.1089

Carty, L., & Mohanty, C. T. (2015). Mapping transnational feminist engagements: Neoliberalism and the politics of solidarity. In R. Baksh & W. Harcourt (Eds.), *The Oxford handbook of transnational feminist movements* (pp. 82–115). New York, NY: Oxford University Press.

Castles, S. (2002). Migration and community formation under conditions of globalization. *The International Migration Review, 36,* 1143–1168. http://dx.doi.org/10.1111/j.1747-7379.2002.tb00121.x

Centre de recherché interdisciplinaire sur la violence familiale et la violence faite aux femmes. (2011). *Violence in the lives of Aboriginal girls and young women in Canada through an intersectional lens* (Fact Sheet, No. 6). Retrieved from http://www.criviff.qc.ca/sites/criviff.qc.ca/files/publications/pub_17012011_154130.pdf

Chowdhury, E. H. (2015). Rethinking patriarchy, culture and masculinity: Transnational narratives of gender violence and human rights advocacy. *Journal of International Women's Studies, 16,* 98–114.

Council of Europe. (2011). *Council of Europe Convention on preventing and combating violence against women and domestic violence.* Retrieved from https://rm.coe.int/168008482e

Crenshaw, K. (1991). Mapping the margins: Internationality, identity politics and violence against women of color. *Stanford Law Review, 43,* 1241–1299. http://dx.doi.org/10.2307/1229039

Dasai, M. (2002). Transnational solidarity: Women's agency, structural adjustment, and globalization. In N. A. Naples & M. Dasai (Eds.), *Women's activism and globalization* (pp. 15–32). New York, NY: Routledge.

Day, A., Jones, R., Nakata, M., & McDermott, D. (2012). Indigenous family violence: An attempt to understand the problems and inform appropriate and effective responses to criminal justice system intervention. *Psychiatry, Psychology and Law, 19,* 104–117. http://dx.doi.org/10.1080/13218719.2010.543754

Dorjee, T., Baig, N., & Ting-Toomey, S. (2013). A social ecological perspective on understanding "honor killing": An intercultural moral dilemma. *Journal of Intercultural Communication Research, 42*, 1–21. http://dx.doi.org/10.1080/17475759.2012.723024

Erez, E., Adelman, M., & Gregory, C. (2009). Intersections of immigration and domestic violence: Voices of battered immigrant women. *Feminist Criminology, 4*, 32–56. http://dx.doi.org/10.1177/1557085108325413

European Union Agency for Fundamental Rights. (2014). *Violence against women: An EU-wide survey.* Retrieved from https://fra.europa.eu/sites/default/files/fra-2014-vaw-survey-main-results_en.pdf

Fulu, E. (2014). *Domestic violence in Asia: Globalization, gender and Islam in the Maldives.* New York, NY: Routledge.

Fulu, E., & Miedema, S. (2015). Violence against women: Globalizing the integrated ecological model. *Violence Against Women, 21*, 1431–1455. http://dx.doi.org/10.1177/1077801215596244

Gangoli, G., Razak, A., & McCarry, M. (2006). *Forced marriage and domestic violence among South Asian communities in North East England.* Bristol, England: University of Bristol.

Garcia-Moreno, C., Jansen, H. A., Ellsberg, M., Heise, L., & Watts, C. H. (2006, October 7). Prevalence of intimate partner violence: Findings from the WHO multi-country study on women's health and domestic violence. *The Lancet, 368*, 1260–1269. http://dx.doi.org/10.1016/S0140-6736(06)69523-8

Gill, A. (2008). 'Crimes of honour' and violence against women in the UK. *International Journal of Comparative and Applied Criminal Justice, 32*, 243–263. http://dx.doi.org/10.1080/01924036.2008.9678788

Grewal, I., & Kaplan, C. (2000). *Postcolonial studies and transnational feminist practices.* Retrieved from https://english.chass.ncsu.edu/jouvert/v5i1/grewal.htm

Harvey, D. (2005). *A brief history of neoliberalism.* Oxford, England: Oxford University Press.

Heise, L., & Garcia-Moreno, C. (2002). Violence by intimate partners. In E. G. Krug, L. L. Dahlberg, J. A. Mercy, A. G. Zwi, & R. Lozano (Eds.), *World report on violence and health* (pp. 87–121). Geneva, Switzerland: World Health Organization.

Held, D. A., McGrew, A., Goldblatt, D., & Perraton, J. (1999). *Global transformations: Politics, economics and culture.* Cambridge, England: Polity Press.

Hester, M. (2005). Transnational influences on domestic violence policy and action: Exploring developments in China and England. *Social Policy and Society, 4*, 447–456. http://dx.doi.org/10.1017/S1474746405002630

Holtzman, J. (2000). *Nuer journeys, Nuer lives: Sudanese refugees in Minnesota.* Boston, MA: Allyn & Bacon.

Ishkanian, A. (2014). Neoliberalism and violence: The Big Society and the changing politics of domestic violence in England. *Critical Social Policy, 34*, 333–353. http://dx.doi.org/10.1177/0261018313515973

Jewkes, R. K., Dunkle, K., Nduna, M., & Shai, N. (2010, July 3). Intimate partner violence, relationship power inequity, and incidence of HIV infection in young women in South Africa: A cohort study. *The Lancet*, *376*, 41–48. http://dx.doi.org/10.1016/S0140-6736(10)60548-X

Johnson, M. E. (2009). Redefining harm, reimagining, remedies, and reclaiming domestic violence law. *U.C. Davis Law Review*, *42*, 1107–1164.

Kanuha, V. K. (2002). Colonization and violence against women. *Asian Pacific Institute on Gender-Based Violence*. Retrieved from https://www.api-gbv.org/resources/colonization-violence-against-women/

Khalideen, R., & Khalideen, N. (2002). Caribbean women in globalization and economic restructuring. *Canadian Women's Studies*, *21*, 108–113.

Khan, A. R. (2015). Women's coping strategies and help-seeking practices: Some observations on domestic violence in rural Bangladesh. *Asian Journal of Women's Studies*, *21*, 252–272. http://dx.doi.org/10.1080/12259276.2015.1072941

Kircher, I. (2013). *Challenges to security, livelihoods, and gender justice in South Sudan: The situation of Dinka agro-pastoralist communities in Lakes and Warrap States.* Retrieved from https://www.oxfam.org/sites/www.oxfam.org/files/rr-challenges-security-livelihoods-gender-south-sudan-130313-en.pdf

Lindio-McGovern, L. (2007). Conclusion: Women and neoliberal globalization inequities and resistance. *Journal of Developing Societies*, *23*, 285–297. http://dx.doi.org/10.1177/0169796X0602300216

Maman, S., Mbwambo, J. K., Hogan, N. M., Kilonzo, G. P., Campbell, J. C., Weiss, E., & Sweat, M. D. (2002). HIV-positive women report more lifetime partner violence: Findings from a voluntary counseling and testing clinic in Dar es Salaam, Tanzania. *American Journal of Public Health*, *92*, 1331–1337. http://dx.doi.org/10.2105/AJPH.92.8.1331

Mazibuko, N. C. (2016). Ilobolo, the bride price that comes 'at a price' and the narratives of gender violence in Mamelodi, a South African township. *Gender & Behaviour*, *14*, 7373–7378.

McDonald, J. (2005). Neo-liberalism and the pathologising of public issues: The displacement of feminist services models in domestic violence support services. *Australian Social Work*, *58*, 275–284. http://dx.doi.org/10.1111/j.1447-0748.2005.00220.x

Mohanty, C. T. (2003). *Feminism without borders: Decolonizing theory, practicing solidarity.* Durham, NC: Duke University Press. http://dx.doi.org/10.1215/9780822384649

Mondesesire, A. (1995). *Towards equity in development: A report on the status of women in sixteen commonwealth Caribbean countries.* Georgetown, Guyana: CARICOM Secretariat.

Nayak, M. (2003). The struggle over gendered meanings in India: How Indian women's networks, the Hindu Nationalist Hegemonic project, and transnational feminists address gender violence. *Women & Politics, 25,* 71–96. http://dx.doi.org/10.1300/J014v25n03_04

Olwan, D. M. (2013). Gendered violence, cultural otherness, and honour crimes in Canadian national logics. *Canadian Journal of Sociology, 38,* 533–556.

Patil, V. (2013). From patriarchy to intersectionality: A transnational feminist assessment of how far we've really come. *Signs, 38,* 847–867. http://dx.doi.org/10.1086/669560

Perreault, S. (2015). *Criminal victimization in Canada, 2014* (Statistics Canada No. 85-002-X). Retrieved from https://www150.statcan.gc.ca/n1/en/pub/85-002-x/2015001/article/14241-eng.pdf

Radford, L., & Tsutsumi, K. (2004). Globalization and violence against women: Inequalities in risks, responsibilities and blame in the UK and Japan. *Women's Studies International Forum, 27,* 1–12. http://dx.doi.org/10.1016/j.wsif.2003.12.008

Rajan, H. (2018). When wife-beating is not necessarily abuse: A feminist and cross-cultural analysis of the concept of abuse as expressed by Tibetan survivors of domestic violence. *Violence Against Women, 24,* 3–27. http://dx.doi.org/10.1177/1077801216675742

Salazar, L. F., & Cook, S. L. (2002). Violence against women: Is psychology part of the problem or the solution? A content analysis of psychological research from 1990 through 1999. *Journal of Community & Applied Social Psychology, 12,* 410–421. http://dx.doi.org/10.1002/casp.691

Saltzman, L. E. (2004). Definitional and methodological issues related to transnational research on intimate partner violence. *Violence Against Women, 10,* 812–830. http://dx.doi.org/10.1177/1077801204265553

Schneider, E. M. (2000). *Battered women and feminist lawmaking.* New Haven, CT: Yale University Press.

Schuller, M. (2015). "Pa manyen fanm nan konsa": Intersectionality, structural violence, and vulnerability before and after Haiti's earthquake. *Feminist Studies, 41,* 184–210. http://dx.doi.org/10.15767/feministstudies.41.1.184

Sedziafa, A. P., Tenkorang, E., Owusu, A. Y., & Sano, Y. (2017). Women's experiences of intimate partner economic abuse in the Eastern region of Ghana. *Journal of Family Issues, 38,* 2620–2641. http://dx.doi.org/10.1177/0192513X16686137

Sokoloff, N. J. (2004). Domestic violence at the crossroads: Violence against poor women and women of color. *Women's Studies Quarterly, 32,* 139–147.

Sokoloff, N. J. (2008). Expanding the intersectional paradigm to better understand domestic violence in immigrant communities. *Critical Criminology, 16,* 229–255. http://dx.doi.org/10.1007/s10612-008-9059-3

Sokoloff, N. J., & Dupont, I. (2005). Domestic violence at the intersections of race, class, and gender: Challenges and contributions to understanding violence against marginalized women in diverse communities. *Violence Against Women*, *11*, 38–64. http://dx.doi.org/10.1177/1077801204271476

Speed, S. (2014). *A dreadful mosaic: Rethinking gender violence through the lives of Indigenous women migrants*. Retrieved from http://www.colectivasos.com/wp-content/uploads/2016/01/Gender-Violence-and-Indigenous-Women-Migrants.pdf

United Nations. (1993). *Declaration on the elimination of violence against women* (General Assembly Resolution A/RES/48/104). Retrieved from http://www.un.org/documents/ga/res/48/a48r104.htm

United Nations International Children's Emergency Fund. (2000). *Domestic violence against women and girls*. Retrieved from http://www.unicef-irc.org/publications/pdf/digest6e.pdf

United Nations Office on Drugs and Crime. (2011). *Global study on homicide*. Retrieved from https://www.unodc.org/documents/congress/background-information/Crime_Statistics/Global_Study_on_Homicide_2011.pdf

Victorian Indigenous Family Violence Task Force. (2003). *Final report*. Retrieved from http://www.deadlyrav.com.au/assets/Uploads/2016-update/vic-indigenous-family-violence-task-force-report-2003-main.pdf

Vidales, G. T. (2010). Arrested justice: The multifaceted plight of immigrant Latinas who faced domestic violence. *Journal of Family Violence*, *25*, 533–544. http://dx.doi.org/10.1007/s10896-010-9309-5

Walby, S., Towers, J., & Francis, B. (2016). Is violent crime increasing or decreasing? A new methodology to measure repeat attacks making visible the significance of gender and domestic relations. *British Journal of Criminology*, *56*, 1203–1234. http://dx.doi.org/10.1093/bjc/azv131

Weissman, D. M. (2007). The personal is political—and economic: Rethinking domestic violence. *BYU Law Review*, *2007*, 387–450. Retrieved from https://digitalcommons.law.byu.edu/cgi/viewcontent.cgi?article=2309&context=lawreview

Women Against Violence Europe. (n.d.). *We are the European network WAVE*. Retrieved from http://www.wave-network.org/?q=content/violence-against-women

The World Bank. (2012). *World development report 2012: Gender equality and development*. http://documents.worldbank.org/curated/en/492221468136792185/pdf/646650WDR0201200Box364543B00PUBLIC0.pdf

World Health Organization. (2013). *Global and regional estimates of violence against women: Prevalence and health effects of intimate partner violence and non-partner sexual violence*. Retrieved from http://apps.who.int/iris/bitstream/10665/85239/1/9789241564625_eng.pdf?ua=1

World Health Organization. (2016). *Violence against women: Intimate partner and sexual violence against women* (Fact Sheet No. 239). Retrieved from http://www.who.int/mediacentre/factsheets/fs239/en/

Yamawaki, N., Ochoa-Shipp, M., Pulsipher, C., Harlos, A., & Swindler, S. (2012). Perceptions of domestic violence: The effects of domestic violence myths, victim's relationship with her abuser, and the decision to return to her abuser. *Journal of Interpersonal Violence, 27*, 3195–3212. http://dx.doi.org/10.1177/0886260512441253

Zhang, L. (2009). Domestic violence network in China: Translating the transnational concept of violence against women into local action. *Women's Studies International Forum, 32*, 227–239. http://dx.doi.org/10.1016/j.wsif.2009.05.017

8

TOWARD A TRANSNATIONAL FEMINIST PSYCHOLOGY OF WOMEN'S REPRODUCTIVE EXPERIENCES

JEANNE MARECEK

In this chapter, I examine aspects of women's reproductive experiences through the lens of transnational feminism. Broadly construed, women's reproductive experiences span much of the life cycle, including menarche and menstruation; sexual debut and sexual activity; contraception, child-spacing, and abortion; fertility issues and the increasing array of assisted reproductive technologies; pregnancy, childbirth, breastfeeding, and adoption; disorders of the reproductive system; and menopause. Each of these topics encompasses a range of issues that psychologists might research. At the same time, few, if any, of the questions are narrowly psychological. Nearly all involve the body and reproductive physiology. All involve the social context, including cultural meanings, state regulation, and the social structural locations of those involved. Because of space limitations, I focus on only a small slice of these topics and only one part of the world. I narrow the focus to communities

http://dx.doi.org/10.1037/0000148-009
Transnational Psychology of Women: Expanding International and Intersectional Approaches, L. H. Collins, S. Machizawa, and J. K. Rice (Editors)

within Sri Lanka, located in South Asia, where I have engaged in research, practical action, and teaching for several years.

I begin with a note on terminology. Like a number of scholars and activists, I use the terms *Majority World* and *Minority World* rather than older terms such as *Third World* and *First World* or *developing countries* and *developed countries*. As Alam (2008) pointed out, these outdated terms embed the presumption that there is a singular linear trajectory of progress with the "developed" (capitalist) world at its pinnacle. These older terms also imply that Western high-income countries serve as the model to which developing (sometimes called *underdeveloped*) countries should aspire. The term *Majority World* further serves to remind us that roughly 80% of the world's population lives in such countries, whereas the countries of the Minority World account for somewhat less than 15% of the world's population.

I set the stage by discussing briefly transnational feminism and, in particular, its commitment to a decolonial perspective and greater reflexivity on the part of Western scholars. In part of this discussion, I reflect on some taken-for-granted characteristics of U.S. psychology. Following that, I turn to women's reproductive experiences outside the Minority World, focusing specifically on South Asia and taking up Sri Lanka as a case study.

TRANSNATIONAL FEMINIST THEORY

Transnational feminist theory emerged over 30 years ago as a critical response to the idealized notion of a *global sisterhood*—that is, a unified universal feminism (Morgan, 1984). *Third World Women and the Politics of Feminism* (Mohanty, Russo, & Torres, 1991) was a foundational text. Since then, transnational feminist theorists have continued to urge that scholars attend to the manifold differences in women's experiences in diverse locales. These differences include both the oppressions that women face and also their strengths, advantages, life satisfactions, and opportunities.

More important, transnational feminist theorists have often criticized feminists in the Minority World for presuming that their theories and practices could be exported from the Minority World to the Majority World (Kurtiş & Adams, 2018; Rutherford, Capdevila, Undurti, & Palmary, 2011). Too often, they charged, feminists in the Minority World have positioned themselves as saviors of the unenlightened or "underdeveloped" women of Majority World countries (Cronin-Furman, Gowrinathan, & Zakaria, 2017, p. 2). For example, international campaigns such as those against female genital cutting, transactional sex, *sati* (i.e., self-immolation by widows, sometimes transliterated as *suttee*), veiling, and child labor have sometimes made exaggerated claims, couched in sensationalistic or inflammatory rhetoric (e.g., *mutilation, trafficking, slavery*; Abu-Lughod, 2002; Mani, 1987; Shell-Duncan, 2008). Further, such campaigns have often disregarded the viewpoints of in-country feminists and ignored local programs of change.

As transnational feminist theory has developed, a variety of definitions, arguments, and practices have emerged (Conway, 2017; Swarr & Nagar, 2010). Rather than insist that one or another definition is correct, we can think of transnational feminisms (in the plural) as resources that offer a critical stance on the knowledge, moral visions, and activist projects formulated by feminists in the Minority World. What, we might then ask, does this stance offer to psychologists?

In the United States, feminists in psychology have been late (and perhaps reluctant) arrivals to transnational theory. A brief look at the intellectual history of the discipline suggests why this is so. Throughout its history, the mainstream of psychology in the United States has set its goal as producing universal generalizations about humans, which are akin to the "laws" of physics. Such universality biases have left little room for research that attends to cultural differences. Colleagues in psychology, for example, have frequently dismissed my work as pointless (e.g., "You study Sri Lankans? Why don't you study people?"), or they have labeled it as "not psychology, just (mere) sociology."

Psychology in the United States has long been criticized for its parochialism and its ethnocentric biases. Forty years ago, Marsella, Tharp, and Ciborowski (1979) expressed the hope that increased international experience would afford psychologists greater reflexivity regarding U.S. psychology's cultural roots. This, unfortunately, did not happen. As Arnett pointed out in 2008, U.S.-based psychologists typically rested their claims about (all) human behavior on evidence gathered from less than 5% of the world's population. Yet again, in 2010, Henrich, Heine, and Norenzayan showed that the corpus of psychological knowledge was based overwhelmingly on studies of "WEIRD" participants (i.e., those from Western, educated, industrialized, rich, and democratic societies). These critiques have frequently been cited, but there is little to suggest that research practices have changed (Marecek & Christopher, 2018; Nielsen, Haun, Kärtner, & Legare, 2017).

There is also reason for skepticism about whether concepts, measures, diagnoses, research technologies, and therapeutic practices formulated for U.S. populations can be exported to other locales (Christopher, Wendt, Marecek, & Goodman, 2014; Marecek & Christopher, 2018; Miller, Wang, Sandel, & Cho, 2002). Cultural psychologists who are feminists have begun to catalog a number of constructs (e.g., shame; self-silencing; self-esteem; depression; autonomy; and sexual empowerment) that cannot be exported uncritically to the Majority World (Abeyasekera & Marecek, in press; Kurtiş

& Adams, 2018). Sometimes, as Miller and her colleagues (2002) pointed out, constructs may have no local meaning at all.

Transnational psychologists have joined with critical scholars to point out U.S. psychology's deep roots in the expressive individualism of middle-class White America (Christopher et al., 2014; Cushman, 1995; Kirschner, 1996; Marecek & Christopher, 2018; Rosner, 2018). This cultural orientation places a high value on liberty, equality, independence, privacy, choice, self-expansion, and untrammeled self-expression. It is an orientation that is not widely shared throughout the world. As cultural psychologists and psychological anthropologists have pointed out, in much of the Majority World, people's self-construals are embedded in relationships and are more connected and interdependent on others (Markus & Kitayama, 1994).

In sum, transnational feminist psychology attends to the "social, cultural, and geographic particularities" of people's experiences (Macleod, Marecek, & Capdevila, 2014, p. 4). It is not an "add-and-stir" approach that contents itself with merely adding to the store of knowledge about women's lives. It demands that feminist psychologists deepen their awareness of the multiplicity of feminisms and psychologies around the world. It also demands that we cultivate a reflexivity that "denaturalizes" the cultural models that shape our knowledge.

WOMEN'S REPRODUCTIVE EXPERIENCES IN SOUTH ASIA

Now I turn to an overview of the reproductive practices, experiences, and expectations of women in South Asia. First, I remind readers that the eight countries (Afghanistan, Bangladesh, Bhutan, India, Maldives, Nepal, Pakistan, and Sri Lanka) that compose South Asia account for fully one quarter of the world's population. (By contrast, the United States accounts for 4.4% of the world's population, and the European Union's 28 countries [inclusive of the United Kingdom, which as of this writing remains in the European Union] account for less than 7%.) India, which is the largest country in South Asia, accounts for about 18% of the world's population. (See United Nations Department of Economic and Social Affairs, Population Division, 2018, for these population data.)

South Asia is a broad region that encompasses considerable religious, political, economic, cultural, and geophysical diversity, as well as multiple language groups. Despite this diversity, the histories of the various parts of the region have long been intertwined. In ancient times, the region was criss-crossed by land and maritime trade routes, as well as by military expeditions. During the lengthy period of European imperialism, territorial boundaries were drawn and redrawn. In addition, colonial rulers transported large numbers of people from one area to another (and even from South Asia to colonies in Africa and the Caribbean). The present-day geopolitics remain intertwined and sometimes contentious. Some territorial demarcations are contested (e.g., Kashmir and Siachen), and some questions of citizenship are unsettled (e.g., the Rohingya in Myanmar/Burma; the Lhotshampas, a Bhutanese group that has lived as refugees in Nepal for many generations).

In South Asia, marriage and kin relations furnish the backdrop for women's sexual and reproductive lives, so that is the first topic I take up. I then take up the matter of female sexual respectability and the gendered power relations it entails, especially for unmarried women. I draw on the example of Sri Lanka to illustrate ideologies and practices of female sexual respectability that reflect a mixture of the Victorian values imposed during the colonial era and Indigenous Buddhist teachings (De Alwis, 1997). I show how such ideologies and practices shape the experiences and desires of girls and women, as well as the conditions of possibility under which they live. The third topic I take up is international labor migration, which involves a burgeoning number of women and men across South Asia. The protracted separations that transnational labor migration involved are reconfiguring many aspects of family life—including marital relations, family planning, child care, joint households, and elder care. Finally, I consider matters of women's reproductive autonomy, particularly access to contraception and abortion.

Marriage and Kinship Relations

From the standpoint of feminists in the Minority World, it might seem archaic, unacceptably heteronormative, and even antifeminist to begin a discussion of women's reproductive lives with a consideration of (hetero-sexual) marriage. However, in much of the Majority World, (heterosexual) marriage—as a legal institution, a foundational social structure, and the normative context for adulthood—figures importantly in the regulation of women's lives, both before and after they are married (Abeyasekera, 2017). A transnational standpoint demands that we study women's desires and strategies regarding sexuality and childbearing as they reflect the local social organization and cultural ethos. From a decolonial standpoint, practices such as arranged or quasi-arranged marriage, cross-cousin marriage, multi-generational households, and polygyny and polyandry and the value placed on premarital chastity ought to be analyzed in terms of the local opportunities, constraints, satisfactions, and lifeways they afford.

As in all feminist scholarship, reflexivity is a key element of trans-national feminist practice. *Reflexivity* is the critical practice of taking stock of one's assumptions, values, standpoint, and social location to assess how these might influence one's views of others (Wilkinson, 1988). For feminist psychologists, it also demands that we take stock of the framework of assumptions embedded in Western-centric psychologies. Assuming that most readers of this text are in the United States, I take a moment to reprise some of the institutions, ideologies, and practices of marriage, (hetero)sexuality, family planning, and fertility regulation that regulate women's experiences in the contemporary United States. My aim is to denaturalize our ways of being by pointing out that they are specific to our time and place.

In North America and Western Europe, the ideologies and practices of heterosexual courtship, marriage, childbearing, and fertility regulation have undergone dramatic and swift changes. Many of these changes were spurred by the resurgence of feminism in the last part of the 20th century. As well, there has been a dramatic increase in the public visibility and popular acceptance of lesbian, gay, and bisexual people; nonbinary genders; and sexual and gender fluidity (Diamond, 2018; Hegarty, Ansara, & Barker, 2018). In several countries, legal rights and protections have been affirmed as well.

Looking specifically at the United States, we can see that until about 60 years ago, marriage and childbearing were thought to be requisites for women's fulfillment and maturity. This idea was enshrined in Freud's theories of women's development and female sexual desire, though it hardly originated with Freud. During the 1950s and 1960s, the theories of Freud and his followers were the reigning framework for psychiatry, clinical psychology, personality psychology, and psychotherapy in the United States, as well as in many other parts of the Minority World. Freud's ideas about the primacy of (heterosexual) marriage and motherhood in women's lives shaped the prescriptions and practices of mental health professionals, as well as the theories of normal adulthood propounded in psychology textbooks (Friedan, 1963). Indeed, some prominent feminist social scientists of the 1970s also espoused this view. One example is the psychologist Judith Bardwick (1971), whose *Psychology of Women* was the first textbook for Psychology of Women courses taught in U.S. colleges and universities.

As readers may know, the changes since then have been profound (Cherlin, 2009). The median age at (first) marriage for women rose from 20 in 1960 to 27 in 2016. Rates of divorce roughly doubled. The median age at which U.S. women first bore a child rose from 21 to 26.4. Family sizes have decreased as well; indeed, the current family size is only 1.74 children per woman (Livingston, 2018). Furthermore, in much of U.S. society, sexual activity outside of marriage is condoned. Few people (and probably few psychologists) believe, as Freud (1925/1961) had claimed, that women's sexual desire derives from the underlying desire to have a child. Moreover, out-of-wedlock births are no longer widely stigmatized, nor are they legally penalized. Roughly 40% of births in the United States now occur outside marriage, compared with only 5% in 1960 (National Center for Health Statistics, 2016).

In the United States, information about preventing unwanted births is now widely available, and such information is included in progressive sex education curricula. This is the result of decades of activism and protracted struggle. Moreover, there are now highly effective contraceptive methods. Emergency contraception (sometimes called the *morning after pill* or *Plan B*) is available at pharmacies without a prescription. Nonetheless, the high cost of certain contraceptive methods and emergency contraception, however, is a significant obstacle for low-income women and girls.

Since 1973, the judicial interpretation of the U.S. Constitution has held that abortion is legal up to 24 weeks of pregnancy. However, as readers know, abortion is a highly contentious issue in the United States. The 1973 judicial decision regarding abortion (*Roe v. Wade*) allowed individual states to impose varying restrictions on abortion. Consequently, women's access to abortion has been severely curtailed by numerous local regulations and restrictions, many of which have no bona fide medical purpose, that have forced the closure of many clinics (Beckman, 2017). At the same time, anti-abortion activists have used threats of harm, harassment, vandalism, arson, and murder to deter providers and patients. As of this writing, politicians' opposition to abortion has raised fears that the judicial decision that gave women in the United States the right to abortion may soon be overturned (Angell, 2017).

In other Western high-income countries, there have been similar patterns of change regarding sexuality, heterosexual and nonheterosexual relations, marriage, and childbearing, although there is considerable variation from country to country. State policies regarding women, gender equality, and family supports vary as well, with the United States lagging far behind most central European countries. Interested readers can consult Eurostat (2016) for information about specific countries. Marecek, Macleod, and Hoggart (2017) offered information regarding legal statues governing women's access to abortion.

Now let us turn back to South Asia, where both marriage and child-bearing are cultural imperatives (Abeyasekera, 2016). Sri Lanka offers an example of how this cultural imperative shapes social practices, the normative life course, and personal desires. There, (heterosexual) marriage is the presumptive status for adult men and women. Indeed, it is thought of as a prerequisite to full adulthood. For instance, young adults who are not (yet) married are referred to as *girls* and *boys*. Divorces are infrequent, even when couples have long lived apart and consider their relationship over. In both rural and urban settings, everyday sociality, as well as political and economic life, is organized around marital alliances and family lineages (Abeyasekera, 2017).

By tradition, getting married and having children are regarded as fulfilling an obligation to one's kin, not a matter of pursuing private sexual or romantic desires. Such obligations are consistent with the cultural model of a relational or interdependent self. Optimally, marriage joins together a man and a woman who are blood relatives (Abeyasekera, 2016). In Sri Lanka (as elsewhere in South Asia), cross-cousin marriages have been considered ideal. Marriages to kin serve the important function of entwining families, consolidating clan alliances, and ensuring the continuation of the family lineage. For the individuals involved, such marriages are not experienced as an infringement on their freedom of choice or a sacrifice of their selfhood. Rather, they are the setting in which one's self can be fully realized. More recently, cosmopolitan elites—numerically, a small minority of the populace—have begun to embrace the Western model of companionate marriage, with its ideals of emotional intimacy, sexual pleasure, and affective bonds. This Western model is consistent with a cultural model of expressive individualism and an ethos that holds that people are (or ought to be) masters of their destinies. However, the companionate model of marriage has not replaced the ideal of marriage as a kin obligation but rather been woven into it (Abeyasekera, 2013).

As in most of South Asia, endogamous marriages, which are arranged (or quasi-arranged) by the partners' families, remain the norm in both preference and practice in Sri Lanka (Abeyasekera, 2017; Fuller & Narasimhan, 2008; Lindberg, 2009; Osella, 2012). "Love marriages" are viewed as risky because they disrupt traditional kinship relations and, in that way, threaten to undermine the social order, possibly leading to intergenerational rifts (Mody, 2008). Moreover, sexual passion and romantic attraction are regarded as temporary and therefore not a solid basis for entering into a lifetime relationship (Mody, 2008).

Given the status of marriage as a kin obligation and the preference for endogamous marriages, it is not surprising that parents and other elders have the duty of securing suitable partners for their children (Abeyasekera, 2017). To be suitable, a prospective partner should be of the same caste, religion, ethnicity, and social status and share consanguineal ties. Prospective partners are also expected to be of good moral character and from a family with an unsullied reputation. These qualities are ascertained a priori by discreet (or not so discreet) investigations by parents and other elders (and sometimes by for-hire marriage brokers). Traditionally, prospective partners had limited opportunities to get to know each other before the marriage took place. Today, it is more common that supervised meetings are arranged and that prospective partners can veto "proposals" gathered by their elders (Abeyasekera, 2017).

In many communities in South Asia, arranged marriages may also entail a dowry. Specific arrangements differ from one locale to another and from one religion to another. Speaking in general, however, dowry involves the transfer of wealth (in the form of land, cash, or valuable consumer goods) from the bride's family to the groom or his family. At one time, a dowry was a gift, but now dowry is often a matter of negotiation between families, sometimes with extortionate demands made by the groom's family (Mitter, 1991). In India, dowry was made illegal in 1961; however, this legal prohibition did little to stop the practice (and may have made things worse by driving dowry giving underground). Dowry and a range of abuses associated with it (such as bride burning) have been a major target of protest and activism by feminists in India. Dowry is not illegal in Sri Lanka, and there are few reports of extortionate demands and no reports of bride-burning.

In South Asia, the meanings and practices associated with marriage and kinship form the basis for many gendered practices throughout the life course regarding women's sexuality and childbearing. Next, I briefly describe one set of such practices, focusing in particular on Sri Lanka: the emphasis on female sexual respectability, restraints on unmarried girls' activities, and the value placed on female chastity.

Female Sexual Respectability

Across South Asia, the honor, good name, and "face" of a family rest on the sexual reputation of its women. Once a daughter reaches menarche, she and her family—especially her mother and other adult females—must be vigilant in guarding her reputation as a "good girl" (Lynch, 2007). After menarche, a girl's freedom of movement, freedom of association, and self-presentation are sharply curtailed, not only in comparison to her same-age brothers but also in comparison to the freedoms she had when she was younger. In public venues, a girl is likely to be accompanied by her mother or other female adults. Usha Menon (2013), whose work is in the Indian state of Orissa, described the custom of mothers sharing a bed with their daughter every night between the daughter's first menstrual period and her wedding night so that there could be no question about the daughter's virginity. In my work in Sri Lanka, I have collected several stories of mothers who promptly quit lucrative jobs in the Persian Gulf States because it was necessary for them to be present in the household once a daughter had her first menstrual period. Similarly, women who did shift work (e.g., nurses) were obliged to quit work when a daughter reached menarche to be at home at night to ensure that her sexual reputation would be unsullied (Kiribamune & Samarasinghe, 1990). A blemish on a girl's sexual reputation (whether deserved or not) not only jeopardizes her chances for a good marriage but is also a blemish on the family's honor (Abeyasekera & Marecek, in press). It diminishes the chances of a good marital match for all the children in the family. In a society in which identities are collective and interdependent, an individual cannot singly determine his or her destiny.

Premarital virginity (or more precisely, the appearance of virginity) remains a prominent value for women in most communities in South Asia. Modest comportment, close maternal supervision, and avoiding the company of boys and men are ways that an unmarried girl projects an image of chastity. In her ethnography of students on a university campus in western Sri Lanka, Ruwanpura (2011) described in detail how female students were vigilant about avoiding situations or appearances that could compromise their reputations and about helping their companions to do the same. Ruwanpura noted that the young women, who were in their early-to-mid 20s, did not chafe under such restrictions. Nor did they long for romantic or sexual liaisons. Furthermore, they did not buy into the idea—which is taken as common sense in much of the Minority World—that unmarried people ought to test out a series of romantic relationships before committing to a lifetime partner. Indeed, such a course of action would jeopardize the possibility of securing any partner. Perhaps more important, young people trust that their parents and elders will put considerable energies into locating a suitable marital partner.

A family may be asked to provide physical evidence of their daughter's virginity. Such documentation of a young woman's virginity is often of more importance to the groom's parents than to the groom himself. There are a number of means by which a bride can demonstrate she is a virgin. For example, a girl from a middle-class urban family may undergo a gynecological exam to certify her virginity, with the certification presented to her future mother-in-law (G. I. Unamboowe, personal communication, July 2015). Bridal dressers (that is, beauticians who take charge of the bride's hairstyle, jewelry, clothing, and makeup during the elaborate wedding celebrations) may supply a vial of chicken blood to smear on the linens from the wedding bed (A. L. Abeyasekera, personal communication, December 2015). In more traditional rural communities, the linens are presented to the bride's mother-in-law the morning after the wedding night (Chapin, 2014).

To sum up, in South Asia, collective interests, mutual obligations, and family solidarity have been and continue to be the basis of social organization, as well as of self and identity. Such obligations are not conceived of as impeding self-realization or self-development. Quite the opposite: They are the means through which selves are actualized (Abeyasekera & Marecek, 2018). Personal autonomy, untrammeled freedom of choice, and liberation from social constraints are not prized as they are in the Minority World. In consequence, feminisms in South Asia are not identical to the feminisms of Western high-income countries.

Marriage, Childbearing, and Child-Rearing in the Era of International Labor Migration

The movement of men, women, and (sometimes) children from poor countries to serve the citizens of wealthy countries (whether by choice or force) is not a new phenomenon. Patterns of labor migration closely parallel the stark economic inequalities across the globe. Today, transnational labor migration involves more than 164 million people worldwide (International Labor Organization, 2018). Several of the countries of South Asia (including Bangladesh, India, Nepal, Pakistan, and Sri Lanka) send sizeable numbers of workers abroad, mainly (though not exclusively) to the oil-rich Gulf States. The workers span the occupational spectrum from surgeons and bankers to laborers, drivers, and housemaids. A disproportionate number of South Asian migrants work in low-wage, low-skilled jobs, such as housemaids, nannies, cooks, drivers, gardeners, and construction workers. Many migrant laborers in the Gulf States are women (Ehrenreich & Hochschild, 2004). Such low-wage workers typically sign multiyear contracts and leave their spouses and children behind. Consequently, a large number of households in South Asia have a spouse or parent who resides in another country. In Sri Lanka, for example, in one household out of eight, either the mother or the father works abroad (and occasionally both do; Gamburd, 2000; Weeraratne, 2017).

Across South Asia, there are wide variations in the degree of state regulation of labor migration and the supports provided to migrants and their families. Moreover, the volatile politics of some receiving countries (e.g., Kuwait, Iraq, Syria) have occasionally imperiled foreign workers of all genders. Women who work abroad as domestic servants are often subjected to particularly intense regulation by government agencies in the sending countries. Because of the private nature of their workplace, they are also subjected to particular risks.

Sri Lanka affords one example of the intricate politics of women's international labor migration. State regulations and requirements reflect the range of societal anxieties associated with women's (but not men's) labor migration. There are concerns about the fate of the children who are left behind, as well as concerns about women's risk of sexual abuse, physical violence, and economic exploitation in the foreign households in which they work. In response to these concerns, state regulations are continually in flux. Unfortunately, thus far, the state has focused mainly on regulating women who seek work and made little or no effort to support women when they are abroad. At different times, the Sri Lankan state has set upper and lower age limits on women who wish to work abroad, prohibited mothers of preschool-age children from migrating, or insisted on proof of husbands' consent (V. Samarasinghe, personal communication, July 2017).

Despite anxieties about the safety of women who work as domestic servants and about the welfare of the children they leave behind, there is little chance that any South Asian state will put an end to female foreign employment. For some sending countries, such as Bangladesh, Nepal, and Sri Lanka, the earnings of international migrant workers constitute a significant component of the country's foreign income earnings (Weeraratne, 2017). Moreover, in many cases, the remittances that workers send home are crucial to their families' day-to-day survival. This is a crucial point to understand. Too often, women who work aboard are vilified as bad mothers who neglect or even "abandon" their children, or they are charged with seeking money for frivolous lifestyles or unnecessary luxury items. However, for families in desperate financial circumstances, earning money by working abroad is hardly neglectful; it is a necessity. One might also note that few if any concerns have been raised about the possible negative impact of fathers' protracted absences from the household.

Foreign employment of wives and mothers also has implications for women's reproductive lives, which have yet to be studied. Long periods (quite possibly 2 decades) when husband and wife live apart quite probably affect child spacing and, ultimately, family size. Indeed, cultural values regarding optimal family size, optimal timing of births, and optimal spacing of children may shift if prolonged foreign employment becomes a normative practice. Moreover, in the mother's absence, the burden of childcare most often falls on female relatives, usually a grandmother or an aunt. In some cases, female caregivers assume fulltime residential care of their grandchildren well into their 60s. Women who might have expected to be cared for by their adult daughters or daughters-in-law instead find themselves taking care of those women's children (Gamburd, 2015). Questions about such new family arrangements remain to be studied.

Another set of questions for social scientists concerns how prolonged foreign work contracts affect marriages. As such prolonged separations become commonplace, how will values, norms, and practices regarding monogamy, sexual infidelity, extramarital births, parallel intimate relationships, and so on change? A recent ethnography of long-term Senegalese labor migration to Italy could pave the way for investigations of South Asian labor migrants (Hannaford, 2017). Furthermore, few readers will be surprised to hear that the codes of sexual morality for male migrant workers in the Gulf States differ dramatically from those for female migrant workers (Frantz, 2011). Beyond that, little is known beyond inflammatory rumors and conjecture. Feminist psychologists are well equipped to address such questions.

Fertility Desires and Family Planning

In South Asia, having children is considered a natural part of adulthood and part of one's kinship obligation (Mitter, 1991). For most women, motherhood is thought of as simply a natural part of adult life. Women also find it is highly valued, highly desired, and deeply rewarding (Caldera, 2017). Like getting married, having children is a kin obligation, not purely a matter of personal choice. In Minority World countries, South Asian women are often portrayed in terms of stereotypes of continual childbearing, large families, and a high risk of maternal and infant mortality. Fortunately, such stereotypes are largely outdated. Moreover, like most stereotypes, they conceal a wide range of variation among South Asian countries and within each country, as I discuss next.

In several South Asian countries, access to family planning education and effective methods of contraception has been a high priority for state health agencies. It has also been a priority for international agencies such as the United Nations Population Fund (UNFPA), UNICEF, and private philanthropies. Sri Lanka, with an overall fertility rate of only 2.06 births per woman, offers one example of a relatively effective program of family planning. A prime reason for Sri Lanka's successful family planning program is its nationalized system of free health care, a legacy of the country's postindependence socialist government. Importantly, maternal health care includes a vigorous countrywide outreach program of home visits by a trained health worker for the duration of a woman's pregnancy and for several months after she has given birth. These visits include not only well-baby check-ups and instructions on infant care but also conversations about contraception, with an eye to informing women about "modern" options (i.e., those other than withdrawal, abstinence, and condoms). Furthermore, birth control pills, condoms, and emergency contraception (the morning after medication, Postinor) are available at pharmacies without a doctor's prescription and highly subsidized. (A Postinor tablet, for example, costs less than $1.00.) Government medical facilities provide intrauterine devices, contraceptive implants, and tubectomies without cost.

Women in Sri Lanka are high users of tubectomies, with rates of women seeking tubectomies at some point in their lives ranging between 25% and 45% across different communities (Departments of Census and Statistics, Ministry of National Policies and Economic Affairs & Health Sector Development Project, Ministry of Health, Nutrition and Indigenous Medicine, 2017). Researchers have speculated about reasons for women's high reliance on tubectomies to control their fertility. On the positive side, low rates of infant mortality (7.45 per 1,000 births) may buoy a couple's confidence that their children will survive to adulthood; therefore, when a woman has borne the desired number of children, a tubectomy seems like the most convenient contraceptive option. However, it has also been noted that the highest use of tubectomies is among Tamil women who work as agricultural laborers on the country's tea plantations—a minoritized ethnic community whose members perform work that is highly stigmatized. Some social activists have voiced suspicions that the government health care providers exert undue pressure on these women to undergo tubectomies in exchange for substantial monetary compensation (Balasundaram, 2011).

Sri Lanka's family planning programs stand in sharp contrast to those of Pakistan. Pakistan is now the fifth most populous country in the world, as well as the country with the highest rate of infant mortality in South Asia (UNICEF, 2018). In recent decades, the overall fertility rate in Pakistan has declined, as it has throughout South Asia. However, the rate of decline has been quite slow. In 2012, women had on average 3.8 children, and many women have reported that they have more children than they desire (Sathar, Singh, Rashida, Shah, & Niazi, 2014).

A primary reason for large family sizes in Pakistan is the taboo on all forms of "artificial" birth control that is preached by Muslim clerics. Some 96% of the population of Pakistan is Muslim, and Islam is the official state religion. Many Muslim clerics in Pakistan preach that the only acceptable means of limiting fertility are spacing children by means of breastfeeding or withdrawal, contraceptive methods that are highly unreliable. Government health ministries have been reluctant to challenge the clergy, and as a result, the development of state-supported family planning services has lagged (Bowen, 2004). Another factor that contributes to the high rate of undesired pregnancies is the low level of education and literacy among women in Pakistan. With only 45% of adult women able to read, it is difficult to provide women with information about birth planning (Saleem & Bobak, 2005).

State Coercion and Women's Reproductive Experiences

In Minority World contexts, feminists have mainly worked to ensure that women and girls have the means to control their fertility—that is, to avoid pregnancies that are unintended or unwanted. However, in some parts of the world, a feminist goal of reproductive justice also demands that women are not forcibly prevented from conceiving or bearing children. Examples of such force include sterilizations carried out without a woman's knowledge or consent; state programs of mass sterilizations in India and Indonesia; and forced abortions in Maoist China.

In the South Asian context, a potent instance of coercive sterilization is India's state-run mass sterilization camps, which were initiated in the 1970s and are still in the process of being dismantled (Mohanty & Bhalla, 2016).

These camps, which were organized by the Indian government with funds from international sources, targeted impoverished rural communities. Some offered inducements such as land, cash, and consumer goods in exchange for undergoing sterilization. Some relied on physical coercion by police. There are documented reports of several deaths due to unsafe and unsterile surgical procedures (Mohanty & Bhalla, 2016).

In sum, contraceptive technologies—like any technology—can be put to benign uses or coercive ones. Family planning technologies can enhance women's control over their lives. However, the coercive or deceptive use of such technologies can diminish human autonomy, dignity, and well-being. The history of compulsory fertility control and the state's disregard for women's health has left some Indian feminists wary of campaigns to persuade poor women to use LARCs (i.e., long-acting reversible contraceptives such as intrauterine devices, subdermal hormonal implants, and injections). Population control experts favor LARCs because they are "user-independent." Seen from another angle, however, this may seem to give control over women's bodies to agents of the state. Given the sordid record of state programs of coerced, deceitful, and medically unsafe sterilization, such wariness is hardly surprising (cf., Gold, 2014; Mohanty & Bhalla, 2016).

Abortion in South Asia

Induced abortion is one of the commonest gynecological procedures worldwide. However, roughly 25% of the world's population lives in countries where abortion is largely prohibited (Center for Reproductive Rights, 2019). Most of these countries are in the Majority World; these countries also account for 80% of the world's unsafe abortions. Outlawing abortions, it seems clear, does not prevent women from seeking them; rather, it compels women to seek clandestine abortions, which are often unsafe (Sedgh, Ashford, & Hussain, 2016).

Legal statutes governing abortion vary widely across South Asian countries. In India, the Medical Termination of Pregnancy Act, enacted in 1971, allows women to terminate a pregnancy up to 20 weeks of gestation (Singh et al., 2018). In Pakistan, the law permits abortions to save the mother's life or to provide "necessary treatment" (Sathar et al., 2014). In Nepal, a liberal abortion law was enacted in 2002. By contrast, in Bangladesh and Sri Lanka, abortion is illegal unless it is necessary to save the life of the mother. In Sri Lanka, the population of which is roughly 70% Buddhist, the Buddhist clergy have consistently denounced efforts to loosen restrictions on abortion. As of this writing, abortion is not legally permitted in Sri Lanka even in cases of rape or incest or to enable women to abort fetuses with fatal abnormalities (Kumar, 2013).

Formal legal codes, however, tell only part of the story regarding women's access to abortion. In Bangladesh, state health clinics allow women who have missed a menstrual period to undergo a procedure called *menstrual regulation* (MR; Whittaker, 2010). MR involves either manual vacuum aspiration of the uterus or the administration of the abortifacient medications mifepristone and misoprostol. A woman is permitted to undergo MR up to 12 weeks after a missed menstrual period (Guttmacher Institute, 2017). Similarly, in Sri Lanka, what is called a "womb wash" (a manual vacuum aspiration of the contents of the uterus) has at times been available to women who have missed a menstrual period (T. Munasinghe, personal communication, July 2017). In both Bangladesh and Sri Lanka, these procedures, although they serve to terminate a pregnancy, are considered a form of contraception and hence not legally prohibited.

Let us look more closely at Sri Lanka to examine one set of practices regarding extralegal abortions. The first thing to note is that researchers who seek to learn about extralegal abortions face formidable hurdles. Providers of such abortions do not come forward to take part in research. Physicians and others who direct pregnant women to such providers remain hidden as well. Further, women who have received abortions are careful to hide that fact, believing that they will be subject to legal reprisals.

Despite Sri Lanka's strict prohibition of abortion, an estimated 256,000 women obtain extralegal abortions every year (Abeykoon, 2009). Considering Sri Lanka's small population (about 20 million), this is a high rate of induced abortion. Clearly, neither legal strictures nor religious proscriptions keep Sri Lankan women from seeking an abortion when they are faced with untenable pregnancies. Many of these extralegal abortions are carried out in secret by qualified biomedical providers (in which case they are likely to be medically safe). Otherwise, women obtain abortions from quacks, untrained midwives, or practitioners of traditional medicine (e.g., Ayurveda, Unani); some women attempt to induce an abortion by means of botanical preparations (Abeykoon, 2009; D. Thoradeniya, personal communication, July 2017).

As elsewhere (including in the United States), most Sri Lankan women who seek abortions are married and have children (Kumar, 2013; Thalagala, 2012). Not infrequently, they report that they had conceived due to a contraceptive failure or because they had been misinformed about their chances of getting pregnant (Thalagala, 2012). For example, many believed that they would not get pregnant as long as they were breast-feeding. Second, the criminalization of abortions constitutes a serious public health problem. Clandestine abortions carried out under unsafe conditions by unqualified providers are a significant cause of maternal mortality (Kumar, 2013). Furthermore, because abortion is a crime, women who have had clandestine abortions delay seeking medical care for complications of such abortions for fear of prosecution (Arambepola & Rajapaksa, 2014). (In actuality, medical personnel do not report women to the police; T. Munasinghe, personal communication, August 2018.) Furthermore, the burdens caused by criminalizing abortion are not borne equally across all social strata. For affluent women, especially urban dwellers, it may be relatively easy to locate a qualified gynecologist in private practice who performs clandestine abortions. Poor, less educated, and rural women may be compelled to resort to unqualified practitioners or to attempt a self-induced abortion.

The psychological aspects of unintended, unwanted, and untenable pregnancies and safe and unsafe abortions deserve more study than they have heretofore received. A first question concerns how embryos and fetuses are construed in the local culture. In the Minority World, opponents of abortion typically insist that life (or personhood) begins at conception, and thus embryos have a "right to life." In this view, MR and womb wash would be regarded as forms of abortion. However, in Bangladesh and Sri Lanka, these procedures are seen as contraception, not abortion. As the embryologists Gilbert and Pinto-Correia (2017) told us, the questions of when life begins and what constitutes life have no scientific answers.

Son Preference and Sex-Selection Abortions

In some South Asian countries, notably India, Pakistan, and Nepal, members of some social groups prefer to give birth to sons rather than daughters. With the availability of technologies that readily permit pre-natal sex determination, such preferences may lead couples to elect to abort female fetuses. The use of sex-selective abortion (in some instances coupled with female infanticide or neglect of female infants) has been sufficiently widespread to produce a noticeable imbalance in the sex ratio in the population at large. The Harvard-based economist Amartya Sen, who was born in India, called attention to this in his assertion that "100 million women" were "missing" from Asia and North Africa (Sen, 1990, p. 1). Although the precise figures are a matter of debate, the use of sex-selective abortion in some countries in South Asia has not been disputed. Nor has been the existence of the selective neglect of infant girls. By now, India, Pakistan, and Nepal all have passed legislation intended to halt the practice of sex-selection abortion, although few would argue that legal prohibitions have been entirely successful.

Sex-selective abortion has generated a good deal of ethical debate, including ethical debate among feminists. For feminists in the Minority World, a woman's "right to choose" has been the central principle in abortion activism. But many feminists are uncomfortable endorsing the right to abort a fetus because it is a female. An important contribution of transnational feminist scholars is the recognition that a preference for sons over daughters is not solely a matter of adherence to primordial patriarchal traditions. Current social practices such as dowry and gender biases in inheritance laws lead couples to limit the number of girls they have (Eklund & Purewal, 2017).

In most of the Minority World, women's right to choose and their rights to bodily autonomy and privacy have been cornerstone principles of reproductive justice. These principles flow from the ethos of individualism and liberal political theory (Marecek et al., 2017). But, as we noted earlier, individualism is quite particular to the Minority World. In South Asia, arguments for legalizing abortion do not rest on women's rights to autonomy, self-determination, or privacy, as in the Minority World. Rather, feminists and others who have advocated for legal abortion more often do so by arguing that safe abortion is essential to women's health.

CONCLUSION

Transnational feminist theorists have been careful to avoid an add-and-stir approach to the study of women's lives. An add-and-stir approach, they say, too easily becomes a kind of cultural tourism that offers glimpses of women in exotic locales. Often such glimpses depict women in the Majority World as benighted victims in need of rescue, "upliftment," or attitudinal adjustment. By contrast, transnational feminist scholars seek nuanced, grounded analyses of those they study, and they often work in collaboration with local scholars. Such analyses consider how the conditions of possibility for women are structured by present-day social, cultural, and international inequalities, as well as by colonial histories.

The lens afforded by transnational feminist psychology is not readily compatible with the conventions of Minority World psychological science. Psychological science usually presumes to discover universal principles of behavior that are broadly applicable to all humans. This presumption has come under increasing attack by movements in psychology such as critical psychology, Indigenous psychology, decolonial psychology, and cultural psychology (Kurtiş & Adams, 2015, 2018; Marecek & Christopher, 2018).

Women's reproductive experiences are part and parcel of their identities and their intimate relationships. However, women's reproductive experiences are not solely private experiences; they are embedded in culture and social life. For psychologists in the Minority World to comprehend the lives of women in the cultural settings of the Majority World, they must bracket their beliefs, meanings, and values about an array of life experiences, such as selfhood, mothering, marriage, generational hierarchies, sexual expression and sexualities, and child-rearing and childhood. This is a necessary first step toward comprehending the lifeworlds and societal contingencies of the people they wish to study. Further, psychologists must step beyond the usual boundaries of disciplinary knowledge to take account of the sociopolitical contexts of women's reproductive experiences (Wallace, Porter, & Ralph-Bowman, 2013).

To close, let us remind ourselves that women's reproductive experiences are situated in the context of global politics and stark global economic inequalities. As the brief discussion of international labor migration pointed out, significant numbers of families in the Majority World cannot survive unless the mother or the father relocates to a wealthy country—an economic strategy with consequences for personal well-being, marriage, sexuality, childbearing, child-rearing, and elder care. India's sterilization program, which I discussed briefly, shows how global politics can shape reproductive experiences. That program was initiated in response to international fears of a "population bomb" set to "explode" in the "Third World," notably in India, fears set in motion by Paul Ehrlich's (1968) fear-mongering book (Connelly, 2008). It was funded heavily by development agencies and private foundations in the Minority World. An even more timely example concerns repeated decisions by the U.S. government to cut off UNFPA funding that supports reproductive health care in Majority World countries. Further, Republican presidents since 1984 have repeatedly imposed global gag rules that cut off funds to health care organizations if their workers mention abortion to their patients. Such policies have impeded women's access to contraceptives, gynecological and obstetric care, and HIV-related care (Starrs, 2017). Ironically, as Bendavid, Avila, and Miller (2011) pointed out, making these services unavailable likely leads to more, not fewer, abortions. These policies are an especially dismal example of realpolitik. They are touted domestically as "pro-life," but in reality, they cavalierly put the health and even the lives of Majority World women at risk.

REFERENCES

Abeyasekera, A. L. (2013). *The choosing person: Marriage, middle-class identities, and modernity in contemporary Sri Lanka* (Unpublished doctoral dissertation). University of Bath, Bath, England.

Abeyasekera, A. L. (2016). Narratives of choice: Marriage, choosing right, and the responsibility of agency in urban middle-class Sri Lanka. *Feminist Review, 113*, 1–16. http://dx.doi.org/10.1057/fr.2016.3

Abeyasekera, A. L. (2017). "Living for others": Narrating agency in the context of failed marriages and singleness in urban Sri Lanka. *Feminism & Psychology, 27,* 427–446. http://dx.doi.org/10.1177/0959353517716951

Abeyasekera, A. L., & Marecek, J. (2018). *Transnational feminisms and psychologies: Selves, suffering, and moral personhood in Sri Lanka.* Manuscript submitted for publication.

Abeyasekera, A. L., & Marecek, J. (in press). Embodied shame and gendered demeanors in young women in Sri Lanka. *Feminism & Psychology.*

Abeykoon, A. T. P. L. (2009). *Estimates of abortion rate in Sri Lanka using Bongaarts model of proximate determinants of fertility.* Colombo: UNFPA Sri Lanka.

Abu-Lughod, L. (2002). Do Muslim women really need saving? Anthropological reflections on cultural relativism and its others. *American Anthropologist, 104,* 783–790. http://dx.doi.org/10.1525/aa.2002.104.3.783

Alam, S. (2008). Majority World: Challenging the West's rhetoric of democracy. *Amerasia Journal, 34,* 87–98. http://dx.doi.org/10.17953/amer.34.1.l3176027k4q614v5

Angell, M. (2017, June 22). The abortion battlefield. *The New York Review of Books.* Retrieved from http://www.nybooks.com/articles/2017/06/22/the-abortion-battlefield/?printpage=true

Arambepola, C., & Rajapaksa, L. C. (2014). Decision making on unsafe abortions in Sri Lanka: A case-control study. *Reproductive Health, 11,* 91–99. http://dx.doi.org/10.1186/1742-4755-11-91

Arnett, J. J. (2008). The neglected 95%: Why American psychology needs to become less American. *American Psychologist, 63,* 602–614. http://dx.doi.org/10.1037/0003-066X.63.7.602

Balasundaram, S. (2011). Stealing wombs: Sterilization abuses and women's reproductive health in Sri Lanka's tea plantations. *Indian Anthropologist, 41,* 57–78.

Bardwick, J. M. (1971). *Psychology of women: A study of bio-cultural conflicts.* New York, NY: Sage.

Beckman, L. (2017). Abortion in the United States: The continuing controversy. *Feminism & Psychology, 27,* 101–113. http://dx.doi.org/10.1177/0959353516685345

Bendavid, E., Avila, P., & Miller, G. (2011). United States aid policy and induced abortion in sub-Saharan Africa. *Bulletin of the World Health Organization, 89,* 873–880. http://dx.doi.org/10.2471/BLT.11.091660

Bowen, D. L. (2004). Islamic law and family planning. In S. P. Heyneman (Ed.), *Islam and social policy* (pp. 118–155). Nashville, TN: Vanderbilt University Press.

Caldera, A. V. (2017). *Perceptions of disciplinary strategies for 6-year-olds: A study of mothers in the Colombo District* (Unpublished master's thesis). University of Colombo, Colombo, Sri Lanka.

Center for Reproductive Rights. (2019). *The world's abortion laws 2019.* Retrieved from http://www.worldabortionlaws.com/

Chapin, B. L. (2014). *Childhood in a Sri Lankan village: Shaping hierarchy and desire.* New Brunswick, NJ: Rutgers University Press.

Cherlin, A. J. (2009). *The marriage-go-round: The state of marriage and the family in America today.* New York, NY: Vintage.

Christopher, J. C., Wendt, D. C., Marecek, J., & Goodman, D. M. (2014). Critical cultural awareness: Contributions to a globalizing psychology. *American Psychologist, 69,* 645–655. http://dx.doi.org/10.1037/a0036851

Connelly, M. (2008). *Fatal misconception: The struggle to control world population.* Cambridge, MA: Harvard University Press.

Conway, J. M. (2017). Troubling transnational feminism(s): Theorising activist praxis. *Feminist Theory, 18,* 205–227. http://dx.doi.org/10.1177/1464700117700536

Cronin-Furman, K., Gowrinathan, N., & Zakaria, R. (2017). *Emissaries of empowerment.* Unpublished manuscript, Colin Powell School for Civic and Global Leadership, The City College of New York, NY.

Cushman, P. (1995). *Constructing the self, constructing America: A cultural history of psychotherapy.* Reading, MA: Addison-Wesley.

De Alwis, M. (1997). The production and embodiment of respectability: Gendered demeanours in colonial Ceylon. In M. Roberts (Ed.), *Sri Lanka. Collective identities revisited* (Vol. I, pp. 105–144). Colombo, Sri Lanka: Marga Institute.

Departments of Census and Statistics, Ministry of National Policies and Economic Affairs & Health Sector Development Project, Ministry of Health, Nutrition and Indigenous Medicine. (2017). *Demographic and Health Survey—2016, Sri Lanka.* Retrieved from http://www.statistics.gov.lk/social/DHS_2016a/Chapter5.pdf

Diamond, L. M. (2018). Contemporary theory in the study of intimacy, desire, and sexuality. In N. K. Dess, J. Marecek, & L. C. Bell (Eds.), *Gender, sex, and sexualities: Psychological perspectives* (pp. 271–294). New York, NY: Oxford University Press. http://dx.doi.org/10.1093/oso/9780190658540.003.0012

Ehrenreich, B., & Hochschild, A. R. (Eds.). (2004). *Global woman: Nannies, maids, and sex workers in the new economy.* New York, NY: Holt.

Ehrlich, P. R. (1968). *The population bomb.* New York, NY: Ballantine.

Eklund, L., & Purewal, N. (2017). The bio-politics of population control and sex-selective abortion in China and India. *Feminism & Psychology, 27,* 34–55. http://dx.doi.org/10.1177/0959353516682262

Eurostat. (2016). *The EU in the world.* Retrieved from https://ec.europa.eu/eurostat/documents/3217494/7589036/KS-EX-16-001-EN-N.pdf/bcacb30c-0be9-4c2e-a06d-4b1daead493e

Frantz, E. A. (2011). *Exporting subservience: Sri Lankan women's migration for domestic work* (Unpublished doctoral dissertation). London School of Economics and Political Science, London, England.

Freud, S. (1961). Some psychical consequences of the anatomical distinction between the sexes. In J. Strachey (Ed.), *The standard edition of the complete psychological works of Sigmund Freud.* London, England: Hogarth Press. (Original work published 1925)

Friedan, B. (1963). *The feminine mystique.* New York, NY: Norton.

Fuller, C. F., & Narasimhan, H. (2008). Companionate marriage in India: The changing marriage system in a middle-class Brahman subcaste. *Journal of the Royal Anthropological Institute, 14,* 736–754. http://dx.doi.org/10.1111/j.1467-9655.2008.00528.x

Gamburd, M. R. (2000). *The kitchen spoon's handle: Transnationalism and Sri Lanka's migrant housemaids.* Ithaca, NY: Cornell University Press.

Gamburd, M. R. (2015). Migrant remittances, population ageing, and intergenerational family obligations in Sri Lanka. In L. A. Hoang & B. S. A. Yeoh (Eds.), *Transnational labor migration, remittances, and the changing family in Asia* (pp. 137–162). London: Palgrave.

Gilbert, S., & Pinto-Correia, C. (2017). *Fear, wonder, and science in the new age of reproductive biotechnology.* New York, NY: Columbia University Press. http://dx.doi.org/10.7312/gilb17094

Gold, R. B. (2014). Guarding against coercion while ensuring access: A delicate balance. *Guttmacher Policy Review, 17*(3), 8–14. Retrieved from https://www.guttmacher.org/sites/default/files/article_files/gpr170308.pdf

Guttmacher Institute. (2017). *Menstrual regulation and unsafe abortion in Bangladesh.* Retrieved from https://www.guttmacher.org/fact-sheet/menstrual-regulation-unsafe-abortion-bangladesh

Hannaford, D. (2017). *Marriage without borders: Transnational spouses in neoliberal Senegal.* Philadelphia: University of Pennsylvania Press. http://dx.doi.org/10.9783/9780812294194

Hegarty, H., Ansara, Y. G., & Barker, M.-J. (2018). Nonbinary gender identities. In N. K. Dess, J. Marecek, & L. C. Bell (Eds.), *Gender, sex, and sexualities: Psychological perspectives* (pp. 53–76). New York, NY: Oxford University Press. http://dx.doi.org/10.1093/oso/9780190658540.003.0003

Henrich, J., Heine, S. J., & Norenzayan, A. (2010). The weirdest people in the world? *Behavioral and Brain Sciences, 33*(2–3), 61–83. http://dx.doi.org/10.1017/S0140525X0999152X

International Labour Organization. (2018). *Labour migration.* Retrieved from http://www.ilo.org/global/topics/labour-migration/lang--en/index.htm

Kiribamune, S., & Samarasinghe, V. (1990). *Women at the crossroads: A Sri Lankan perspective.* New Delhi, India: Vikas.

Kirschner, S. R. (1996). *The religious and romantic origins of psychoanalysis: Individuation and integration in post-Freudian theory.* Cambridge, England: Cambridge University Press.

Kumar, R. (2013). Abortion in Sri Lanka: The double standard. *American Journal of Public Health, 103,* 400–404. http://dx.doi.org/10.2105/AJPH.2012.301154

Kurtiş, T., & Adams, G. (2015). Decolonizing liberation: Toward a transnational feminist psychology. *Journal of Social and Political Psychology*, 3, 388–413. http://dx.doi.org/10.5964/jspp.v3i1.326

Kurtiş, T., & Adams, G. (2018). Gender and sex(ualities): A cultural psychology approach. In N. K. Dess, J. Marecek, & L. C. Bell (Eds.), *Gender, sex and sexualities* (pp. 105–125). New York, NY: Oxford University Press.

Lindberg, A. (2009). Islamisation, modernisation, or globalisation? Changed gender relations among South Indian Muslims. *South Asia: Journal of South Asian Studies*, 32, 86–109. http://dx.doi.org/10.1080/00856400802709292

Livingston, G. (2018, January 18). *Is U.S. fertility at an all-time low? It depends*. Retrieved from Pew Research Center website: http://www.pewresearch.org/fact-tank/2018/01/18/is-u-s-fertility-at-an-all-time-low-it-depends/

Lynch, C. (2007). *Juki girls, good girls: Gender and cultural politics in Sri Lanka's global garment industry*. Ithaca, NY: Cornell University Press.

Macleod, C., Marecek, J., & Capdevila, R. (2014). *Feminism & Psychology* going forward. *Feminism & Psychology*, 24, 3–17. http://dx.doi.org/10.1177/0959353513515308

Mani, L. (1987). Contentious traditions: The debate on sati in colonial India. *Cultural Critique*, 7, 119–156. http://dx.doi.org/10.2307/1354153

Marecek, J., & Christopher, J. C. (2018). Is positive psychology an indigenous psychology? In N. J. L. Brown, T. Lomas, & F. J. Eiroá-Orosa (Eds.), *The Routledge international handbook of critical positive psychology* (pp. 84–98). London, England: Routledge.

Marecek, J., Macleod, C., & Hoggart, L. (2017). Abortion in legal, social, and healthcare contexts. *Feminism & Psychology*, 27, 4–14. http://dx.doi.org/10.1177/0959353516689521

Markus, H. R., & Kitayama, S. (1994). A collective fear of the collective: Implications of selves and theories of selves. *Personality and Social Psychology Bulletin*, 20, 568–579. http://dx.doi.org/10.1177/0146167294205013

Marsella, A. J., Tharp, R. G., & Ciborowski, T. J. (1979). *Perspectives on cross-cultural psychology*. New York, NY: Academic Press.

Menon, U. (2013). *Women, wellbeing, and the ethics of domesticity in an Odia Hindu temple town*. New York, NY: Springer. http://dx.doi.org/10.1007/978-81-322-0885-3

Miller, P. J., Wang, S., Sandel, T., & Cho, G. E. (2002). Self-esteem as folk theory: A comparison of European American and Taiwanese mothers' beliefs. *Parenting: Science and Practice*, 2, 209–239. http://dx.doi.org/10.1207/S15327922PAR0203_02

Mitter, S. S. (1991). *Dharma's daughters: Contemporary Indian women and Hindu culture*. New Brunswick, NJ: Rutgers University Press.

Mody, P. (2008). *The intimate state: Love-marriage and the law in Delhi*. London, England: Routledge. http://dx.doi.org/10.4324/9780203874691

Mohanty, C. T., & Bhalla, N. (2016, September 16). *Indian activists welcome top court ban on 'sterilization camps' after women's deaths*. Retrieved from Reuters website: https://www.reuters.com/article/us-india-women-sterilisation/indian-activists-welcome-top-court-ban-on-sterilization-camps-after-womens-deaths-idUSKCN11M1YT

Mohanty, C. T., Russo, A., & Torres, L. (1991). *Third World women and the politics of feminism*. Bloomington: Indiana University Press.

Morgan, R. (1984). *Sisterhood is global*. New York, NY: Feminist Press.

National Center for Health Statistics. (2016). *Unmarried childbearing*. Retrieved from http://www.cdc.gov/nchs/fastats/unmarried-childbearing.htm

Nielsen, M., Haun, D., Kärtner, J., & Legare, C. H. (2017). The persistent sampling bias in developmental psychology: A call to action. *Journal of Experimental Child Psychology, 162*, 31–38. http://dx.doi.org/10.1016/j.jecp.2017.04.017

Osella, C. (2012). Desires under reform: Contemporary reconfigurations of family, marriage, love and gendering in a transnational south Indian matrilineal Muslim community. *Culture and Religion, 13*, 241–264. http://dx.doi.org/10.1080/14755610.2012.675508

Rosner, R. I. (2018). History and the topsy-turvy world of psychotherapy. *History of Psychology, 21*, 177–186. http://dx.doi.org/10.1037/hop0000102

Rutherford, A., Capdevila, R., Undurti, V., & Palmary, I. (Eds.). (2011). *Handbook of international feminisms*. New York, NY: Springer. http://dx.doi.org/10.1007/978-1-4419-9869-9

Ruwanpura, E. (2011). *Sex or sensibility? The making of chaste women and promiscuous men in a Sri Lankan university setting* (Unpublished doctoral dissertation). University of Edinburgh, Edinburgh, Scotland.

Saleem, S., & Bobak, M. (2005). Women's autonomy, education and contraception use in Pakistan: A national study. *Reproductive Health, 2*, 8. http://dx.doi.org/10.1186/1742-4755-2-8

Sathar, Z., Singh, S., Rashida, G., Shah, Z., & Niazi, R. (2014). Induced abortions and unintended pregnancies in Pakistan. *Studies in Family Planning, 45*, 471–491. http://dx.doi.org/10.1111/j.1728-4465.2014.00004.x

Sedgh, G., Ashford, L. S., & Hussain, R. (2016). *Unmet need for contraception in developing countries: Examining women's reasons for not using a method*. Retrieved from Guttmacher Institute website: https://www.guttmacher.org/report/unmet-need-for-contraception-in-developing-countries

Sen, A. (1990, December 20). More than 100 million women are missing. *The New York Review of Books*. Retrieved from http://www.nybooks.com/articles/1990/12/20/more-than-100-million-women-are-missing/?printpage=true

Shell-Duncan, B. (2008). From health rights to human rights: Female genital cutting and the politics of intervention. *American Anthropologist, 110*, 225–236. http://dx.doi.org/10.1111/j.1548-1433.2008.00028.x

Singh, S., Shekhar, C., Acharya, R., Moore, A. M., Stillman, M., Pradhan, M. R., . . . Browne, A. (2018, January 1). The incidence of abortion and unintended pregnancy in India, 2015. *The Lancet, 6*(1), e111–e120. http://dx.doi.org/ 10.1016/S2214-109X(17)30453-9

Starrs, A. M. (2017, February 4). The Trump global gag rule: An attack on US family planning and global health aid. *The Lancet, 389*(10068), 485–486. http://dx.doi.org/10.1016/S0140-6736(17)30270-2

Swarr, A. L., & Nagar, R. (2010). *Critical transnational feminist praxis.* Albany, NY: SUNY Press.

Thalagala, N. (2012). Unsafe abortions in Sri Lanka—facts and risk profile. *Journal of the College of Community Physicians of Sri Lanka, 15*, 1–12. http://dx.doi.org/ 10.4038/jccpsl.v15i1.4934

UNICEF. (2018). *Pakistan.* Retrieved from https://data.unicef.org/country/pak/

United Nations Department of Economic and Social Affairs, Population Division. (2018). *United Nations expert group meeting for the review and appraisal of the programme of action of the international conference on population and development and its contribution to the follow-up and review of the 2030 agenda for sustainable development.* Retrieved from http://www.un.org/en/development/desa/ population/events/pdf/expert/28/EGM_Frank_Swiaczny_ppt.pdf

Wallace, T., Porter, F., & Ralph-Bowman, M. (Eds.). (2013). *Aid, NGOs and the realities of women's lives: A perfect storm.* Rugby, England: Practical Action. http://dx.doi.org/10.3362/9781780447780

Weeraratne, B. (2017). Globalization of family: The role of the state. Unpublished manuscript, Institute of Policy Studies of Sri Lanka, Colombo.

Whittaker, A. (2010). *Abortion in Asia: Local dilemmas, global politics.* Oxford, England: Berghahn Books.

Wilkinson, S. (1988). The role of reflexivity in feminist psychology. *Women's Studies International Forum, 11*, 493–502. http://dx.doi.org/10.1016/0277-5395(88)90024-6

9

TRANSNATIONAL FEMINIST PERSPECTIVES ON HUMAN TRAFFICKING: CENTERING STRUCTURES, INSTITUTIONS, AND SUBJECTS

JULIETTA HUA AND JESSICA TJIU

In the nearly 2 decades since the passage of a United Nations (UN; 2000) human trafficking protocol and the myriad national antitrafficking laws, programs, and policies criminalizing human trafficking, we have seen the growth of media, organizational, and legal infrastructures addressing human trafficking.[1] Feminist criticisms of the UN Protocol and antitrafficking discourses have examined the significance of singling out sex, as well as the language that collapses women with children.

---

[1]According to the UN Protocol, human trafficking is generally defined as

> Recruitment, transportation, transfer, harbouring or receipt of persons, by means of the threat or use of force or other forms of coercion, of abduction, of fraud or deception, of the abuse of power or of a position of vulnerability or of the giving or receiving of payments or benefits to achieve the consent of a person having control over another person, for the purpose of exploitation. Exploitation shall include, at a minimum, the exploitation of the prostitution of others or other forms of sexual exploitation, forced labour or services, slavery or practices similar to slavery, servitude or the removal of organs. (UN, 2000, Article 3, para. 1).

http://dx.doi.org/10.1037/0000148-010

Transnational Psychology of Women: Expanding International and Intersectional Approaches, L. H. Collins, S. Machizawa, and J. K. Rice (Editors)

Feminist interventions into human trafficking also include transnational feminist calls to refrain from universalization, understand the importance of history and context, and consider linkages rather than one-to-one comparisons. Thus, "transnational feminism" has been taken up by feminist scholars of human trafficking in ways that engage what Grewal and Kaplan (1994) term *scattered hegemonies* that illuminate the uneven routings of power both across and within categorical units, all while focusing on the making of such categories. Doing so reveals the limits of universalization and categorical binaries ("West" or the rest, North or South, center or periphery, global or local, trafficked or trafficker, victim or criminal) and the ways categories enforce a notion of stability that, in fact, undermines, hides, and erases heterogeneity, complexity, and contradiction. These critiques of binaries and the universalization of the category "woman" build on the works of U.S. Women of Color feminists. Women of Color feminisms draw attention to the invisibilizing of racial privilege (Whiteness) within mainstreamed feminisms and characterize the interventions of scholars such as Barbara Smith, Beverly Guy-Sheftall, and Paula Giddings (2014); Kimberle Crenshaw (1989); Patricia Hill Collins (1990); Cherrie Moraga and Gloria Anzaldua (1983); and many other Women of Color feminists. Moraga and Anzaldua's work also draws attention to Third World feminism. In this chapter, we outline some of the main threads of these transnational and Women of Color feminist interventions into human trafficking.

DECONSTRUCTING CATEGORIES

As scholars of social construction have long pointed out, power tends to be organized in ways that naturalize categorical difference. This does not make the experience of citizenship, race, gender, sexuality, or the myriad social categories at work in the world any less real in organizing power relations or senses of the self; it is to simply point out that such categories come to have significance and coherence through social, historical, and political machinations. Chandra Mohanty and Jacqui Alexander (1997), in their reformulation of Simone de Beauvoir's (1949) famous passage that one is not born a woman but rather becomes one, articulated it this way: "We were not born women of color, but became women of color here [in the United States]" (p. 492). They explained that although they each had distinct experiences growing up in formerly British colonial spaces and experienced class or caste, religious, and racial fractures in these spaces, the kind of racial terrain they experienced when they moved to the United States was different. Thus, they drew the distinction of becoming "Women of Color" to signal both the distinct, national meanings about race anchored in their migrations to the

United States, as well as the political aspect of claiming "Woman of Color"; it signals a political and intellectual formation, not simply an identity.

As Grewal and Kaplan (1994) further explained, "transnational" is evoked as a way to signal a challenge to "inadequate and inaccurate binary divisions" (p. 13) that might presume a "West versus the rest" or "U.S. versus non-U.S." terrain. Rather, like Mohanty and Alexander's (1997) call to understand how one becomes a "Woman of Color," Grewal and Kaplan's (1994) "transnational feminism" works to destabilize and deconstruct taken-for-granted categories. Grewal and Kaplan (1996) are critical, for instance, of the ways U.S. Women of Color, such as Alice Walker, can also homogenize and universalize meanings of patriarchy and Blackness that flatten the important historical, geopolitical relationships that make understandings of gender, sexuality, race, and ethnicity in Africa related, yet distinct, from the United States.[2] Writing specifically against international relations, political science, area studies, and other U.S.-centric disciplinary knowledge formations that for too long built perspectives that naturalized a West versus the rest paradigm, Grewal and Kaplan (1996) proposed instead how circuits of power situate subjects relationally (to each other as well as with and through the many categories we use to organize society). Such perspectives, shared with many feminist scholars including Nancy Naples and Manisha Desai (2002) and Kum-Kum Bhavnani (2001), to name a few, approach feminism as plural and interconnected; they challenge how feminism can and has supported colonial power relations but need not continue to do so.

Following in the traditions of critiques such as Mohanty's (1988), as well as feminist literature on rape and sexual violence, feminist criticisms of human trafficking often begin by unpacking the "victim label" and asking how such labels are made, experienced, and policed (see Haynes, 2007; Hill, 2016; Jackson, 2016; Murray, 1998; Shih, 2016; Showden & Majic, 2014). The binarism of the worthy trafficking victim posed against the (criminal) illegal or smuggled alien (Bernstein & Schaffner, 2004; Kempadoo & Doezema, 1998; Kempadoo, Sanghera, & Pattanaik, 2012; Sharma, 2003) is one that informs the different positioning of many human trafficking interventions, especially on the level of nation-states attempting to balance the human rights impulse (of protecting people from violence) against the desire to police borders. For example, Thaddeus Gregory Blanchette and Ana Paula da Silva (2014) pointed out the ways Brazil's 21st-century efforts to address human trafficking come alongside post-9/11 geopolitical changes that

---

[2]This is similar to Patricia Hill Collins's *Black Feminist Thought* (1990), which offers a critique of the way Afrocentric frameworks for understanding "African American" presume heteropatriarchy as the terms for reclaiming "African-ness."

impacted migration and migrants. The war on terror, in other words, had global resonance in rendering certain migrant subjects suspect and criminal and altering migration patterns (namely, when key states restrict or change entry conditions), as Julie Kaye (2017) explained.

Like many nations, Brazil's ratification of the UN protocol in 2004, although ostensibly a "human rights" effort, was also one deeply situated in the growth of the surveillance state. The context of the growing influence of the surveillance state has meant that innocence becomes the singular axis through which trafficked subjects can be rendered. Although "the transnational migrant subject is deeply shaped by notions of criminality, criminalizing processes, and the criminal justice system" and migrants are always "produc[ing] and produced by the racial and gender schemas in sending and destination countries that define them as 'criminal,' 'illegal' and the antithesis to the nation-states' project of citizen-subjects" (Fukushima, 2019, p. xx), this aspect is heightened within the context of the war on terror.

Innocence and victimization render trafficked subjects unthreatening and in opposition to the (terrorist threat of the) criminal alien. In the context of Brazil,

> Discussions about the trafficking of persons in the media are replete with stories in which Brazilian innocents (generally represented as poor, dark skinned, or black) are lured by false promises made by foreigners (typically presented as 'false princes' who are seemingly well-to-do foreign men with 'blond hair and blue eyes') who offer opportunity for work and/or fame abroad. (Blanchette & da Silva, 2014, p. 126)

Against this construction of innocent trafficked victims, Article 231 of the Brazilian penal code

> stipulates that prostitution is a sine qua non of trafficking, with the crime [trafficking] described solely as "promoting or facilitating the entry, into national territory, of a person to work as a prostitute or in other forms of sexual exploitation, or the departure of a person from the country for the same purpose abroad" (Brazilian Penal Code, Article 231). (Blanchette & da Silva, 2014, p. 125)

This law also includes an addendum to include persons moving about within the national territory. The fact that the legal tradition criminalizes anyone who facilitates sex work has meant that, in Brazil, as in many other national legal contexts, the way many antitrafficking campaigns imagine and represent victims further harm one of the populations most vulnerable to violence— sex workers.

In this context, much antitrafficking enforcement comes in the form of the closure or raid of brothels and the restriction of movement of those suspected as sex workers. Police seek the rescue of "innocents" and in doing so criminalize sex workers, establishing situations where police officers can demand "bribes from prostitutes in exchange for 'protection,' a situation that is made even more problematic by the fact that police officers are often involved in brothel ownership and management in Brazil" (Blanchette & da Silva, 2014, p. 125). Outside the locale of the brothel, this has meant that police engaging in antitrafficking efforts judge for themselves who might be a trafficked victim. This "training" about how to identify trafficking thus make the visual rhetoric all the more important because it shapes who the police (or any viewer) imagines as the purported and potential "victim." As Annie Fukushima (2019) pointed out, how we see trafficking is "not merely passive. Witnesses construct, participate in and create the normative visions of what it means to experience contemporary violence and human rights violations in the twenty-first century" (p. xxiii). In Brazil, this has meant "that 'trafficking victims' have a class (working or poor), gender (female), color (black or brown), and profession (prostitute). In strictly legal terms, this strategy involves the attribution of victimization before a crime has even taken place" (Blanchette & da Silva, 2014, p. 139).

Thus, one important critique provided by transnational feminist analyses is to suggest that the violence of trafficking is not just in the condition of being exploited and abused but also in the ways legal and discursive systems of accounting delimit how victimhood can be claimed and by whom. Although the ideal victim is often posed through assumptions of moral and sexual worthiness, these same systems of accounting make it impossible for other subjects to be read as anything but victims. The opposition between the worthy trafficking victim and the illegal alien or criminal is one that proliferates "womanchild" or the collapsing of "women and children" into women-as-children (Mahdavi & Sargent, 2011). In fact, the desire to cast a social issue like trafficking through gendered and sexualized frames of women-in-need-of-rescue not only infantilizes women (Hesford, 2011) but also works alongside colonial and racial constructions that reproduce "Third World women" as only objects of "Western" intervention (Hua, 2011; Kaye, 2017; Sharma, 2005; Yea, 2013). Some subjects can never claim to be a victim, whereas others can never escape it. Both positions are antifeminist in that they disallow complexity. Rather than take for granted sex trafficking, transnational feminist perspectives instead look at how certain definitions become attached to sex trafficking and what impact such definition building might have on a community (and on different stakeholders within a community). The work of such representation, and the stakes of representing in particular ways, are thus a key intervention of transnational feminist perspectives into human trafficking.

SEXUALITY, LABOR, AND ELISIONS

For feminists and women's advocates, the rise of human trafficking discourse has added a different dimension to already existing debates around sex work (see Agustin, 2007; Jackson, 2016; Kempadoo & Doezema, 1998; Kempadoo, Sanghera, & Pattanaik, 2012; Showden & Majic, 2014). For example, in August 2015, Amnesty International proposed a plan to decriminalize sex work, arguing that criminalization harms sex workers. This plan, however, resonated with and remains controversial amongst anti-trafficking organizations. A well-known antitrafficking organization, Coalition Against Trafficking in Women (CATW; 2015), has opposed decriminalizing sex work and Amnesty International's plan, noting that decriminalization supports the exploitation of sex trafficking victims. Thus, although some sex worker advocates and social service providers have argued to keep sex work distinct from sex trafficking (Amnesty International, 2015), other organizations and providers have argued that there is no distinction between sex work and sex trafficking (CATW's, 2015, position, often referred to as *abolitionist feminism*).

In many Global South locations, antitrafficking efforts are complicated by the dense network of antitrafficking nongovernmental organizations, which are financed through foreign state aid (e.g., U.S. Agency for International Development) or foundation wealth (tax shelters for the world's 1%; INCITE!, 2007). This is one way the infrastructures set up to address human trafficking can reinforce colonial divisions of "those in need of rescue and intervention" versus "those who only rescue and intervene." Such presumptions, which naturalize intervention, have been heavily critiqued by feminist and postcolonial scholars as justifying the imposition of Global North priorities and frameworks to Global South locales in ways that do not take seriously "the rescued" as decision makers and knowledge producers (Bernal & Grewal, 2014; Choudry & Kapoor, 2013; Kinney, 2014; Yea, 2013). Given this economic structure of funding that underpins where and how human trafficking can be addressed, it is no surprise that sexualized violence and exploitation become the center of attention. Drawing attention draws resources for the implementation of antitrafficking infrastructures, which are about not only the criminal justice systems but also international nongovernmental organizations that sometimes participate in policing and often provide victim services (Bernal & Grewal, 2014).

Human trafficking is often represented in public discourse primarily through sex trafficking, demonstrating what feminist critiques have pointed out as the moral preoccupation with the policing of (female) sexuality (Chapkis, 2005; Vance, 2011). As Micol Seigel (2018) put it,

> Mainstream anti–human trafficking discourse all too easily slips its object over to the subset of sex trafficking, offering titillation and (melo)drama, harnessing the productive power of moral outrage and female victimization to projects of gender policing and category-border control. (p. 4)

At stake are two competing perspectives, one that understands sex work as distinct from sex trafficking and the other that argues the inherently patriarchal and oppressive nature of all sex work. Against these poles, transnational feminist perspectives suggest approaches that understand sex work as work (and in fact, part of a broader set of domestic and sexualized labors), even as the conditions for work can be, and often are, exploitative, undervalued, and criminalized. In this tradition, Laura M. Agustin (2007) argued that sex trafficking, as well as labor migration discussions, often renders sex work migrants invisible. Sex work migrants either are rendered trafficking victims (in much mainstream, especially abolitionist, trafficking efforts), or they are written out of labor migration literature (that assume sex work is outside the scope of "labor").

This tension between labor migration and sex trafficking is another important site of transnational feminist interventions because it draws attention to the limits of consent, choice, and agency. As Kamala Kempadoo's (2001) early work outlined, the tendency to make sex work synonymous with sex trafficking or sexual slavery tends to be an argument made in ways that reproduce colonial notions of Global South underdevelopment. Thus, sex workers in the Global South contest this conflation, arguing that it has been "inadequate to capture the various histories, oppressions, and experiences of women of color" (Kempadoo, 2001, pp. 36–37). In another example, although sex trafficking generally implies coercion or force, how we recognize coercion is not clear cut. Women who choose to cross the U.S.–Mexico border, and who often pay to do so, are extremely vulnerable to being sexually exploited and abused. Rape becomes the price of crossing (and of survival), and rape is often perpetrated by authority figures such as border patrol agents (Falcon, 2007; Luibheid, 2002). On the one hand, stories of women choosing to cross the U.S.–Mexico border are often rendered through labor migration frames, despite the coerced and exploitative sexual terms of that migration, ignoring or diminishing the possibility that these women may be trafficking victims. On the other hand, trafficking frames often fail to recognize that women often report being aware of the terms of their border crossing. Women raped as part of the cost of crossing the U.S.–Mexico border are victims of sexualized violence but also are making decisions that make them more than only victims. If transnational feminist methodologies situate such incidents within a broader context of global wealth inequalities, what does it mean when persons in impoverished conditions "choose" to migrate for greater economic opportunity? And what happens when such choices make migrants vulnerable to sexual abuse and exploitation? Further, how might we account for the instances when the violence of sex trafficking takes place in legitimated and contracted labor contexts? Jennifer Suchland (2015), as have others interested in transnational feminist lenses, argued that "what we need is a more critical approach to the economic and social dynamics of trafficking as a symptom of—not as distinct from—our political and economic systems" (p. 5).

THE CALIFORNIANS AGAINST SEXUAL EXPLOITATION ACT EXAMPLE: CENTERING STRUCTURES

To demonstrate how transnational feminist perspectives on human trafficking discourses—which question rather than take for granted the terms of intervention—shape our research as scholars situated in the United States, we briefly recount one structural and legal attempt to address human trafficking, the Californians Against Sexual Exploitation (CASE) Act (2012). We analyze the assumptions underlying the CASE Act, the way such assumptions limit (or not) who can claim protections and rights, and how such frameworks resonate with global contexts of uneven power relations. Though we do not deny that human trafficking inflicts sexualized violence in uneven ways, we do argue that adding to or increasing criminal penalties does not necessarily change or alter systemic violence or state-inflicted violence, effectively placing trafficked subjects in a position where they experience violence not only from traffickers but also from state actors.

Proposition 35, or the CASE Act, passed with 81% of the vote in November 2012 (California Against Slavery, http://www.caseact.org/about/). The Act increased prison terms, fines, and law enforcement programs for human trafficking–related cases. Daphne Phung, then-executive director of the nonprofit California Against Slavery, proposed and promoted the proposition, which had bipartisan support in the state legislature. The Act emphasizes longer incarceration and higher financial fines for traffickers, as well as mandates that convicted traffickers register on the state sex offenders list. The CASE Act follows and bolsters the 2005 California Trafficking Victims Protection Act (AB 22), specifically extending a special focus on child sex trafficking and prioritizing longer prison terms for cases involving children. Although labor trafficking has prison terms of 5, 8, or 12 years, prison terms for sex trafficking are 8, 14, or 20 years (SEC 8. Section 236.1, http://www.caseact.org). Although minors cannot legally consent to sex, the Act increases prison terms by transforming minors into trafficked victims, with the harshest punishments attached to instances of child sex trafficking with coercion (Tjiu, 2017).

As feminists such as Julia Sudbury (2005) have illustrated, presumptions of criminality are unevenly enforced; some communities are viewed as more likely to harbor criminality, and thus, enforcement, surveillance, and the adjudication of punishment are also unevenly administered and distributed. This kind of logic, one that is taking for granted our already existing presumptions about criminality, can inform the policing of human trafficking, where poor Black and Brown women are more likely to be treated as criminal prostitutes, even when they report being victims of violence. At the same time, racial and sexual logics can pigeonhole other non-White women as perpetual victims. Asian women, particularly, are often treated in this manner because the "Western" or "orientalist" presumption of Asian cultures and nations as hyper-patriarchal predisposes viewers to see Asian women as likely victims of trafficking and sexual exploitation (Hua, 2011). In both cases—the stereotype of Black and Brown poor women as criminal and the stereotype of Asian women as sexually exploitable—rely on longstanding colonial, sexual meanings that render these women subjects in need of intervention.

Visual images reproduce and reaffirm the ideal sex trafficking victim: an unfortunate young girl who is manipulated into soliciting sex for profit and, in the process, loses her innocence and her bright future. This ideal victim becomes the rhetorical justification for increasing criminal sentencing against traffickers. During the campaign to pass Proposition 35, Californians Against Slavery produced several political campaign advertisements, including "Classroom" (Casjustice, 2012), which features a high school–age female protagonist. The advertisement takes place mostly in the context of a school and depicts the protagonist studying; she is looking down and scribbling, modeling the "good student" who has a bright and successful future ahead of her. The advertisement then shifts to a silhouette of a cityscape, with text that reads, "Slavery exists in California today." The ad returns to the student, this time with the text "Thousands of Children" across her face. As she looks down and scribbles at her desk, words appear and disappear in succession: *enslaved, abused, sold*. She slowly looks up at the moment when the word *sold* comes to the screen, and the camera freezes. In the next scene, she is depicted in black and white with hands tied to a bed frame as she struggles to get out of her bonds. The camera zooms out to her entire body on the bed, and the advertisement encourages California voters to support Proposition 35 to "stop human trafficking in California." This imminent fear of (child) sex trafficking produces a visceral response from the audience as the advertisement switches from a brightly lit, in-color classroom to a dark, black-and-white enclosed bedroom where the student is turned into a helpless and vulnerable victim.

The CASE Act's adding to and increasing criminal sentencing, as well as its particular emphasis on sex trafficking, focuses the harm as a matter of the (otherwise innocent) individual. This particular focus is one that scholars such as Carol Vance have tied to moral panic, particularly around sexuality. As Elizabeth Bernstein's (2010) critique of the alliance between Christian conservatives and abolitionist feminists around anti–sex trafficking noted, both are drawn together by a shared political ideology about female sexuality, morality, and family, as well as an investment in carceral strategies. The special focus on children and women is one that facilitates representations of "womanchild" as the individualized site of harm (Mahdavi & Sargent, 2011). The pro-Prop 35 ad, "Classroom," for example, depicts the victim through gendered, infantilizing tropes of helplessness. The setting of the school provides a backdrop rather than an active (state) player in the story. This is in line with antitrafficking abolition feminists who insist that the only solution to human trafficking is increasing law enforcement, police surveillance, and incarceration—solutions focused on individuals rather than social structures.

Attention to structural conditions would implicate law enforcement and criminal legal systems as actors in the story. A key transnational feminist intervention into human trafficking focuses on the issue of criminalization. These arguments are also about social structures, representations (of victims vs. prostitutes), and sex work and the ways antitrafficking efforts, particularly those focused on policing sex trafficking, problematically expand and reinforce the criminal justice system (see Bernstein, 2010; Musto, 2010). Violence at the hands of state entities include abuse or mistreatment by police, inside jails and prisons (where many victims are held until processed), and even mistreatment in shelters and by social service providers. As noted by Toni Eby (2017), outreach and training manager at a San Francisco women's shelter serving "homeless women escaping sexual exploitation, prostitution, and sex trafficking" (San Francisco Safehouse, 2017, para. 1),

> Many shelter programmes focus only on the psychological effects of male domination instead of on those pertaining to socioeconomic structures. While addressing psychological trauma is important, it is equally important to address the day-to-day barriers that many women face, like discriminatory housing, policing, and employment practices. (para. 6)

Attention to structural violence recognizes that the trauma of sexual exploitation comes not simply from "male domination" but from the discrimination that (cis- and trans-) women might face (by other women, not only men) in seeking housing, employment, health care, and so on. These are structural factors that can lead to sexually exploitative situations and are thus central to address if we want to find alternative ways to survive and thrive.

The centering of law-and-order approaches demonstrates the narrow rendering of human trafficking in public discourse and politics. Instead, transnational feminist analyses of human trafficking have questioned the conventions of representation and knowledge production that pose false binaries between coercion and choice, rescued and rescuer, victim and criminal prostitute, "Third World" and "First World." Against these binaries, transnational feminist interventions instead locate sex trafficking within structures and systems (political, economic, media). As Jennifer Suchland (2015) pointed out, although "representations of trafficking have heightened our sensitivity to violence on an individual level" this is at the cost of "obscuring the structural" (p. 4). Instead, a structural, transnational feminist view would be attentive to the work of stereotypes informing how and who we identify as victims, and it would shift the focus away from individualized victims, focusing instead on how social structures and institutions work to place subjects in vulnerability differently and relationally.

RETHINKING CRIMINALITY, RETHINKING LEGALITY

In this final section, we consider how centering transnational feminist perspectives on human trafficking can shift and reverse the gaze. Centering the work of worker-led, transnational activist organizations such as the International Migrants Alliance, this section highlights how people are made vulnerable to trafficking and violence for a multitude of reasons, and trafficking-like conditions and acts of violence can take place in many settings, including, as international labor activist Eni Lestari (2016), pointed out, some legal ones. Chairperson of the International Migrants Alliance and former domestic worker in Hong Kong, Lestari drew attention to the structural failure to protect and recognize migrant labor. Migrants often are at the center of exploitative conditions, experiencing transport across national borders and rape and sexualized violence—conditions otherwise named "sex trafficking"—even in legally arranged workplaces.

In the absence of any international legal mechanism to protect migrant workers, workers often find themselves in vulnerable situations, which can include the withholding of wages, sexual abuse and rape on the job, forced signing of documents, isolation to the point of confinement, and so on. These conditions are often legal, bringing to the fore important questions about what it means to distinguish legalized arrangements of exploitative labor from criminal trafficking (Lestari, 2016). What we propose, given the many aspects of transnational feminist criticisms of human trafficking, is a perspective from which we can think about how gendered and sexualized violence becomes expected and commonplace and that seeks to address this by destabilizing what we currently take for granted as human trafficking.

Though migration happens everywhere, within and across national borders, the economic distributions of globalized wealth tend to situate what sociologists often term *labor migration* along the lines of relative wealth. Thus, locales with greater concentrations of wealth tend to draw migrants from impoverished locales. As Lestari (2016) noted about Indonesia, relative national wealth or poverty has meant that Indonesia provides the second largest supply, just behind the Philippines, of migrant laborers, who leave Indonesia to work elsewhere. In addition to uneven distributions of globalized wealth, much of which is intricately tied to colonial histories, are the legacies of militarism, imperialism, and (sexual) tourism that provide structural context to understanding why certain Global South locales become "supply" centers for domestic, sex, and reproductive labors (e.g., activities related to having children and caregiving; Kempadoo, 2001).

As Kamala Kempadoo (2001) noted, colonial and imperial histories of war have meant that "sex with local women has a longstanding history for the armed forces" (p. 37) and has thus also impacted the representation of mainly Asian, Black, and Brown women as both exotic and sexually available. The importance of relative wealth and poverty means that, for instance, circuits of migration, travel, and border crossing not only happen between the Global North and Global South but also within and between the Global South (Indonesia workers in Malaysia, South and Southeast Asian migrants who transit to Kuwait, or ethnic minorities who might transit within a territory). The fact that exploitation and migration take place within, between, and beyond categorical units (Global South or Global North) does not, however, diminish the importance of historical, geopolitical formations that continue to shape economic realities (e.g., the colonial occupation of the Philippines by Spain and the United States).

Such is the context for Filipina domestic workers in Singapore. The Singaporean state's investment in particular forms of economic production is part of the backdrop of their domestic labor importation program, as is the fact that both the Philippines and Singapore share anglophonic colonial histories. The terms of globalized economic organization, encouraged through International Monetary Fund 1980s- and 1990s-driven agendas to "develop" so-called underdeveloped regions of the world, encouraged export-oriented production centered in some global places (e.g., the so-called Asian Tiger nations). These structural forces not only reified certain kinds of migration relationships between "high- and low-growth countries" that precipitated "the acceleration of labor migration in Southeast Asia" (Cheah, 2006, p. 185), but they also encouraged sex and domestic work industries to attract "foreign exchange or as an export commodity servicing industries abroad. Remittances from migrant women to their families and home communities [are] a staple of small national economies" (Kempadoo, 2001, p. 33).

Like Hong Kong, the Singaporean state structured a labor importation program to help with domestic and child care labor for middle-class Singaporean citizens. To enable economic growth, the Singapore government encouraged Singaporean citizen-women to work outside the home. At the same time, the state targeted the importation of workers from the Philippines to provide domestic work and childcare for Singaporean families where mothers joined the Singapore formal economy. The naturalizing of domestic and childcare labor as female meant that this labor importation program targeted Filipinas. As a place formerly colonized by the United States, the Philippines not only shares English with Singapore, a former British colony, but also has an informalized sexual labor sector precipitated by the presence of U.S. military bases in the country (Kempadoo, 2001, p. 37).

The relationality of Filipina domestic worker and Singaporean state-citizen provides the key to understanding the vulnerability and precarity of the domestic worker to sexual abuse. The "foreign domestic worker" program in Singapore provides work permits to Filipina migrants under certain conditions, including the prohibition of marriage to a citizen or permanent resident and regular medical examinations for pregnancy and sexually transmitted diseases (Cheah, 2006, p. 210). The state requirement of an employer bond works as a mechanism to ensure employers police and monitor their foreign domestic worker: "From the start, therefore, the FDW [foreign domestic worker] is viewed as a minor or delinquent, someone without a fully moral personality who needs to be trained, corrected, and policed so that she will not err" (Cheah, 2006, p. 210).

The example of the Singapore domestic worker program is important because it makes clear an important transnational feminist insight into sex trafficking: The violence and abuse we use to define "sex trafficking" can be legitimated into legal and contractual labor relationships. The Singapore program did not lessen but instead enabled the routinizing of sexual abuse and exploitation of workers, who had little recourse because they are framed as consenting and free individual workers in legally contracted arrangements (the opposite of how human trafficking discourse and law defines the victim). The systemic nature of the problem, embedded in the conditions of the labor importation program, is thus at issue from a transnational feminist perspective, whereas the employee–employer relationship functions as a cosmetic distraction (Cheah, 2006, p. 223). As Sallie Yea (2012) pointed out, these conditions that structure migration and labor in Singapore mean that the binary of the victim of trafficking versus the empowered sex worker cannot capture the ambiguity that situates consent and coercion.

The limitations of dualistic understandings of human trafficking as criminal, posed against the legal, contractual arrangement, is in fact, the transnational (feminist) political project that Lestari (2016) engaged. Recounting her experience at an event and interview I (JH) attended, Lestari discussed many of the conundrums about legality and criminality that also define the context of Filipina domestic work in Singapore. Although her experience was as an Indonesian domestic worker in Hong Kong, Lestari pointed to the ways her legal status as a worker (employed through an agency) did not protect her from trafficking-like acts of violence, including having her papers confiscated by her employer once arriving in Hong Kong, being forced to sign documents she did not understand or know how to read, and living in virtual isolation and confinement with her employers. As Lestari pointed out, Hong Kong is the only place in Asia where domestic workers are included in general labor protections. The legal and "protected" labor migration Lestari engaged in is nonetheless similar to the violent and coercive conditions we associate with human trafficking. Lestari further recounted that when she decided to run away, conditions attached to living in a shelter meant she could not work. Without work, Lestari lost her visa status, and with no visa, she became illegal and was not able to access public services like hospital care.

CONCLUSION

Although the specific context and conditions of workers engaged in household and childcare labor in Hong Kong differ from those in Singapore, transnational feminisms enable us to see the many global flows of power that draw relationality between workers like Lestari with Filipina workers in Singapore. These connections provide the basis for the global scale of organizing for groups such as the International Migrants Alliance. However, transnational feminist perspectives also caution against universalization. The specific terms, experiences, and discourses through which workers such as Lestari understand themselves are not collapsible to each other, nor are they singular. A transnational feminist perspective instead looks for how the historical, economic, political, cultural, and social contexts of human trafficking, sex work, and labor migration draw on and produce interdependencies. A transnational feminist perspective thus also rejects a rescued or rescuer paradigm (as well as other simplistic and binary frames), asking instead for social justice tools and visions generated out of collaborative strategies. Further, transnational feminist perspectives center social structures and, in doing so, recognize state and institutional violence as creating shared interdependencies that provide a broader context for interpersonal violence. Transnational feminist perspectives destabilize taken-for-granted understandings of human trafficking and center methodologies and knowledge that complicate how we understand ourselves, others, and our relations to each other, seeing such projects as always political. In other words, like Lestari's migrant labor organizing, a transnational feminist human trafficking project centers and strives for solidarity.

REFERENCES

Agustin, L. M. (2007). *Sex at the margins: Migration, labour markets and the rescue industry*. New York, NY: Zed Books.

Amnesty International. (2015, August 11). *Global movement votes to adopt policy to protect human rights of sex workers*. Retrieved from https://www.amnesty.org/en/latest/news/2015/08/global-movement-votes-to-adopt-policy-to-protect-human-rights-of-sex-workers/

Bernal, V., & Grewal, I. (Eds.). (2014). *Theorizing NGOs: States, feminisms and neoliberalism*. Durham, NC: Duke University Press. http://dx.doi.org/10.1215/9780822377191

Bernstein, E. (2010). Militarized humanitarianism meets carceral feminism: The politics of sex, rights, and freedom in contemporary antitrafficking campaigns. *Signs, 36*, 45–71. http://dx.doi.org/10.1086/652918

Bernstein, E., & Schaffner, L. (Eds.). (2004). *Regulating sex: The politics of intimacy and identity*. New York, NY: Routledge.

Bhavnani, K. (Ed.). (2001). *Feminism and 'race.'* New York, NY: Oxford University Press.

Blanchette, T. G., & da Silva, A. P. (2014). Bad girls and vulnerable women: An anthropological analysis of narratives regarding prostitution and human trafficking in Brazil. In C. R. Showden & S. Majic (Eds.), *Negotiating sex work* (pp. 121–143). Minneapolis: University of Minnesota Press.

CASE Act. (2012). *Prop 35 is law!* Retrieved from http://www.caseact.org

Casjustice. (2012, October 8). *Classroom* [Video file]. Retrieved from https://www.youtube.com/watch?v=dPN2ugUX1u8&index=12&list=PL0yeGqi5MejAw_ds3NsJcxEIEP6A9kHAu

Chapkis, W. (2005). Soft glove, punishing fist: The trafficking victims protection act. In E. Bernstein & L. Schaffner (Eds.), *Regulating sex* (pp. 51–66). New York, NY: Routledge.

Cheah, P. (2006). *Inhuman conditions: On cosmopolitanism and human rights*. Cambridge, MA: Harvard. http://dx.doi.org/10.4159/9780674029460

Choudry, A., & Kapoor, D. (Eds.). (2013). *NGO-izations: Complicitiy, contradictions and prospects*. New York, NY: Zed Books.

Coalition Against Trafficking in Women. (2015). *CATW responds: Amnesty International turned its back on women.* Retrieved from http://www.catwinternational. org/Home/Article/624-catw-responds-amnesty-international-turned-its-back-on-women

Collins, P. H. (1990). *Black feminist thought.* New York, NY: Routledge.

Crenshaw, K. (1989). Demarginalizing the intersection of race and sex. *University of Chicago Legal Forum.* Retrieved from https://chicagounbound.uchicago.edu/uclf/vol1989/iss1/8/

de Beauvoir, S. (1949). *The second sex.* Paris, France: Gallimard.

Eby, T. (2017). Using an intersectional approach to raid and rescue. *Open Democracy.* Retrieved from https://www.opendemocracy.net/beyondslavery/using-intersectional-approach-to-raid-and-rescue

Falcon, S. M. (2007). Rape as a weapon of war: Militarized rape at the U.S.–Mexico border. In D. Segura & P. Zavella (Eds.), *Women and migration in U.S.–Mexico borderlands* (pp. 201–223). Durham, NC: Duke.

Fukushima, A. (2019). *Migrant crossings.* Palo Alto, CA: Stanford University Press.

Grewal, I., & Kaplan, C. (Eds.). (1994). *Scattered hegemonies: Postmodernity and transnational feminist practices.* Minneapolis: University of Minnesota Press.

Grewal, I., & Kaplan, C. (1996). *Warrior Marks*: Global womanism's neo-colonial discourse in a multicultural context. *Camera Obscura, 13*(3), 4–33. http://dx.doi.org/10.1215/02705346-13-3_39-4

Haynes, D. F. (2007). (Not) found chained to a bed in a brothel: Conceptual, procedural and legal failures fulfill the promise of the Trafficking Victims Protection Act. *Georgetown Immigration Law Journal, 21,* 337–380.

Hesford, W. (2011). *Spectacular rhetorics: Human rights visions, recognitions, feminisms.* Durham, NC: Duke. http://dx.doi.org/10.1215/9780822393818

Hill, A. (2016). How to stage a raid: Police, media and the master narrative of trafficking. *Anti-Trafficking Review, 7,* 39–55.

Hua, J. (2011). *Trafficking women's human rights.* Minneapolis: University of Minnesota Press. http://dx.doi.org/10.5749/minnesota/9780816675609.001.0001

INCITE! (2007). *The revolution will not be funded: Beyond the non-profit industrial complex.* Cambridge, MA: South End Press.

Jackson, C. (2016). Framing sex worker rights. *Sociological Perspectives, 59,* 27–45. http://dx.doi.org/10.1177/0731121416628553

Kaye, J. (2017). *Responding to human trafficking: Dispossession, colonial violence, and resistance among Indigenous and racialized women.* Toronto, Ontario, Canada: University of Toronto Press. http://dx.doi.org/10.3138/9781487513863

Kempadoo, K. (2001). Women of color and the global sex trade: Transnational feminist perspectives. *Meridians, 1,* 28–51.

Kempadoo, K., & Doezema, J. (Eds.). (1998). *Global sex workers: Rights, resistance and redefinition.* New York, NY: Routledge.

Kempadoo, K., Sanghera, J., & Pattanaik, B. (Eds.). (2012). *Trafficking and prostitution reconsidered: New perspectives on migration, sex work, and human rights*. Boulder, CO: Paradigm.

Kinney, E. (2014). Raids, rescues, and resistance: Women's rights and Thailand's response to human trafficking. In C. Showden & S. Majic (Eds.), *Negotiating sex work* (pp. 145–166). Minneapolis: University of Minnesota Press.

Lestari, E. (2016, May). *A sharing with Eni Lestari, chairperson of the International Migrants Alliance*. Mujeres Unidas y Activas, Oakland, CA.

Luibheid, E. (2002). *Entry denied: Controlling sexuality at the border*. Minneapolis: University of Minnesota Press.

Mahdavi, P., & Sargent, C. (2011). Questioning the discursive construction of trafficking and forced labor in the United Arab Emirates. *Journal of Middle East Women's Studies*, 7(3), 6–35. http://dx.doi.org/10.2979/jmiddeastwomstud.7.3.6

Mohanty, C. (1988). Under Western eyes: Feminist scholarship and colonial discourses. *Feminist Review*, 30, 61–88. http://dx.doi.org/10.1057/fr.1988.42

Mohanty, C., & Alexander, J. (1997). Introduction: Genealogies, legacies, movements. In C. Mohanty & J. Alexander (Eds.), *Feminist genealogies, colonial legacies, democratic futures* (pp. xiii–xlii). New York, NY: Routledge.

Moraga, C., & Anzaldua, G. (1983). *This bridge called my back*. Cambridge, MA: Kitchen Table Press.

Murray, A. (1998). Debt-bondage and trafficking: Don't believe the hype. In K. Kempadoo & J. Doezema (Eds.), *Global sex workers* (pp. 51–64). New York, NY: Routledge.

Musto, J. (2010). Carceral protectionism and multi-professional anti-trafficking human rights work in the Netherlands. *International Feminist Journal of Politics*, 12, 381–400. http://dx.doi.org/10.1080/14616742.2010.513107

Naples, N., & Desai, M. (Eds.). (2002). *Women's activism and globalization*. New York, NY: Routledge.

San Francisco Safehouse. (2017). *Mission*. Retrieved from https://www.sfsafehouse.org/our-mission.html

Seigel, M. (2018). Global moral panics and the affective contours of power. In M. Seigel (Ed.), *Panic, transnational cultural studies, and the affective contours of power* (pp. 1–16). New York, NY: Routledge.

Sharma, N. (2003). Travel agency: A critique of anti-trafficking campaigns. *Refuge: Canada's Periodical on Refugees*, 21(3), 53–65.

Sharma, N. (2005). Anti-trafficking rhetoric in the making of global apartheid. *National Women's Studies Association Journal*, 17, 88–112.

Shih, E. (2016). Not in my "backyard abolitionism." *Sociological Perspectives*, 59, 66–90. http://dx.doi.org/10.1177/0731121416628551

Showden, C., & Majic, S. (Eds.). (2014). *Negotiating sex work*. Minneapolis: University of Minnesota Press. http://dx.doi.org/10.5749/minnesota/9780816689583.001.0001

Smith, B., Guy-Sheftall, B., & Giddings, P. (2014). What would Harriet do? A legacy of resistance and activism. *Meridians: Feminism, Race, Transnationalism, 12*, 123–141.

Suchland, J. (2015). *Economies of violence: Transnational feminism, postsocialism, and the politics of sex trafficking.* Durham, NC: Duke. http://dx.doi.org/10.1215/9780822375289

Sudbury, J. (Ed.). (2005). *Global lockdown: Race, gender and the prison-industrial complex.* New York, NY: Routledge.

Tjiu, J. (2017). *The discursive power of anti-trafficking laws: Restructuring social justice outside neoliberalism* (Unpublished master's thesis). San Francisco State University, San Francisco, California.

United Nations. (2000). *Protocol to Prevent, Suppress and Punish Trafficking in Persons Especially Women and Children, supplementing the United Nations Convention against Transnational Organized Crime.* Retrieved from https://www.ohchr.org/EN/ProfessionalInterest/Pages/ProtocolTraffickingInPersons.aspx

Vance, C. (2011). Thinking trafficking, thinking sex. *GLQ, 17*, 135–143. http://dx.doi.org/10.1215/10642684-2010-024

Yea, S. (2012). "Shades of grey": Spaces in and beyond trafficking for Thai women involved in commercial sexual labor in Sydney and Singapore. *Gender, Place and Culture, 19*, 42–60. http://dx.doi.org/10.1080/0966369X.2011.617906

Yea, S. (2013). Mobilising the child victim: The localisation of human trafficking in Singapore through global activism. *Environment and Planning D: Society & Space, 31*, 988–1003. http://dx.doi.org/10.1068/d15411

10

TRANSNATIONAL PSYCHOLOGY IN THE CLASSROOM: A PLURALISTIC APPROACH

LYNN H. COLLINS, JENNIFER J. MOOTZ, JEANNE MARECEK,
ALISHA GUTHERY, SAYAKA MACHIZAWA, OLIVA M. ESPÍN,
ANDREA L. DOTTOLO, JULIETTA HUA, SARA CRANN,
NICOLE JEFFREY, AND ELIZABETH SCHWAB

In this chapter, we suggest ways to help instructors and students understand transnational concepts more fully and hopefully adopt a more transnational research program and psychological perspective. Teaching transnational psychology requires a transformation in instructors' and students' appreciation for the range of impacts of globalization on individuals and communities and the extent to which globalization and power asymmetries may influence psychological phenomena. Transnational psychological perspectives require the rejection of assumptions of universality and greater examination of reciprocal interactions among multiple dynamic, intersecting factors. Through the assignments and activities described in this chapter, instructors can help students "disrupt" their belief systems and look at psychological constructs and data from the perspectives of Global Majority communities.

http://dx.doi.org/10.1037/0000148-011
Transnational Psychology of Women: Expanding International and Intersectional Approaches, L. H. Collins,
S. Machizawa, and J. K. Rice (Editors)

This chapter describes readings, assignments, and classroom activities that can be used in any class in which transnational psychology is covered. Thus, it is useful in infusing transnational psychology into the curriculum generally, as well as enriching a dedicated course on the topic. Although primarily written for undergraduate- and graduate-level classes, some of the suggestions can be tweaked to be used with middle and high school students. Although transnational psychology might not typically be a stand-alone topic on a syllabus in middle and high school, students at that level take courses in social studies, which may include human geography, world history, nation-state history (e.g., U.S. history), government and politics, comparative government and politics, psychology, anthropology, sociology, and/or new languages. In the process, students learn about communities around the world, colonization, imperialism, governance, social change, privilege and oppression, immigration, and globalization. They can explore the varied migratory routes of groups with whom they identify and transnational influences on their identities. All these topics are related to transnational psychology. The exercises related to these topics may help prevent the development of xenophobic attitudes and narrow nationalistic identities. Students can learn to ask themselves, "What assumptions am I making because of my own ethnicity, class, education level, cultural and religious backgrounds, sex, theoretical perspective, life experiences, and so forth, and how do these assumptions influence my opinions and decisions?" Teachers and professors can also use some of the suggestions for personal and professional development.

Mohanty (2003) described three pedagogical approaches to internationalizing the curriculum and analyzing "the politics of knowledge at work" (p. 518). The first is the common tourist, consumer, or add-and-stir model (Mohanty, 2003, p. 518), in which examples of Global Majority cultures are added to Global Minority narratives. This model tends to focus on sensationalized issues (e.g., child labor, honor killings) rather than providing a comprehensive picture of day-to-day life in a community. This results in students feeling removed and superior instead of connected to the community. In the tourist, consumer, or add-and-stir model, students do not learn how to challenge and critique nationalistic and Global Minority assumptions. The second approach is called the explorer model. It focuses solely on Majority World local and global phenomena. Although this model allows for a deeper understanding, it separates racial and ethnic issues from international issues. Students still feel disconnected and are not taught how to identify and critique issues of power, agency, and justice (Mohanty, 2003). This is problematic because globalization is a dynamic economic, political, and ideological phenomenon connecting communities around the world and should be examined and critiqued with attention to these interconnections.

Mohanty (2003) recommended a third approach, the comparative or solidarity model, which builds a complex relational understanding of experience, location, and history that considers specific contexts. In this model, the local and global are not seen as defined by nation-state boundaries but exist simultaneously and interact with one another. They are seen as coexisting and interconnected, with differences, commonalities, interests, and responsibilities. Mohanty recommended that the one-third and two-thirds or Minority World and Majority World paradigm be used instead of nation-state or directional (e.g., East, West, North, South) labels to represent points of connection and distance. The resources and techniques described in this chapter are stepping-stones toward the goal of teaching a more relational and interactive understanding of the local and global.

Psychologists teaching transnational psychological approaches have to not only be generally well informed about macrolevel regional and global contexts but also specifically well versed regarding communities' immediate, local contexts and the relationship among these contexts. Therefore, psychologists should include personal accounts of daily life and information about local politics, religions, ethnic groups, and military presence in their lectures and classroom activities. They should portray the common and unique interwoven histories, experiences, and challenges present in the community's context of power relations. Individual and collective experiences of oppression, exploitation, and resistance should be described to make accounts of globalization's impacts more salient and relatable so that students will develop and experience a sense of empathy and connection with those affected by globalization.

TEACHING SUGGESTIONS AND RESOURCES

The classroom can be used as a microcosm of applied transnational psychological principles. Transnational psychology's emphasis on pluralism and egalitarianism can be modeled in the classroom by ensuring that all students in the classroom "community" are heard, especially those with any reason to feel silenced. Students can be empowered to develop the classroom guidelines to both produce and critique their knowledge and identify the assumptions that influence their thinking and feelings. A helpful resource for developing a healthy classroom climate and dealing with defensiveness is Dottolo's (2019) "Overcoming Student Defensiveness in Social Psychology Courses: A Collaborative Workshop for Discussing Privilege and Prejudice." The chapter creatively addresses issues related to power asymmetries, preparing students to engage with material addressing difference. In addition to enlisting students' help in developing classroom ground rules, the chapter describes how to provide students with the conceptual tools and language to understand and identify reactions to challenging material, especially in discussions.

Students should be given assignments that give them hands-on experience with transnational psychology's phenomena and research techniques. After receiving classroom exposure to transnational approaches, students should be encouraged to participate in service-learning experiences in which they partner with other communities to explore issues. Unlike traditional practicum and field experiences, transnational service-learning and research experiences are action oriented and designed to mutually benefit both the students and the community.

Teaching Resources

What follows is a series of demonstrations, readings, and videos that may be useful in teaching transnational psychology. The resources can help illustrate the histories, social dynamics, and economic situations of communities, as well as clarify the nature of transnational perspectives, from the macro to the micro level. Resources range from basic information about colonization and decolonization that could be used as a quick historical introduction or review for high school students or undergraduates, through lists of suggested readings for doctoral classes. In addition to the ideas in this chapter, there are also videos of lectures, conferences, quick lessons, and other content online, especially on YouTube. General recommendations are followed by resources organized by chapter topic. Transnational psychological service-learning and research experiences are described after the classroom recommendations.

Introduction to Transnational Psychology

To begin to teach transnational perspectives, especially in the context of globalization, it is helpful to assign Chapter 1, "Transnational Psychology of Women," by Collins, Machizawa, and Rice, and Chapter 2, "The Transnational Turn: Looking Back and Looking Ahead," by Conway. They both review the history and impact of globalization and the perspective's history within feminist studies, especially postmodern and postcolonial feminisms, from which transnational feminism draws its terminology. Chapter 1 provides a history of transnational psychology in basic terms and is useful for introducing undergraduates to transnational psychology. Chapter 2 is more suitable for advanced undergraduates and graduate students. The last chapter in the book, Chapter 11, "Toward an Inclusive, Affirmative Transnational Psychology," by Rice and Grabe, provides a critique of transnational psychology and could be assigned later in the semester in an advanced undergraduate or graduate class. Instructors should also introduce the vocabulary of postcolonial feminism, especially the terms listed at the end of this chapter. A chapter in Mena and Quina's (2019) *Integrating Multiculturalism and Intersectionality Into the Psychology Curriculum: Strategies for Instructors* entitled "Teaching Cultural and Transnational Psychology: Taking Intersectionality Across the Globe" (Collins, 2019) lists and defines these terms, as does the Glossary in this volume. This chapter builds on that chapter by introducing a variety of activities and assignments.

Multidirectional Learning (Class Activity). For this first activity, contact an instructor from a Majority World community (regardless of your location, more attention to Majority World communities is needed) who ideally teaches gender studies or a psychology of women class to arrange a virtual transnational cross-community discussion for students. Such a partnership could potentially provide the platform for practicing rapid ethnographies and qualitative interviewing and holding discussions related to a topic of mutual interest. Participants could also discuss transnational identities, including how these identities impacted the relationship across the semester. A partnership could also allow for discussions about sexuality and reproductive health and domestic violence. It might provide opportunities for engaging in other activities that all instructors involved would find mutually educational or meaningful for students. For example, a research class might hold a weekly call with their Majority World partner. A translator may have to be present. During one of those calls, they could engage in a conversation about research, taking turns sharing using the following prompts: What do you think about psychological research? Have you participated in any studies either as a participant or researcher? What were your research experiences like? If you could research any topic, what would you research and why? If you could change anything about research, what would you change and why? What do you see as benefits of research, if any? How do your research interests relate to who you are as a person? At the end of the semester, students could write a reflection paper on what they have learned about the partner and themselves through the process of transnational dialogue and sharing.

It is important to increase the visibility and understanding of Global Majority perspectives. Some of the challenges to implementing this demonstration include language differences, technology limitations, and the risk of the inquiry being one-way, primarily benefiting Minority World students. In addition, traditional approaches to revealing Majority World perspectives sometimes result in the interrogation of that group, rather than a respectful mutual exchange. Furthermore, the language differences may require an interpreter, which can impede the dialogue. Schools, government agencies, and organizations are developing networks of individuals who are members of various communities, are familiar with their communities' "particularities," share a common language, and are interested in having this type of exchange for reasons that serve their communities' interests. Multidirectional learning can occur through such networks, which can improve intercommunity understanding and help identify and use more forms of knowledge production. It is important, however, that such exchanges occur in a collaborative, mutually respectful, mutually beneficial, egalitarian manner in which all participants engage in strong reflexivity (critical awareness of how one's background, status, etc., shapes their perspectives and their relationship to the discipline, its theories, and its data).

Decolonization (Assignment). Decolonization is the process through which communities reclaim their culture and characteristics by freeing themselves from the philosophies and practices—the scattered hegemonies— forced on them. Extricating a community from colonization ideally involves a democratic process through which people rethink, reevaluate, and reclaim their self, community, and governance structures (McHugh, 2007; also find helpful videos at thecrashcourse.com). Students can write a paper or brainstorm ways that people in more recently colonized communities and regions might reverse that colonization. Resources for this assignment can be found on the website of the U.S. Department of State (from https://history.state.gov; search for "decolonization") and on the global issues page of the United Nations website (http://www.un.org/en/sections/issues-depth/global-issues-overview/index.html). Examples are the decolonization of Asia and Africa, India and Pakistan, and Angola from their European rulers. CrashCourse (2012) video #40 describes decolonization; CrashCourse (2015) video #228 describes nonviolent decolonization movements.

Readings. The following readings are becoming classics on the topic. Kurtiş and Adams (2015) is the most accessible of the group. *Under Western Eyes* (Mohanty, 1986) is the piece that set transnational feminism in motion, but Mohanty's writing is challenging for many psychology students. *"Under Western Eyes" Revisited: Feminist Solidarity Through Anticapitalist Struggles* (Mohanty, 2003) is an update of the piece but is equally challenging for students. Still, after reading the first two chapters of this book and a few more, students may be better prepared to read the classics:

Kurtiş T., & Adams, G. (2015). Decolonizing liberation: Toward a transnational feminist psychology. *Journal of Social and Political Psychology*, 3, 338–413. http:// dx.doi.org/10.5964/jspp.v3i1.326

Martín-Baró, I. (1996). Toward a liberation psychology. In A. Aron & S. Corne (Eds.), *Writings for a liberation psychology: Ignacio Martín-Baró* (pp. 17–32). Cambridge, MA: Harvard University Press.

Mohanty, C. T. (1991). Under Western eyes: Feminist scholarship and colonial discourses. In C. T. Mohanty, A. Russo, & L. Torres (Eds.), *Third World women and the politics of feminism* (pp. 51–80). Bloomington: Indiana University Press.

Mohanty, C. T. (2002). "Under Western eyes" revisited: Feminist solidarity through anti-capitalist struggles. *Signs, 28*, 499–535. http://dx.doi.org/10.1086/342914

Ralston, M. (2009). Towards a truly transnational feminism. *European Journal of Women's Studies, 16*, 400–401.

Videos. Khan Academy (http://www.kahnacademy.org), and Crash Course both offer free online educational videos that help students understand the dynamics of globalization, world history, imperialism, colonization, decolonization, and many other topics. There are two sources of Crash Course videos: Hank Green and John Green, who created the VlogBrothers channel (http://www.thecrashcourse.com), and the Public Broadcasting Service (https://www.pbslearningmedia.org/collection/crash-course/). These videos can be used to supplement academic history readings to provide an efficient, lively review or introduction to these topics. The videos can also be used to stimulate class discussions about similar contemporary controversies and dynamics in the news. Students can also review historical timelines for topics such as imperialism, migration, and trade at http://www.historyworld.net. Perspectives regarding the arrival of Europeans in the Americas are useful examples for Global Minority students to examine regarding their countries' histories (Sellers & Arrigo, 2016).

Other examples of imperialism and colonization related to the recent acceleration of globalization include military occupations, mass immigrations, relocating companies and production sites to reduce costs (Chen, 2015; Yuval-Davis, 2009), natural resource exploration, and gentrification in specific areas of Asia and the Middle East. In each case, students could be asked, "What was the imperialistic country seeking? How did its values and customs impact the community? How is this country different than it was before the intrusion? Are the changes helpful or harmful to its citizens?" (Collins, 2019).

"Critical" Vocabulary. The following vocabulary list can be helpful to students reading the professional literature on transnational psychology and thinking about how to decolonize psychology. Students might be given this list of terms and asked to research their definitions; the process of attaching meaning to a word increases the likelihood that it will be remembered. Extended explanations can be found in Collins (2019) and *Feminist Philosophies A–Z* (McHugh, 2007), as well as in the literature and various online resources. Key terms include *colonization, decolonization, feminism, Global Majority, Global Minority, hegemony, imperialism, Majority World, Minority World, monoculture, othering, postcolonialism, postmodernism, situated knowledge,*

standpoint epistemology, and *strong reflexivity.* There is a more extensive list of important terms and definitions in the Glossary.

Transnational Research Methods

Some of the most common characteristics of transnational psychological research are the creation of partnerships with the community being studied, use of ethnographies to understand the community (Craven & Davis, 2013; Manning, 2016), use of qualitative research methods, and consideration of factors ranging from local, community-level phenomena through how the community is affected by macro or global phenomena. It is of utmost importance that research collaborations be egalitarian and of benefit to both the researchers and community. Unlike most traditional academic research, which is primarily concerned with knowledge production for the advancement of the field, transnational research is action oriented and community based. It usually creates knowledge that brings direct benefits to the community being studied and addresses relevant social and community issues.

The concepts of standpoint epistemology, strong reflexivity, and othering are key to understanding the processes that encourage and support egalitarian collaborations between researchers and communities. Chapter 3, "Strategies and Considerations for Transnational Feminist Research: Reflections From Research in Uganda," by Mootz and Stabb, is relevant, especially for its detailed table of research considerations entitled, "Research Areas and Transnational Feminist Strategies and Considerations." General readings about ethnography and qualitative methods (e.g., Creswell & Poth, 2017), as well as examples of transnational research cited by this book, are valuable. Bolton and Tang's (2004) article "Using Ethnographic Methods in the Selection of Post-Disaster, Mental Health Interventions" is a good resource on ethnography.

In transnational psychology, knowing communities' particularities (e.g., unique characteristics, details, nuances) is important to understanding them. Rather than make relativistic cross-cultural comparisons, transnational psychology takes a case study–like, comparative approach that examines the particularities of life in each community. For example, after a rise in suicides in Sri Lanka drew worldwide attention, teams of researchers arrived to study the phenomena. Marecek and Senadheera (2012) took a comparative transnational approach to studying the rise of suicide in Sri Lanka. The two other teams took a more top down, traditional approach based on Western universalist assumptions. Knipe et al. (2014) assumed beforehand that the increased suicide rates were due to access to highly toxic pesticides and used a traditional archival research approach. Samaraweera, Sumathipala, Siribaddana, Sivayogan, and Bhugra (2008) relied on psychiatric diagnoses, coroners' reports, and interviews of each suicidal individual's closest relatives or friends and reviewing coroners' reports but not any survivor interviews. Each reached a different conclusion. The three articles resulting from the studies serve as useful examples of how different methodologies can lead to different results and conclusions. The articles can be assigned and serve as the basis for a class discussion of research approaches and assumptions, Global Minority perspectives, and test validity.

Critical Article Review (Assignment). Students can be asked to identify a research study in a peer-reviewed journal that was conducted with women who have migrated or women living in the Majority World and to write a three- to five-page critique from a transnational perspective. Have students consider the different stages and areas of research (formulating questions, constructs and measurement, data analysis and interpretation, and dissemination, representation, and action). Refer the students to Table 3.1 from Chapter 3 (this volume) on conducting transnational research and have them use the transnational strategies and considerations outlined in Table 3.1 to guide their critiques.

Article and Chapter Critiques (Assignment). Most academic research on oppressed, marginalized groups is conducted or supervised by researchers from WEIRD (Western, educated, industrialized, rich, democratic) countries rather than the communities of the group studied (Henrich, Heine, & Norenzayan, 2010). Researchers bring their biases and expectations to their research. Their subjective perspectives can be a resource for mutual understanding (Hirsh & Olson, 1995) if their perspectives are made explicit and subjected to examination. Students can discuss whether the concept of objectivity exists. They can be asked to identify their "positions" with their classmates. They can also be assigned or select articles and identify the position of the authors. Students can be asked whether authors of articles are engaging in *othering*, which can range from stereotyping people from different regions based on perceived differences to claiming to speak for them while oppressing them.

Many measures and observational categories are not valid when used with non-Western populations, raising questions about construct equivalence (e.g., Spielberger, 2006). Other potential sources of errors include different cultural and linguistic meanings, technical and methodological problems, and interpretation of test results (Hambleton & Kanjee, 1995). Students can be asked to identify these issues in articles as well.

Community Guest Speaker and Transnational Reflection (Class Activity and Assignment). Invite a representative from a local community advocacy group or agency that supports refugees' and/or migrants' well-being. Ask the representative to talk about the organization's mission and work and any research with which the organization has been involved. Have the representative discuss what kind of research would be helpful for the organization and its work. Break students into small groups and discuss some of the research ideas posed by the presenter. Questions for discussion might include the following: In which ways do the presenters' ideas align with transnational feminist principles? How could the research ideas be modified so that they more closely align with transnational tenets? What transnational psychological research questions could guide a hypothetical study? Which constructs would be important to measure? How would you measure these constructs? What methods would you use to collect data? What are the policy implications of this hypothetical study, if any?

Adaptable Research Project (Class Activity and Assignment). This project can be adapted as an assignment for any of the following topics. Students could be assigned readings about rapid ethnography and community research partnerships. They could be asked to choose a phenomenon present within their classroom, a school, or a community group. It might also be possible to partner with a more distant community online. After getting Institutional Review Board approval, under supervision, students can form a "partnership" that allows them and their partner to explore issues and answer questions of interest. They should be supervised and provided with Mootz and Stabb's Table 3.1 (Chapter 3, this volume) to ensure that they follow transnational psychology principles. This exercise also potentially gives students and their partners the experience of creating new knowledge.

Classroom exercises could also introduce students to *standpoint epistemology*, which decenters the thinking of people from WEIRD countries by making the views of oppressed groups more visible and important than those of dominant groups. In their research, students can be encouraged to draw out individuals whose views tend to be overlooked or silenced. Members of dominant, privileged groups are more likely to be invested in protecting the status quo from which they are benefitting, conforming to their dominant culture, and therefore are more likely to obscure reality (Miller, 1986). Oppressed groups are less invested in the status quo and therefore more likely to reveal its limitations. Research experience, in this way, can include teaching students to recognize the partiality of their perspectives.

Strong Reflexivity Exercise (Assignment). Students can also be asked to keep a journal during the research project to develop strong reflexivity. Students can be encouraged to ask themselves, "What assumptions am I making because of my ethnicity, class, education level, sex, theoretical perspective, life experiences, and so forth? How does my perspective lead me to select and conceptualize my research and scholarship? How can I use my awareness of my situated knowledge to conceptualize the issues in a better way? How has studying this topic changed how I think about it?" (Collins, 2019). Amer, Howarth, and Sen (2015), Moon (2008), and Ortlipp (2008) provided examples of such journals.

Mock Research Dissemination Meetings (Class Activity). In small groups, identify a research paper from a peer-reviewed journal that was conducted with women who have migrated to or are living in the Majority World. Create a plan for disseminating the research findings. Conduct a mock dissemination meeting with the class. Who would you invite to this meeting? How would you conduct it? What findings would be important to share? How would you share the results?

Readings. The following books and articles may be especially helpful:

Bolton, P., & Tang, A. M. (2004). Using ethnographic methods in the selection of post-disaster, mental health interventions. *Prehospital and Disaster Medicine, 19*, 97–101. http://dx.doi.org/10.1017/S1049023X00001540

Dawson, A., Toombs, E., & Mushquash, C. (2017). Indigenous research methods: A systematic review. *International Indigenous Policy Journal, 8*(2). http://dx.doi.org/10.18584/iipj.2017.8.2.5

Dottolo, A. L., & Tillery, S. M. (2015). Reflexivity and research: Feminist interventions and their practical implications. In J. L. Amoreaux & B. J. Steele (Eds.), *Reflexivity and international relations: Positionality, critique, and practice* (pp. 123–141). New York, NY: Routledge.

Israel, B. A., Schulz, A., Parker, E., Becker, A., Allen, A., III, & Guzman, R. (2008). Critical issues in developing and following CBPR principles. In M. Minkler & N. Wallerstein (Eds.), *Community-based participatory research for health: From process to outcomes* (pp. 47–66). San Francisco, CA: Jossey-Bass.

Kovach, M. (2010). Conversational method in indigenous research. *First Peoples Child & Family Review, 5*, 40–48.

Minkler, M., & Wallerstein, N. (2008). Introduction to community-based participatory research: New issues and emphases. In M. Minkler & N. Wallerstein (Eds.), *Community-based participatory research for health: From process to outcomes* (pp. 5–24). San Francisco, CA: Jossey-Bass.

Seehawer, M. K. (2018). Decolonising research in a sub-Saharan African context: Exploring Ubuntu as a foundation for research methodology, ethics and agenda. *International Journal of Social Research Methodology, 21*, 453–466. http://dx.doi.org/10.1080/13645579.2018.1432404

Simonds, V. W., & Christopher, S. (2013). Adapting Western research methods to Indigenous ways of knowing. *American Journal of Public Health, 103*, 2185–2192. http://dx.doi.org/10.2105/AJPH.2012.301157

Smith, L. T. (2012). *Decolonizing methodologies: Research and indigenous peoples* (2nd ed.). New York, NY: Zed Books.

Sprague, J. (2016). *Feminist methodologies for critical researchers*. New York, NY: Rowman & Littlefield.

Wallerstein, N., & Duran, B. (2010). Community-based participatory research contributions to intervention research: The intersection of science and practice to improve health equity. *American Journal of Public Health, 100*, 40–46. http://dx.doi.org/10.2105/AJPH.2009.184036

Organizations and Websites. The following organizations do research and programming with women and gender. Some may provide service-learning opportunities as well. Promundo does extraordinary research in low- and middle-income countries with men and gender equality.

- American Indigenous Research Association: https://www.americanindigenousresearchassociation.org/
- International Center for Research on Women: http://www.icrw.org
- International Rescue Committee: http://www.rescue.org
- Promundo: http://www.promundoglobal.org
- UN Women: http://www.unwomen.org

Collaborative Transnational Conceptualization and Intervention

Chapter 4, "Transnational Psychological Perspectives on Assessment and Intervention," by Collins, is a helpful overview of this topic. The Global Minority has dominated psychology and psychiatry in a manner that forces its beliefs and practices onto others for whom their assessment, diagnostic, and treatment methodologies may not only fail to help but may also be harmful (Christopher, Wendt, Marecek, & Goodman, 2014; Morgan-Consoli, Inman, Bullock, & Nolan, 2018; Wessells, 2009). The acceleration of globalization and migration makes it difficult to identify valid assessment instruments because populations are increasingly less static and less homogeneous. New approaches are required to understand people in the context of these population shifts, especially in relation to the ethical practice of psychology. As mentioned previously, qualitative studies are critical to transnational research. Rapid ethnographies may soon become a regular part of assessment batteries. Therapeutic techniques have always been shaped by global influences. As rates of migration escalate, it is important to learn and incorporate new approaches into our repertoires and to think both critically and creatively regarding our work with clients to ensure therapeutic approaches are accessible, comfortable, and culturally appropriate for clients (Peters, Straits, & Gauthier, 2015). The following teaching ideas relate to these new realities.

Rapid Ethnographies in Pairs (Class Activity and Assignment). Have students conduct a rapid ethnography (inquiring about definitions and priority of problems) about problems associated with being a student (or other common experience). Have them write these problems and definitions down and later discuss as a class. What was it like conducting the rapid ethnographies? What kinds of problems emerged? What types of problems tended to rank most highly? What types of problems tended to rank as the least important? What do these problems say about the culture of the classroom and how students make meaning? In which research settings would rapid ethnographies be more or less useful? What changes would you want to make to improve or alter this method, depending on the clinical context? Bolton and Tang's (2004) article "Using Ethnographic Methods in the Selection of Post-Disaster, Mental Health Interventions" is a helpful resource for this.

From Macro to Micro: Transnational Feminist Case Conceptualization (Assignment). Ask students to do a case conceptualization that includes information about a person's (a client's, friend's, or even their own) personal perspective, the nature of their community, the characteristics of their country and its region, and an analysis of the local (e.g., personal, community) through global forces that may be impinging on them. Also incorporate information about the intersections of their identities, including those added by transnational feminist perspectives: historical, national, political, economic, and other global influences. After the papers are completed, hold a class discussion about the experience and what they learned.

The Evolution of Therapeutic Approaches (Assignment). Many Western approaches to psychotherapy have roots in Indigenous healing practices. Have students pick a therapeutic technique and trace its origins both by what the literature says and by how it resembles approaches from around the world. Have them comment on the culture, values, and practices the techniques reflect and where they may have come from. Have students imagine how an approach may have to be enhanced or altered to respond to rapid change due to globalization.

Transnational Psychology of Migration

Chapter 5 in this book, Espín and Dottolo's "A Transnational Feminist Perspective on the Psychology of Migration," provides a comprehensive description of transnational psychological viewpoints on globalization and migration, including the multitude of reasons people migrate to other locations. Diasporic communities are displaced people who share a history of having left a common location. The communities often construct narratives or legends about their country of origin to which they may hope to return. Migrants are often subjected to discrimination in their new environment and survive partly by close ties and loyalty to their displaced community. Students can be asked to come up with historical and contemporary examples. Students can discuss why those who migrate from the Minority World (West) are typically called *expatriates* or *expats*, whereas those migrating from the Majority World are called *migrants* (Koutonin, 2015).

Helping Students Discover Their Migrant Ancestors (Assignment). Students may "other" the migrants they see on television and feel little if any connection to them. In reality, few people's ancestors are originally from where they currently reside. This exercise may help decenter and disrupt students' ethnic and racial identities, as well as help them identify more with the migrant communities they study.

Students can either participate in the National Geographic's Genographic Project (https://genographic.nationalgeographic.com/about/), which reveals individuals' deep ancestry, including ancestors' migration patterns thousands of years ago. The Genographic Project traces ancestors' migratory paths from Mitochondrial Eve of East Africa, the most recent common matrilineal ancestor of all living humans, up through their locations 500 years ago. Ancestry.com and 23andMe pick up the trail at the 500-year mark and can provide more detailed information about ancestors from the last 500 years, including the connection between the DNA and paper trails, but entail privacy risks. There are also free resources that allow students to trace their ancestors via a paper trail. If students have financial limitations or privacy concerns, have them share the name of the group (e.g., national or ethnic) they most closely identify with, then look up common DNA types for that population. If there are several students with the same stated national or ethnic origin, assign them different DNA types associated with that same group. Using that information, they can use Internet resources to follow the migratory path of their ancestors out of Africa, read about the theories of why various groups migrated, and learn about experiences they may have had. Students should read about the economic, military, religious, cultural, governmental, and environmental forces that may have influenced their ancestors' identities and led them to migrate. Students can also research their ancestors' culture and reflect on whether artifacts from their ancestors' experiences, traditions, skills, and art forms are represented in their thinking, behavior, and preferences today. Have students with similar stated nationalities report their DNA-based histories in groups for comparison and contrast.

Although this chapter was written with instructors of undergraduate and graduate students in mind, introducing this material earlier may help prevent the development of xenophobic attitudes and narrow nationalistic identities that are based on recent family history. This demonstration can even be adapted for use in elementary and middle school. For the youngest children, teachers can ask where students' ancestors came from or display a map of the world and ask where they are from. Regardless of whether students say they come from a city, state, country, or region, there are resources available to trace the migratory paths of people landing in that place. Older students may be able to find information on the Internet themselves. For younger students, teachers can prepare a set of materials for the most common locations to use year after year. The materials can contain the most common migratory histories to that place, and the cultural and other influences along the way, as well as tales of seeking a better life, challenges, achievements, escaping violence, and so forth. In addition to common DNA types for a region, it is important to include examples of strikingly different migratory paths to the same location to draw attention to the hidden heterogeneity of populations.

Asymmetrical Power (Assignment). After completing the previously described exercise, students can write a paper about their history of oppression and privilege. In this assignment, they are asked to identify situations in which their ancestors may have been privileged, oppressed, or discriminated against based on the history revealed by their DNA assignment. Students can also write about times when they found themselves in subordinate and dominant positions across their lifetimes, naming the demographic categories and roles associated with privilege or oppression. Students can describe how the various categories and roles affected their chances of being heard or offered opportunities and had consequences for them and those around them. Once papers are handed in, hold a class discussion of what they learned from the experience, especially in terms of how their different characteristics dynamically interacted within particular contexts to produce different outcomes and how their status has shifted across contexts. For Global Minority students, Jean Baker Miller's (1986) *Towards a New Psychology of Women* (second edition) provides good descriptions of the dynamics that occur between subordinate and dominant status individuals.

Artistic Representation of Self From a Transnational Perspective (Assignment). Debra Mollen (2018) from Texas Woman's University developed a cultural self-portrait project. An important component of transnational research is reflection on one's multifaceted, hybridized, fluctuating, and sometimes fragmented transnational identities, including race or ethnicity, socioeconomic status, gender and sexual orientation identities, national identity, migratory history, and disciplinary training and affiliation, among others. Have students create a visual (e.g., collage, painting, photography, sculpture), written (e.g., poem, children's story), musical (e.g., song), or dramatic representation of intersecting and hybridized identities. Also have students write an accompanying reflection paper on the process of creating an artistic representation and how these identities influence their research and scholarly interests.

Small Group Discussion on Transnational Feminist Performances (Class Activity). Bhattacharya (2009) used performance ethnography to examine two female Indian graduate students' experiences in the United States. The front stage was the space of performances (the part shown to others), and the back stage was where internal thoughts, tensions, and contradictions existed.

Have students read Bhattacharya's article and write a paper reflecting on their "performances" for others and internal experiences (Bhattacharya, 2009) by answering the following questions. On the day they turn them in, have them share their insights with the class.

- What identities are most salient for you?
- How do these identities relate to your history (upbringing, family, cultural background)?
- In which situations or contexts do you perceive yourself as performing (i.e., highlighting or strengthening) certain aspects of your identities?
- In which ways do you think others might strengthen or highlight certain aspects of their identities when interacting with you?
- What kinds of tensions and contradictions do you reserve for back stage (the intern experience)?

How Contiguous and Noncontiguous Flows Impact Us (Assignment). Have students write papers on how they are exposed to other cultures and communities in contiguous and noncontiguous manners and how other cultures and communities influence them. Have them describe how these exposures have influenced their lives, and have them predict future consequences. Also, have students consider how they influence others through direct and remote contact. On the day they turn their papers in, have the whole class share and discuss what they wrote.

Locating Migrant Communities (Assignment). Students can gather information about migrant groups residing within their area using census data and then use a world map to trace their routes from their places of origin. Helpful reports can be found by searching the United Nations Development Programme website (http://www.undp.org) and http://www.migrationpolicy.org for information about migration, refugees, and displacement.

Transnational Case Studies (Assignment). Students can also create in-depth case studies of individual members of migrant groups who have left their homes due to war, poverty, or persecution or for school or better opportunities or who have been acutely affected by globalization (e.g., economic or cultural instability in their home region). Individually or as a class, students might begin by collecting information about groups' composition (e.g., gender, strengths, resources, religion, socioeconomic status, ethnicity, age, sexuality, and place of origin) and contrast locations and migration paths. Students can describe the political, economic, and social issues affecting the regions in which the groups have lived, including power struggles involving corporate and governmental entities. If students stopped there, they might essentialize everyone from that group. Although information about a region or group can be useful in expanding knowledge about some possible life trajectories, it can also lead to the formation of inaccurate stereotypes. It is therefore important that students are exposed to a variety of narratives by members of that group. They can then contrast the personal narratives of individual group members with the characteristics of the larger group, asking themselves how the individuals are similar to or different from the picture created of the group to which they belong to draw attention to within-group diversity.

Instructors can invite members of the groups or an affiliated organization representative to class and interview them using preselected questions from students. The questions can help explore cultural ideologies, inequalities, struggles, sources of empowerment and pride, and experiences of migration of multiple individuals within the group, including how they were received in their new country. Global communications systems offer additional opportunities to connect with people across the world. International organization websites, social media, and blogs also provide options for learning from people in other regions. Google Translate® can be a useful tool for navigating language boundaries, although its translation ability has limitations.

Websites offer powerful first-person accounts. Organizations such as the Peace Corps, Doctors Without Borders, and UNESCO post stories and videos about the day-to-day lives of individuals on their websites. Before reaching out to people to better understand their lives and contexts, students should read Grabe and Else-Quest's (2012) suggestions for culturally sensitive investigative and data collection techniques, including appropriate personal contact.

Violence Against Women and Girls

Chapter 7 in this book, "Using Transnational Feminist Theory to Expand Domestic Violence Understandings," by Guthery, Jeffrey, Crann, and Schwab, is an excellent resource for this topic. Chapter 9, "Transnational Perspectives on Human Trafficking: Centering Structures, Institutions, and Subjects," by Hua and Tjiu, discusses a particular form of violence against women and girls: human trafficking. Both expand readers' perspectives regarding these phenomena.

Exploring the Many Forms of Domestic Violence (Classroom Activity and Assignment). Not enough is known about the many forms that domestic violence takes. Guthery and her collaborators (A. Guthery, personal communication, June 8, 2018) suggested that students brainstorm all the tactics and elements they believe to be involved with domestic violence (either through experience, by proxy, or through media). Students should also read the legal definition and then interview people with as many different origins as possible, asking them the same questions. Students could then compare the sets of answers and discuss the similarities and differences. Students then could also discuss why there is a difference and discuss known cultural and local norms pertaining to violence against women to keep the discussion informed rather than allowing it to stray into stereotypical notions.

Exploring the Dynamics Behind Domestic Violence (Class Activity). Perhaps the most obvious place to begin a discussion about domestic violence is to discuss the dynamics present within the context of violence against women and children. The discussion could focus on the dynamics within relationships, as well as the dynamics that exist outside relationships that intentionally or unintentionally sustain this violence (e.g., laws and policies, culture). It would also be useful to use narrative accounts to illustrate real-life experiences and further personalize the context and highlight the issues.

Violence Against Women Policy (Assignment). Have students research treaties and guidelines on violence against women originated by the United Nations (United Nations, 1979) and associated laws and policies adopted by a country in the Majority World and answer the following questions: Who was involved in the development of the international treaties (e.g., What countries were represented?)? How do the international treaties and local policy and legislation compare with one another (e.g., Did the local country ratify all sections? Why or why not?)? What do local media say about the passing of these laws in [name of selected country]? What laws have not been passed? How was research used to support (or not) the development of United Nations treaties and in-country legislation? How were these laws informed by international organizations and guidelines for violence against women? How do these laws and policies impact specific local communities?

Film and Small Group Discussion on Violence Against Women and Girls (Activity). Have students watch *V-Day: Until the Violence Stops* (Ensler, Mitchell, Shalit, & Epstein, 2003). This documentary features interviews and footage from the 2002 international grassroots movement inspired by Ensler's (1998) *The Vagina Monologues* to end violence against girls and women. The documentary highlights grassroots movements in several different countries and diverse settings within the United States. In small groups, discuss the film. Ask the students, What were your thoughts and reactions? What was surprising? What stands out as most important? In which ways does the approach of the movement and director resonate with a transnational feminist perspective? In which ways could the approach of the movement and documentary be modified to more closely align with transnational feminist principles? What research ideas does this film generate for you?

Film (Class Activity). An estimated 40,000 women and children were trafficked into host cities before the first 2010 World Cup soccer match in

South Africa. *Don't Shout Too Loud* (Campbell, 2011) raises difficult questions about the human trafficking in South Africa in the days leading up to the 2010 FIFA World Cup from the perspectives of public officials and activists.

Readings on Domestic Violence. The authors of the chapter on domestic violence found the following readings especially helpful:

Adams, M. E., & Campbell, J. (2012). Being undocumented & intimate partner violence (IPV): Multiple vulnerabilities through the lens of feminist intersectionality. *Women's Health & Urban Life, 11,* 15–34.

Bovarnick, S. (2007). Universal human rights and non-Western normative systems: A comparative analysis of violence against women in Mexico and Pakistan. *Review of International Studies, 33,* 59–74. http://dx.doi.org/10.1017/S0260210507007309

Brenner, J. (2003). Transnational feminism and the struggle for global justice. *New Politics, 9*(2), 78.

Carty, L., & Mohanty, C. T. (2015). Mapping transnational feminist engagements: Neoliberalism and the politics of solidarity. In R. Baksh & W. Harcourt (Eds.), *The Oxford handbook of transnational feminist movements* (pp. 82–115). Oxford, England: Oxford University Press.

Chowdhury, E. H. (2015). Rethinking patriarchy, culture and masculinity: Transnational narratives of gender violence and human rights advocacy. *Journal of International Women's Studies, 16,* 98–114. http://dx.doi.org/10.1163/15692086-12341253

Dasai, M. (2002). Transnational solidarity: Women's agency, structural adjustment, and globalization. In N. A. Naples & M. Dasai (Eds.), *Women's activism and globalization* (pp. 15–33). New York, NY: Routledge.

Dorjee, T., Baig, N., & Ting-Tommey, S. (2013). A social ecological perspective on understanding "honor killing": An intercultural moral dilemma. *Journal of Intercultural Communication Research, 42,* 1–21. http://dx.doi.org/10.1080/17475759.2012.723024

Fulu, E. (2014). *Domestic violence in Asia: Globalization, gender and Islam in the Maldives.* New York, NY: Routledge.

Fulu, E., & Miedema, S. (2015). Violence against women: Globalizing the integrated ecological model. *Violence Against Women, 21,* 1431–1455. http://dx.doi.org/10.1177/1077801215596244

Jewkes, R. K., Dunkle, K., Nduna, M., & Shai, N. (2010). Intimate partner violence, relationship power inequity, and incidence of HIV infection in young women in South Africa: A cohort study. *The Lancet, 376,* 41–48. http://dx.doi.org/10.1016/S0140-6736(10)60548-X

McDonald, J. (2005). Neo-liberalism and the pathologizing of public issues: The displacement of feminist services models in domestic violence support services. *Australian Social Work, 58,* 275–284.

Adaptable Research Project (Assignment). Have students use the research project format described earlier to partner with a group concerned about violence in relationships and use qualitative methods to examine the meanings of relationships and domestic violence.

Women's Reproductive Experiences

Chapter 8, "Toward a Transnational Feminist Psychology of Women's Reproductive Experiences," by Jeanne Marecek, can serve as the primary reading when covering reproductive health.

Decolonizing Sexuality and Reproduction (Assignment). When *Our Bodies, Ourselves* (Boston Women's Health Book Collective, 2009) was introduced to the Global Majority, it was viewed as hegemonic and insulting in ways that varied depending on the background of the individual (Davis, 2007). Women exposed to Latin American culture, which tends to be collectivistic, raised concerns that *Our Bodies, Ourselves* endorsed individualistic and androcentric norms of sexuality. Women from Eastern Europe were accepting of the individualistic tone but uncomfortable with collectivist ideas of communal sisterhood, which were reminiscent of their experiences with totalitarian regimes. Davis (2007) described how the authors had to confront how their WEIRD-situated perspectives had influenced how they understood and approached women's sexuality, health, and relationships. The most recent *Our Bodies, Ourselves* website now includes a map of the world with links to each region's page, some of which describe the process of adaptation for that region (https://www.ourbodiesourselves.org/global-projects/). Google Translate or a similar application can be used to roughly translate versions into students' preferred languages. Students can read different versions and reflect on how women's views of their bodies and sexuality change as they interact with cultures and outside forces. Students can then do additional research to uncover more detailed information about sexuality and reproductive attitudes and practices within particular communities.

Additional Readings. Ehrenreich and Hochschild (2003) and Burman (2008) are helpful in understanding this topic. Another three pieces are from a special issue entitled *Feminism & Psychology in the Nordic States* (2005, Volume 15(2)). They are examples of work that is very explicit in putting feminist psychology in the context of the social welfare politics of the Nordic state.

Andenæs, A. (2005). Neutral claims—gendered meanings: Parenthood and developmental psychology in a modern welfare state. *Feminism & Psychology in the Nordic States, 15,* 209–226. http://dx.doi.org/10.1177/0959353505051729

Burman, B. (2008). *Developments: Child, image, nation.* London, England: Routledge.

Ehrenreich, B., & Hochschild, A. R. (2003). *Global woman: Nannies, maids, and sex workers in the new economy.* New York, NY: Metropolitan Books.

Haavind, H., & Magnusson, E. (2005). Feminism, psychology and identity transformations in the Nordic countries. *Feminism & Psychology in the Nordic States, 15,* 236–247. http://dx.doi.org/10.1177/0959353505051731

Haavind, H., & Magnusson, E. (2005) The Nordic countries—Welfare paradises for women and children. *Feminism & Psychology in the Nordic States, 15,* 227–235. http://dx.doi.org/10.1177/0959353505051730

Film. Nilita Vachani's *When Mother Comes Home for Christmas* (1995) is a documentary film about a Sri Lankan housemaid working abroad in the Middle East who visits home after many years away. The film can be used to illustrate aspects of marital traditions and transnational *reproductive labor* (activities related to having children, caregiving, cooking, and housekeeping) for Sri Lankans. It includes a sequence of a traditional marriage proposal, though this is presented subtly.

Transnational Service-Learning Experiences

One of the approaches to achieving a deeper understanding of communities is service learning. *Service learning* is a pedagogy in which students apply academic knowledge and skills to address community needs that are linked to broader social justice issues. One of the core principles of service learning is an equal focus on service and learning. Traditional practicum and field experiences focus primarily on students' learning through experiences in the community and run the risk of using communities for students' learning without bringing many benefits to the community. Transnational service learning focuses more on developing an egalitarian and mutually beneficial relationship with communities, with an equal focus on student learning in the community and student service to the community. Service learning involves critical reflection guided through classroom discussions and assignments (e.g., reflective journals and papers) that help students develop what Irvin Altman (1996) called "socially responsive knowledge" (Altman, 1996, p. 371). Socially responsive knowledge connects students' perspectives with content within particular social contexts, teaches them ways to approach and resolve social problems, and fosters their sense of responsibility as global citizens. The section on research includes websites for organizations that may provide such opportunities. In addition, many colleges, universities, and other institutions offer global service-learning opportunities. Such opportunities have new significance and added weight in the context of global migration trends.

Service learning is not just for students. Instructors can also benefit from participating in such programs both as leaders and participants. It is essential that instructors be well prepared both academically and experientially to teach classes on transnational psychology and serve as role models of global citizens. It is imperative that instructors develop self-awareness about their multiple social identities and how they have been shaped by their gender, geopolitical, economic, and current and historical contexts. Instructors should understand how those identities and contexts have influenced their access to economic, political, gender-based, social, and other sources of power and privilege. If instructors understand the nature of privilege and its impact on culture and practices, they should be more able to decenter its influence and instead attend to the experiences of those from Majority World cultures, including their views of members of the Global Minority (Mohanty, 1991). They will also be less likely to abuse their power.

This process can be facilitated by reading, participation in professional organizations, and participation in international travel, study, and conferences. Instructors can also participate in service-learning experiences themselves. Cultural immersion experiences are also helpful in decentering one's cultural perspectives and practices. Through these activities, instructors will have the opportunity to develop personal and professional relationships, including mentoring and collaborative partnerships (Machizawa & Enns, 2015).

CONCLUSION

These suggested activities, assignments, readings, and service-learning experiences are just a beginning. As more psychologists begin to use transnational psychological paradigms, ideas about how to teach them will proliferate. It is vital that people representing a variety of perspectives (e.g., many positions and situations) are included in dialogue and educational and research efforts. According to the principle of pluralism, the more perspectives and voices that are accessed and shared, the more accurate our knowledge base will be, enhancing the quality of information and our notions of "truth" (McHugh, 2007). These exercises model this spirit of pluralism by emphasizing not only the production of ideas and knowledge but also the sharing of this information with a larger group. Furthermore, merely broadening and deepening students' understanding of transnational phenomena is not enough. We should provide students with the knowledge, experience, and skills with the goal of enabling them to take effective action on social justice issues related to globalization and to foster their sense of civic responsibility as global citizens.

Understanding the psychological dynamics and implications of globalization and *glocalization* (ideas and practices reflecting a mixture of local and global influences) will require the real-life practice of multidirectional learning and research. With collective action and common commitment, global networks of citizens, including students and scholars, can create better understandings of peoples' realities as well as enhance potential solutions to problems. As Hill-Collins (1990) said, an inclusive, pluralistic approach is necessary to keep pace with the escalation of globalization and its psychological impacts. Exposure to transnational approaches and principles will hopefully also inspire students to become well-informed, active global citizens in the service of democracy and justice (Mohanty, 2003).

REFERENCES

Adams, M. E., & Campbell, J. (2012). Being undocumented & intimate partner violence (IPV): Multiple vulnerabilities through the lens of feminist intersectionality. *Women's Health & Urban Life, 11*, 15–34.

Altman, I. (1996). Higher education and psychology in the millennium. *American Psychologist, 51*, 371–378. http://dx.doi.org/10.1037/0003-066X.51.4.371

Amer, A., Howarth, C., & Sen, R. (2015). Diasporic virginities: Social representations of virginity and identity formation amongst British Arab Muslim women. *Culture & Psychology, 21*, 3–19. http://dx.doi.org/10.1177/1354067X14551297

Andenæs, A. (2005). Neutral claims—gendered meanings: Parenthood and developmental psychology in a modern welfare state. *Feminism & Psychology in the Nordic States, 15*, 209–226. http://dx.doi.org/10.1177/0959353505051729

Bhattacharya, K. (2009). Negotiating shuttling between transnational experiences: A de/colonizing approach to performance ethnography. *Qualitative Inquiry, 15*, 1061–1083. http://dx.doi.org/10.1177/1077800409332746

Bolton, P., & Tang, A. M. (2004). Using ethnographic methods in the selection of post-disaster, mental health interventions. *Prehospital and Disaster Medicine, 19*, 97–101. http://dx.doi.org/10.1017/S1049023X00001540

Boston Women's Health Book Collective. (2009). *Our bodies, ourselves: A book by and for women.* New York, NY: Paw Prints.

Bovarnick, S. (2007). Universal human rights and non-Western normative systems: A comparative analysis of violence against women in Mexico and Pakistan. *Review of International Studies, 33*, 59–74. http://dx.doi.org/10.1017/S0260210507007309

Brenner, J. (2003). Transnational feminism and the struggle for global justice. *New Politics, 9*(2), 78.

Burman, B. (2008). *Developments: Child, image, nation.* London, England: Routledge.

Campbell, C. (Director). (2011). *Don't shout too loud* [Motion picture]. United States: Changing Direction Films.

Carty, L., & Mohanty, C. T. (2015). Mapping transnational feminist engagements: Neoliberalism and the politics of solidarity. In R. Baksh & W. Harcourt (Eds.),

The Oxford handbook of transnational feminist movements (pp. 82–115). Oxford, England: Oxford University Press.

Chen, S. (2015, April 5). *U.S. wages will be 58 times Indonesia's by 2019.* Retrieved from http://www.bloomberg.com/news/articles/2015-04-06/u-s-wages-will-be-58-times-indonesia-s-by-2019

Chowdhury, E. H. (2015). Rethinking patriarchy, culture and masculinity: Transnational narratives of gender violence and human rights advocacy. *Journal of International Women's Studies, 16,* 98–114. http://dx.doi.org/10.1163/15692086-12341253

Christopher, J. C., Wendt, D. C., Marecek, J., & Goodman, D. M. (2014). Critical cultural awareness: Contributions to a globalizing psychology. *American Psychologist, 69,* 645–655. http://dx.doi.org/10.1037/a0036851

Collins, L. H. (2019). Teaching cultural and transnational psychology: Taking intersectionality across the globe. In J. A. Mena & K. Quina (Eds.), *Integrating multiculturalism and intersectionality into the psychology curriculum: Strategies for instructors* (pp. 181–196). Washington, DC: American Psychological Association.

CrashCourse. (2012, October 25). *Decolonization and nationalism triumphant: Crash Course World History #40* [Video file]. Retrieved from https://youtu.be/T_sGTspaF4Y

CrashCourse. (2015, March 13). *Nonviolence and peace movements: Crash Course World History #228* [Video file]. Retrieved from https://www.youtube.com/watch?v=eP-mv5IjFzY

Craven, C., & Davis, D. (2013). Introduction: Feminist activist ethnography. In C. Craven & D. Davis (Eds.), *Feminist activist ethnography: Counterpoints to neoliberalism in North America* (pp. 1–20). Lanham, MD: Lexington Books.

Creswell, J. W., & Poth, C. N. (2017). *Qualitative inquiry and research design: Choosing among five approaches.* Los Angeles, CA: Sage.

Dasai, M. (2002). Transnational solidarity: Women's agency, structural adjustment, and globalization. In N. A. Naples & M. Dasai (Eds.), *Women's activism and globalization* (pp. 15–33). New York, NY: Routledge.

Davis, K. (2007). *The making of Our Bodies, Ourselves: How feminism travels across borders.* Durham, NC: Duke University Press. http://dx.doi.org/10.1215/9780822390251

Dawson, A., Toombs, E., & Mushquash, C. (2017). Indigenous research methods: A systematic review. *International Indigenous Policy Journal, 8*(2). https://dx.doi.org/10.18584/iipj.2017.8.2.5

Dorjee, T., Baig, N., & Ting-Tommey, S. (2013). A social ecological perspective on understanding "honor killing": An intercultural moral dilemma. *Journal of Intercultural Communication Research, 42,* 1–21. http://dx.doi.org/10.1080/17475759.2012.723024

Dottolo, A. L. (2019). Overcoming student defensiveness in social psychology courses: A collaborative workshop for discussing privilege and prejudice.

In J. A. Mena & K. Quina (Eds.), *Integrating multiculturalism and inter-sectionality into the psychology curriculum: Strategies for instructors* (pp. 257–268). Washington, DC: American Psychological Association.

Dottolo, A. L., & Tillery, S. M. (2015). Reflexivity and research: Feminist interventions and their practical implications. In J. L. Amoreaux & B. J. Steele (Eds.), *Reflexivity and international relations: Positionality, critique, and practice* (pp. 123–141). New York, NY: Routledge.

Ehrenreich, B., & Hochschild, A. R. (2003). *Global woman: Nannies, maids, and sex workers in the new economy.* New York, NY: Metropolitan Books.

Ensler, E. (1998). *The vagina monologues.* New York, NY: Villard.

Ensler, E. (Producer), Mitchell, P. (Producer), Shalit, W. (Producer), & Epstein, A. (Director). (2003). *V-day: Until the violence stops* [Motion picture]. United States: Docurama.

Fulu, E. (2014). *Domestic violence in Asia: Globalization, gender and Islam in the Maldives.* New York, NY: Routledge.

Fulu, E., & Miedema, S. (2015). Violence against women: Globalizing the integrated ecological model. *Violence Against Women, 21,* 1431–1455. http://dx.doi.org/10.1177/1077801215596244

Grabe, S., & Else-Quest, N. M. (2012). The role of transnational feminism in psychology: Complementary visions. *Psychology of Women Quarterly, 36,* 158–161. http://dx.doi.org/10.1177/0361684312442164

Hambleton, R. K., & Kanjee, A. (1995). Increasing the validity of cross-cultural assessments: Use of improved methods for test adaptations. *European Journal of Psychological Assessment, 11,* 147–157. http://dx.doi.org/10.1027/1015-5759.11.3.147

Haavind, H., & Magnusson, E. (2005a). Feminism, psychology and identity transformations in the Nordic countries. *Feminism & Psychology in the Nordic States, 15,* 236–247. http://dx.doi.org/10.1177/0959353505051731

Haavind, H., & Magnusson, E. (2005b) The Nordic countries—Welfare paradises for women and children. *Feminism & Psychology in the Nordic States, 15,* 227–235. http://dx.doi.org/10.1177/0959353505051730

Henrich, J., Heine, S. J., & Norenzayan, A. (2010). The weirdest people in the world? *Behavioral and Brain Sciences, 33,* 61–83. http://dx.doi.org/10.1017/S0140525X0999152X

Hill-Collins, P. (1990). *Black feminist thought: Consciousness and the politics of empowerment.* London, England: HarperCollins.

Hirsh, E., & Olson, G. A. (1995). Starting from marginalized lives: A conversation with Sandra Harding. *Journal of Advanced Composition, 15,* 193–225.

Israel, B. A., Schulz, A., Parker, E., Becker, A., Allen, A., III, & Guzman, R. (2008). Critical issues in developing and following CBPR principles. In M. Minkler & N. Wallerstein (Eds.), *Community-based participatory research for health: From process to outcomes* (pp. 47–66). San Francisco, CA: Jossey-Bass.

Jewkes, R. K., Dunkle, K., Nduna, M., & Shai, N. (2010). Intimate partner violence, relationship power inequity, and incidence of HIV infection in young women in South Africa: A cohort study. *The Lancet, 376*, 41–48. http://dx.doi.org/10.1016/S0140-6736(10)60548-X

Knipe, D. W., Metcalfe, C., Fernando, R., Pearson, M., Konradsen, F., Eddleston, M., & Gunnell, D. (2014). Suicide in Sri Lanka 1975–2012: Age, period and cohort analysis of police and hospital data. *BMC Public Health, 14*, 839. http://dx.doi.org/10.1186/1471-2458-14-839

Koutonin, M. R. (2015, March). Why are white people expats when the rest of us are immigrants? *The Guardian*. Retrieved from http://www.theguardian.com/global-development-professionals-network/2015/mar/13/white-people-expats-immigrants-migration

Kovach, M. (2010). Conversational method in indigenous research. *First Peoples Child & Family Review, 5*, 40–48.

Kurtiş, T., & Adams, G. (2015). Decolonizing liberation: Toward a transnational feminist psychology. *Journal of Social and Political Psychology, 3*, 388–413. http://dx.doi.org/10.5964/jspp.v3i1.326

Machizawa, S., & Enns, C. Z. (2015). Transnational psychological practice with women: Perspectives from East Asia and Japan. In C. Z. Enns, J. K. Rice, & R. L. Nutt (Eds.), *Psychological practice with women: Guidelines, diversity, empowerment* (pp. 225–256). Washington, DC: American Psychological Association. http://dx.doi.org/10.1037/14460-009

Manning, J. (2016). Constructing a postcolonial feminist ethnography. *Journal of Organizational Ethnography, 5*, 90–105. http://dx.doi.org/10.1108/JOE-01-2016-0002

Marecek, J., & Senadheera, C. (2012). 'I drank it to put an end to me': Narrating girls' suicide and self-harm in Sri Lanka. *Contributions to Indian Sociology, 46*, 53–82. http://dx.doi.org/10.1177/006996671104600204

Martín-Baró, I. (1996). Toward a liberation psychology. In A. Aron & S. Corne (Eds.), *Writings for a liberation psychology: Ignacio Martín-Baró* (pp. 17–32). Cambridge, MA: Harvard University Press.

McDonald, J. (2005). Neo-liberalism and the pathologizing of public issues: The displacement of feminist services models in domestic violence support services. *Australian Social Work, 58*, 275–284.

McHugh, N. A. (2007). *Feminist philosophies A–Z*. Edinburgh, Scotland: Edinburgh University Press.

Mena, J. A., & Quina, K. (Eds.). (2019). *Integrating multiculturalism and intersectionality into the psychology curriculum: Strategies for instructors*. Washington, DC: American Psychological Association.

Miller, J. B. (1986). *Toward a new psychology of women* (2nd ed.). Boston, MA: Beacon Press.

Minkler, M., & Wallerstein, N. (2008). Introduction to community-based participatory research: New issues and emphases. In M. Minkler & N. Wallerstein

(Eds.), *Community-based participatory research for health: From process to outcomes* (pp. 5–24). San Francisco, CA: Jossey-Bass.

Mohanty, C. T. (1986). Under Western eyes: Feminist scholarship and colonial discourses. *Boundary 2, 12,* 333–358. http://dx.doi.org/10.2307/302821

Mohanty, C. T. (1991). Under Western eyes: Feminist scholarship and colonial discourses. In C. T. Mohanty, A. Russo, L. Torres, L. (Eds.), *Third World women and the politics of feminism* (pp. 51–80). Bloomington: Indiana University Press.

Mohanty, C. T. (2003). "Under Western eyes" revisited: Feminist solidarity through anticapitalist struggles. *Signs, 28,* 499–535. http://dx.doi.org/10.1086/342914

Mollen, D. (2018). *Artistic representation of self from a transnational feminist perspective.* Teaching demonstration presented at the Psychology Department, Texas Woman's University, Denton.

Moon, T. (2008). Reflexivity and its usefulness when conducting a secondary analysis of existing data. *Psychology & Society, 1,* 77–83.

Morgan-Consoli, M. L., Inman, A. G., Bullock, M., & Nolan, S. A. (2018). Framework for competencies for U.S. psychologists engaging internationally. *International Perspectives in Psychology: Research, Practice, Consultation, 7,* 174–188. http://dx.doi.org/10.1037/ipp0000090

Ortlipp, M. (2008). Keeping and using reflective journals in the qualitative research process. Qualitative Report, 13, 695–705. Retrieved from http://www.nova.edu/ssss/QR/QR13-4/ortlipp.pdf

Peters, W. M. K., Straits, K. J. E., & Gauthier, P. E. (2015). Psychological practice with Native women. In C. Z. Enns, J. K. Rice, & R. L. Nutt (Eds.), *Psychological practice with women: Guidelines, diversity, empowerment* (pp. 191–256). Washington, DC: American Psychological Association. http://dx.doi.org/10.1037/14460-008

Ralston, M. (2009). Towards a truly transnational feminism. *European Journal of Women's Studies, 16,* 400–401.

Samaraweera, S., Sumathipala, A., Siribaddana, S., Sivayogan, S., & Bhugra, D. (2008). Completed suicide among Sinhalese in Sri Lanka: A psychological autopsy study. *Suicide and Life-Threatening Behavior, 38,* 221–228. http://dx.doi.org/10.1521/suli.2008.38.2.221

Seehawer, M. K. (2018). Decolonising research in a sub-Saharan African context: Exploring Ubuntu as a foundation for research methodology, ethics and agenda. *International Journal of Social Research Methodology, 21,* 453–466. http://dx.doi.org/10.1080/13645579.2018.1432404

Sellers, B. G., & Arrigo, B. A. (2016). Economic nomads: A theoretical deconstruction of the immigration debacle. *Journal of Philosophical & Theoretical Criminology, 8,* 37–56.

Simonds, V. W., & Christopher, S. (2013). Adapting Western research methods to Indigenous ways of knowing. *American Journal of Public Health, 103,* 2185–2192. http://dx.doi.org/10.2105/AJPH.2012.301157

Smith, L. T. (2012). *Decolonizing methodologies: Research and indigenous peoples* (2nd ed.). New York, NY: Zed Books.

Spielberger, C. D. (2006). Cross-cultural assessment of emotional states and personality traits. *European Psychologist, 11*, 297–303. http://dx.doi.org/10.1027/1016-9040.11.4.297

Sprague, J. (2016). *Feminist methodologies for critical researchers.* New York, NY: Rowman & Littlefield.

United Nations. (1979). *Convention on the elimination of all forms of discrimination against women.* Retrieved from http://www.un.org/womenwatch/daw/cedaw/

Vachani, N. (Producer & Director). (1995). *When mother comes home for Christmas* [Motion picture]. Mainz-Lerchenberg, Germany: FilmSixteen.

Wallerstein, N., & Duran, B. (2010). Community-based participatory research contributions to intervention research: The intersection of science and practice to improve health equity. *American Journal of Public Health, 100*, 40–46. http://dx.doi.org/10.2105/AJPH.2009.184036

Wessells, M. G. (2009). Do no harm: Toward contextually appropriate psychosocial support in international emergencies. *American Psychologist, 64*, 842–854. http://dx.doi.org/10.1037/0003-066X.64.8.842

Yuval-Davis, N. (2009). Women, globalization and contemporary politics of belonging. *Gender, Technology and Development, 13*, 1–19. http://dx.doi.org/10.1177/097185240901300101

11

TOWARD AN INCLUSIVE, AFFIRMATIVE TRANSNATIONAL PSYCHOLOGY

JOY K. RICE AND SHELLY GRABE

In this final chapter, we have several aims. Although the purpose of this first volume on transnational perspectives in psychology is to begin a transformation of purview and practice in the psychology of women, it is critical to understand why the application of this perspective is likely to be a slow endeavor and one that may meet with some neglect, resistance, and/or sparse usage; the current limited use of intersectionality in feminist psychology provides an instructive example. The chapter then discusses the transnational perspective as a "feminism across borders" and addresses salient, important advantages and possible limitations of the transnational perspective

This book was conceived and nurtured and finally born through the exciting and inspiring work of feminist scholars collaborating in a summit in 2015 sponsored by the Society for the Psychology of Women (SPW) of the American Psychological Association (APA); Canadian Psychological Association, Section on Women and Psychology; Division International Activities Grant Program; APA International Office; Committee on International Relations in Psychology; APA Division 2, Society for the Teaching of Psychology; Association for Women in Psychology; La Salle University; The Chicago School of Professional Psychology; APA Division 17, Counseling Psychology; and APA Division 52, International Psychology.

http://dx.doi.org/10.1037/0000148-012
Transnational Psychology of Women: Expanding International and Intersectional Approaches, L. H. Collins, S. Machizawa, and J. K. Rice (Editors)

for research and practice in the psychology of women. Conclusions and future recommendations for research, teaching, and practice are then presented with cross-references made to the other chapters in the book. As feminist psychologists, we begin this chapter in the tradition of giving voice to our experiences in how we came to this endeavor.

As we noted, this book has an ambitious goal: to facilitate and provide guidance for an evolving paradigm shift from an international toward a transnational psychology of women. Although elated at the progress of feminist thought, methods, and perspectives throughout the field of psychology, I (JKR) was correspondingly disappointed and dismayed by the lack of interdisciplinary and global perspectives throughout theory and research in the psychology of women, women and mental health, and generally in the field of psychology (Rice & Ballou, 2004; Rice & Russo, 2010). Thus, working with like-minded colleagues and then-SPW president, Jean Lau Chin, in 2002, I brought together a panel of women leaders from sociology, political science, business, and international psychology to speak on and share contrasting and complementary approaches to advancing the leadership and status of women nationally and internationally; our goal was also action driven, and in the work groups following the panel, we aimed to formulate and implement collaborative action projects (Rice & Austria, 2007, pp. 165–167).

Although the 2002 panel and work groups were a milestone of sorts in helping to open up more global and interdisciplinary perspectives for our division and resulted in many APA presentations and a book on leadership and collaboration (Chin, Lott, Rice, & Sanchez-Hucles, 2007), the work did not lead to a more fundamental shift in international and interdisciplinary focus in the division, APA, or psychology. Thus, more recently, the coeditors of this book, Collins, Machizawa, and Rice, organized meetings with other psychologists to develop what became the 2015 summit on "From International to Transnational: Transforming the Psychology of Women," which ultimately led to the inspiration for this book. Shelly Grabe was the only scholar from the discipline of psychology invited to give one of the keynotes, a fact that reflects the nascent stages of attention to transnational feminism within psychology. As one of the first psychologists to apply a transnational perspective in research, her work continues to provide helpful and creative examples of this paradigm.

I (JKR) also previously worked with other colleagues to apply the construct of intersectionality to formulating a set of *Guidelines for Psychological Practice With Girls and Women* that were ultimately adopted by APA in 2007 (American Psychological Association, 2007) and led to a book (Enns, Rice, & Nutt, 2015). In this book, Machizawa and Enns (2015) wrote a chapter on "Transnational Psychological Practice With Women: Perspectives From East Asia and Japan," which called on future groups to consider the relevance of the Guidelines to cultures beyond the Global North. They began that process by exploring the implications, modifications, and extensions of the Guidelines for working with women in East Asia of Japanese descent, illustrating how transnational perspectives can advance our understanding about the importance of attending to the unique life experiences of diverse women and girls that are the result of multiple interacting factors related to culture, migration, immigration, and oppression.

A SLOW PROCESS OF CHANGE AND ACCEPTANCE

To understand and apply a feminist transnational approach in psychology and better anticipate its potential for actual use and application in psychology, it is important and illuminating to analyze the use and acceptance of one of its close predecessors in the discipline, intersectional theory. Such an analysis helps us to appreciate and unravel possible reasons for the sparse and limited use of the transnational paradigm.

More than a decade ago, feminist psychology had advanced to realizing that studying any social construct such as gender or race did not provide an understanding and appreciation of the rich interplay of all the various layers and intersections of a woman's or person's life. Intersectionality became an approach that was widely accepted and increasingly applied to research paradigms and questions within feminist psychology (Bowleg & Bauer, 2016; Ceballo, Graham, & Hart, 2015; Cole, 2009; Eagly, Eaton, Rose, Riger, & McHugh, 2012; Else-Quest & Hyde, 2016a, 2016b; Enns et al., 2015; Yoder & Kahn, 2003). Intersectionality as theory was first articulated as a lens to analyze the oppressions faced by American Women of Color,[1] with the significant observation that Black women were socially located at the crossroads of multiple oppressions (Collins, 1990; Crenshaw, 1989). Cole's (2009) brief, cogent definition of intersectionality as "analytic approaches that simultaneously consider the meaning and consequences of multiple categories of identity, difference and disadvantage" (p. 17) is a useful one. One would have to understand, for example, that a social identity formed in the context of a migration and diaspora community could well be multifaceted, fluctuating, and possibly fragmented (Bhatia, 2009; see also Chapter 5, this volume).

Although the emphasis on intersectionality is and was one of the most important advances in feminist psychology in the last 15 years or so, most of

---

[1]Following the suggestion of Aida Hurtado (1996), we have capitalized *Color* in this chapter because it is used in reference to specific ethnic groups (e.g., Chicanos, Asians, Blacks).

the work using the paradigm remains U.S.-centric (Patil, 2013). Attention is given and limited to analyzing ethnic and racial dynamics within U.S. settings rather than among Majority World[2] women, and a Eurocentric lens is commonly used to explain cultural or national others (Kurtiş & Adams, 2015). A survey of the types of studies for the past decade (2006–2017) in the highly regarded, leading academic journal in feminist psychology, the *Psychology of Women Quarterly* (PWQ), is instructive here. In 2010, the journal was positively characterized as "a feminist journal at the cutting edge of a psychology for women" (p. 2) both in terms of its standards for scholarship and its feminist values (Yoder, 2010) and as "the premiere feminist journal in psychology" (Rutherford & Yoder, 2011, p. 174). In her 2010 editorial, the editor also noted, "I welcome (and encourage) manuscripts that explore the intersection of gender with other social categorizations, such as sexuality, race and ethnicity, (dis)ability, socio-cultural, and so on" (Yoder, 2010, p. 2).

This clarion call was not immediately answered. An examination of the research published and books reviewed up until 2016 in PWQ finds only a few studies that explicitly use an intersectional lens to formulate the design and goals of the research, such as a comparison of cultural interactions by different ethnic minority groups regarding body image (Sabik, Cole, & Ward, 2010); an intersectional analysis studying race, social class, and religion in relation to infertility experience (Ceballo et al., 2015); an analysis of Asian women's body image (Brady et al., 2017); and a review of a book on readings relevant to intersectionality (Segal & Martinez, 2007). However, more recently, a comprehensive, in-depth special section devoted to intersectionality research and feminist psychology was published in PWQ, with key articles exploring the use of intersectionality in both quantitative research (Else-Quest & Hyde, 2016a) and qualitative research (Else-Quest & Hyde, 2016b). This analysis, in turn, inspired a dialectical conversation and a host of invited reflections on contested interpretations and methodological choices in the application of intersectional theory (Bowleg & Bauer, 2016; Marecek, 2016, Warner, 2016) that have advanced our understanding of this paradigm in feminist psychology.

Nonetheless, PWQ has remained primarily U.S.-based in its purview; rarely does research about women in other cultures appear. And when these studies do appear, they typically use one nation samples rather than

---

[2]Given that the commonly used terms *developing* and *Third World* are often used by so-called *First World* nations to describe the relatively low economic well-being of another country in a manner that implies inferiority, the term *Majority World*, borrowed from Cigdem Kagitçibasi (2002) and Kurtiş and Adams (2015) is used in this book because individuals from "developing" countries constitute the majority of the world's population.

cross-national or transnational analysis (Fang, Chang, & Shu, 2014; Lewis, Robkin, Gaska, & Njoki, 2011; Mootz, Stabb, & Mollen, 2017; Murthi, 2009) or a design using a U.S. or non-U.S. comparison (Killeen, Lopez-Zafra, & Eagly, 2006). A more recent exception would be Grabe's 2015 cross-national analysis of women's land ownership in Nicaragua and Tanzania. These observations mirror the more systematic findings of Eagly et al. (2012) in their analysis of a half century of research on women and gender derived from searches of journal articles cataloged by PsycINFO for 1960–2009. On the positive side, Eagly et al. found significant changes in psychology since the 1960s second wave of feminism that called for efforts to develop bias-free theories and methods in psychology. A large and diverse body of research on the psychology of women and gender has emerged from an area receiving almost no attention to a position of considerable popularity. Contemporary feminism has called for scholarship on the diversity of genders and their interaction with other social category memberships. Here, however, further analysis of the content of research in regard to diversity of gender reveals a paucity of research that challenges a binary approach, with only a minority of the articles including intersectionality as a salient theme and these, mostly and not unexpectedly, from more recent articles after 1990.

These findings are also in line with Cortina, Curtin, and Stewart (2012), who found that social-structural analyses rarely appeared in highly cited psychology journals devoted specifically to personality research, with social class and sexual orientation particularly neglected. The "silo" effect is evident, with research on gender being automatically diverted to gender journals and race or People of Color to race and ethnicity journals, and so forth. Thus, the method and process of separation by journal focus is one big deterrent to the call of feminist scholars to other researchers to include the intersectionalities of gender with race, social class, sexual orientation, and other social categories (Eagly & Riger, 2014).

Another phenomenon also may strongly mitigate against this call. This is the fact that post-positivism remains the bedrock of mainstream psychological research. *Postpositivism* refers to the belief that the existence of human biases and the influence of social context does not prevent scholars and scientists from mapping external reality and generalizations across settings through laboratory experimentation and empirical methods. Although methodological diversification of psychology as a field occurs in many subareas, experimentation that permits the researcher to draw conclusions about causal relationships remains psychology's prototypical method. An intersectional approach (and a transnational one, as will be discussed later) may use not only quantitative methods but also qualitative and mixed methods that seek an understanding of how participants see, voice, and interpret their social locations and experiences in context-specific settings without recourse to causal relationships (Gergen, 2010).

A FEMINISM ACROSS BORDERS

As the coeditors of this book read and analyzed feminist research outside of psychology and collaborated and shared perspectives with women colleagues from other related disciplines, it also became evident that psychology had not yet embraced an even broader perspective, one that went beyond both an international and intersectional analysis. New to psychology, but not to other social sciences such as sociology, economics, and political science, this perspective has become known as *transnational*. Transnational feminist theories have been based on the work of writers and researchers from a variety of disciplines such as social psychology, sociology, economics, law, political science, philosophy, arts, cross-cultural, migration and population studies, history, education, and women's studies (Briggs, McCormick, & Way, 2008; Cole, 2009; Crenshaw, 1989; Dunn, 2005; Espín & Dottolo, 2015; Grabe & Else-Quest, 2012; Iriye & Saunier, 2009; Kurtiş & Adams, 2015; McConaghy, 2000; Ozkul, 2012; Powell, 2005; Swarr & Nagar, 2010) and used in applied fields such as nursing, health, and social work (Anderson, 2004; Deepak, 2012; Gupta, 2006). A comprehensive history of transnational feminist movements, definitions, strategies, and social contexts in which they have emerged and evolved, particularly in political science and politics, can be found in Baksh and Harcourt (2015). Transnational feminism arose during the 1980s out of the interplay between global and local practices influenced by neoliberalism that were denying women's rights, permitting exploitation, and reproducing subjugation, regardless of the respective location or country (Alexander & Mohanty, 1997; Naples & Desai, 2002; see also Chapters 1 and 2, this volume).

Thus, transnationalism is hardly a new approach—new to psychology but not to other fields. We can trace the roots of transnational feminism to over 30 years ago with Mohanty's seminal 1984 essay, "Under Western Eyes: Feminist Scholarship and Colonial Discourses," in which she critiqued Western feminism and its construction of the category of the "Third World woman" as a generic, homogenous, victimized stereotype that Western feminists must save. She cogently highlighted how the experience of oppression is incredibly diverse and contingent on historical, cultural, and individual factors and experiences. Mohanty (2003) followed that up with her widely cited book, *Feminism Without Borders: Decolonizing Theory, Practicing Solidarity*, that explored how her views on transnational feminism had evolved and shifted with changing critical views on globalism, significantly underlining that the business of capitalistic globalization known as *neoliberalism* was built on the backs and labor of poor women around the world. Reference was also made to the failure of the "sisterhood is powerful" movement that served to highlight the division between Western women's interests from Third World women. In her final section, "Reorienting Feminism," Mohanty (2003), however, offered a more positive view affirming her belief in the real possibility and necessity of building common goals and political projects between Western and Third World feminisms.

To take that a step further, we might conceive, then, of "a feminist psychology across borders." What does that mean? How could it be applied to the psychology of women? And what are the advantages as well as the limitations of such an approach? How, one might ask, does it differ from intersectionality or the post-structuralist approach of second wave feminism? Or is it just a new "buzzword"? The answers to these questions can be partially found in the many in-depth explorations of the chapters in this book. Here, we try to provide a helpful summary of how one might understand this approach and the powerful and broad perspective it can provide us as psychologists and as feminists, as well as some limitations in application, ending with a look toward the future of the transnational paradigm in feminist psychology.

As previously noted, transnational feminist theory has been based on the work of feminist writers and researchers from many fields, including women's studies and, more recently, psychology. Transnationalism is also built on the concept of intersectionality, which approaches the understanding of a person's life space and course by looking at social location and embracing myriad variables beyond gender and race. However, a transnational perspective goes beyond the typical social location analysis that is more local or national to a lens that is transnational—that is, one that transcends countries, nations, and borders. The term *transnational feminism* also inherently points to a multiplicity of feminisms across the world as well as a movement to politicize women's issues beyond the border state as, for example, in the United Nations Women's Conferences (see also Chapter 2, this volume). However, it also has come to be identified with antiglobalism in the sense that the processes of economic globalization have penalized women by exploiting their underpaid labor (Mendoza, 2002). As Swarr and Nagar (2010) noted,

> Whereas international feminisms are seen as rigidly adhering to nation-state borders and paying inadequate attention to the forces of globalization, global feminisms have been subjected to critical scrutiny for prioritizing northern feminist agendas and perspectives for homogenizing women's struggles. (p. 4)

Although the discussion of transnational feminism has been present in other disciplines for nearly 3 decades, it was explicitly introduced into psychology less than 10 years ago, its introduction being brought, in part, by Grabe (2010, 2016a, 2016b, 2017; Grabe & Else-Quest, 2012; see also Kurtiş & Adams, 2015; Marecek, 2012). Before this introduction, scholars had argued that contributions from psychology that integrate feminist scholarship and grassroots community action aimed at transforming the structural inequities that put women at risk and that such transformations were necessary to make the progress critical to advancing women's rights (e.g., Lykes & Moane, 2009). For example, one of the first scholars to bring these ideas together in psychology was Geraldine Moane (1999) in her book *Gender and Colonialism: A Psychological Analysis of Oppression and Liberation.* Although Moane's book was published almost 2 decades ago, empirical examinations in psychology that take a transnational or feminist liberation approach are still in nascent stages. Psychology, however, may have the potential to provide the currently missing, but necessary, links between transnational feminism and the discourse on women's human rights and neoliberalism to contribute to systematic change in the actualization of women's rights worldwide (Grabe, 2016a, 2017).

It has been argued by critical feminist psychologists that, in response to globalization, the discussion of women's rights has become ever more relevant to presenting a "political urgency of critical research" (Fine, 2006, p. 86). To contribute to research on women's issues in this context, scholars will have to embrace a culturally grounded and inclusive vision of justice for women. A transnational feminist approach embraced by scholars across disciplines thus represents an important attempt toward just such inclusivity. Given the multiplicity of knowledge and practices that emerge from a transnational perspective, feminist scholars interested in an inclusive vision of rights for women underscore that there is and must be a diversity of feminisms—responsive to the varying needs and concerns of women throughout the world and defined by them for themselves (Sen & Grown, 1987). Moreover, because transnational feminism involves understanding gender in the context of unfavorable global systems in which the United States participates, this perspective can and should also be applied when conducting research and intervention in the United States (see also Chapters 3 and 4, this volume).

It should be evident that broadening our lens to include the application of transnational feminism may provide many advantages. Transnational feminism, as applied to psychology, however, is not without important limitations for the scholar studying this perspective and seeking to implement it in research, teaching, or practice. We attempt to address both the advantages and limitations of this approach for psychological application.

ADVANTAGES OF TRANSNATIONAL FEMINIST APPROACHES

A Broader Paradigm

One powerful benefit of the transnational approach to the study of the psychology of women is that it offers us a far broader paradigm to study the position of women and to advocate for the interests and rights of women in multiple contexts and settings locally, nationally, and globally. Transnational feminist psychology can provide a lens to examine power and hegemonic[3] practices and resistance to those practices across borders that are cutting edge and can provide both disadvantages and advantages for women. For example, in modern globalization, power has shifted tremendously and exponentially from nation-state to transnational corporations, unsettling national boundaries "whereby a single unitary supranational political power can gain sovereignty over the world's nations and over-determine the distinct centers of power of capitalism in a way it could not do previously" (Mendoza, 2002, p. 298). Transnationalism in general, then, offers a new perspective in psychology and the social sciences not because it identifies new networks of people but because it examines, analyzes, and calls attention to multidirectional movement and flows that have been unexamined or overlooked in the past, such as migrant transnationalism (Dunn, 2005; Ozkul, 2012).[4] Because it seems apparent that identities are formed by geographic or migratory movements as much as they are by the long-term relationship between people and place (Hiebert, 2000, p. 39), a transnational perspective in psychology opens up new opportunities to analyze and better understand these complex relationships (see also Chapters 5 and 9, this volume).

Interdisciplinary Insights and Challenges

Transnational feminist psychology is also inherently interdisciplinary. As Alexander (2005) noted in considering transnational feminism, "If there were ever a moment when interdisciplinary is most needed it is now" (p. 253). Transnational feminist theorizing traverses the social sciences and humanities with sociological, literary, cultural, historical, and legal approaches all represented and embedded in the discourse. Thus, an approach from a number of disciplinary and interdisciplinary perspectives forces scholars to

---

[3]The term *hegemonic* is used following the suggestion of Kurtiş and Adams (2015) to refer to dominant forms of global feminist discourse that originate in Western settings and become applied universally in diverse local contexts.
[4]*Transnationalism* is in the title of hundreds of academic journal articles; a 2007 search of commercial academic databases revealed that the overwhelming majority of them concern the field of human migration (Briggs et al., 2008).

look beyond the narrow confines of their discipline and its epistemology and hegemonic assumptions to understand the multiple related contributions of feminist scholars across disciplines and, one might say, the borders of disciplines. This is quite a challenge, in part because *transnational* has taken on different meanings. Many various disciplines are discussing transnationalism, "but those working in these fields are not seen necessarily mutually conversant; terms such as *glocal*, so crucial to geography's working out of what is meant by transnationalism in that field, is only occasionally even intelligible to historians" (Briggs et al., 2008, p. 625).

Feminist Collaborative Practice

Transnational feminist psychology's focus is on collaborative practice, reinforcing a basic tenet of classical feminism. It challenges three sets of dichotomies: the academic and activist, theory and method, and individual and collective process of knowledge making (Swarr & Nagar, 2010). An important avenue that can be more fully explored and opened up is the collaboration of academics and researchers located in the United States and Europe (who enjoy ready public international access) with feminists in the Majority World, where research is more often of strictly "local" province (Briggs et al., 2008). Thus, transnational feminist psychology has the potential to promote a redefinition of *solidarity* among both Western women and Majority World women that emphasizes empowerment and agency. Further, transnational feminist networks can link women across national borders regarding common economic, social, policy, and identity issues in collective analysis and action while simultaneously also being attentive to the needs of women who experience fewer common challenges (Moghadam, 2005).

An Alternative Vision for Human Rights

Transnational feminist psychology can provide an alternative vision for broad human liberation, not just women's rights but human rights. The goal, in essence, becomes "liberating liberation" (Kurtiş & Adams, 2015). Thus, the quest becomes one that seeks collective liberties and global social justice. This goal is in contrast to a liberal one advocating individual human rights and the fulfillment of individual needs and desires, an optimum goal so prevalent in mainstream psychology but one that is based on privilege and neocolonial domination (Kurtiş & Adams, 2015). Transnational feminist psychology, then, represents an intellectual inquiry that inherently embraces both advocacy and social activism as important components of any scholarship and, as such, it has the potential to address human suffering and paths to healing (Anderson, 2004; Grabe, 2017).

A Dynamic Scholarship

Transnational feminist psychology implicitly requires a self-reflexive approach to research, study, and advocacy by the scholar or practitioner (see Chapter 3, this volume, for examples), but it is also characterized as an inherently unstable praxis that continuously evolves rather than resolves and reaches closure (Swarr & Nagar, 2010). Other transnational scholars have noted that transnational feminist psychology is a "concept in the making . . . postcolonial scholarship is still a work in progress, crafted from divergent positions, with shifting conceptual boundaries" (Anderson, 2004, pp. 239–40) and that we must constantly ask ourselves whether the concept framed captures the fluid and varied contexts and whether the analysis adequately reflects the voices of marginalized groups (Kim, 2006). This can be seen both as an advantage (a *dynamism* that makes it promising for future exploration, modification, and adaptation) and a *limitation* (antithetical to an empiricist approach). Note that the *post* in postcolonial does not refer to time nor era but instead to the idea of working against and beyond colonialism (McConaghy, 2000).

LIMITATIONS OF TRANSNATIONAL FEMINIST APPROACHES

Participant Involvement May Be Problematic

Feminist transnationalism is a lens that, when applied to research, teaching, or practice, assumes that the psychologist is comfortable with modeling a scholar–activist stance that advocates for the advancing status and welfare of women. The research project and goal are not seen as divorced from the overall goal of actively and collaboratively working to improve women's lives. Further, a feminist transnational approach may involve the participants themselves in the formulation of the goals, methodology, and interpretation of the research (Else-Quest & Hyde, 2016b; Grabe, 2016a; Mohanty, 2003). Such a process and an approach are seen as critically important to valuing and giving voice to women's concerns, perceptions, and solutions to their problems. However, psychologists who do not see themselves as activists or advocates or as trained to take the lead in formulating design and hypothesis testing may be quite uncomfortable or wary of such an intertwined enterprise.

Unequal Status of Knowledge Access, Production, and Privilege

Transnationalism is a much used and abused term. For feminists, the transnational has been described as a paradigm that recognizes differences and borders while building solidarity and transcending those borders (Alexander,

2005). Yet *transnationalism* has also been used as a celebratory descriptor for the forces of globalization that make for easy economic access and transfer, instantaneous communication and knowledge production, and a new lens to understand the dynamics of the modern world (P. Levitt & Jaworsky, 2007). In this sense, transnational feminism may be seen as complicit in replicating the very phenomenon it has critiqued. For example, transnational feminist studies have mainly developed and been institutionalized in the U.S. academy (Nadkarni, 2017). As such, it participates and promotes itself within an unequal system of knowledge access, production, and privilege. Even when the researchers are from different countries, their collaborative scholarship, which requires flying to multiple nations with easy access to visas, can be seen as a model of imperial privilege and potential advantage. Further, in the post–Cold War decades, U.S. academics, colleges, and universities all were invited and funded to map the transnational, and thus, academic transnationalism in part has had to serve the goals of government or business (Briggs et al., 2008).

Questionable Applicability to All Fields Within Psychology

The conceptual strength of transnationalism is most obvious in the field of migration and immigration studies in its strong concordance with the multiple attachments and movements of migrants (Dunn, 2005; see also Chapters 5, 8, and 9, this volume). Transnational feminist psychology might be seen as a perspective more applicable to comparative, political, and social psychology than, for example, to clinical, child, or medical psychology, particularly if the clientele is White and American. One could counter that perspective as reinforcing the status quo and instead encourage the use of the idea of the "other" and "othering" to reframe and expand not only our own but also our WEIRD (Western, educated, industrialized, rich, and democratic) clients' limited frameworks (Henrich, Heine, & Norenzayan, 2010). Bhabha's (1990) idea of the "third space" where two cultures or the colonizer and the colonized come together to create a new culture that is a hybridity has application here. He noted that the "third space" displaces the prior histories that constitute it and "gives rise to something different, new and unrecognizable, a new era of negotiation of meaning and representation" (p. 211). Moreover, the methodologies more frequently conducive to clinical and applied research are also ones amenable to the transnational perspective, namely those that are ethnographic, qualitative, and community based.

Women Divided

It is likely that important differences in class, religion, and economic position will continue to divide women, complicating, though not negating,

Mohanty's (2003) transnational call to build common goals and political projects between Western and Majority World feminisms. Certainly, there are broad issues that almost universally impact and unite women in global feminist solidarity and future alliances for advocacy on topics such as violence against women, global sex trafficking, equal opportunity in education and employment and health (see Chapter 2, 6, 7, and 9, this volume), and security and environmental concerns, to name the most salient. Yet other issues can divide women on opposite sides of the fence. They include translocation and outsourcing of jobs and services to the Global South and religious and fundamentalist prescriptions about dress, sexuality, abortion, movement, and communication, as well as the evolving development and globalization of technologies for artificial reproduction and reproductive body parts and their inherent multiple and divisive challenges (Gupta, 2006). In this volume, Chapters 5 and 8 also warn against the pitfalls of minimizing important cultural, theoretical, and political stances among women under the umbrella of *transnationalism*.

Dismissing the Importance of the Nation-State and Borders

Although the feminist transnational approach cautions about avoiding universalist assumptions and conclusions, "a feminism without borders," nation-states and borders cannot simply be dismissed as irrelevant to feminism or to feminist research (Herr, 2013; see also Chapter 2, this volume). The relationship between transnationalism and the nation-state is a complex one. It inherently embraces a critique of the nation-state as a restrictive variable of study that potentially silences narratives and stories both smaller and larger than the state. However, in some contradiction, it simultaneously relies on the existence of nation-states for analyzing, tracing, and understanding the movement and flow of ideas and actions, peoples and practices across the borders of these states (Bender, 2006). Although the nation can be seen as but one of many forms of power and dominance, meaning and containment, it remains as a powerful ideological and economic force in the lives of real people that cannot be ignored. For example, one only has to review the current divisive, fearful, and angry array of attitudes toward immigration across the globe but particularly in Western Europe and the United States, where the proposal to build actual walls protecting the nation-state from illegal immigration and the legal and political opposition to the DREAM Act (Development, Relief, and Education for Alien Minors Act) remain strong realities.[5]

---

[5]The DREAM Act, first introduced in the U.S. Senate on August 1, 2001, S.1291, is an American legislative proposal for a multiphase process for qualifying alien minors in the United States that would first grant conditional residency and, on meeting further qualifications, permanent residency. It has since been reintroduced several times but has failed to pass. In 2017, the 2012 DACA (Deferred Action for Childhood Arrivals) program was also rescinded (https://www.dhs.gov/news/2017/09/05/memorandum-rescission-daca)

CONCLUSIONS AND RECOMMENDATIONS
FOR RESEARCH AND APPLICATION

Although there appears ample theoretical reason to proceed with the investigation of women's experiences through a transnational lens, in particular, those related to the denial of rights and exploitation, little exists in psychology to understand women's experience from this perspective (see Grabe, 2017, for exceptions). Why have investigations of women's rights been conspicuously missing from our discipline? Michelle Fine (2012) suggested that in an increasingly neoliberalized context in social science, questions of method and what counts as evidence have contributed to the narrowing of investigations related to matters of justice for women. Fine stated, "Dominant methodologies systematically strip women (and men) of the material and political contexts of their lives; randomly assigning them to condition and/or assessing their outcomes on standardized indicators deemed appropriate by 'experts'" (p. 10). The result of this narrowing is that social structures and systems of power (e.g., patriarchy, neoliberalism) related to women's experiences cannot easily be considered through the use of standard approaches to research (Grabe, 2017). Based on an urgency for critical research in this area, we offer several areas of focus for transnational feminist researchers and practitioners in psychology: (a) intersectionality, (b) structural analyses, (c) processes of resistance, (d) abandoning the West-as-the-norm approach, (e) privileging local knowledge, (f) understanding how power relates to the research process, and (g) avoiding common pitfalls.

Credit the Importance of Intersectional Approaches

As discussed previously, in an example of a grounded and inclusive agenda, many scholars, including ones in psychology, have urged thinking beyond the homogenization of the category gender to understand the intersectional effects that other social locations related to power—such as race and ethnicity, sexual orientation, and social class—have on women's lives (Cole, 2009; Crenshaw, 1989; Hare-Mustin & Marecek, 1994; Hurtado, 1989). In other words, it has become increasingly clear that gender must be understood in the context of power relations embedded in multiple social categories, a theme emphasized by many authors in this volume. As important as the growing use of intersectional approaches to the study of gender and power within psychology has been (Bowleg, 2008; Cole, 2009; Fine & Sirin, 2007; Hurtado, 1989; Hurtado & Sinha, 2008; Mahalingam, Balan, & Haritatos, 2008; Stewart & McDermott, 2004), many initial investigations have reflected a largely Western bias. In addition to the other dimensions of social location that are often the focus in a U.S. context, transnational and decolonial feminist scholars, including those in this volume, have suggested that women's experience is also inextricably linked to systemic inequities of global power (e.g., colonialism, globalization; Bose, 2012; Grabe & Else-Quest, 2012; Grabe, Grose, & Dutt, 2015; Lugones, 2010; Narayan, 1997; Sen & Grown, 1987). Therefore, research, teaching, and training in psychology that centers women's experience has to take into account the theoretical frameworks offered by Majority World feminisms, which argue that gender oppression operates through unfavorable social systems, such as global power, that exacerbate or maintain violations of women's human rights (Crenshaw, 1989; Lugones, 2010; Sen & Grown, 1987; see also useful teaching applications in Chapter 10, this volume).

Similarly, scholarship and intervention in psychology should not be based on the notion that women have universal experiences; rather, it should be rooted in a shared criticism of and resistance to how policies and societal practices create structural conditions that limit women's rights in their respective communities and locations. Although there are clearly documented inequalities based on gender, notions of universalism in regard to women's experience can raise concern for several reasons. First, a central idea behind what constitutes desirable outcomes, such as the recognition of women's rights, is that they are afforded to autonomous individuals who are assumed to be free of historical and social conditions (e.g., poverty, heterosexist discrimination). An obvious consequence of this is that in many cases women's oppression is not only a matter of gender but is also influenced by factors that may include sexual orientation, class, race and ethnicity, and global economic exploitation, which their male counterparts also experience. As such, an intersectional perspective interrupts a homogenous or universalizing feminism that assumes the focus on achieving women's rights should be placed solely on power imbalances between men and women and directs that the focus has to consider the multiple locations of power that may be contributing to women's risk and vulnerability. Such a perspective is implicit in the contributions of all the authors in this volume.

Focus Analyses at the Structural Level

Critical feminist psychologists have suggested that an individual-level focus on women downplays sociohistorical and cultural context and overlooks an intersectional analysis of the roles of multiple, simultaneous power injustices in women's rights violations (Cole, 2009; Griscom, 1992; Stewart, 1998; Yoder & Kahn, 2003). Similarly, social psychologists have argued for decades that sociostructural factors should be examined to understand well-being instead of focusing on variables that assess individual differences alone (Apfelbaum, 1979; Pettigrew, 1991). Nevertheless, the bulk of mainstream psychology continues to conduct investigations and interventions that separate individuals from their social context, with near neglect of social structures such as gender (Cortina et al., 2012).

Because a main tenet of transnational feminism involves a critique of how systems of global power exacerbate or sustain gender oppression, a focus on social structures and systems of power in understanding women's experience is crucial (Grabe, 2016b, 2016c). For example, across countries and cultures, one of the most ubiquitous group-based inequalities is based on gender, whereby men and women hold different roles that reflect the bias of male structural and social power (Pratto, Sidanius, Stallworth, & Malle, 1994). A glance at international data immediately demonstrates that almost without exception women everywhere in the world, regardless of race or ethnicity, sexual orientation, income level, and so forth, are, on average, disadvantaged by power differentials and are in more subordinate positions than are men (Acosta-Belén & Bose, 1990). Globally, women hold only 24% of seats in national parliaments (The World Bank, 2016). International percentages of women in parliament range from a high of around 41% in Nordic countries, to 27% and 24% in the Americas and Europe, respectively, to 18% in the Arab States (The World Bank, 2016). It has also been consistently demonstrated across the world, including in the United States, that women's earnings are approximately 70% of men's earnings (United Nations, 2010; see also Chapter 6, this volume, for global educational differentials). Approaches to research and intervention taken from a transnational psychology perspective, therefore, have to attend to the social conditions that are embedded in global structures of gender inequality by examining structural power differences at local, national, and transnational levels (Lykes & Moane, 2009; Moane, 1999). Findings from such programs of research should also be aimed at influencing social change rather than used to implement Band-Aid interventions. For example, rather than providing interventions or shelter for women who have been trafficked or have experienced domestic violence, from a transnational psychological framework, findings should target the structural conditions in which such abuse exists (see also Chapters 7 and 9, this volume).

Further, although transnational feminists have cause to remain suspicious of analysis based on nations and nation-states, Dhamoon (2015) argued, "The specificities of nation and the global have to be contextualized to assess their liberatory potential: nationalism is not intrinsically good or intrinsically bad across all struggles for justice" (p. 29). Relations between Indigenous nations may be key to the facilitation of production and socio-family structures and obligations and critical to the maintenance of identity and peoplehood. In some instances, nationhood, for example, is inseparable from native people's relationship to and protection of their land and its borders with cultural mores and traditions and kinship networks and customs all rooted in the intranational alliances, treaties, and relationships among the peoples and other Indigenous nations (Bauerkemper & Stark, 2012). Thus, in future transnational studies, psychologists will have to contextualize the specifics of nation and state to access their positive or negative impact on women and peoples of the Majority World (see also Chapter 2, this volume).

Examine Processes of Resistance

Given the persistence of injustice that women experience globally, it is imperative to understand the psychosocial conditions in which structural inequalities and human rights violations are sustained, as well as how processes of resistance can contribute to conditions that lead to justice. In this manner, resistance to oppressive structures would not be the end goal of political struggle but rather its beginning—an emergent behavior that moves toward justice and liberation. Decolonial theorist María Lugones (2010) defined resistance as the tension between "subjectification (the forming of the subject) and active subjectivity, that minimal sense of agency required, without appeal to the maximal sense of agency of the modern subject" (p. 746). Discussion of topics such as empowerment and agency in traditional psychology has to include an analysis and understanding of how processes of resistance can help women deal with and overcome oppressive social conditions (Grabe, 2016a, 2016b).

A rich body of investigation has emerged in the past couple decades from within the discipline of sociology to document that women in communities all over the world are experiencing the negative effects of globalization and are using a transnational political stage to press for social, educational, economic, and political justice (Moghadam, 2005; Naples & Desai, 2002; see also Chapters 1, 2, 6, and 7, this volume). However, less well documented are the patterns in society associated with oppression that are relevant for understanding the psychosocial processes that lead to social change (Grabe, 2016a). In particular, processes of resistance that have fueled individuals committed to collective action aimed at social justice for women have received only limited attention from the discipline of psychology (Grabe, 2016a, 2017). This may be in part because much of mainstream Western feminist psychology has, with few exceptions, largely neglected the voices of marginalized women and Women of Color in understanding feminist dynamics of resistance and oppression (Kurtiş & Adams, 2015; see Cole & Stewart, 1996; Grabe, Dutt, & Dworkin, 2014; Hurtado, 1996; White & Rastogi, 2009, for exceptions). Emphasizing the role of women's resistance in social justice highlights the importance of psychological processes in the development of strategies for action that suit local capacities and interests aimed at women's rights

(Grabe, 2016c). Research and teaching in psychology can shed light on the diverse experiences of women engaging in resistance and help to understand the role of psychological processes in more effectively challenging the broader structures of power that sustain gender inequalities (Grabe, 2017). Transnational feminist psychologists, therefore, have to document the diverse ways women in different parts of the world creatively resist and confront the challenges posed by the economic and political changes associated with globalization.

Abandon the West-As-Norm Approach

Transnational feminist scholar Leela Fernandes (2013) suggested that despite the interest in transnational feminism moving away from stereotypical views of non-Western women, a narrow focus exists in much interdisciplinary scholarship that has created a binary of marginalized women from the Majority World and elite scholars. This West–rest dichotomy shields from scrutiny the cultural roots of gender inequality that are played out in women's lives everywhere and calls into question the implications of a transnational feminist approach to the feminist production of knowledge (Grabe, 2016c). For example, one consequence of the West-as-norm approach is that it conflates women's rights with those defined by the West. Therefore, through much of the writings about women's human rights, we have come to understand rights violations as a non-U.S.-based phenomenon (Powell, 2005). This is reflected in the widely used examples (in teaching and research) meant to represent violations of women's rights. Although practices such as veiling or genital cutting have been commonly used as examples of violations of women's rights, the imbalanced focus on these examples in Western media and scholarship suggests that the West is assumed to have a culturally neutral baseline against which to evaluate other women's rights (Grabe, 2013). Moreover, these examples also reflect how various countries or cultures are positioned in terms of having human rights monitored by international bodies such as the United Nations. Specifically, Western countries, whose status as harbingers of rights is seldom questioned, are comfortably positioned to discuss women's human rights violations in countries from the rest of the world. Overusing certain examples in Western scholarship contributes to the dichotomy whereby the West evaluates the rest of the world.

Future research, teaching, training, and practice in transnational feminism within psychology has to interrupt the West–rest notion that the United States is the norm by which women's rights and resistance ought to be understood. The West–rest dichotomy limits a comprehensive structural analysis of what contributes to violations against women or the upholding of their rights. Recently, it has been suggested that the liberatory potential of feminism within psychology has fallen short because of its grounding in (neo) colonial legacies of hegemonic feminism (Kurtiş & Adams, 2015). For example, much of mainstream feminist work in psychology has developed theories and understandings of gender oppression in WEIRD (Henrich et al., 2010) contexts and imposed those perspectives across varied settings for understanding what has been conceptualized as "universal" gendered oppression (Kurtiş & Adams, 2015). Moreover, and not unrelated to the first point, mainstream feminist psychology has largely used methodologies that involve sampling predominately White undergraduate college students studying at U.S. universities (Marecek, 2012). These traditional approaches to understanding gendered injustice within psychology are problematic not only because they develop understandings that might not be applicable across varied contexts but also because they tend to treat women in Majority World settings as powerless, thereby serving to legitimize structures of domination (Kagitcibasi, 2002; Kurtiş & Adams, 2015; see also Chapters 8, 9, and 10, this volume, on teaching about asymmetrical power, reflexivity, and decolonization from a transnational perspective).

Transnational feminism in psychology should discuss women's inequities as structural issues to be understood within a human rights framework, regardless of the region of the world in which the women live. Human rights discourse, though widely used in other countries when understanding women's experiences (Grabe, 2017), is conspicuously missing in the discourse in the United States. Although several theorists have traced gender-based violence to inequitable relationships between women and men that are based on normalized ideologies of male dominance and female submission (e.g., Morash, Bui, & Santiago, 2000), violence against women within the United States has often been discussed as a public health problem rather than a violation of women's human rights (e.g., Heise, Raikes, Watts, & Zwi, 1994; Koss, 1990; Krantz, 2002; see also Chapter 7, this volume). Thus, the political structures that perpetuate gender inequality and that fail to recognize or guarantee the rights of women must be recognized and addressed.

Privilege Local Partnerships and Knowledge by Taking a Scholar–Activist Approach

To safeguard against the risk of transnational feminist psychologists further legitimizing structures of domination when conducting investigations, it is imperative that academics take a scholar–activist approach by using methodology in the name of social justice. In *Activist Scholarship: Antiracism, Feminisms, and Social Change*, Sudbury and Okazawa-Rey (2009) defined *activist scholarship* as "the production of knowledge and pedagogical practices through active engagements with, and in the service of, progressive social movements" (p. 3). As a mode of scholarship, social justice research entails movement and intellectual exchange between academic and activist spaces, privileging the knowledge that emerges from the grassroots in that it creates new possibilities for the production of emancipatory knowledge. As such, several authors have suggested that researchers not work with elite organizations but rather prioritize grassroots social change agents who are mobilized within social movements (e.g., Cooke, 2004; Grabe, 2016a, 2017).

According to Geraldine Moane (1999), "liberating modes of psychology are aimed at contributing to changing, developing, and maintaining a society that allows people to become full citizens who can exert their rights" (p. 527). Because women from diverse local contexts all over the world have demonstrated that they are not mere victims but rather have worked actively to resist oppression and promote women's rights (Brodsky et al., 2012), research partnerships should be established with local grassroots organizations or social change agents. Given that self-mobilized groups of women across the world use a complex understanding of the interaction between local and global impacts on women's human rights, feminist psychologists interested in global social change have to work alongside women and build alliances that center local knowledge. The aim in scholar–activist partnerships, therefore, is to develop a synergistic relationship whereby activists develop their agendas and research questions or strategies for action, and psychologists use the discipline in the service of social justice by focusing on the oppressive reality of social structures (Martín-Baró, Aron, & Corne, 1994; see also a list of "best practices" for working in communities in Grabe, 2016b).

A major consideration for transnational feminist psychologists is in asking how, as scholar–activists, they might collaborate with women outside the academy who are setting their own agendas (Grabe, 2016a, 2016c). Traditionally, when academic and community partnerships have been used in psychology, the structure of the relationship encourages instrumentalist involvements whereby communities, and the individuals within them, are positioned as extractable data sources, rather than true partners in collective social change efforts (Nelson, Prilleltensky, & MacGillivary, 2001). However, the goal of social justice scholarship is to foster meaningful alliances with others working outside the academy in joint pursuit of liberation (Prilleltensky, 2008). Because the transnationalization of feminisms requires local knowledge and experience to establish commonalities on which alliances and relations may be built, this approach is particularly important in transnational feminist psychology (Montenegro, Capdevila, & Sarriera, 2012). Feminist researchers working from the perspective of transnational psychology do not determine an agenda for working with marginalized women but rather work in collaboration with community partners to reveal and understand inherent power imbalances that prevent genuinely liberatory action (see also Chapter 3, this volume, for a discussion and research examples of partnering with community locals; Chapter 4, on community intervention; and Chapter 10, on teaching about community partnerships).

Understand the Role of Power

In much community-based work, researchers rarely explicitly recognize that there is a power imbalance between professionals and the oppressed groups with whom they work (Nelson et al., 2001; see Chapter 3, this volume, for exceptions). One of the aims of transnational feminist scholarship is to break through the strangleholds imposed by mainstream academia and universalizing feminisms to elevate the voices of marginalized women in the production of liberatory knowledge. This is not possible if scholars come to research projects with "ready-made" theories, especially if those theories represent those of a fairly small handful of privileged women. Decolonial feminist scholars María Lugones and Elizabeth Spelman (1983) pointedly noted that "if other women's voices do not sing in harmony with the theory, they aren't counted as women's voices—rather they are the voices of the woman as Hispana, Black, Jew, etc." (p. 575). Lugones suggested this happens when those who are producing theory (i.e., the "experts") presume to know more about the phenomenon under study than those who are being theorized about. Those interested in pursuing transnational research in psychology should not fall prey to the falsehoods of "expert" or "knower" but rather work in collaboration with community partners and engage in "political listening," thereby challenging subject–researcher power imbalances that determine the knower and expert (Shayne, 2014).

Transnational feminist scholars in psychology should establish a commitment to a research process that is attentive to the boundaries between researchers and partners and the power those boundaries have to marginalize (Ackerly & True, 2008). Future research should attempt to break down traditional academic boundaries by interrogating forms of inclusion and exclusion in the research process. In particular, if scholars and community partners are going to create knowledge together, space has to be made for women in the community to articulate, interpret, theorize, and reflect about what is under investigation (Lugones & Spelman, 1983). And more specific, because scholar–activist partnerships should be aimed at being genuinely transformative, the needs and interests of the marginalized group should be what guides the research question rather than the scholar's academic agenda. In other words, the research project should not be based on the need to complete a dissertation, advance a program of research, fulfill a grant obligation, or get tenure (Lugones & Spelman, 1983). Transnational feminist collaborations that are rooted in shared criticisms and commitment to social change should be rooted in ideas, concerns, and understandings that are driven by a local community and not imported from outside.

Avoid Common Pitfalls

In the 1980s, Julian Rappaport challenged the field of community psychology to adopt empowerment as a guiding concept and introduced a framework for investigating processes whereby groups, in particular, those outside the mainstream of society, took control over their lives (Rappaport, 1987). However, early conceptualizations and investigations of empowerment within psychology focused primarily on individual factors, thereby giving limited attention to context and social structures (Perkins & Zimmerman, 1995; Riger, 1993). Moreover, many empowerment interventions within community psychology have typically not been designed to transform inequitable social structures but rather to help "victims" (Prilleltensky, 2008). Similarly, a majority of international development interventions aimed at empowerment use a "rescue narrative" by intending to rectify injustices experienced due to "tradition" that women, in particular, are presumably unable to confront without outside help (Alexander, 2005). Despite the intent to improve the social conditions in which people live their lives, these approaches have been limited in demonstrating how those with less structural power take action to improve their lives and also contribute little to understanding the transformation of social structures that maintain gender inequity (see Chapter 6, this volume, for illuminative case examples).

Moving forward, transnational feminist psychologists have to take great care not to enter the same pitfalls, for example, by labeling research or teaching that takes place in an international context as *transnational* simply because it appears trendy or more progressive to do so. Scholars across disciplines have made a concerted effort to distinguish *transnational* feminism from *international* feminism or *global sisterhood* because international and global models of feminism have traditionally turned a blind eye to diverse expressions of feminism, instead favoring a Western model that universalizes women's experiences (Alexander & Mohanty, 1997; Grewal & Kaplan, 1994; Naples & Desai, 2002).

To help assess the risk of pitfalls, feminist scholars should engage in *reflexivity*—or the process of examining oneself as a researcher, as well as examining the research or intervention relationship—before beginning a transnational project. This starts with asking questions about the role of psychology or academia—at large—in perpetuating existing power imbalances (Marecek, 2012). For example, in what ways does the work of scholars inadvertently support and reinforce hierarchies that help contribute to the global order? Psychologists should also be self-reflexive by situating themselves in the context of global power dynamics (Ackerly & True, 2008). What is the psychologist's social location in relation to globalization? And how will that impact how she believes the research project or intervention should be conducted or her ability to engage authentically, conceptualize the issue under investigation, interpret the findings, or conduct the intervention? (See also Chapter 4, this volume.)

Perhaps more important, given the power disparities that exist between the researcher or teacher and research partner(s), psychologists should also ask themselves why they want to do this work. What is the motivation? Are there self-interests? As a scholar, can parts of one's privilege be abandoned to engage in "political listening"? Psychologists should also consider in advance when they speak, write, publish, or teach about other women to whom will they be accountable (Lugones & Spelman, 1983). These questions may not have easy answers, but they (and others, see Grabe, 2016b) should be asked before engaging in work that has transnational aims.

CLOSING REFLECTIONS AND GOALS

As previously discussed, intersectional and interdisciplinary perspectives, and now transnational approaches, have not been widely applied in the field of psychology. The individual level focus of our field has, until recently, limited our vision, assumptions, and conclusions (Eagly et al., 2012). The rhetoric and the call for this broader lens is increasingly frequent. For example, the first principle of the new 2017 APA Multicultural Guidelines (APA, 2017) called for an appreciation that intersectionality is shaped by the multiplicity of the individual's social context.

This written recognition, however, finds less frequent and sparser representation in actual application in psychological research (Cortina et al., 2012; Eagly et al., 2012). An application of the transnational lens is likely to be a slow process. Adopting a transnational perspective inherently involves acknowledging a fluid and shifting phenomenology of multiple realities and an openness and comfort with such a flexible stance. This can be challenging to psychologists trained, grounded, and wedded to a postpositive view of research and a corresponding belief that generalizations contribute more to understanding people and the world than do partial, fluid, and changing observations. Such a perspective, however, has been roundly criticized by postmodern feminist psychologists as reflecting a somewhat grandiose vision of what psychology can bring to the rest of the world. WEIRD psychology as projected onto the Majority World has failed to accurately portray the perspectives, life realities, and actual concerns of individuals in those locations.

That failure, perhaps not coincidentally, parallels the failure of 21st-century global economics and politics to include the global poor and disenfranchised. Capturing the diverse perspectives of Majority World peoples may require the use of multi-methodologies, including qualitative research methods and qualitative meta-analysis in psychology. Thus, it is encouraging to see that in 2019 as this book goes to press, for the first time in its history, the APA Publications and Communications Board has recommended and issued reporting standards for qualitative research appropriate for a wide range of methods within the discipline of psychology that have possible utility in a broad range of social sciences (H. M. Levitt et al., 2018). The historical and practical significance of this development cannot be underestimated because it will mean that qualitative research in APA Style will be included in future editions of the *Publication Manual of the American Psychological Association* (APA, 2010). This is one of many steps that will hopefully not only encourage psychologists to embrace a broader perspective in attempts to understand and include underrepresented groups and populations but also to honor a range of tools, traditions, methods, and reporting styles within that endeavor. It is indicative of flexibility and humility rather than rigidity and hubris.

So, this book, in essence, represents a call for humility (Gallardo, 2014). Humbleness is not a popular stance, particularly among the elite of a profession or discipline who have worked hard and struggled long to reach their positions of power and influence. Humility calls for openness and self-reflexivity; for modest acknowledgment of the validity of different feminisms, multiple pluralities, and alternative methodologies; and for interdisciplinary and community partnerships. The purpose of adopting a feminist transnational perspective is not necessarily one that seeks the goal of elusive equality or multi-meaning social justice, although these utopic visions find strong and meaningful expression in the values underlying feminist transnationalism. The goal is a more modest one—one of encompassing, understanding, and appreciating the missing voices in documenting people's lives and concerns, both locally and globally, and thus one that fosters an inclusive, affirmative transnational psychology. The big picture includes acknowledging our myopia as scholars, researchers, and practitioners projecting our vision of a better world based on WEIRD perspectives and concerns, as well as recognizing the colonialism of Western feminism as it has been defined and applied to other women.

We hope that this book, the first in psychology and the psychology of women to consider and analyze a transnational approach, will serve as a modest beginning to inspire and encourage others to study these ideas and to use and expand on them in many various settings, practices, and future studies. Although transforming the psychology of women from an international to a transnational perspective seems, at first blush, also a grandiose goal, it is a goal that reiterates and builds on the long-standing call of multi-cultural, liberation, and feminist psychology for a humble appreciation of multiple lens perspectives and a reaffirmation of pluralism (Rice & Ballou, 2004), intersectionality (Cole, 2009; Yoder & Kahn, 2003), and a continuous practice of reflexivity (Mootz et al., 2017). It also calls for taking the next and challenging step of forming partnerships with participants in giving voice to their authentic experiences, for embracing activism in scholarship, and for recognizing both the limitations and the positive contributions of our work. We have much to learn from our colleagues in other disciplines, our international partners, and the voices of women around the world that transcend borders and nations.

REFERENCES

Ackerly, B., & True, J. (2008). Reflexivity in practice: Power and ethics in feminist research on international relations. *International Studies Review*, *10*, 693–707. http://dx.doi.org/10.1111/j.1468-2486.2008.00826.x

Acosta-Belén, E., & Bose, C. B. (1990). From structural subordination to empowerment: Women and development in Third World contexts. *Gender & Society*, *4*, 299–320. http://dx.doi.org/10.1177/089124390004003003

Alexander, M. J. (2005). *Pedagogies of crossing: Meditations on feminism, sexual politics, memory, and the sacred.* Durham, NC: Duke University Press.

Alexander, M. J., & Mohanty, C. T. (1997). *Feminist genealogies, colonial legacies, democratic futures.* New York, NY: Routledge.

American Psychological Association. (2007). Guidelines for psychological practice with girls and women. *American Psychologist*, *62*, 949–979. http://dx.doi.org/10.1037/0003-066X.62.9.949

American Psychological Association. (2010). *Publication manual of the American Psychological Association* (6th ed.). Washington, DC: Author.

American Psychological Association. (2017). *Multicultural guidelines: An ecological approach to context, identity, and intersectionality.* Washington, DC: Author.

Anderson, J. M. (2004). Lessons from a postcolonial-feminist perspective: Suffering and a path to healing. *Nursing Inquiry*, *11*, 238–246. http://dx.doi.org/10.1111/j.1440-1800.2004.00231.x

Apfelbaum, E. (1979). Relations of domination and movements for liberation: An analysis of power between groups. In W. G. Austin & S. Worchel (Eds.), *The social psychology of intergroup relations* (pp. 188–204). Monterey, CA: Brooks/Cole.

Baksh, R., & Harcourt, W. (Eds.). (2015). *The Oxford handbook of transnational feminist movements.* New York, NY: Oxford University Press.

Bauerkemper, J., & Stark, H. K. (2012). The trans/national terrain of Anishinaable law and diplomacy. *Journal of Transnational American Studies, 4,* 1–21.

Bender, T. (2006). *A nation among nations: America's place in world history.* New York, NY: Farrar, Strauss & Giroux.

Bhabha, H. (1990). The third space: Interview with Homi Bhabha. In J. Rutherford (Ed.), *Identity, community, culture difference* (pp. 207–221). New York, NY: Routledge.

Bhatia, S. (2009). Theorizing identity in transnational and diaspora cultures: A critical approach to acculturation. *International Journal of Intercultural Relations, 33,* 140–149. http://dx.doi.org/10.1016/j.ijintrel.2008.12.009

Bose, C. E. (2012). Intersectionality and global gender inequality. *Gender & Society, 26,* 67–72. http://dx.doi.org/10.1177/0891243211426722

Bowleg, L. (2008). When Black + lesbian + woman ≠ Black lesbian woman: The methodological challenges of qualitative and quantitative intersectionality research. *Sex Roles, 59,* 312–325. http://dx.doi.org/10.1007/s11199-008-9400-z

Bowleg, L., & Bauer, G. (2016). Invited reflection: Quantifying intersectionality. *Psychology of Women Quarterly, 40,* 337–341. http://dx.doi.org/10.1177/0361684316654282

Brady, J. L., Kaya, A., Iwamoto, D., Park, A., Fox, L., & Moorhead, M. (2017). Asian American women's body image experiences: A qualitative intersectionality study. *Psychology of Women Quarterly, 41,* 479–496. http://dx.doi.org/10.1177/0361684317725311

Briggs, L., McCormick, G., & Way, J. T. (2008). Transnationalism: A category of analysis. *American Quarterly, 60,* 625–648. http://dx.doi.org/10.1353/aq.0.0038

Brodsky, A. E., Portnoy, G. A., Scheibler, J. E., Welsh, E. A., Talwar, G., & Carrillo, A. (2012). Beyond (the ABCs): Education, community, and feminism in Afghanistan. *Journal of Community Psychology, 40,* 159–181. http://dx.doi.org/10.1002/jcop.20480

Ceballo, R., Graham, E. T., & Hart, J. (2015). Silent and infertile: An intersectional analysis of the experiences of socioeconomically diverse African American women with infertility. *Psychology of Women Quarterly, 39,* 497–511. http://dx.doi.org/10.1177/0361684315581169

Chin, J. L., Lott, B., Rice, J. K., & Sanchez-Hucles, J. (Eds.). (2007). *Women and leadership: Transforming visions and diverse voices.* Washington, DC: American Psychological Association.

Cole, E. R. (2009). Intersectionality and research in psychology. *American Psychologist, 64,* 170–180. http://dx.doi.org/10.1037/a0014564

Cole, E. R., & Stewart, A. J. (1996). Meanings of political participation among Black and White women: Political identity and social responsibility. *Journal of Personality and Social Psychology, 71,* 130–140. http://dx.doi.org/10.1037/0022-3514.71.1.130

Collins, P. H. (1990). *Black feminist thought: Knowledge, consciousness and the politics of empowerment.* New York, NY: Routledge.

Cooke, B. (2004). Rules of thumb for participatory change agents. In S. Hickey & G. Mohan (Eds.), *Participation: From tyranny to transformation?* (pp. 42–56). New York, NY: Zed Books.

Cortina, L. M., Curtin, N., & Stewart, A. J. (2012). Where is social structure in personality research? A feminist analysis of publication trends. *Psychology of Women Quarterly, 36*, 259–273. http://dx.doi.org/10.1177/0361684312448056

Crenshaw, K. (1989). Demarginalizing the intersection of race and sex: A Black feminist critique of Antidiscrimination doctrine, feminist theory and antiracist politics. *University of Chicago Legal Forum, 140*, 139–167.

Deepak, A. C. (2012). Globalization, power and resistance: Postcolonial and transnational feminist perspectives for social work practice. *International Social Work, 55*, 779–793. http://dx.doi.org/10.1177/0020872811414038

Dhamoon, R. (2015). A feminist approach to decolonizing anti-racism: Rethinking transnationalism, intersectionality and settler colonialism. *Feral Feminisms, 4*, 20–36.

Dunn, K. M. (2005). A paradigm of transnationalism for migration studies. *New Zealand Population Review, 31*, 15–31.

Eagly, A. H., Eaton, A., Rose, S. M., Riger, S., & McHugh, M. C. (2012). Feminism and psychology: Analysis of a half-century of research on women and gender. *American Psychologist, 67*, 211–230. http://dx.doi.org/10.1037/a0027260

Eagly, A. H., & Riger, S. (2014). Feminism and psychology: Critiques of methods and epistemology. *American Psychologist, 69*, 685–702. http://dx.doi.org/10.1037/a0037372

Else-Quest, N. M., & Hyde, J. S. (2016a). Intersectionality in quantitative psychological research: I. Theoretical and epistemological issues. *Psychology of Women Quarterly, 40*, 319–336. http://dx.doi.org/10.1177/0361684316647953

Else-Quest, N. M., & Hyde, J. S. (2016b). Intersectionality in quantitative psychological research: II. Methods and techniques. *Psychology of Women Quarterly, 40*, 319–336. http://dx.doi.org/10.1177/0361684316647953

Enns, C. Z., Rice, J. K., & Nutt, R. L. (Eds.). (2015). *Psychological practice with women: Guidelines, diversity and empowerment.* Washington, DC: American Psychological Association. http://dx.doi.org/10.1037/14460-000

Espín, O. M., & Dottolo, A. L. (Eds.). (2015). *Gendered journeys: Women, migration, and feminist psychology.* New York, NY: Palgrave Macmillan.

Fang, S., Chang, H., & Shu, B. (2014). Objectified body consciousness, body image discomfort and depressive symptoms among breast cancer survivors in Taiwan. *Psychology of Women Quarterly, 38*, 563–574. http://dx.doi.org/10.1177/0361684314552652

Fernandes, L. (2013). *Transnational feminism in the United States: Knowledge, ethics, and power.* New York: New York University Press.

Fine, M. (2006). Bearing witness: Methods for researching oppression and resistance: A textbook for critical research. *Social Justice Research, 19*, 83–108.

Fine, M. (2012). Troubling calls for evidence: A critical race, class and gender analysis of whose evidence counts. *Feminism & Psychology, 22*, 3–19. http://dx.doi.org/10.1177/0959353511435475

Fine, M., & Sirin, S. R. (2007). Theorizing hyphenated selves: Researching youth development in and across contentious political contexts. *Social and Personality Psychology Compass, 1*, 16–38. http://dx.doi.org/10.1111/j.1751-9004.2007.00032.x

Gallardo, M. E. (Ed.). (2014). *Developing cultural humility: Embracing race, privilege, and power*. Los Angeles, CA: Sage.

Gergen, M. M. (2010). Qualitative inquiry in gender studies. In J. C. Chrisler & D. R. McCreary (Eds.), *Handbook of gender research in psychology* (pp. 103–131). New York, NY: Springer. http://dx.doi.org/10.1007/978-1-4419-1465-1_6

Grabe, S. (2010). Women's human rights and empowerment in a transnational, globalized context: What's psychology got to do with it? In M. A. Paludi (Ed.), *Feminism and women's rights worldwide* (pp. 17–46). Westport, CT: Praeger.

Grabe, S. (2013). Psychological cliterodectomy: Body objectification as a human rights violation. In M. K. Ryan & N. R. Branscombe (Eds.), *The Sage handbook of gender and psychology* (pp. 412–427). Los Angeles, CA: Sage. http://dx.doi.org/10.4135/9781446269930.n25

Grabe, S. (2016a). *Narrating a psychology of resistance: Voices from the compañeras in Nicaragua*. New York, NY: Oxford University Press.

Grabe, S. (2016b). Transnational feminism in psychology: Moving beyond difference to investigate processes of power at the intersection of the global and local. In T. A. Roberts, N. Curtin, L. Cortina, & L. Duncan (Eds.), *Feminist perspectives on building a better psychological science of gender* (pp. 295–318). New York, NY: Springer. http://dx.doi.org/10.1007/978-3-319-32141-7_17

Grabe, S. (2016c). Transnational feminism in psychology: Women's human rights, liberation, and social justice. In P. Hammack (Ed.), *The Oxford handbook of social psychology and social justice* (pp. 193–203). New York, NY: Oxford University Press.

Grabe, S. (Ed.). (2017). *Women's human rights: A social psychological perspective on resistance, liberation, and justice*. New York, NY: Oxford University Press.

Grabe, S., Dutt, A., & Dworkin, S. (2014). Women's community mobilization and well-being: Local resistance gendered social inequities in Nicaragua and Tanzania. *Journal of Community Psychology, 42*, 379–397. http://dx.doi.org/10.1002/jcop.21616

Grabe, S., & Else-Quest, N. M. (2012). The role of transnational feminism in psychology: Complimentary visions. *Psychology of Women Quarterly, 36*, 158–161. http://dx.doi.org/10.1177/0361684312442164

Grabe, S., Grose, R., & Dutt, A. (2015). Women's land ownership and relationship power: A mixed methods approach to understanding structural inequities and violence against women. *Psychology of Women Quarterly, 39,* 7–19. http://dx.doi.org/10.1177/0361684314533485

Grewal, I., & Kaplan, C. (1994). *Scattered hegemonies: Postmodernity and transnational feminist practices.* Minneapolis: University of Minnesota Press.

Griscom, J. L. (1992). Women and power: Definition, dualism and difference. *Psychology of Women Quarterly, 16,* 389–414. http://dx.doi.org/10.1111/j.1471-6402.1992.tb00264.x

Gupta, J. A. (2006). Toward transnational feminisms: Some reflections and concerns in relation to the globalization of reproductive technologies. *European Journal of Women's Studies, 13,* 23–38. http://dx.doi.org/10.1177/1350506806060004

Hare-Mustin, R. T., & Marecek, J. (1994). Asking the right questions: Feminist psychology and sex differences. *Feminism & Psychology, 4,* 531–537. http://dx.doi.org/10.1177/0959353594044007

Heise, L. L., Raikes, A., Watts, C. H., & Zwi, A. B. (1994). Violence against women: A neglected public health issue in less developed countries. *Social Science & Medicine, 39,* 1165–1179. http://dx.doi.org/10.1016/0277-9536(94)90349-2

Henrich, J., Heine, S. J., & Norenzayan, A. (2010). The weirdest people in the world? *Behavioral and Brain Sciences, 33,* 61–83. http://dx.doi.org/10.1017/S0140525X0999152X

Herr, R. S. (2013). "Third World," transnational, and global feminisms. In P. Mason (Ed.), *Encyclopedia of race and racism* (2nd ed., pp. 190–195). New York, NY: Macmillan.

Hiebert, D. (2000). Immigration and the changing Canadian city. *The Canadian Geographer/Le Geographe Canadien, 44,* 25–43. http://dx.doi.org/10.1111/j.1541-0064.2000.tb00691.x

Hurtado, A. (1989). Relating to privilege: Seduction and rejection in the subordination of white women and women of color. *Signs, 14,* 833–855. http://dx.doi.org/10.1086/494546

Hurtado, A. (1996). *The color of privilege: Three blasphemies on race and feminism.* Ann Arbor: University of Michigan Press.

Hurtado, A., & Sinha, M. (2008). More than men: Latino feminist masculinities and intersectionality. *Sex Roles, 59,* 337–349. http://dx.doi.org/10.1007/s11199-008-9405-7

Iriye, A., & Saunier, P. (Eds.). (2009). *The Palgrave dictionary of transnational history: From the mid-19th century to the present day.* New York, NY: Palgrave Macmillan.

Kagitcibasi, C. (2002). Psychology and human competence development. *Applied Psychology, 51,* 5–22. http://dx.doi.org/10.1111/1464-0597.0076z

Killeen, L. A., Lopez-Zafra, E., & Eagly, A. H. (2006). Envisioning oneself as a leader: Comparisons of women and men in Spain and the United States. *Psychology of Women Quarterly, 30,* 312–322. http://dx.doi.org/10.1111/j.1471-6402.2006.00299.x

Kim, H. S. (2006). The politics of border crossings: Black, postcolonial, and transnational feminist perspectives. In S. N. Hesse-Biber (Ed.), *Handbook of feminist research* (pp. 107–122). Thousand Oaks, CA: Sage.

Koss, M. P. (1990). The women's mental health research agenda: Violence against women. *American Psychologist, 45,* 374–380. http://dx.doi.org/10.1037/0003-066X.45.3.374

Krantz, G. (2002). Violence against women: A global public health issue! *Journal of Epidemiology and Community Health, 56,* 242–243. http://dx.doi.org/10.1136/jech.56.4.242

Kurtiş, T., & Adams, G. (2015). Decolonizing liberation: Toward a transnational feminist psychology. *Journal of Social and Political Psychology, 3,* 388–413. http://dx.doi.org/10.5964/jspp.v3i1.326

Levitt, H. M., Bamberg, M., Creswell, J. W., Frost, D. M., Josselson, R., & Suárez-Orozco, C. (2018). Journal article reporting standards for qualitative primary, qualitative meta-analytic, and mixed methods research in psychology: The APA Publications and Communications Board task force report. *American Psychologist, 73,* 26–46. http://dx.doi.org/10.1037/amp0000151

Levitt, P., & Jaworsky, B. N. (2007). Transnational migration studies: Past developments and future trends. *Annual Review of Sociology, 33,* 129–156. http://dx.doi.org/10.1146/annurev.soc.33.040406.131816

Lewis, K. M., Robkin, N., Gaska, K., & Njoki, L. C. (2011). Investigating motivations for women's skin bleaching in Tanzania. *Psychology of Women Quarterly, 35,* 29–37. http://dx.doi.org/10.1177/0361684310392356

Lugones, M. (2010). Toward a decolonial feminism. *Hypatia, 25,* 742–759. http://dx.doi.org/10.1111/j.1527-2001.2010.01137.x

Lugones, M. C., & Spelman, E. V. (1983). Have we got a theory for you! Feminist theory, cultural imperialism, and the demand for "the woman's voice." *Women's Studies International Forum, 6,* 573–581. http://dx.doi.org/10.1016/0277-5395(83)90019-5

Lykes, M. B., & Moane, G. (2009). Editors' introduction: Whither feminist liberation psychology? Critical explorations of feminist and liberation psychologies for a globalizing world. *Feminism & Psychology, 19,* 283–297. http://dx.doi.org/10.1177/0959353509105620

Machizawa, S., & Enns, C. Z. (2015). Transnational psychological practice with women: Perspectives from East Asia and Japan. In C. Z. Enns, J. K. Rice, & R. L. Nutt (Eds.), *Psychological practice with women: Guidelines, diversity, empowerment* (pp. 225–256). Washington, DC: American Psychological Association. http://dx.doi.org/10.1037/14460-009

Mahalingam, R., Balan, S., & Haritatos, J. (2008). Engendering immigrant psychology: An intersectionality perspective. *Sex Roles, 59,* 326–336. http://dx.doi.org/10.1007/s11199-008-9495-2

Marecek, J. (2012). The global is local: Adding culture, ideology and context to international psychology. *Psychology of Women Quarterly, 36*, 149–153. http://dx.doi.org/10.1177/0361684312441775

Marecek, J. (2016). Invited reflection: Intersectionality theory and feminist psychology. *Psychology of Women Quarterly, 40*, 177–181. http://dx.doi.org/10.1177/0361684316641090

Martín-Baró, I., Aron, A., & Corne, S. (1994). *Writings for a liberation psychology.* Cambridge, MA: Harvard University Press.

McConaghy, C. (2000). *Rethinking indigenous education: Culturalism, colonialism and the politics of knowing.* Flaxton, Australia: Post Pressed.

Mendoza, B. (2002). Transnational feminisms in question. *Feminist Theory, 3,* 295–314. http://dx.doi.org/10.1177/146470002762492015

Moane, G. (1999). *Gender and colonialism: A psychological analysis of oppression and liberation.* London, England: Macmillan.

Moghadam, V. M. (2005). *Globalizing women: Transnational feminist networks.* Baltimore, MD: Johns Hopkins University Press.

Mohanty, C. T. (1984). Under Western eyes: Feminist scholarship and colonial discourses. *Boundary 2, 12–13,* 333–358. http://dx.doi.org/10.2307/302821

Mohanty, C. T. (2003). *Feminism without borders: Decolonizing theory, practicing solidarity.* Durham, NC: Duke University Press.

Montenegro, M., Capdevila, R., & Sarriera, H. F. (2012). Editorial introduction: Towards a transnational feminism: Dialogues on feminisms and psychologies in a Latin American context. *Feminism & Psychology, 22,* 220–227. http://dx.doi.org/10.1177/0959353511415830

Mootz, J. J., Stabb, S. D., & Mollen, D. (2017). Gender-based violence and armed conflict: A community-informed socioecological conceptual model from Northeastern Uganda. *Psychology of Women Quarterly, 41,* 368–388. http://dx.doi.org/10.1177/0361684317705086

Morash, M., Bui, H. N., & Santiago, A. (2000). Cultural-specific gender ideology and wife abuse in Mexican-descent families. *International Review of Victimology, 7,* 67–91. http://dx.doi.org/10.1177/026975800000700305

Murthi, M. (2009). Who is to blame? Rape of Hindu–Muslim women in inter-ethnic violence in India. (2009). *Psychology of Women Quarterly, 33,* 453–462. http://dx.doi.org/10.1111/j.1471-6402.2009.01523.x

Nadkarni, A. (2017). Transnational feminism. *Oxford Bibliographies.* Retrieved from http://www.oxfordbibliographies.com/view/document/obo-9780190221911/obo-9780190221911-0006.xml

Naples, N. A., & Desai, M. (2002). *Women's activism and globalization: Linking local struggles and transnational politics.* New York, NY: Routledge.

Narayan, U. (1997). *Dislocating cultures: Identities, traditions, and Third World feminism.* New York, NY: Routledge.

Nelson, G., Prilleltensky, I., & MacGillivary, H. (2001). Building value-based partnerships: Toward solidarity with oppressed groups. *American Journal of Community Psychology, 29,* 649–677. http://dx.doi.org/10.1023/A:1010406400101

Ozkul, D. (2012). Transnational migration research. *Sociopedia.isa.* Retrieved from http://www.sagepub.net/isa/resources/pdf/TransnationalMigrationResearch.pdf

Patil, V. (2013). From patriarch to intersectionality: A transnational feminist assessment of how far we've really come. *Signs, 38,* 847–867. http://dx.doi.org/10.1086/669560

Perkins, D. D., & Zimmerman, M. A. (1995). Empowerment theory, research, and application. *American Journal of Community Psychology, 23,* 569–579. http://dx.doi.org/10.1007/BF02506982

Pettigrew, T. F. (1991). Toward unity and bold theory: Popperian suggestions for two persistent problems of social psychology. In C. W. Stephan, W. G. Stephan, & T. F. Pettigrew (Eds.), *The future of social psychology* (pp. 13–27). New York, NY: Springer-Verlag. http://dx.doi.org/10.1007/978-1-4612-3120-2_2

Powell, C. (2005). Lifting our veil of ignorance: Culture, constitutionalism and women's human rights in post-September 11 America. *The Hastings Law Journal, 57,* 331–387.

Pratto, F., Sidanius, J., Stallworth, L. M., & Malle, B. F. (1994). Social dominance orientation: A personality variable predicting social and political attitudes. *Journal of Personality and Social Psychology, 67,* 741–763. http://dx.doi.org/10.1037/0022-3514.67.4.741

Prilleltensky, I. (2008). The role of power in wellness, oppression and liberation: The promise of psychopolitical validity. *Journal of Community Psychology, 36,* 116–136. http://dx.doi.org/10.1002/jcop.20225

Rappaport, J. (1987). Terms of empowerment/exemplars of prevention: Toward a theory for community psychology. *American Journal of Community Psychology, 15,* 121–148. http://dx.doi.org/10.1007/BF00919275

Rice, J. K., & Austria, S. (2007). Collaborative leadership and social advocacy among women's organizations. In J. L. Chin, B. Lott, J. K. Rice, & J. Sanchez-Hucles (Eds.), *Women and leadership: Transforming visions and diverse voices* (pp. 157–176). Hoboken, NJ: Wiley. http://dx.doi.org/10.1002/9780470692332.ch7

Rice, J. K., & Ballou, M. (2004). *APA resolution on culture and gender awareness in international psychology.* Washington, DC: American Psychological Association.

Rice, J. K., & Russo, N. K. (2010). International perspectives on women and mental health. In M. Paulidi (Ed.), *Handbook of feminism and women's rights worldwide* (Vol. 2, pp. 1–24). New York, NY: Praeger.

Riger, S. (1993). What's wrong with empowerment? *American Journal of Community Psychology, 21,* 279–292. http://dx.doi.org/10.1007/BF00941504

Rutherford, A., & Yoder, J. D. (2011). Thirty-five years and counting: Feminist psychology in PWQ, a job for the long haul. *Psychology of Women Quarterly, 35,* 171–174. http://dx.doi.org/10.1177/0361684310395915

Sabik, N. J., Cole, E. R., & Ward, L. M. (2010). Are all minority women equally buffered from negative body image? Intra-ethnic moderators of the buffering hypothesis. *Psychology of Women Quarterly, 34*, 139–151. http://dx.doi.org/10.1111/j.1471-6402.2010.01557.x

Segal, M. T., & Martinez, T. A. (2007). Intersections of gender, race, and class: Readings for a changing landscape. *Psychology of Women Quarterly, 31*, 437–438. http://dx.doi.org/10.1111/j.1471-6402.2007.00392_2.x

Sen, G., & Grown, C. (1987). *Development, crisis, and alternative visions: Third World women's perspectives*. New York, NY: Monthly Review Press.

Shayne, J. (2014). *Taking risks: Feminist stories of social justice research in the Americas*. Albany, NY: SUNY Press.

Stewart, A. J. (1998). Doing personality research: How can feminist theories help? In J. K. Norem & B. M. Clinchy (Eds.), *The gender and psychology reader* (pp. 54–68). New York: New York University Press.

Stewart, A. J., & McDermott, C. (2004). Gender in psychology. *Annual Review of Psychology, 55*, 519–544. http://dx.doi.org/10.1146/annurev.psych.55.090902.141537

Sudbury, J., & Okazawa-Rey, M. (2009). *Activist scholarship: Antiracism, feminism, and social change*. Boulder, CO: Paradigm Publishers.

Swarr, A., & Nagar, R. (2010). *Critical transnational feminist praxis*. Albany, NY: SUNY Press.

United Nations. (2010). *Statistic and indicators on men and women*. Retrieved from http://unstats.un.org/unsd/demographic/products/indwm/

Warner, L. R. (2016). Invited reflection: Contested interpretations and methodological choices in quantitative research. *Psychology of Women Quarterly, 40*, 342–346. http://dx.doi.org/10.1177/0361684316655453

White, A., & Rastogi, S. (2009). Justice by any means necessary: Vigilantism among Indian women. *Feminism & Psychology, 19*, 313–327. http://dx.doi.org/10.1177/0959353509105622

The World Bank. (2016). *Proportion of seats held by women in national parliaments*. Retrieved from https://data.worldbank.org/indicator/SG.GEN.PARL.ZS

Yoder, J. D. (2010). Editorial: A feminist journal at the cutting edge of a psychology for women. *Psychology of Women Quarterly, 34*, 1–4. http://dx.doi.org/10.1111/j.1471-6402.2009.01535.x

Yoder, J. D., & Kahn, A. S. (2003). Making gender comparisons more meaningful: A call for more attention to social context. *Psychology of Women Quarterly, 27*, 281–290. http://dx.doi.org/10.1111/1471-6402.00108

GLOSSARY

binary, binaries: Divided into two groups, classes, or categories that are considered diametrically opposed. Examples of binaries include male/female, straight/gay, good/bad, West/the rest, North/South, East/West, global/local, victim/criminal, us/them, and so forth (Binary, n.d.; see Introduction, Chapter 1).

colonization: A process of oppression and domination that is often violent and racially based, in which Indigenous people, land, and ideas are controlled and occupied through power. Colonization of ideas can take place without colonization of land. For example, Mohanty (2003a) criticized Western mainstream feminisms for colonizing Third World women through appropriating and systematizing knowledge about Third World women (McHugh, 2007).

critical race theory: In critical race theory (CRT) the relationship among race, racism, and power is studied and transformed. Although CRT originates from legal scholarship, it has been developed into an interdisciplinary, eclectic framework incorporating other intellectual traditions such as feminism, liberalism, Marxism, poststructuralism, critical legal theory, neopragmatism, and the law and society movement (Matsuda, Lawrence, Delgado, & Crenshaw, 1993). CRT theorists attempt to challenge institutional racism by including the voices of marginalized group members through storytelling or what they call *naming one's own reality* (Ladson-Billings & Tate, 1995).

cross-cultural psychology: Whereas cross-cultural psychology and cultural psychology are similar in that they both involve cultural influence on human behavior, they are different in that the former uses a relativistic approach, comparing cultures to understand variations and universals, whereas in the latter, the link between culture and psychological phenomena within a specific culture is studied. Cross-cultural psychologists are interested in general dimensions that cut across cultures, such as collectivism versus individualism (Ratner, 2008).

cultural psychology: The study of how cultural factors and practices are interconnected with individual human psychologies. Whereas in cross-cultural psychology the patterns in psychological phenomena are identified and compared among different cultures, cultural psychology takes a comparative approach and focuses on how cultural factors shape psychological phenomena and how psychological phenomena influence cultural practices within a culture (Ratner, 2008).

decolonial: Decolonial thinking questions or problematizes the histories of patriarchy, heterosexuality, colonialism, racism, capitalism, power, political, and cultural domination established by Europeans. Decolonial feminism analyzes and attempts to overcome oppression stemming from this history by separating from existing hegemonic colonial structures (McHugh, 2007; Mohanty, 2003a; Schutte, 1998).

decolonization: The process of dismantling and deconstructing colonialist power and institutional as well as hidden, cultural forces that maintain colonial power after political independence. Decolonization is a complex and continuing process that is not automatically achieved at the moment of political independence because colonialist values, as well as political, economic, and cultural models introduced during colonization, often persist after independence (Ashcroft, Griffiths, & Tiffin, 2000). Mohanty (2003a) argued that decolonization is a democratic process that facilitates the transformation of social structures as well as the individual and collective identity of colonized people and community.

decolonize: To release from the colonizing state. See *decolonization*.

diaspora: The dispersion of a population from its indigenous territories or original geographic location to new regions. Diasporas are often created by globalization and colonization. The dispersal can be involuntary, voluntary, temporary, or permanent. The descendants of diasporas may develop distinctive cultures that are often a hybrid of indigenous cultures with new ones. The notion of a *diasporic identity* has been used as a positive affirmation of their hybridity in postcolonial literature (Ashcroft et al., 2000; Bhatia, 2007; Chapter 1, this volume).

essentialism: In modern social science, essentialism is a philosophical concept that asserts certain phenomena such as race, gender, and sexuality are natural, inevitable, universal, and biologically determined (Irvine, 1990). The concept of essentialism, however, originates in Plato's work. Plato believed that unchanging distinct forms, or *eide*, which was later renamed *essences*, compose natural phenomena (DeLamater & Hyde, 1998). Essentialism has been criticized by social constructivists who believe that these phenomena are socially constructed—that they are concepts with meanings developed in conjunction with others and influenced by culture (Gergen, 2001) rather than based on "objective" facts arrived at through scientific investigation. Social constructionists believe that there is no universal, unchangeable essence (see *social constructivism*). *Essentialist* means consistent with or supporting essentialism.

feminism: Various movements and ideologies that aim to define and achieve social, political, and economic equality between men and women. It is a misconception that feminism only benefits women because patriarchy, hegemony, and imperialism can be harmful, disempowering, and oppressive to many men. Feminism and postcolonialism are closely related; both see imperialism and patriarchy as forms of domination and oppression (Ashcroft et al., 2000).

First World: First used to designate the dominant economic power of the Euro-American nations aligned with the North Atlantic Treaty Organization as opposed to the Soviet Union and its satellites that were termed *Second World*. Since the end of the Cold War, the term *First World* has often been used to refer to economically successful, highly developed, and industrialized countries (Ashcroft et al., 2000).

Foucauldian theory: Developed by Michel Foucault (1926–1984), a French historian, psychologist, and philosopher. He rejected the view of power as something held by particular actors or institutions; instead, he suggested that power operates within a network of relations and "individuals are the vehicles of power, not its points of application" (Foucault, 1980, p. 98). Foucauldian discourse analysis, a methodology of discourse analysis based on Foucauldian theories, is used to understand power relationships in society expressed through language.

Global East: Countries that are between the Global North and Global South and do not belong to either of these categories. The concept of Global East emerged in opposition to the binary of Global North and South (Muller, 2018).

Global Majority: People from Majority World settings based on Mohanty's (1991) one-third/two-thirds global paradigm (e.g., from Africa, Asia, South and Central America, and the Caribbean; Akpovo & Nganga, 2018). This paradigm was also described by Gustavo Esteva and Madhu Suri Prakash (1998). Global Minority and Majority also refer to what Esteva and Prakash called *social minorities* and *social majorities*. These terms are associated with the relative quality of life led by peoples and communities in different regions (Mohanty, 2003b). The term Global Majority is controversial because of the heterogeneity of these populations, which is why Mohanty refers to them as *Global Majorities* (plural). The individual communities do not represent true majorities, however. It is important that this label not be used in a reductionist, dichotomous manner—attention should be paid to diversity and complexity within these categories (Kurtiş & Adams, 2013).

Global Minority: People from Minority World settings based on Mohanty's (1991) one-third/two-thirds global paradigm (e.g., from the United States, Canada, Australia, and Europe; Akpovo & Nganga, 2018). Like *Global Majority*, this term is controversial because of the heterogeneity of these populations. It is important that this label not be used in a reductionist, dichotomous manner—attention should be paid to diversity and complexity within these categories (Kurtiş & Adams, 2013).

Global North: Global North and Global South countries are divided by an imaginary line called the Brandt Line that was proposed in the 1980s to distinguish economically wealthier countries located in the northern hemisphere and economically poorer countries in the southern hemisphere. The term also emphasizes the geographical split in global economies, politics, and health conditions. However, because this division is too simplistic, the term *Global North* normally includes economically developed countries regardless of geographic locations such as the United States, England, Japan, Spain, Belgium, Israel, South Africa, and Norway (Odeh, 2010). See also *Global South*.

global sisterhood: An idea envisioned and proposed by Robin Morgan (1984) that women around the world share the common experience of gender oppressions, and this commonality can unite them in working toward addressing these oppressions. Transnational feminists resist the utopic idea of global sisterhood and criticize its tendency to promote essentialist and homogenous views of women that neglect economic and sociopolitical divisions and inequitable global systems (see Chapter 1, this volume; Mohanty, 1991, 2003b).

Global South: Economically underdeveloped countries that are often located in the southern hemisphere, such as African nations, India, Brazil, and Mexico (Odeh, 2010). See also *Global North*.

globalization: The emergence of an international network of economic systems and the increasing interaction between people on a worldwide scale due to advances in transportation and communication technology. Whereas economic changes may be the most salient aspect of globalization, globalization also results in ideological, technological, political, social, and cultural shifts (Kacowicz, 2007).

glocalization: A concept introduced by sociologist Roland Robertson to problematize the tension between *global* and *local* in the concept of globalization. According to Robertson (1995), there is an assumption within the term *globalization* that *global* excludes the local as if the global overrides localities. He argued that the idea of glocalization implies that "globalization—in the broad sense, the compression of the world—has involved and increasingly involves the creation and the incorporation of locality, processes which themselves largely shape, in turn, the compression of the world as a whole" (Robertson, 1995, p. 40). In other words, *local* and *global* are not separable, and they should be understood in relation to their interconnected, interdependent processes. Inderpal Grewal and Caren Kaplan (1994) also argued that global and local are permeable constructs because "transnational linkages influence every level of social existence" (p. 13).

hegemony: The command, influence, or predominance of one group over another. The term *hegemony* is often used to describe the domination of the ruling class over other classes. Such domination is often maintained not by military force or persuasion but by subtle power over the economy, education, and media that present the interest of the ruling class as the common one shared by other classes (Ashcroft et al., 2000).

hybridities: The cross-breeding of two species to form a third, hybrid species. Although the term originates from biology, it is used in various disciplines to describe a mixture of more than one genre, culture, race, identity, or language. In postcolonial theory, hybridity describes "the creation of new transcultural forms within the contact zone produced by colonization" (Ashcroft et al., 2000, p. 108). Homi K. Bhabha, a postcolonial scholar, sees hybridity as a subversive tool that can be used by colonized people to challenge oppression. The concept of hybridity is also used to emphasize the mutual and interactive nature of cultures in colonial and postcolonial processes (Ashcroft et al., 2000; Bhabha, 1994).

imperialism: When a group expands its power, authority, or influence through land acquisition, diplomacy, gaining control over political or economic systems, or other forces (Imperialism, n.d.).

Indigenous feminism: Concerned with identities and attachments to territory deemed central to Indigenous peoples' (variously called *Indigenous, Aboriginal, First-Nation, Indian,* or *Native*) struggle against dispossession and for their cultural, political, and economic existence as peoples. Postcolonial feminism assumes that colonized peoples are not still struggling for their right to exist as political entities even though Indigenous people remain colonized and under threat. Indigenous feminisms critique transnational feminism's de-emphasis of nations and nationalism for neglecting Indigenous peoples and settler colonialism and Indigenous peoples' political claims that are anchored to particular territories. Indigenous feminist scholars criticize transnational feminism's scholarly focus on mobility, migration, and consequent diasporic identities for its neglect and delegitimization of Indigenous land claims in settler colonial societies (Chapter 2, this volume). Indigenous feminisms are antipatriarchal, antiheterosexist, anticolonial, and antiracist. They critique White supremacist practices against Indigenous communities (Lin, 2016).

internationalism: Moves beyond nationalism and embraces greater cooperation and collaboration between nations in the interest of international interdependence and solidarity. Internationalism includes form (national-scale associations), site (international federation; interstate organizations), and axis (national–international) modes of organizing, with an advocacy focus primarily on national institutions underpinned by a political commitment to national sovereignty but oriented toward international solidarity (Chapter 2, this volume).

international psychology: Phenomena are typically considered *international* when they involve interactions or transfers between nation-states. Diplomacy, contracts, disputes, and other interactions involving the governing bodies of nation-states and the movement and comparison of people and things between two nation-states are considered international (Vertovec, 2011). Consistent with this, *international psychology* refers to any number of psychology-related activities (e.g., research, meetings, businesses, organizations) conducted across nation-state borders rather than a unique theoretical perspective (Bullock, 2013). International psychology research typically focuses on comparisons between nation-states as defined by geographical and governmental borders. Whereas international psychology views patterns within a nation-state or region as universal, homogeneous, and static, transnational psychology focuses on the unique local and global influences on individual communities, which are not defined by nation-state borders (Chapter 1, this volume; Bullock, 2013).

intersectionality: An analytic framework that considers that the various forms of oppression associated with social stratification, such as class, race, sexual orientation, disability, and gender, do not exist separately from each other but are interwoven in complex interactions. Although the concept of intersectionality had been discussed by feminists before, the term was first coined by Kimberlé Crenshaw in 1989 in her paper "Demarginalizing the Intersection of Race and Sex: A Black Feminist Critique of Antidiscrimination Doctrine, Feminist Theory, and Antiracist Politics," which pointed out the multidimensional, intersecting nature of oppressions women face.

kyriarchy: Like intersectionality, kyriarchy moves beyond Western feminism's focus on patriarchy and examines how multiple systems of discrimination and oppression, such as those associated with race, gender, class, age, sexual orientation, and ability, overlap and are compounded when individuals are members of more than one disadvantaged social category or group (Chapter 1, this volume; Pui-lan, 2009).

liberation psychology: Scholars from this perspective aim to resist oppression and poverty through collaborating with individuals who are most affected by such oppression and incorporating their voices in theory and practice. Liberation psychology was influenced by Paolo Freire's work in adult education and the theology of liberation movement in Latin America and later articulated by the Spanish-Salvadoran social psychologist Ignacio Martín-Baró (Moghaddam, Erneling, Montero, & Lee, 2007).

located, location: According to Harding (1991), one's perspective is shaped by experiences in one's location, position, or place in the world, which warrants examination and critique. One's location is defined by such things as class, race, sexual orientation, disability, gender, education, ethnicity, local and global historical influences, sociopolitical context, human rights, and personal experiences. These influences can create different perspectives (Chapter 1, this volume; Haraway, 1988).

Majority World: Those countries where the majority of the world's population lives, based on Mohanty's (1991) one-third/two-thirds global paradigm (e.g., Africa, Asia, South America, Central America, and the Caribbean). *Majority World* and *developing country* are often used interchangeably, but *Majority World* is preferred because the term *developing country* assumes that there is a linear process of economic development and that achieving such development is a shared goal for all countries. *Majority World* has also replaced *Third World* because the latter term is also part of the discourse about certain countries being less developed or advanced than others (Akpovo & Nganga, 2018; Alam, 2008; Ashcroft et al., 2000).

Minority World: Those countries where a minority of the world's population lives, based on Mohanty's (1991) one-third/two-thirds global paradigm (e.g., the United States, Canada, Australia, and Europe).

monoculture: Although its original meaning is to grow a single crop in an agricultural practice, a feminist ecologist, Vandana Shiva (1993), used this term to refer to a lack of diversity in values, ideas, and knowledge, often as a result of globalization (McHugh, 2007; Norberg-Hodge, 1999; Shiva, 1993).

nation-states: Sovereign states in which the great majority of people share a particular national culture and identity. The cultural boundaries match up with the political boundaries in the nation-state (UNESCO, 2017).

neocolonialism: A form of imperialism, a process of indirect control or dominance by a Minority World country over a Majority World country through exploiting rules and regulations (Rahaman, Yeazdani, & Mahmud, 2017).

neoliberalism: A political ideology or philosophy that holds that expanding individual economic freedom within an institutional framework that promotes strong private property rights and free trade and free markets will advance human well-being (Harvey, 2005).

noncolonizing: To refrain from engaging in oppression, domination, and the appropriation and systematization of knowledge when dealing with people.

other, othering: *Othering* is a term first used by Jean-Paul Sartre to indicate the negative relationship that may develop when a person has selfhood and sees those different from him- or herself as other, different, and not-self (McHugh, 2007). In *The Second Sex* (1949), Simone de Beauvoir said that women are othered because men declare themselves the norm and with selfhood but socially construct women as deviant—therefore, other and without selfhood (McHugh, 2007; Simons, 2000). Third World feminists use the term *alternity* in a similar way (McHugh, 2007).

positionality: Describes how an individual's understanding of the world is colored by personal values, beliefs, different aspects of identities, and location in time and space. It also describes the position a researcher has chosen to adopt in the context of a given research study (Savin-Baden & Major, 2013). The importance of positionality in qualitative research has been emphasized because the position adopted by a researcher can have an impact on every aspect and phase of the research process. Positionality is fluid and is highly dependent on situation and context (Foote & Bartell, 2011).

postcolonialism: The academic study of the enduring effects and consequences of European imperialism on societies and cultures. It often includes the analysis of the process of the extension of European territories and institutions and the manner in which the empire controlled information, discussion, and debate in the process of expanding into new regions. It considers the nature of social constructions within the information shared, discussed, and debated. It also examines the resistance of colonized subjects and the different responses to the invasions. Finally, it analyses the current state of colonial legacies in nations and communities before and after achieving independence (Ashcroft et al., 2000). Postcolonialism emerged from the discourses of minorities and postcolonial scholars' critiques of the uneven development, histories, and cultural differences that are normalized by various forms of imperialism (Rukundwa & van Aarde, 2007).

postcolonial feminism: Like Third World feminism, postcolonial feminism emerged in opposition to mainstream Western feminism or second wave feminisms that misrepresented women in the Majority World and silenced their voices. Postcolonial feminism challenges the self–other binaries that were common in classic critiques of imperialism. Postcolonial feminists strategically use the colonizers' tools against them to challenge the structure of social domination and oppressions. Unlike transnational feminisms that deemphasize nation-state borders, in postcolonial feminism, the intersection of gender, postcolonial nation-state, and national identity is analyzed (McHugh, 2007; Rukundwa & van Aarde, 2007).

postessentialist: A perspective that takes a social constructivist view in which scholars focus less on alleged "facts" and more on how people come to make sense of their world and how they interact with others to create their "truth." This perspective entails two approaches: reflexivity in research and a constructivist approach (Bettiza, 2015).

postmodern feminism: Emerged in France in the 1970s. It incorporates postmodern philosophy, such as work by Simone de Beauvoir, that views gender as a discursive construction rather than a fixed biological fact. Postmodern feminists resist defining *women* as a universal concept; instead, they emphasize the plurality of women's experiences and resulting positioning (McHugh, 2007).

postmodernism: A movement that began in the late 20th century that critiqued Western positivistic, modern, scientific rationality and its role in perpetuating social hierarchies. It rejected the notion of neutrality and objectivity in science, holding that "facts" are influenced by researchers' perspectives, situations, choice of techniques, language, and social factors. It also rejected universality, emphasizing the impact of contexts and social factors on the variability of human beings. Similarly, language was seen as relative and contextual. Postmodernism rejected the idea that any statement could be proven purely true or false. It held that science was not necessarily liberatory but could be used for destructive, oppressive purposes. Postmodernism is consistent with a social constructionist rather than essentialist perspective, holding that human characteristics are not biologically determined (e.g., gender differences are socially constructed rather than based in biological characteristics; Foucault, 1980; Gergen, 2001; Hare-Mustin & Marecek, 1988; Ubach, 2004).

poststructuralism: A literary criticism and philosophy that emerged in France around the 1960s and developed in critical response to structuralism. Jacques Derrida, a French deconstructionist and poststructuralist, developed an analytical method called *deconstruction*. Deconstructionists claim that texts have a multiplicity of voices with no unitary interpretation because all texts are interpreted by people in the context of complex social structures and histories. Deconstruction has been incorporated by postmodern feminists such as Judith Butler (McHugh, 2007).

praxis: The process by which a theory, lesson, or skill is enacted, practiced, embodied, or realized.

problematizing: To perceive something as a problem, challenge, or issue and to consequently seek a solution for it.

representation: Transnational feminists tend to be concerned with representation and are interested in the issues of how stories of other women's lives are told, how their images are produced, and how they are classified and conceptualized. Mohanty (2003a) pointed out in her essay "Under Western Eyes" that Western feminist scholarship often engages in representational practices that homogenize Third World women who are viewed as victims of traditional, patriarchal culture.

reproductive labor: Activities related to having children, caregiving, cooking, and housekeeping that are often uncompensated (Duffy, 2007).

self-reflexivity: A practice in feminist methodology that examines the role that researchers' intersecting identities have in shaping analysis and interpretations in all phases of the research process. It is used to develop a critical consciousness of intersecting areas of power, privilege, and marginalization. The term *self-reflexivity* is similar to *reflexivity*, but some drop the *self* because the self is a concept associated with Western individualism and is not emphasized or even recognized in some cultures (Chapter 1, this volume). See also *strong reflexivity*.

situated knowledge: A concept originally proposed by feminist anthropologist Donna Haraway (1988) in her essay "Situated Knowledges: The Science Question in Feminism and the Privilege of Partial Perspective." It is one of the key concepts in feminist epistemology. Situated knowledge is the idea that one's perspective is shaped by experiences in one's location, position, or place in the world, which warrants examination and critique. What one "knows" about a group (knowledge) depends on opinions (perspectives) developed by virtue of one's characteristics (e.g., race, gender, socioeconomic status, education, ethnicity) and personal experiences, and it is thus subject to biases. Situated knowledge denies the neutrality of researchers and highlights the influence of contextual factors in knowledge production (Chapter 1, this volume; Haraway, 1988).

social constructivism: Emerged from the disciplines of the history of science, sociology of knowledge, critical theory, feminism, literary theory, and rhetoric. Social constructivism continues to be developed across disciplines. It critiques positivist and empiricist science traditions. Scientific knowledge was previously assumed to be "objective" and uncontaminated by culture, history, and ideology. Social constructionists counter that science is influenced by the processes of relationship—that meanings are developed in conjunction with others. It challenges the assumption that science is free from cultural influences and examines purported "facts" arrived at through scientific investigation (Gergen, 2001).

standpoint theory/epistemology: American feminist theorist Sandra Harding (1991) coined the term *standpoint theory* to categorize epistemologies that emphasize women's knowledge. A *standpoint* refers to is an individual's unique world perspective. Standpoint theory emerged from Marx's writings in the 1970s and became influential in feminist writing in the 1980s. It holds that a person's social position influences their knowledge and research. The theory denies the objectivity of traditional science, suggesting that research and theory have ignored and marginalized the perspectives of oppressed groups (Borland, 2019). According to Miller (1976), oppressed, "subordinated" groups have unique information from having to be observant to survive. It is easier for those with privilege to miss or ignore aspects of social reality and therefore not ask good questions in their scholarship.

strong reflexivity: A term Sandra Harding (1991) used to specify a rigorous form of reflexivity, one that requires acknowledging, critically evaluating, and openly admitting the conceptual, political, historical, and other frameworks that shape our beliefs. The term *strong reflexivity* is similar to the postcolonial feminist term *reflexivity* and the postmodern term *self-reflexivity*, except that it is more thorough (Harding, 1991; McHugh, 2007). Strong reflexivity requires critical consciousness regarding one's position in the world and its relationship to what and how one knows. It involves acute awareness of how the observer changes as they interact with the object of their observation and acknowledges that subjective elements of experience are not necessarily negative. Although subjective elements make the results of research less "objective," strong reflexivity increases our understanding of the inherent subjectivity resulting from one's situation and perspective. This allows us to use that awareness of potential bias to improve our methods, essentially improving objectivity through this awareness (Brooks & Hesse-Biber, 2006).

Third World: This term emerged during the Cold War period to designate those countries that did not align with either the United States or the Soviet Union. However, since the end of the Cold War, it has often been used as a general term referring to any underdeveloped country and society. Such use of the term reinforces the pejorative stereotyping of those countries that constitute about two thirds of United Nations members (Ashcroft et al., 2000). Because of the term's association with the problematic discourse about certain countries being less developed or advanced than others, the term *Majority World* is increasingly used instead of the term *Third World* (Akpovo & Nganga, 2018; Alam, 2008; Ashcroft et al., 2000).

Third World feminism: Both Third World feminism and transnational feminism emerged as new feminist paradigms to counter Western, White feminisms that homogenized and universalized women's oppression (Herr, 2014). Third World feminism was created in response to White second wave feminism, which continued the Western feminist tradition of analyzing only gender oppression. In contrast, Third World feminists examine multiple oppressions in the context of various social locations (Herr, 2014). Third World feminism historically situates Third World women's oppression and resistance and respects their agency and voices. Unlike the currently more dominant transnational feminism, Third World feminism tends to concentrate on local and national contexts and does not consider nation-states and nationalism as necessarily detrimental to feminism (Herr, 2014).

transnationalism: Characterized by multiple ties and transactions connecting people and institutions across nation-state borders. Transnational activities can take place on a national, organizational, or individual level. They may include but are not limited to economic, political, cultural, and religious initiatives (Portes, 1999; UNESCO, n.d.).

transnational feminism: An interdisciplinary feminist paradigm that emerged to decolonize, deconstruct, and dismantle Western, White feminisms that universalized and homogenized "multiple, overlapping, and discrete oppressions" of Third World women (Grewal & Kaplan, 1994, p. 17). It evolved out of postcolonial and Third World feminist movements (McHugh, 2007) in the 1990s when globalization and Western imperialism escalated. Transnational feminism rejects the utopic idea of "global sisterhood" (as presented in Morgan, 1984), which was developed by feminists in the Minority World. Instead, it promotes building a decolonizing transnational feminist solidarity that attends to the diversity and multiplicity of women's experiences and respects and elevates silenced voices of oppressed groups.

transnational intersectionality: Extends the intersections identified by Women of Color feminists to those associated with economic exploitation and social hierarchies associated with imperialism, colonialism, and globalization. Transnational intersectionality adds consideration of local and global historical, sociopolitical, human rights, nationhood, economic, and political forces to the analysis of how oppressive institutions are interconnected. The resulting influences and experiences are dynamic, fluid, and synergistic rather than merely additive. (Chapters 1, 4, and 5, this volume; Grabe & Else-Quest, 2012).

universalism: A notion that there are common, shared features of human life and experience that apply to all humanity regardless of context and conditions. In postcolonial studies, universalism is seen as a crucial feature of imperial hegemony because it assumes applicability and generalizability of experiences, values, and expectations of a dominant culture or group to all others (Ashcroft et al., 2000).

universalization: Assuming that there are common, shared features of human life and experience that apply to all humanity regardless of local cultural conditions and making generalizations about a population based on those features (Ashcroft et al., 2000).

WEIRD: An acronym referring to Western, educated, industrialized, rich, democratic societies. This concept was originally introduced by Henrich, Heine, and Norenzayan (2010), who pointed out that most psychological research is based on samples drawn from WEIRD societies. They noted that people from WEIRD societies are particularly unusual and not representative of populations around the globe.

Western: *Western* and the *West* are often used to refer to North America and Western Europe.

Women of Color: A term created during the 1977 National Women's Conference in Houston, Texas. A group of Black women created "The Black Women's Agenda" to replace the conference organizer's "Minority Women's Plank." Other women members of minority groups (e.g., Asian, Hispanic, American Indian) wanted to endorse and be included in the Black Women's Agenda. During the conference, these women met and created a "Minority Caucus." After some debate, the term *Women of Color* was selected to symbolize the solidarity and commitment of the Women of Color to collaborate and support each other (Wade, 2011). It began to be used in academic circles when Moraga and Anzaldúa used it in *This Bridge Called My Back* in 1981 (McHugh, 2007; Moraga & Anzaldu̶a, 1981; Spruill, 2017; Wade, 2011).

REFERENCES

Akpovo, S. M., & Nganga, L. (2018). Minority-world professionals in majority-world early childhood contexts: How do international field experiences promote intercultural competence or reinforce "professional" ethnocentrism?

Contemporary Issues in Early Childhood, 19, 199–205. http://dx.doi.org/ 10.1177/1463949118778024

Alam, S. (2008). Majority World: Challenging the West's rhetoric of democracy. *Amerasia Journal, 34,* 87–98. http://dx.doi.org/10.17953/amer.34.1.l3176027k4q614v5

Ashcroft, B., Griffiths, G., & Tiffin, H. (2000). *Key concepts in post-colonial studies.* New York, NY: Routledge.

Bettiza, G. (2015). Constructing civilisations: Embedding and reproducing the 'Muslim world' in American foreign policy practices and institutions since 9/11. *Review of International Studies, 41,* 575–600. http://dx.doi.org/10.1017/ S0260210514000400

Bhabha, H. K. (1994). *The location of culture.* New York, NY: Routledge.

Bhatia, S. (2007). Rethinking culture and identity in psychology: Towards a transnational cultural psychology. *Journal of Theoretical and Philosophical Psychology, 27–28,* 301–321. http://dx.doi.org/10.1037/h0091298

Binary. (n.d.). In *Merriam-Webster's online dictionary.* Retrieved from https:// www.merriam-webster.com/dictionary/binary

Borland, E. (2019). Standpoint theory. In *Encyclopedia Britannica.* Retrieved from https://www.britannica.com/topic/standpoint-theory

Brooks, A., & Hesse-Biber, S. N. (2006). An invitation to feminist research. In S. Hesse-Biber (Ed.), *Feminist research practice: A primer* (pp. 1–24). Newcastle Upon Tyne, England: Sage.

Bullock, M. (2013). International psychology. In D. K. Freedheim & I. B. Weiner (Eds.), *Handbook of psychology: History of psychology* (pp. 562–596). Hoboken, NJ: Wiley.

Crenshaw, K. (1989). Demarginalizing the intersection of race and sex: A Black feminist critique of antidiscrimination doctrine, feminist theory and antiracist politics. *University of Chicago Legal Forum, 1,* 139–160. Retrieved from http:// chicagounbound.uchicago.edu/uclf/vol1989/iss1/8

de Beauvoir, S. (1949). *Le deuxieme sexe* [The second sex]. Paris, France: Gallimard.

DeLamater, J. D., & Hyde, J. S. (1998). Essentialism vs. social constructionism in the study of human sexuality. *The Journal of Sex Research, 1,* 10–18. http:// dx.doi.org/10.1080/00224499809551913

Duffy, M. (2007). Doing the dirty work: Gender, race, and reproductive labor in historical perspective. *Gender and Society, 21,* 313–336. Retrieved from http:// www.jstor.org/stable/27640972

Esteva, G., & Prakash, M. (1998). Beyond development, what? (Au-delà du développement, qu'y-a-t-il?/Além do desenvolvimento, o que acontece?/ Mas allá del desarrollo, øCómo?). *Development in Practice, 8,* 280–296. Retrieved from http://www.jstor.org/stable/4028743

Foote, M. Q., & Bartell, T. G. (2011). Pathways to equity in mathematics education: How life experiences impact researcher positionality. *Educational Studies in Mathematics, 78,* 45–68. http://dx.doi.org/10.1007/s10649-011-9309-2

Foucault, M. (1980). Power/knowledge: Selected interviews and other writings 1972–1977. London, England: Harvester Press.

Gergen, K. J. (2001). *Social construction in context*. London, England: Sage.

Grabe, S., & Else-Quest, N. M. (2012). The role of transnational feminism in psychology: Complementary visions. *Psychology of Women Quarterly, 36*, 158–161. http://dx.doi.org/10.1177/0361684312442164

Grewal, I., & Kaplan, C. (1994). *Scattered hegemonies*. Minneapolis: University of Minnesota Press.

Haraway, D. (1988). Situated knowledges: The science question in feminism and the privilege of partial perspective. *Feminist Studies, 14*, 575–599. http://dx.doi.org/10.2307/3178066

Harding, S. (1991). *Whose science? Whose knowledge?* Ithaca, NY: Cornell University Press.

Hare-Mustin, R. T., & Marecek, J. (1988). The meaning of difference: Gender theory, postmodernism, and psychology. *American Psychologist, 43*, 455–464. http://dx.doi.org/10.1037//0003-066X.43.6.455

Harvey, D. (2005). *A brief history of neoliberalism*. Oxford, England: Oxford University Press.

Henrich, J., Heine, S. J., & Norenzayan, A. (2010). The weirdest people in the world? *Behavioral and Brain Sciences, 33*, 1–75. Retrieved from https://www2.psych.ubc.ca/~henrich/pdfs/WeirdPeople.pdf

Herr, R. S. (2014). Reclaiming Third World feminism: Or why transnational feminism needs Third World feminism. *Meridians, 12*, 1–30. http://dx.doi.org/10.2979/meridians.12.1.1

Imperialism. (n.d.). In *Merriam-Webster's online dictionary*. Retrieved from https://www.merriam-webster.com/dictionary/imperialism

Irvine, J. M. (1990). *Disorders of desire: Sex and gender in modern American sexology* (Vol. 49). Philadelphia, PA: Temple University Press.

Kacowicz, A. M. (2007). Globalization, poverty, and the North–South divide. *International Studies Review, 9*, 565–580. http://dx.doi.org/10.1002/9781444302936.ch2

Kurtiş, T., & Adams, G. (2013). A cultural psychology of relationship: Toward a transnational feminist psychology. In M. K. Ryan & N. R. Branscombe (Eds.), *Handbook of gender and psychology* (pp. 251–269). London, England: Sage. http://dx.doi.org/10.4135/9781446269930.n16

Ladson-Billings, G., & Tate, W. F. (1995). Toward a critical race theory of education. *Teacher's College Record, 97*, 47–68. http://dx.doi.org/10.4324/9781315709796-2

Lin, Y. T. (2016). An introduction: "Indigenous feminisms: Why transnational? Why now?" *Lectora, 22*, 9–12.

Matsuda, M. J., Lawrence, C. R., Delgado, R., & Crenshaw, K. W. (1993). *Words that wound: Critical race theory, assaultive speech, and the First Amendment*. Boulder, CO: Westview Press.

McHugh, N. A. (2007). *Feminist philosophies A–Z*. Edinburgh, Scotland: Edinburgh University Press.

Miller, J. B. (1976). *Toward a new psychology of women*. Oxford, England: Beacon.

Moghaddam, F. M., Erneling, C. E., Montero, M., & Lee, N. (2007). Toward a conceptual foundation for a global psychology. In M. J. Stevens & U. P. Gielen (Eds.), *Toward a global psychology: Theory, research, intervention, and pedagogy* (pp. 179–206). Mahwah, NJ: Erlbaum.

Mohanty, C. T. (1991). Under Western eyes: Feminist scholarship and colonial discourses. In C. T. Mohanty, A. Russo, & L. Lourdes Torres (Eds.), *Third World women and the politics of feminism* (pp. 51–78). Bloomington: Indiana University Press.

Mohanty, C. T. (2003a). *Feminism without borders: Decolonizing theory, practicing solidarity*. Durham, NC: Duke University Press.

Mohanty, C. (2003b). "Under Western eyes" revisited: Feminist solidarity through anticapitalist struggles. *Signs, 28*, 499–535. http://dx.doi.org/10.1086/342914

Moraga, C., & Anzaldua, G. (1981). *This bridge called my back: Writings by radical women of color*. Watertown, MA: Persephone Press.

Morgan, R. (1984). *Sisterhood is global*. New York, NY: Feminist Press at CUNY.

Muller, M. (2018). In search of the Global East: Thinking between North and South. *Geopolitics*. Retrieved from https://www.tandfonline.com/doi/full/10.1080/14650045.2018.1477757

Norberg-Hodge, H. (1999). Consumer monoculture: The destruction of tradition. *Global Dialogue, 1*, 70–77.

Odeh, L. K. (2010). A comparative analysis of Global North and Global South economics. *Journal of Sustainable Development in Africa, 12*, 338–347. Retrieved from https://pdfs.semanticscholar.org/3629/a2898d4dc51902de3b8bd6b1c3b553fe7fff.pdf

Portes, A. (1999). Conclusion: Towards a new world—the origins and effects of transnational activities. *Ethnic and Racial Studies, 22*, 463–477. http://dx.doi.org/10.1080/014198799329567

Pui-lan, K. (2009). Elisabeth Schüssler Fiorenza and postcolonial studies. *Journal of Feminist Studies in Religion, 25*, 191–197. http://dx.doi.org/10.2979/fsr.2009.25.1.191

Rahaman, M. S., Yeazdani, M. R., & Mahmud, R. (2017). The untold history of neocolonialism in Africa (1960–2011). *History Research, 5*, 9–16.

Ratner, C. (2008). *Cultural psychology, cross-cultural psychology, indigenous psychology*. Hauppauge, NY: Nova Science.

Robertson, R. (1995). Global modalities. In M. Featherstone, S. Lash, & R. Robertson (Eds.), *Glocalization* (pp. 25–44). London, England: Sage.

Rukundwa, L. S., & van Aarde, A. G. (2007). The formation of postcolonial theory. *HTS Teologies Studies, 63*, 1171–1194. http://dx.doi.org/10.4102/hts.v63i3.237

Savin-Baden, M., & Major, C. H. (2013). *Qualitative research: The essential guide to theory and practice*. Abingdon, England: Routledge.

Schutte, O. (1998). Cultural alternity: Cross-cultural communication and feminist thought in North–South dialogue. *Hypatia, 2*, 53–72. http://dx.doi.org/10.1111/j.1527-2001.1998.tb01225.x

Shiva, V. (1993). *Monocultures of the mind*. London, England: Zed Books.

Simons, M. A. (2000). Beauvoir's philosophical independence in a dialogue with Sartre. *The Journal of Speculative Philosophy, 14*, 87–103. http://dx.doi.org/10.1353/jsp.2000.0015

Spruill, M. (2017, January 20). *Women Unite! Lessons from 1977 for 2017*. Retrieved from http://www.processhistory.org/women-unite-spruill/

Ubach, T. C. (2004). Postmodernism in psychology. In C. D. Spielberger (Ed.), *Encyclopedia of applied psychology* (pp. 67–73). Oxford, England: Elsevier Science & Technology.

UNESCO. (n.d.). *Trans-nationalism*. Retrieved from http://www.unesco.org/new/en/social-and-human-sciences/themes/international-migration/glossary/trans-nationalism/

UNESCO. (2017). *Nation-state*. Retrieved from http://www.unesco.org/new/en/social-and-human-sciences/themes/international-migration/glossary/nation-state/

Vertovec, S. (2011). Transnationalism. In G. T. Kurian (Ed.), *The encyclopedia of political science* (p. 1684). Washington, DC: CQ Press. http://dx.doi.org/10.4135/9781608712434.n1576

Wade, L. (2011, March 26). *Loretta Ross on the phrase "women of color."* Retrieved from https://thesocietypages.org/socimages/2011/03/26/loreta-ross-on-the-phrase-women-of-color/

INDEX

socially constructed knowledge in, 101–103
transnational considerations in, 94–110
Coalition Against Trafficking in Women (CATW), 216
Coercion, state, 198–199
Cole, E. R., 259
Collaborative conceptualization, 240–241
Collectivist cultures, 108
Collins, Lynn, 4, 235
Collins, P. H., 258
Colonial difference, defined, 56
Colonialism, 174, 222
Colonization, 235, 291
Communism, 45
Communities
    defining, 93
    and disaster response, 112–113
    legislation on, impact of, 34
    in treatment research, 102–103
Community guest speaker (class activity), 237–238
Community participatory approaches, 68–69, 73
Comparative analytic approach, defined, 20
Comparative model, 231
Congo, Democratic Republic of, 75
Conscientization, defined, 31
Constructivism, social, 292, 299
Consumer model, 230
Contiguous flows, defined, 24
Contiguous globalization, defined, 63
Contraception. *See* Family planning
Contraceptive technologies, 199
Convention on the Elimination of All Forms of Discrimination Against Women (CEDAW), 79
Cook, S. L., 167
Cortina, L. M., 261
Crash Course, 234–235
Craven, C., 97
Crazy Like Us (Watters), 74
Crenshaw, Kimberlé, 295
Creolization, 24
Criminality, of human trafficking, 221–224

Critical Article Review (assignment), 237
Critical globalization studies, 44
Critical race theory (CRT), 27, 145, 159, 291
Critical realism, defined, 31
Cross-cultural psychology, 29–30, 122, 291
CRT. *See* Critical race theory
Cultural norms, 131–132
Cultural psychology, 31, 291
Cultures, collectivist, 108
Curtin, N., 261

Da Silva, Ana Paula, 213–214
Data analysis and interpretation, 66, 71–72
Data collection, techniques for, 71
Datzberger, S., 160
Davis, K., 97, 248
Decolonial (term), 291
Decolonial feminism, 291
Decolonization, 5, 6, 56–57, 292
Decolonization (assignment), 234
"Decolonizing Liberation" (Kurtiş & Adams), 143
Decolonizing Sexuality and Reproduction (assignment), 248
Deconstruction, 298
De Jong, J. T., 76
"Demarginalizing the Intersection of Race and Sex" (Crenshaw), 295
Democratic Republic of Congo, 75
Derrida, Jacques, 298
Desai, J., 123, 125
Desai, Manisha, 213
Deterritorialization, defined, 47
Detournay, D., 123
Development, Relief, and Education for Alien Minors (DREAM) Act, 269
Dhamoon, R., 272
Diagnostic and Statistical Manual of Mental Disorders, Fifth Edition (*DSM-5*), 110
Diaspora
    in clinical practice, 95–96
    culture/knowledge spreading through, 22

Fernandes, Leela, 274
Fertility, 197–198
Film (class activity), 246–247
Fine, Michelle, 270
Finlay, L., 18
First-Nation peoples. *See* Indigenous
        feminism
First World, defined, 292
Fogarty International Center, 77
Form mode of organizing, 295
Foucauldian theory, 48, 292–293
Foucault, Michel, 292–293
Freud, S., 190
Friere, Paolo, 296
"From International to Transnational"
        summit, 4
From Macro to Micro (assignment),
        240–241
Fukushima, Annie, 215

GBV. *See* Gender-based violence
Gender
        and migration, 128–129
        oppressions based on, 293
        in postmodern feminism, 298
        roles set by, 122–123, 130–132
Gender and Colonialism (Moane), 264
Gender-based exclusion, from
        education, 147
Gender-based violence (GBV), 77–80,
        165–166. *See also* Domestic
        violence (DV)
Gender gap, in educational attainment,
        145–146
Genocide, 62
Genographic Project, 242
Global East, defined, 293
Global Gender Gap Report (WEF, 2017),
        146
Global influences, in clinical practice,
        103–104
Globalization
        in 1990s, 44–47
        in clinical practice, 95–96
        contiguous, defined, 63
        defined, 294
        DV impacted by, 172–173
        escalation of, 3–4
        impact of, 23–25, 249–250
        noncontiguous, defined, 63–64

research proliferation from, 61
and transnationalism, 19
transnational psychology addressing,
        32
Global Majority
        advantages of, 33
        complexities in, 145
        defined, 93, 293
        globalization affecting, 25
        in liberation psychology, 31
        oppressive entities of, 28
        perspectives of, 15
        in psychological research, 4
Global mental health, 75–76, 85
Global Minority
        assessment practices with, 107–108
        defined, 293
        evidence-based treatments in, 114
        focus on, 240
        globalization affecting, 25
        in psychological research, 4
        women's well-being in, 93–94
Global North, defined, 293
Global sisterhood
        in clinical practice, 96–97
        defined, 186, 293
        issues with, 32, 51
        transnational feminism rejecting,
        19–20
Global South, defined, 294
Glocalization, 24, 249–250, 294
God Loves Uganda (Williams), 81
Goldberger, N. R., 123
Gómez, L. H., 122
Grabe, Shelly
        on intersectionality, 28, 64, 134, 144
        intervention research by, 111
        on multi-level analysis, 30, 35
        in research partnerships, 71
        and transnational feminism
                development, 21, 264
Green, Hank, 235
Green, John, 235
Grewal, Inderpal
        on glocalization, 294
        on hegemonies, 28, 96
        on scattered hegemonies, 212–213
        and transnational psychology
                development, 52, 54
Guinea, 146

Scattered hegemonies, 13, 32, 37, 212
Scattered Hegemonies (Grewal
    & Kaplan), 52
Schiller, N. G., 22
Scholar–activist approaches, 275–277
Science, perspectives on, 298–299
Secondary school enrollment, 149–151
The Second Sex (Beauvoir), 297
Second wave feminism, 300
Second World, 292
Seigel, Micol, 217
Self, in research, 74–75
Self-reflexivity, 72, 298–299
Sen, Amartya, 201
Sen, R., 18
Senadheera, C., 74, 111–112, 236
Service-learning experiences, 249–250
Sex Roles (journal), 124
Sex-selection abortions, 201–202
Sexual assault, 77–78
Sexual respectability, female, 193–195
Sex work, 216–218
Shiva, Vandana, 7–8, 141, 296
Shweder, R. A., 122
Silenced voices, addressing, 32–33,
    97–98
Singapore, 222–223
Singh, 149
Siribaddana, S., 236–237
Sisterhood, global. *See* Global
    sisterhood
Site mode of organizing, 295
Situated knowledge, 18, 299
"Situated Knowledges" (Haraway),
    299
Sivayogan, S., 236–237
Small Group Discussion on
    Transnational Feminist
    Performances (class activity),
    243–244
Small Group Discussion on Violence
    Against Women and Girls
    (class activity), 246
Social constructivism, 292, 299
Social forces, in DV, 169–175
Socially constructed knowledge,
    101–103
Social majorities, 293
Social minorities, 293

Society for the Psychology of Women
    (SPW), 43–44, 258
Society for the Psychology of Women's
    Global Issues Committee, 4
Socioeconomic context, for educational
    attainment, 145–146
Sociostructural factors, for research,
    271–272
Solidarity model, 231
Son preference, 201–202
South Africa, 171
South Asia, 149, 188–202
    Bangladesh. *See* Bangladesh
    India. *See* India
    Pakistan. *See* Pakistan
    Sri Lanka. *See* Sri Lanka
Special economic zones, 23
Spielberger, C. D., 108–109
Spirals of influence, of educational
    attainment, 158–160
Spivak, Gayatri, 134, 143
SPW (Society for the Psychology of
    Women), 43–44, 258
Sri Lanka. *See also* South Asia
    abortion in, 199–201
    family planning in, 197
    labor migration in, 195–196
    marriage in, 191–192
    research in, 111–112
Ssewakiryanga, R., 70
Stabb, S. D., 100, 105
Stacey, J., 107
Standardized assessments, 108
Standpoint, defined, 299
Standpoint theory (epistemology),
    238, 299
State coercion, 198–199
Stereotypes, 73
Sterilizations, 198–199
Stewart, A. J., 261
Strategic essentialism, defined, 56
Strong reflexivity, 5, 18, 299–300
Strong reflexivity exercise (assignment),
    238
Structural violence, 220–221
Sub-Saharan Africa, 4
Suchland, Jennifer, 218, 221
Sudan, 76, 171

ABOUT THE EDITORS

Lynn H. Collins, PhD, is an associate professor of psychology at La Salle University in Philadelphia, Pennsylvania. Dr. Collins is a Fellow of the American Psychological Association (APA) and a recipient of the Association for Women in Psychology's Christine Ladd-Franklin Award. She has served as president of APA Division 52 (International Psychology) and APA Division 35 (Society for the Psychology of Women). Dr. Collins oversaw the creation of the Division 52 journal, *International Perspectives in Psychology: Research, Practice, Consultation*, and has served on the editorial boards of *Psychological Assessment*; *Psychology of Women Quarterly*; *Sex Roles*; *Journal of Genetic Psychology*; and *Genetic, Social, and General Psychology Monographs*.

Sayaka Machizawa, PsyD, is senior clinical scientist at Bracket Global. Born in Tokyo, Japan, and trained in the United States, she is fully bilingual and uses her transmigrant background to ensure the development of culturally appropriate clinical content for rater training and qualification programs in global clinical trials by major pharmaceutical companies. Until 2016, Dr. Machizawa worked at The Chicago School of Professional Psychology as associate director of community partnerships and international faculty lead, where she designed and taught study abroad courses in Japan and oversaw service learning and community-based participatory research projects. She has served in numerous leadership roles in the American Psychological Association.

Joy K. Rice, PhD, is a clinical psychologist, emerita professor, and clinical professor at the University of Wisconsin–Madison School of Medicine and Public Health. She is a recipient of the Educational Press Association Distinguished Achievement Award, the Florence L. Denmark and Mary E. Reuder Award for outstanding international contributions to the psychology of women and gender, and the 2008 Woman of the Year Award from the American Psychological Association Section for the Advancement of Women in Counseling Psychology. Dr. Rice is coauthor of *Living Through Divorce: A Developmental Approach to Divorce Therapy*; coeditor of *Women and Leadership: Transforming Visions and Diverse Voices*; and coeditor of *Psychological Practice With Women: Guidelines, Diversity, Empowerment.*